Creative Learning Activities

FOR

Young Children

Creative
Learning
Activities

FOR
Young Children

Dr. Judy Herr

DELMAR
CENGAGE Learning™

Australia • Brazil • Japan • Korea • Mexico • Singapore • Spain • United Kingdom • United States

DELMAR
CENGAGE Learning

Creative Learning Activities for Young Children
Judy Herr

Business Unit Director: Susan L. Simpfenderfer

Acquisitions Editor: Erin O'Connor Traylor

Developmental Editor: Sandy Woods

Editorial Assistant: Alexis Ferraro

Executive Marketing Manager: Donna J. Lewis

Channel Manager: Nigar Hale

Executive Production Manager: Wendy A. Troeger

Production Editor: J. P. Henkel

Cover Design: Dutton & Sherman

For product information and technology assistance, contact us at
Cengage Learning Customer & Sales Support, 1-800-354-9706
For permission to use material from this text or product,
submit all requests online at **www.cengage.com/permissions**
Further permissions questions can be emailed to
permissionrequest@cengage.com

Library of Congress Control Number: 00-050899

ISBN-13: 978-0-7668-1613-8

ISBN-10: 0-7668-1613-3

Delmar
Executive Woods
5 Maxwell Drive
Clifton Park, NY 12065
USA

Cengage Learning is a leading provider of customized learning solutions with office locations around the globe, including Singapore, the United Kingdom, Australia, Mexico, Brazil, and Japan. Locate your local office at **www.cengage.com/global**

Cengage Learning products are represented in Canada by Nelson Education, Ltd.

To learn more about Delmar, visit **www.cengage.com/delmar**

Purchase any of our products at your local bookstore or at our preferred online store **www.ichapters.com**

Notice to the Reader

Printed in the United States of America
3 4 5 6 7 11 10 09

Contents

Contents by Activities

ART

Arts and Crafts

Collage

Easel Painting

Finger and Hand Painting Recipes

Gifts and/or Decorations

Painting

Printing with Paint

COOKING

Beverages

Breads

Spread

DRAMATIC PLAY THEMES

Animals

Home and Family

Our Community

Plants

Seasons and Weather

Sports and Hobbies

Transportation

EXCURSIONS AND RESOURCE PEOPLE

Excursions

Resource People

FINGERPLAY ACTIVITIES

GAMES

MATH

MOVEMENT

NURSERY RHYMES

People

Seasons

Traditional

Transportation

Weather

SENSORY

Water

Sensory

SCIENCE

Weather Experiences

Other Interesting Science Activities

SOCIAL STUDIES

SONGS

All about Me

Animals

Preface

My life's work has always focused on the young child. Thus, while reviewing resources for caregivers, including nannies, parents, grandparents, and teachers, in large bookstores and libraries, it became apparent that few books were available that coupled the understanding of child development with hundreds of activities for promoting children's optimal growth and development. Because of my in-depth knowledge and experience in the field as a college professor and the director of a Child and Family Study Center that provided practicum and student teaching experiences for students majoring in early childhood education, friends and colleagues continually have encouraged me to write a book that would be tailored to this market. Since I had already written numerous books, including a premier book for educating preschool–child care teachers and one of the most sought-after curriculum books in the field, which is used for training teachers as well as for designing curriculum in preschool programs, I felt a responsibility for sharing this information with adults who are working with children in home settings.

Before beginning to outline and prepare the manuscript, I interviewed many parents, nannies, and grandparents, as well as prospective parents, to find out what they wanted and needed to know. Knowing that all caregivers need information, support, and encouragement to do the job well, my response has been to design and write a book that has been especially tailored to their concerns and needs. The inside covers of the book contain developmental norms for two-, three-, four-, five-, and six-year-old children. Moreover, the introduction contains important information on brain development that anyone working with young children needs to know. Suggestions for guiding children, tips for promoting their child's self-esteem, and criteria for selecting developmentally appropriate toys are also all included in this section of the book.

The first chapter of the book focuses on the development of art in the young child. Discussed are the developmental progression and characteristics of the stages of art for young children and the beginning of self-expression. Vocabularies of young children often fall short of their accomplishments. Therefore, tips are included for the adults working with the child. Following the introduction chapter there are chapters on painting, doughs and clays, drawing, collages, and arts and crafts. Successful recipes, activities, and methodology for introducing and working with these materials with young children are all included.

A chapter focusing on the value of cooking with young children is also provided. Suggestions for cooking with young children are outlined. Children's favorite recipes for beverages, breads, candy, cakes, salads, sandwiches, snacks, and ethnic recipes are all included. Moreover, vocabulary words to acquaint young children with cooking processes and utensils are profiled.

An introduction to storytelling is provided in another chapter. Children's interests at different stages of development are delineated. Suggestions for choosing books for children of different ages are included. Hints are outlined for successful storytelling experiences. Classic and/or popular children's books that have been carefully chosen by a literature specialist at a university are conveniently listed by concept or topic area. This listing will be helpful when attempting to select books according to the child's interests. Likewise, common vocabulary words for young children are simply defined.

Play is highlighted in a chapter with an emphasis on the stages and importance of dramatic play. Hints are outlined for the adult's role in fostering play and activities for young children. Since play is the work of young children, a list of suggested activities is included to foster dramatic play.

Other chapters include fingerplays, games, math, music, social studies, excursions, and science. For each of these chapters, there is an introduction, including the value of each topic for the child, and accompanied by numerous related activities. Hints are also provided for the adult(s) working with the child.

The detailed introduction of the book is designed to help caregivers, including nannies, parents, grandparents, and teachers. It includes:

▶ a discussion of the use of the developmental norms for young children described on the book's inside covers.

▶ a review of the recent research on brain development and the importance of providing nurturing and stimulation for young children, including the windows of opportunity to different developmental areas.

▶ tips for guiding young children and promoting positive self-esteem.

▶ criteria for selecting developmentally appropriate toys and equipment.

Acknowledgments

Throughout the long months of preparing this manuscript, there were many individuals whose encouragement, support, and expertise helped me immeasurably. My sincere thanks go to all of them.

First, I would like to dedicate this book to my grandmother, Amanda Larson, who has been an inspiration to me. She was a wonderful mentor and model. Thanks also go to my parents, Charles and Melba Rolland, for their nurturing, encouragement, and support, and to Lynda Herrmeyer, who was the nanny to my children.

Thanks to my husband, Dr. James Herr, who supported and nurtured me throughout the process.

Thanks to my sons, John and Mark, who by their development and accomplishments have reinforced the value of the book's contents and the importance of nurturing young children. They have earned all of the appreciation that I can give them; both have become independent, productive, and fascinating young adults.

Thanks to my grandchildren, Jeffrey and Eva, who keep reminding me of the importance, beauty, and promise of childhood. Thanks to my daughter-in-law May and son John, for bringing them into my life. Thanks to my daughter-in-law Molly, who shares my love for young children.

Thanks to Debbie Hass, my administrative assistant, who assisted me throughout the process. Clearly, her insights and recommendations have enhanced the quality of the book.

Thanks to all of the early childhood professionals who assisted me in making this book a reality. Particularly, I want to thank all of the laboratory teachers and students who have been professionally engaged in the Child and Family Study Center at the University of Wisconsin–Stout. Their interest and encouragement have been constant. For thirty years, they have welcomed me into their laboratories and discussed best practices, while sharing their children and families. Likewise, I would like to thank the students majoring in early childhood at the university. They have challenged me and also have been an inspiration. Without them, this book would not have been possible.

Thanks to Erin O'Connor Traylor, my editor at Delmar, who was a constant support in the inception and development of this book. Her creativity, patience, and support made the book a reality. Melissa Reveglia and Sandy Woods also deserve special recognition for their assistance. Likewise, the reviewers need special recognition.

Thanks to Earlychildhood.com and Ron Elliott, CEO and president; Judy McGuinn, chief operating officer; Megan Shaw, editor of *Early Childhood News;* Jessica Callahan, educational program coordinator; and Lisa

Derian, art director; for the use of their wonderful photographs. I also thank Elaine Murphy, director of sales and marketing at Kimbo Records, Kimbo Educational.

Finally, thanks to University of Wisconsin–Stout Chancellor Charles Sorensen; Vice Chancellor Bob Sedlak; and John Wesolek, Dean of the College of Human Development; for their continuous support of the early childhood program.

Introduction

The purpose of this introduction is to share the importance of brain development and, subsequently, the importance of the early years. Suggestions for positive guidance for promoting healthy self-esteem and an "I can do it" attitude are also included. Moreover, criteria for choosing appropriate activities and toys for stimulating the child's growth and development are outlined. Adults need to nourish children's curiosity about themselves, other people, and their environment.

A child's development is influenced by his environment—people, objects, opportunities, etc. In order to reach their full potential and beyond, young children need:

- a predictable, consistent, and stimulating environment.

- a loving relationship with the caregivers and family members in their lives.

- praise and positive guidance from their caregivers.

- opportunities for self-expression and creativity through hands-on learning and play.

- experiences to promote their curiosity, self-awareness, and problem-solving abilities.

- age-appropriate toys, books, and activities that assure success and encourage challenge.

Brain Development

Recent developments in neuroscience and powerful new research tools have provided us with dramatic new insights on brain development during the early years. Using modern technology, researchers can literally look into a child's brain. What they have discovered about how the brain works and develops will have a profound impact on how we raise our children.

Brain development occurs as a result of the interplay between nature (the genes) and nurture (the environment). Genes do play an important role; however, early experiences will either enhance or diminish the brain's development. The architecture and size of the child's brain is a result of the interaction between her genetic inheritance and everything experienced in the external environment. Therefore, the brain's development is influenced by a child's early interactions with adults in her environment, including nannies, parents, and grandparents.

Importance of Early Years

Although brain development occurs throughout life, the early years are very, very important. A child's optimal development is dependent on the interactions and experiences provided primarily during the first three years of life. During this period, 90 percent of the brain's development takes place. Our healthy interactions, or lack of healthy interactions, with young children will affect them for the rest of their lives since a child's brain develops in response to experience. Moreover, how children develop their ability to learn and to govern their emotions is dependent on their early care and learning. Warm, consistent care helps young children grow into self-assured, confident learners.

A generation or two ago, people thought that a child's real ability to learn emerged at about six or seven years of age. However, we now know it is during the early years that the most dramatic growth in a child's brain occurs. Unlike other major organs in the body, the human brain is not fully developed at birth. At birth, the growth of the human brain stem is completed, however. This center controls the vital wiring for breathing and the heartbeat. The connections or circuitry to the other part of the brain's circuit, which can be compared to electrical wiring, is weak. These circuits govern all language, emotions, math, and music. Since the circuits for developing emotions are some of the first to be constructed, the right kind of emotional stimulation is essential.

Studies

Studies show that there are sensitive periods during which the brain must be stimulated in order to create or stabilize long-lasting structures. Different parts of the brain develop at different ages, creating various windows of opportunity. Brain development is a "use it or lose it" operation. Timing is crucial for optimal development. Proper stimulation during the fertile period of the early years of life, through interacting with people and objects in his environment, is vital for an infant's healthy brain growth and development. Even a prodigy like Mozart could not have composed had he never heard music during his first years of life. The following chart on brain development stages shows the windows of opportunity when the brain must be stimulated.

Windows of Opportunity in Brain Development

Area of Development	Time Frame
Vision	Birth to 6 months
Emotional control	Birth to 18 months
Vocabulary	Birth to 3 years
Math and logic	1 to 4 years
Motor development	Birth to 6 years
Music	3 to 10 years
Second language	Birth to 5 years

This research has also taught us why early nurturing experiences are so vital to a child's development. Relationships are primary to development. Young children are dependent on close, warm, ongoing relationships for their positive emotional, social, intellectual, and physical growth and development. Depression, poor impulse control, and heightened aggression in later life can be a result of a lack of, or inappropriate, nurturing in infancy.

To construct knowledge and learn, young children need to build curiosity. Their brain development is stimulated when responding to caregivers and playthings in their environment. Therefore, they like to investigate. They need many daily opportunities for seeing, touching, tasting, learning, and self-expression to enhance their environment. They ask questions. They dump, fill, take apart, and refill. This is why young children need opportunities for manipulating their environment.

Parent's, Nanny's, Grandparent's, and Caregiver's Roles

To provide these daily opportunities, the parent, nanny, grandparent, and/or caregiver needs to actively nurture and manipulate young children's environment to meet their changing needs and interests as they grow and develop. *Webster's Dictionary* defines nurturing as "to feel or nourish, to promote the

development of, to raise by educating, training, etc." Nurturing requires providing many experiences that will stimulate children's senses and curiosity. Children learn by doing, and play is their work. As a result, it is the author's intention that you will use this book as a resource. Specifically, the ideas in this book should help you to enrich, organize, and structure children's environment, providing them an opportunity to make choices among a wide variety of activities that stimulate their natural curiosity. The book also includes hints for introducing activities and interacting with children.

Guiding Young Children

The National Association for the Education of Young Children has a saying that "Good beginnings never end." According to the famous philosopher Plato, a good beginning is essential. He said, "You know that the beginning is the most important part of any work, especially in the case of young and tender things." Thus, the early years are instrumental in building a child's healthy self-esteem, which is the belief that the child is worthwhile as a person. It is formed by perceptions about one's social, emotional, physical, and intellectual competence.

Promoting Healthy Self-Esteem

Your interactions with a child are important in shaping her self-esteem. You probably have heard of two different terms in regard to self: self-concept and self-esteem. Self-concept can be defined as the qualities that the child believes she possesses. The child's self-concept is formed at an early age. By eight or nine years of age, it appears to be well developed. A child's self-concept is formed as a result of perceptions, beliefs, and feelings. Perceptions of self are largely based on experiences that an individual has had with a person who is important to her.

A positive self-concept is one in which the child perceives himself as capable and important. As a result, the child is able to perform at a normal or superior level. During the early years, a positive self-concept is essential since young children develop important dispositions and attitudes about themselves and learning. A child with a negative self-concept will perceive himself as unimportant or incapable. As a result, this child will have a difficult time reaching his full potential.

Self-Esteem

What is self-esteem and how can we foster it in others? Self-esteem is the personal judgment that a child constantly makes about her self-worth. Self-esteem develops from the inside out. For the child, it accrues slowly from the wealth of experiences she accumulates. It is possible for a child to go through life with poor self-esteem, but this is like riding a bicycle with flat tires.

Self-esteem builds up with repeated experiences of success and failure. It includes other people's impressions and treatment. In short, self-esteem involves how a child thinks and feels about himself. It means having confidence and satisfaction in oneself. It is influenced by performance, abilities, appearance, and the judgment of significant others. All of these forces acting on the child affect his self-esteem.

If you were taught by the caregivers in your life that you must be perfect, then your sense of self-esteem may be low. Children, like adults, who have low self-esteem are in effect carrying with them the adults who were disapproving and harshly critical of their failures. These individuals experience only short-lived pleasure when they succeed.

On the other hand, if you were taught that everything you do is wonderful or even perfect, then your self-esteem may be pretty high. People with high self-esteem carry with them loving significant others who were proud of their successes and tolerant of their failures. People with high self-esteem are accepting of themselves.

Children's thoughts, feelings, goals, and actions are constantly being sharpened by the adults they live with. When they interact with critical people, they will be critical. When they interact with happy people, they will be happy. When they interact with anxious and angry people, they will be anxious and angry. Likewise, when they interact with accepting and positive people, they will be accepting and positive. The following chart contains a list of behaviors that undermine a child's self-concept.

Behaviors That Undermine Self-Concept

Rejection	Lack of discipline
Ridiculing	Sarcasm
Constant nagging	Favoritism
Constant reprimands	Demands for perfection
Excessive strictness	

Certainly, children are not born with a value system. This is learned through time. Their original image of themselves is formed in the family circle. Children develop their notions of who they are in relation to the behavior of those around them, particularly through the ways in which their behavior is received by adults who are important to them.

The most important determinant of whether a child will develop feelings of comfort is the general feeling that exists in the home. Long before a child can think things through or reason—even before she is clear about the physical boundaries of her own body—she is aware of the feelings that exist around her. A major drive of the human body is to reach and maintain a state of balance. Periods of imbalance, such as hunger, pain, and poor body position, are periods of pain. On the other hand, periods of being full, warm, held, and rocked are all periods of comfort and promote trust.

Time is important in the development of comfort and control. Feelings are built up over a period of years and are not strictly related to single specific happenings. If, day after day, a child experiences more comfort than discomfort and more attention than lack thereof, chances are that he will see himself and the world positively.

Typically, as the child develops language and reaches out for more experiences, her need for love and warmth continues. By the third year of life, she sees herself as distinct from others. Therefore, her need for support is important. Since the child is growing and constantly being exposed to new experiences both from within and without, her self is not static. It is constantly in the process of being organized—of taking in new ideas, feelings, attitudes, and adding these to her already developed personality.

"I Can Do It" Attitude

One of the most important attitudes a child can learn is an "I can do it" attitude. Observing young children, you will note that some children have a high sense of self-worth. These children feel valued, loved, and worthwhile as a person. Cues about their self-esteem are reflected in their behavior. When children have low self-esteem, their behavior may reflect unjustified anger, unrealistic fears; inability to get along with others; and avoidance of particular activities. They may also appear overly dependent, anxious, and hostile and have a constant need for attention. Their body language may reveal their lack of confidence. Then, too, they may avoid certain activities because of their fear of failure.

To promote positive self-esteem in young children, it is important that you provide the child with warmth, empathy, respect, and acceptance. Praise the child for his efforts, as well as for accomplishments. This praise, however, needs to be genuine. A realistic sense of one's identity is important. Motivation can actually be diminished in young children when given praise that is not genuine. Young children also need to be recognized for a positive approach to their work. Understanding the correlation between hard work and accomplishment is important.

A child's self-esteem is enhanced when she feels she can influence and control her environment. Therefore, the role of the adult is to provide choices, as opposed to imposing order on a child's play. This involves choosing developmentally appropriate toys, which should allow the child to be successful. At the same time, they need to challenge the child's growing abilities.

Encouragement. Parents, nannies, and grandparents can encourage children to build confidence in themselves. For young children, enjoyment often emerges from trying and mastering new skills. To assist them in this process, caregivers should use encouragement. Encouragement is a strategy that helps children have confidence in themselves. One way to encourage young children is by helping them to reflect positively on their own good qualities and accomplishments. Encouraging comments that you can make include:

> ⏵ "You did it yesterday."

> ⏵ "How clean you wiped the table!"

> ⏵ "You know how to put it together."

> ⏵ "You must be proud."

> ⏵ "I liked the way you cleaned up yesterday."

Helping over Hurdles

Sometimes you need to help children experience success by helping them over the hurdles. This often involves helping a child complete a task. It could be that the child picked up and then dumped a sibling's puzzle that was developmentally inappropriate for him. You notice that he is struggling. Consequently, you can step in and assist the child in completing the task. However, waiting and instead letting the child put the last puzzle piece in place is important. It should provide self-satisfaction.

Essential to self-confidence and a healthy self-esteem is self-pride. Accomplishments and efforts need to be commended. Therefore, if the child is doing a good job, let her know that she should be proud of herself. Be specific in your feedback. If the child has been struggling with a puzzle for a long time, say, "You have really worked hard on the puzzle."

Another positive technique for promoting positive self-esteem is to take pictures of the child engaged in different activities. Then create an album using these pictures. While looking at the album, you can tell a story. Children love to hear stories that begin with, "Once when you . . ." These stories are like a fairy tale to a child.

You might also want to consider making a picture board of the child on the refrigerator, on a wall in the child's room, or in the hallway. Once displayed, chances are the child will look at the pictures. Chances are he will also ask questions about the pictures. You can check on the child's memory and perceptions by encouraging him to tell you a story about the pictures.

Building Trust. Young children thrive in a trusting environment that is consistent and predictable. How can you build trust within your child? Begin by keeping your promises to the child. Therefore, it is important to only make promises that you can keep. If you promise that after dinner you will go to the park, make every effort to take the child to the park after dinner.

Modeling Effective Listening Skills. Model effective listening skills for the child. Much of what preschool children learn is a result of watching other people. Observe. Children who are always listened to, listen. Effective listening involves giving the child your full attention. Before talking, stoop down to let her know that you are listening. Likewise, provide other verbal cues, such as nodding.

One form of listening is called *active listening*. This form of listening lets the child know that you are listening to him. Begin by listening to what the child is saying to you. Then respond by repeating what you just heard. To illustrate, John might say, "I want to go outside." You might respond by saying, "John, we can go outdoors right after lunch." Then remain silent long enough so that the child may continue the circle of communication by responding.

Plan and provide experiences that encourage the child to listen. Do this by reading stories and poems, playing music and games, and engaging in one-to-one conversation. Set aside time each day for listening activities. To teach listening, encourage the child to listen to and identify different sounds. These sounds may include blowing a whistle, clapping hands, a rattle, a knock on the door, traffic sounds, animal sounds, household appliance sounds, musical instruments, and even clocks. If you have a tape recorder, record sounds around your home. The dishwasher, doorbell, vacuum cleaner, washing machine, food

processor, telephone, alarm clock, and other items around the home can be recorded. Play the tape for the child and encourage her to recall the items.

Using Positive Guidance. Always use positive guidance with young children. Like adults, children feel more comfortable when they receive positive comments. It is always important to focus on telling the child what to do, as opposed to what not to do; otherwise, the child may become confused. To illustrate, instead of saying, "Don't put the scissors on the floor," say, "Place the scissors on the table." If you have been in the habit of providing negative guidance, you may have to work on rephrasing your comments. The following chart provides examples of how negative comments can be rephrased into positive comments.

Replacing Negative Comments with Positive Comments

Negative	Positive
Quit yelling.	Use your inside voice.
Stop running.	Walk indoors.
Don't stand.	Sit down.
Do not use your fingers.	Use your spoon.
Do not eat with dirty hands.	Wash your hands.
Don't step on the crayon.	Pick the crayon up.
Don't get paint on your shirt.	Put on an apron.
Don't swallow the marble.	Take the marble out of your mouth.

Following Directions. Help your child to follow simple directions by using simple language. Before giving directions, always consider the age of the child. Since children have limited vocabularies, speak using simple language. To effectively communicate, your vocabulary needs to be adjusted to the age of the child you are speaking to. Then, too, your directions need to be provided sequentially. To illustrate, if you say, "We are going outside to play," and then you add, "But first we need to have lunch," the young child may immediately walk toward the door to go outside. He is responding to the first words that he heard.

Providing Choices. Listen. Adults often confuse children by offering them a choice when they do not intend to give them one. Examples include, "Do you want to go to bed?," "Do you want to turn the television off?," "Do you want to have lunch?," or "Do you want to take a shower?" Exercise care when offering young children choices. Only offer them a choice when you fully intend to let them make one. Otherwise, you should say, "You need to go to bed."

Promoting Independence. Always provide the child with the least amount of assistance so that he has the maximum opportunity to grow in independence. If your goal is to have the child become independent and develop an "I can do it" attitude, you need to encourage behaviors that lead to independence. Delay providing help until the child seems ready for it. Then ask, "How would you feel about my helping you?"

Toddlers can be encouraged to dress and feed themselves. They can also be encouraged to assist in picking up toys and returning them to their appropriate places. You might be surprised at the competence of young children. However, to encourage independence, you need to be consistent and follow through with your expectations.

Introducing Successful Transitions. When children are engaged in one activity, it is often difficult for them to make the transition to another. They need time. One way to do this is to provide time for them to prepare themselves for this change. You may say, "In five minutes we are going to have to put the toys away and go to bed." Depending upon the development level of the child, you may have to assist in picking up and storing the toys. Be consistent. If the child is capable of picking them up himself, encourage and expect this behavior. Since children are good at testing adults, they may want to revert back to a previous stage of development when you provided assistance.

Transition Activities. Children enjoy predictability. You may use different transition activities depending upon the activity that will follow. To illustrate, a popular transition for young children before nap- or bedtime often is reading them a storybook. The following transition activities can be used for clean up time, meals, and going on a walk. Encourage the child to learn the songs and join you.

Cleanup Time

"Cleanup Time I"

(Sing to the tune of "Hot Cross Buns")

Cleanup time.
Cleanup time.
Put all of the toys away.
It's cleanup time.

"Cleanup Time II"

(Sing to the tune of "London Bridge")

Cleanup time is already here,
Already here, already here.
Cleanup time is already here,
Already here.

"Do You Know What Time It Is?"

(Sing to the tune of "The Muffin Man")

Oh, do you know what time it is,
What time it is, what time it is?
Oh, do you know what time it is?
It's almost cleanup time.
(Or, It's time to clean up.)

"A Helper I Will Be"

(Sing to the tune of "The Farmer in the Dell")

A helper I will be.
A helper I will be.
I'll pick up the toys and put them
*   away.*
A helper I will be.

"It's Cleanup Time"

(Sing to the chorus of "Looby Loo")

It's cleanup time at school.
It's time for boys and girls
To stop what they are doing
And put away their toys.

"Oh, It's Cleanup Time"

(Sing to the tune of "Oh, My Darling Clementine")

Oh, it's cleanup time,
Oh, it's cleanup time,
Oh, it's cleanup time right now.
It's time to put the toys away,
It is cleanup time right now.

"This Is the Way"

(Sing to the tune of "Mulberry Bush")

This is the way we pick up our
*   toys,*
Pick up our toys, pick up our
*   toys.*
This is the way we pick up our
*   toys,*
At cleanup time each day.

"Time to Clean Up"

(Sing to the tune of "Are You Sleeping?")

Time to clean up.
Time to clean up.

Everybody help.
Everybody help.
Put the toys away,
Put the toys away.
Then sit down.
(Or, Then come here.)

Note: Specific toys can be
mentioned in place of "toys."

"We're Cleaning Up Our Room"

(Sing to the tune of "The Farmer in
the Dell")

We're cleaning up our room.
We're cleaning up our room.
We're putting all the toys away.
We're cleaning up our room.

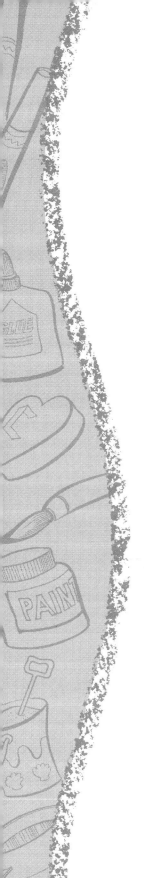

Routines

"It's Time to Change"

(Sing to the tune of "Hello Everybody")

It's time to change, yes indeed,
Yes indeed, yes indeed.
It's time to change, yes indeed,
Time to go outside.

"Passing Around"

(Sing to the tune of "Skip to My Loo")

Brad, take a napkin and pass them
to Sara.
Sara, take a napkin and pass them
to Tina.
Tina, take a napkin and pass them
to Eric,
Passing around the napkins.

(Fill in the appropriate child's name, and for napkin substitute any object that needs to be passed at meal-time.)

"Put Your Coat On"

(Sing to the tune of "Oh, My Darling Clementine")

Put your coat on.
Put your coat on.
Put your winter coat on now.
We are going to play outside.
Put your coat on right now.

(Change "coat" to any article of clothing.)

"Time to Go Outside"

(Sing to the tune of "When Johnny Comes Marching Home")

When it's time for us to go outside
To play, to play,
We find a place to put our toys
Away, away.
We'll march so quietly to the door.
We know exactly what's in store
When we go outside to play for a
little while.

"Walk Along"

(Sing to the tune of "Clap Your Hands")

Walk, walk, walk along,
Walk along to the bathroom.
——— and ——— walk along,
Walk along to the bathroom.

(Variation: Change "walk" to any other types of movement, such as jump, hop, skip, or crawl.)

"We're Going"

(Sing to the tune of "Go in and out the Window")

We're going to the bathroom,
We're going to the bathroom,
We're going to the bathroom,
And then we'll wash our hands.

"We're Going on a Walk"

(Sing to the tune of "The Farmer in the Dell")

We're going for a walk.
We're going for a walk.
Hi-ho, the dairy-o,
We're going for a walk.

Additional verses:

What will we wear?
What will we see?
How will we go?
Who knows the way?

Selecting Toys

Toys for young children are expensive. In some cases, they cost as much, if not more, than small appliances. Based on price alone, they need to be given careful consideration. Since toys can promote positive, as well as negative, learning, they should never be purchased on impulse. To get the best value, shop around. If you have not already done so, you will discover that toy prices vary from one vendor to another. Check prices in catalogs, stores, and e-commerce toy stores on the Internet.

Toys for young children need to be selected with care. You need to match the toy to the child's developmental stages, needs, interests, and abilities. A child's physical age may vary from his developmental age. While the physical age is determined by the child's birth rate, the developmental age is different. It refers to a child's growth and skill level compared to what is thought of as normal for that physical age. The right toy given at the right time can stimulate the child's development. It will provide the right kind and amount of stimulation to appeal to his curiosity. Toys that are developmentally appropriate foster success. Before selecting toys, refer to the inside covers of this book and review the typical development benchmarks. This information can provide a framework for selecting appropriate toys.

Do's and Don'ts for Choosing Safe Toys

- Do buy toys that match the child's needs, developing interests, and abilities.
- Do select toys that are open ended and versatile.
- Do buy toys that stimulate the child's imagination.
- Do buy toys that teach the child new skills.
- Do look for some toys that will involve the child with other people.
- Don't buy on impulse.
- Don't believe the manufacturer's claims, either for the age of the child or for how the toy works.
- Avoid buying toys that work automatically with no interaction from the child.
- Don't buy hard plastic toys. When they break, the resulting sharp edges can cause cuts.
- Don't buy toys unless they are nonflammable.
- Don't buy dolls or stuffed animals with glued-on or pop-out eyes.
- Don't buy electrical toys.
- Don't buy toy weapons such as guns, slingshots, or bow and arrow sets.

When selecting toys, there are numerous questions that you need to ask yourself. Safety is the most important factor. Check the toy for sharp edges. Does it have parts that could be swallowed? One way to check for safety is to try to put the toy or toy parts through the cardboard core in a roll of toilet paper. If the part fits inside this core, it is not safe for infants and toddlers. This size piece could get lodged in the child's windpipe, causing choking. Also, small pieces or detachable parts could get lodged in a child's ear or nose. The chart on page 14 contains do's and don'ts for choosing safe toys for preschool children.

Many items commonly found around the house can be used as educational toys. Listed in the following chart are common items that can be used as educational devices and the skills that they can teach young children.

Common Household Items	Skills That Can Be Learned
Clothespins	Patterning, number concepts, and fine motor coordination
Pots, pans, and fitted lids	Sequencing, matching, "What is missing?," big and little, repositions, and sounds
Cans (various sizes)	Nesting, building, sorting
Aluminum pie tins	Sorting and matching
Mirrors	Self-image, self-concept, hide and seek
Cereal boxes	Prepositions, matching, and sorting
Buttons	Matching or sorting by size, color, and textures
Magazine pictures	Classification, labeling of foods and furniture, etc.
Silverware	Sorting, matching, and patterning
Clothing	Self-help skills, matching, and color matching
Clothes with buttons, buttonholes, zippers, snaps, and laces	Fine motor development
Foods	Colors, shapes, sizes, textures, and tastes
Plastic food containers	Seriation
Plastic deli containers	Water play, nesting, stacking

Whenever possible, inspect toys prior to purchasing them. Although this is simple advice, it is difficult to follow. Many toys, especially the expensive and complicated ones, are packaged so that they cannot be opened in the store. They may be shrink wrapped or stapled closed. If this is the case, ask the salesperson if there is a demonstration model available for your examination. Rather than buying the toy sight unseen, if there is no demonstration model, ask the salesperson to open the package so that you can examine the toy. The following chart contains criteria for selecting toys for young children.

Criteria for Selecting Toys for Young Children

	Yes	No
Is it safe?		
Is it developmentally appropriate?		
Does it require a minimum of supervision?		
Is it constructed from nontoxic materials?		
Is it easy to maintain?		
Is it durable?		
Does it involve the child?		
Does it teach multiple skills?		
Is it nongender biased?		
Does it promote nonviolent play?		
Is it suitable for the space available?		
Does it add balance to existing toys?		
Is there sufficient quantity?		
Does it complement the child's existing toys?		

Adapted from Herr, J. (1998). *Working with Young Children Teacher's Resource Binder.* Tinley, IL: Goodheart Wilcox.

In addition to the criteria in the chart, make sure to carefully study the toy. Examine the small parts and how the toy works. Then imagine the child interacting with the toy. A rule of thumb is that the child should be able to master it. On the other hand, the toy should not be so simple that the child will quickly lose interest. Also, consider the purpose of the toy. Good toys are interactive. They also encourage interactive and imaginative play. Toys that are the least effective are those with a single purpose. These toys usually are close ended. Moreover, they encourage the children to be spectators.

Some of the best toys are open ended. These toys have a variety of functions. They are so simple that young children will find a variety of ways to use them on their own. A set of blocks is an example of an excellent open-ended toy that helps children learn. Blocks assist young children in the development of their vocabularies as they learn to describe colors, sizes, shapes, and positions. Young children also learn math skills while interacting with blocks. They do this by adding, subtracting, and grouping. Blocks also foster imaginative play and encourage children to make their own designs and structures. When observing young children playing with blocks, you will see that they will play for extended periods of time.

An Introduction to Children's Art

Young children flourish when provided with an environment that cultivates their curiosity and imagination. They delight in engaging in art experiences. They are active learners. Remember your own experiences as a child. Art provided you with an opportunity to create, explore, and experiment. It also provided you with active involvement and self-expression. Chances are you found art to be an intrinsically motivating experience. It provided you with an opportunity to fulfill a need for purposeful involvement and self-expression. You could communicate your thoughts and feelings in art before expressing them in words. No doubt you probably were grinning with joy as you shared your products with others.

Value of Art

Art experiences stimulate children's expressiveness. Their art is free, unafraid, messy, honest, and personal. Watch them while engaged in these activities. Art provides children with the opportunity to examine the complexities of the real world by:

- experimenting and discovering new ways of using materials.

- gaining a sense of accomplishment and self-confidence.

- mixing materials.

- sensually exploring many materials.

- learning to make artistic visual symbols—scribbles, lines, circles, etc.

- learning color concepts.

- learning shape concepts.

- developing the ability to make choices.

- learning the physical nature of materials.

- learning to appreciate the value of tools in the human hands.

- using a variety of tools: brushes, scissors, markers, crayons, etc.

- using and learning the terms for a variety of adhesives: paste, glue, cellophane tape, and masking tape.

- expressing their feelings, exploring, and experimenting.

- developing pride in one's own creativity.

- heightening perceptual powers.

- developing small muscle coordination skills.

- developing hand-eye coordination skills.

- becoming aware of texture, form, and line.

- appreciating aesthetic elements in the environment.

- learning to think in an original way.

Young children's thinking is action oriented and, consequently, they are interested in the process of art. You will note that the process of art allows children to express their emotions. Watch. Often young children find it easier to communicate their feelings through art than through words. They will squeeze and pound play dough; likewise, they will slide a felt-tip marker back and forth across paper. Observing them, you will note how they enjoy using vibrant colors in their paintings. Engaging in the use of these hands-on tools and materials is educational, as well as fun and entertaining.

While the process of art allows children to express their feelings, the product allows them to share their expressions. Together, the process of engaging in art activities and the resulting products help build their self-concept and feelings about their self. The most important trait you can develop in a child is a positive self-concept and the resulting self-confidence. Observe. Self-confidence is reflected in an "I can do it" attitude. Children who feel good about themselves are constructive in their approach to life. They focus their attention and energy on learning.

Promoting Development

Art is a wonderful sensory medium for self-expression. Through art, children learn to express their own individuality and creativity. They use the materials as a means of self-expression. As a result, art cannot be taught. Each child develops his own style. Art experiences contribute to all areas of a child's growth and development—physical, cognitive, social/emotional, perceptual, and creative. Art experiences promote the development of cognitive skills such as problem solving. These experiences also promote the development of physical skills as art tools such as scissors, crayons, and felt-tip markers are manipulated.

Young children enjoy scribbling and drawing shapes that are unrecognizable. Observe and you will discover that the art reflects their development. To illustrate, watch a two-year-old child with a pencil. Children at this age use a whole-hand approach to gripping the marking tool. They also use shoulder motions when marking a paper. You will also observe the young child using limited finger movements as she makes random marks, lines, and scribbles while motorically exploring. Gradually as the child's small muscles develop, her artwork will appear more controlled. Observing the child, you will note a principle of child development: Large motor development proceeds fine motor development.

Physical Development

Creating art helps the child develop physical, cognitive, and perceptual skills. By making large, sweeping arm motions, the child develops and gains muscular and large, or gross, motor development. Likewise, by making small, discrete motions with his fingers, the child develops small muscle, or fine motor, development. While tearing paper, cutting, pounding clay, and pasting, children are developing the muscles in their hands. These activities are important in developing the finger, hand, and wrist muscles that are needed for holding and gaining control while using marking tools. Gradually, the child will show improved control of arm and hand movements. Concurrently, he will be developing hand-eye coordination skills. These skills are prerequisites for writing and reading.

Cognitive Development

Through art, children discover new ways of using materials, tools, and problem-solving skills. They also develop language concepts as they provide names for art tools, materials, and processes. As they mix materials, they learn prediction skills and cause-and-effect principles. By exploring art and using art materials, they gradually become aware of texture and form and develop an interest in learning. As their sensitivity to visual and auditory stimuli improves, their imagination and creativity are fostered.

Social/Emotional Development

By engaging in art, young children are learning social and language skills as they interact with other adults and children. Through art, children learn what they can do and what they like. They learn to share and respect property rights. Art also provides young children with an opportunity to express their emotions. Their likes, fears, and frustrations can be expressed because art is an acceptable outlet for expressing negative impulses and feelings.

Perceptual Development

During the process of exploring and creating art, children are constantly learning. They learn about colors, including their names. By observing their own and other's work, they also learn about textures, shapes, form, size, space, and patterns. Perceptual development is a necessary skill for learning to read and write.

Stages of Development

Observing young children, you will note that there are observable, predictable characteristics and stages of art. Artistic expression keeps changing as the child grows. The characteristics of the artwork a child creates varies depending on the child's stage of development. When comparing the work of a two-year-old and five-year-old, you will observe marked differences. A two-year-old lacks the hand-eye coordination skills and the motor control of a five-year-old. The art of a two-year-old lacks purpose. Her scribbles are made for the physical sensation of movement. The child is primarily interested in exploring the tool and materials; she holds the tool with her whole hand. The child at this stage of development does not mentally connect her own movements to marks on the page. Comparing the work of a two-year-old and a five-year-old, you will also note improved line control and details in the work of the older child. The chart on the following page shows motor control and purpose at different ages during early childhood.

One-and-One-Half- to Three-Year-Olds

Children as young as one year of age are known for boldly investigating basic writing tools such as crayons, pens, and markers. By holding a writing tool, they can randomly make lines. This stage is called the emergence of **random scribbling**, or chance forms. Examples of scribbling include simple, random marks. Gradually, the young child's hand-eye coordination and small muscular control improve. As this development occurs, you will observe that the child's work reflects improved control and stronger lines. Observe a child's first attempts. He may even hold a crayon in each hand. Some children will enjoy holding the tool so much that they fail to notice the marks on the paper. **Controlled scribbling** follows the random scribbling stage of development. Now the children are aware of the connection between the marks on the page and their marking movements. Between two and three years of age, a young child can copy circles and make single lines and multiple crossings. These lines only create a variety of unrecognizable patterns. Moreover, they may be placed on various positions on the paper. The children have discovered seeing the results of doing.

Art Stages

Age	Motor Control	Purpose
One-and-one-half to three-year-olds	• Disordered scribbles followed by controlled scribbles • Hold marking tool with the whole hand • Make random lines and marks • Copy circles • Make multiple crossings	Scribble for the pure physical sensation of the movement
Three- and four-year-olds	• Hold marking tool with their fingers • Copy basic shapes: circle, oval, square, and rectangle • Use lines to draw human figures	Enjoy mastery over the line
Five- and six-year-olds	• Combine two basic shapes • Draw triangles	Shapes are combined to represent objects or people
Seven- and eight-year-olds	• Make stick drawings • Make recognizable geometric shapes	Express personality and relationship to the symbols drawn

Three- and Four-Year-Olds

Gradually, children between the ages of three to four will begin to hold their marking tool with their fingers. Their scribbling now becomes more intentional. As their thinking develops, they also begin giving a name to their scribbles. You will notice that most children between three and four years of age can copy a single cross. Space may become enclosed with scribbles. During this time, there is an emergence of **basic forms**. Circles, squares, and rectangles all are emerging. Now the child's hands and eyes are working together as they are producing the shapes.

The developmental stages of art—**random scribbling**, **controlled scribbling**, and **basic forms**—often overlap. Children will move backward. A three-year-old might begin making basic forms that require the control of lines. Then she may begin making repeated circular scribbles. Later, she will move forward, producing art that requires the control of lines for making basic forms.

Observe. You probably have already noticed that by age four, children are developing more control. Motor control is improving as the child begins using more hand movements and free arm movements. As a result, the child is physically developing; he will use full arm movements during this stage.

Circles now may be drawn as suns. These "suns" may have additional lines. Human figures will be drawn with lines. These first human figures are typically crudely drawn. The arms and legs may be represented with sticks,

while circles will usually represent the body. Gradually, children at this age begin developing control over the direction and size of a line. They are also discovering the connections between their own movements and marks on the page.

Children at this stage recognize that the objects they are creating can represent objects in the real world. As a result, they may name their objects. However, the process, as opposed to the representation, is still most important. At this stage of development, celebrate the child's progress and work. Begin by asking her to "tell me about your picture." This statement shows that you are interested in her work. Frequently the child will enjoy telling a story about her picture. Listen. Often there is not a direct relationship between the symbols and story. Children at this stage often exaggerate shapes, sizes, and relationships. Thus, as a result, their art may be either realistic or nonrealistic.

Listen carefully to three- to five-year-old children as they explain their drawings. Their comments and descriptions are a clue to their mental growth. In fact, the comments about their drawings and paintings reveal far more about their intellectual development than do their pictures. A child's verbal description can show how advanced his thinking is and how he puts information together.

Some children's motor development limits their ability to depict their subjects. Often, there is a surprising gap between what a child is able to show and what she knows. Therefore, a child's conversation may reveal her level of cognitive development.

Five- and Six-Year-Olds

At five and six years of age, the child's art is becoming increasingly more interesting. Now they are beginning to use drawing as a form of communication. Many children begin to combine two shapes by the time of their fifth birthday. To illustrate, they may be able to combine two circles to create a snowman or an inverted triangle and a circle to form an ice cream cone. Animals, boats, and cars will begin to appear in their drawings. Crude houses and trees also begin to appear. By six years of age, children typically can successfully draw triangles. They are now communicating with their outside world through drawings. In the process, they are expressing their personality and relationship to the symbols drawn.

Avoid erring at this stage of development. Once the child's art forms become recognizable, avoid making verbal requests. To illustrate, asking the child to draw a cat, horse, or sun will curtail her imagination and communication. When encouraging imitation, adults may be causing the child to become insecure in creating art. As a result, she may lose interest in this form of expression.

Seven- and Eight-Year-Olds

Stick drawings continue appearing in children's art from four to seven years of age. Although the size is out of proportion, the geometric shapes are recognizable. Emerging in the drawings are meaningful and important objects. Examples include friends, family, pets, homes, and toys. You are also likely to see gender differences in the art of seven-year-olds. As the child creates, your role is to be observant and supportive. By keeping materials available and providing positive reinforcement, you will be encouraging the creation of art.

Selecting and Collecting Art Materials

Exercise care when selecting art materials and tools for young children. Developmental levels affect the selection of media, size of paper, and tools, as well as the most effective experiences for promoting growth. Typically, children of this age are lacking in hand and fine motor coordination. One-, two-, and three-year-old children need larger, thick pieces of paper since they use their entire arm to make movements. Also, thicker paper is easier for them to pick up and manipulate. Moreover, they need paintbrushes with thick, long handles. They also need larger marking tools, pencils, crayons, and felt-tip markers. Avoid using thin, long pencils or crayons. The points of these marking tools break easily since young children cannot control the pressure. Moreover, thin pencils are hard for young children to control. In addition to marking tools, the following chart shows the materials you can collect to promote art experiences. Some caregivers place the materials in art boxes or baskets and make them constantly available to the children.

Materials to Collect for Art Activities

Aluminum foil	Clay	Glass	Nails
Ball bearings	Cloth	Gloves	Necklaces
Barrel hoops	Colored pictures	Golf balls	Neckties
Beads	Confetti	Gourds	Oilcloth
Belts	Containers	Hat boxes	Ornaments
Bottle caps	Copper foil	Hooks	Pans
Bottles (plastic)	Cord	Inner tubes	Paper, corrugated
Bracelets	Corn husks	Jars	Paper bags
Braiding	Corn stalks	Jugs	Paper boxes
Brass	Costume	Lace	Paper dishes
Buckles	jewelry	Lacing	Paper doilies
Burlap	Cotton balls	Lampshades	Paper napkins
Buttons	Crayon pieces	Leather	Paper
Candles	Crystals	remnants	newspaper
Canvas	Emery board	Linoleum	Paper plates
Cardboard	Eyelets	Magazines	Paper tissue
Cartons	Fabrics	Marbles	Paper towels
Cellophane	Feathers	Masonite	Paper tubes
Cereal boxes	Felt	Material	Paper wrapping
Chains	Felt hats	Metal foil	Pebbles
Chalk	Flannel	Mirrors	Phonograph
Chamois	Floor covering	Muslin	records

Materials to Collect for Art Activities (continued)

Photographs	Seashells	Tape	Wire eyelets
Picture frames	Seeds	Thread	Wire hairpins
Pine cones	Sequins	Tiles	Wire hooks
Pins	Sheepskin	Tin cans	Wire mesh
Pipe cleaners	Shoe boxes	Tin foil	Wire paper clips
Plastic bags	Shoelaces	Tongue	Wire screen
Plastic board	Shoe polish	depressors	Wire staples
Plastic paint	Snaps	Towels	Wood scraps
Pocket books	Soap	Trays (clear	Wooden beads
Reeds	Socks	plastic)	Wooden blocks
Ribbon	Sponges	Trays	Wooden
Rings	Spools	(Styrofoam)	clothespins
Rope	Stickers	Tubes	Wooden sticks
Rubber bands	Stockings	Twine	Wool
Rug yarn	Stones and	Wallpaper	Yarn
Safety pins	pebbles	books	Zippers
Sand	Straws	Wallpaper rolls	
Sandpaper	Sweaters	Wax	
Scrap paper	Tacks	Window blinds	
		Wire	

Sources of Art Materials

Some different, and perhaps unlikely, places in which to find materials for children's art activities include:

- ▶ lumberyards (wood scraps, sawdust, wood shavings).
- ▶ dressmakers (discarded spools, scraps, trimmings).
- ▶ print shops (scrap paper).
- ▶ second-hand stores (almost anything, depending on the store).
- ▶ drugstores (cotton balls, cotton swabs, tongue depressors).
- ▶ art, craft, and hobby shops (bulk quantities of leather, paint, clay, pictures).
- ▶ hardware stores (woodworking tools, sandpaper).
- ▶ supermarkets (macaroni, paper baking cups, foil, toothpicks).
- ▶ paint store and interior design shops (wallpaper books, painting containers, paint caps).

- ▶ school supply stores and catalogs (paper, paint, clay).

- ▶ gas stations (bottle caps).

- ▶ telephone company (scrap wire).

- ▶ office computer paper.

Coloring Books

Children under six years of age, or prior to entering first grade, should not be provided with coloring books, worksheets, or dot-to-dot sheets. These materials block a child's creative impulses. They may have limited merit in promoting the development of hand-eye coordination skills and the fine motor skills of the hand. Moreover, these structured materials fail to provide artistic merit. Consequently, it is better to have children draw their own pictures and add color to them within their own lines.

Remember that coloring book pages reflect an artist's representation of objects. The focus of these materials is on the artist's concept, as opposed to the child's. Over time, coloring books and other structured, adult-directed activities create a dependency on the child's part. They develop a stereotype of how an object should appear and deprive the child of an ability for self-expression.

Adult Interaction

Art activities are excellent prewriting activities for young children. An adult's role is important in encouraging and supporting the child's efforts, as well as accomplishments. It is important to be an interested observer who enjoys the experience. First, provide the child with developmentally appropriate materials in order to encourage self-expression. Be available to the child. Work or sit near enough to be ready to listen and help him, if needed. To do this, you must appreciate the stages of art through which the child progresses.

When providing art materials for the child, exercise caution. Remember, young children are primarily interested in the process, not the product. They enjoy moving pencils, rolling play dough, and manipulating scissors. For every action, children experience a reaction. Let them play. Let them experiment and enjoy the media. Compliment them by posting their work on the refrigerator, bulletin board, or wall. Furthermore, always give them a minimum amount of help so they have the maximum opportunity to grow in independence.

Guidelines

Remember that feelings will come out, one way or another. For young children, like adults, strains and tensions tend to mount. Art has therapeutic avenues since it is an important means for the expression of feelings. Like adults, young children are happier when they are being creative.

Avoid blocking the child's creativity. Studies show that creativity in childhood reaches a peak between four and four-and-one-half years of age. Then there is a drop at about five years of age, when the child begins formal schooling. The most important rule for guiding young children's art activities is that the process is always more important than the product. For this reason, avoid making models in any type of medium for the child to copy. When models

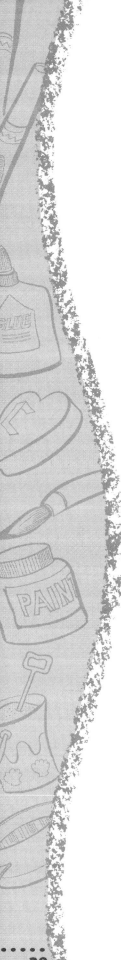

are available, the child may become blocked in using art as a means of self-expression.

Give the child the minimum amount of help in order that she will have the maximum chance to grow in independence. This means giving the child enough time to work out a problem rather than stepping in and solving it for her. Children like to solve their own problems. Moreover, their self-confidence is increased when they can do so independently.

Comments

Comments on the children's experiences should always focus on the process. You want him to have confidence in his own judgment. At all times, your goal should be to make the child feel confident and successful. Therefore, it is important to avoid asking questions such as, "What are you making?" or "Let me guess what you are making." This may cause the child to lose confidence. Remember that one-, two- and three-year-old children are not interested in the product. Their drawings are not intentional. So avoid confusing them. Children at this stage are experimenting with marking tools and creative art materials. Therefore, it is important to avoid helping, correcting, or making suggestions to improve the child's work. Given maturation and experience, his work will gradually become more refined.

Feeding-In. *Feeding-in* is an effective strategy you can use while the child is engaged in art activities. Using this strategy, you can comment on the process with comments such as:

"You are using a red color."

"I like the color blue."

"I like your work."

"Your work is fun."

"Your work is interesting."

"I always like art with the color yellow."

Open-Ended Questions. You can also investigate the child's work by asking open-ended questions. These questions should be constructed to require more than a one-word response. For example, say, "Tell me about your picture," or "Tell me about your work."

Rules and Limits. For safety and the protection of furniture, reasonable rules need to be introduced. It is important that the child know the rules and the reasons for them. If the child breaks a rule, a reminder may be helpful. If the child intentionally breaks a rule, she should not be allowed to continue with the activity. To illustrate, if a child throws play dough, you will need to provide a warning. You may say something like: "Dough is for playing with at the table. It is not for throwing." Then, if the child throws the dough again, take it away while explaining your actions.

Rules need to vary. They should vary with the age of the child, as well as the environment in which the activity is occurring. For example, you may introduce fewer restrictions for art activities outdoors as opposed to indoor activities. Caregivers, too, may have different expectations of the children, depending on the environment in which the activities are occurring. Some homes have playrooms for children; others do not. When guiding young children, regardless of environment, consistency in expectations is always important.

Rules and limits of art may include:

- Wear an apron during painting, pasting, collage, and other messy activities.

- Keep art materials at the table.

- Use tools as intended.

- Wipe up spills immediately.

- Clean up when finished by returning tools and materials to their proper storage place.

Portfolios

Besides displaying the child's art in your home on the refrigerator door and bulletin board, you may develop a portfolio. A portfolio may be in the form of a scrapbook, three-ring binder, or even a large cardboard box or plastic container. By saving the child's art, you can observe his development. Like photographs, artwork tells us a story about our children. It tells us about their development— their physical, cognitive, perceptual, emotional, and social growth.

Always label the child's artwork. Until she is able to print, record her name and print the date on the artwork. Consistently record this information in the upper right-hand corner since in the English language we learn to read by using left-to-right progress; thus, these are skills that you can model for the children. This is the way text will appear for the children when they begin reading. Also, remember that only the first letter of a name needs to be formed with an uppercase letter. The remainder of the letters should be in lowercase letters. When letters are incorrectly formed at home, children often have difficulty in recognizing their names later while attending preschool or kindergarten programs.

Drawing

Young children's drawings can be divided into two broad groups. Early **scribbling**, or the **kinesthetic stage**, represents the first stage, which begins at approximately twelve to fifteen months of age. This stage begins when the child can hold a writing tool, usually with the whole hand, and make a mark or marks. The second stage is referred to as the **representational stage**. This stage emerges sometime between three and four years of age. Gradually, children will gain mastery of the tools. Before a tool can be used to make meaningful representations, mastery is necessary.

31

Drawing

Thus, mastery is dependent upon development, as well as on being in an environment that is rich in opportunity.

Universally, children are similar in their drawings and artistic development worldwide. They all begin with basic forms. Approximately twenty different combinations of circles represent preschool children's drawings. Once the child has mastered the circle, it is used to represent the sun, humans, snowmen, flowers, and other basic forms. After the child has mastered drawing circles, he will master a cross. This progression of young children's drawings is shown in the following chart.

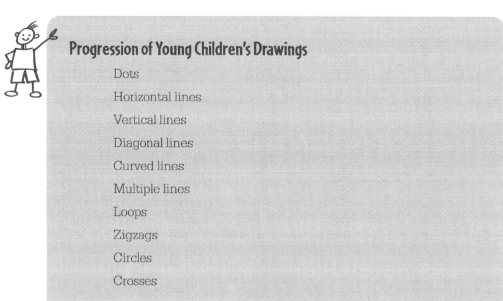

Progression of Young Children's Drawings

Dots

Horizontal lines

Vertical lines

Diagonal lines

Curved lines

Multiple lines

Loops

Zigzags

Circles

Crosses

The main goal of art experiences for young children is the process of creating, as opposed to the production of an end product. Therefore, you should encourage them to work with many different types of writing tools and papers. They will enjoy crayons; nontoxic, washable, felt-tip colored markers; grease pens; pencils; and chalk. With these tools, provide a variety of types and colors of paper. However, consider the size of the paper. The rule of thumb is, the younger the child, the larger the piece of paper is needed. Young children do not have the necessary motor control to confine their scribblings to a small piece of paper. Therefore, it is important to provide them with large sheets that, hopefully, will confine their random markings.

Two-Year-Olds

During this stage, children explore the art materials. Watch them. Prior to this stage, a young child will pick any color of paper or marking tool. By two years of age, many children are beginning to pay attention to the color of crayon or marking tool selected. Children at this age will hold the crayon in a number of different positions. Some children will hold the tool with an overhand grip, while others will hold it like a hammer between the fingers. Observing, you will notice that neither the fingers nor the wrist move. Since two-year-olds do not hold the paper with one hand, it is likely to move. If the paper does move, this will not bother the child. Usually, two-year-olds spend less than a minute on a drawing. They may even look around the room during the process. At this time, the drawing act or process is sufficient in itself.

Study the movements of the toddler. They are large, muscular, random movements. At this stage, the child enjoys the feeling of the marking tool in his hand. Gradually, the child's work will change with milestones in physical and cognitive development.

Three-Year-Olds

During the third year of life, children are beginning to take pride and express pleasure with some of their artwork. Now they are beginning to control materials and tools. Using the free hand, a three-year-old is capable of steadying the paper. At this age, the child's grasp on the drawing tool is always changing. The child's grasp is more like an adult's. Opposed to just making random lines with no concern for filling the page, the child now focuses on filling the entire paper.

Four-Year-Olds

By four years of age, the child's attention span is increasing. Now the child is spending approximately two and a half minutes on a crayon drawing. At this stage, scribbles appear most frequently, although their appearance is changing. With increased wrist and finger motion, children can create more designs. There may be short lines and long lines. These lines may also be thick or thin and straight or curvy. Care is taken in choosing the color of the marking tool, although the choice bears no relationship to the content of the drawing.

Five-Year-Olds

Observing the five-year-old: you will notice that the time spent at drawing increases. By this time, the child has complete control over the drawing tool. The necessary motor control for both direction and pressure has been mastered. Moreover, representational symbols are now appearing.

Choosing Drawing Tools

As a creative media, crayons are less valuable than paint. To make a crayon do what they want, young children have to work harder. Crayons must be pushed with the small finger muscles, which are not as well developed. Paint flow, on the other hand, will flow easily in response to the child's movements.

Toddlers will explore materials. Observing them, you will note how they enjoy tasting crayons. Therefore, it is important to select the nontoxic variety. Crayons for the younger children should also be the heavy type. Large, unwrapped, round crayons are easier to manipulate. Children at this age do not have the small-muscle coordination skills to regulate the pressure on a crayon. As a result, they may put too much pressure on a thin crayon and it will break. Moreover, they still have a challenging time holding a thin writing tool. The thicker tools are easier to handle. Since these children are inclined to make random marks on any surface, toddlers need to be carefully supervised.•

Exercise caution when purchasing felt-tip markers. They come in two types: permanent and washable. For preschool children, always select the washable type. The tip of the marker can leave a stain on the child's hands, and the permanent marker is very difficult to remove. Typically, with a little effort, the washable variety of felt-tip marker will wash off. The following chart contains a list of marking and drawing materials.

Marking and Drawing Tools

Charcoal	Jumbo crayons
Colored chalk	Liquid watercolor refillable markers
Colored pencils	Multicultural crayons
Crayons	Multicultural pencils*
Dustless chalk	Washable sidewalk chalk
Fluorescent crayons	Watercolor markers
Hexagon crayons	Watercolor pencils

*These materials can be obtained through http://www.earlychildhood.com.

Preschool children need to be taught how to care for felt-tip markers. To prevent drying out, they need to be stored with their cap on. As a result, it is important that you show the child how to replace the cap.

Removing Art Stains

To help prevent staining of the children's clothing from art materials, encourage the child to wear a plastic apron. Otherwise, have them wear old clothing. If stains should occur, treat them while fresh for best results. Stains from permanent felt-tip markers or dried paint may be impossible for any laundry stain treatment to remove. Suggestions for removing stains include:

Acrylic Paint: Wash out while still wet. Some acrylics are permanent.

Ballpoint Pen: Wet thoroughly with hairspray or follow directions on the liquid laundry stain remover.

Clay: Let clay dry, then brush the area on the garment until clean. Wash the garment as usual.

Crayon or Melted Crayon: Lay a piece of plain cotton fabric over the material. Using a hot iron, press until the crayon is removed.

Dye: Wash with hot water and chlorine bleach. It will fade.

Finger Paint: Let paint dry, then brush area to remove paint. Soak spot in cold water, apply liquid laundry stain remover, and then work area with hands. Wash as usual.

Glue and Paste: Soak in warm to boiling water as necessary. For nonwashable fabrics, sponge with a nonflammable cleaning fluid. Wash as usual.

Ink: Soak spot in a small amount of milk. Hand-scrub, then wash as usual.

Oil Paint, Oil-Base Ink, and Enamel: Place garment on newspaper. Using a stiff toothbrush, dab with turpentine. Paint will soak into the paper.

Permanent Felt-tip Marker: Try a liquid laundry stain remover, but these materials can never be entirely removed from most fabrics.

Rubber Cement: Rub the area with your finger until all of the cement is balled up and then launder as usual.

Tempera, Poster, Watercolor, and Waterbase Ink: Apply laundry stain remover and follow the directions on the container. If necessary, work area with hands. Wash as usual. A magenta pigment in tempera paint may leave a pink stain that takes numerous washings to remove.

Helpful Hints!

The following are helpful hints while working with drawing tools and materials:

▶ Store crayons in boxes or transparent plastic containers.

▶ Remove the paper coverings from crayons. This allows the children to use all sides of the crayons, in addition to the tip.

▶ Thin crayons are easier to break and are less manageable for young children.

▶ Keep broken crayons. You can melt them down and create new ones. When doing this, exercise caution. Since crayons are highly flammable, never place them directly over heat. Instead, line muffin tins with tinfoil. Place the crayon pieces inside the individual cups. Heat in an oven that has been preheated to 250 degrees Fahrenheit until the crayons have melted. When the crayons are melted, remove from the oven and place out of the reach of the children while they cool.

▶ Felt-tip markers dry out quickly when left uncovered. Consequently, encourage the child to replace the covers after use. If the child forgets and the marker appears to be dried out, try getting a flow of ink by dipping the tip in luke-warm water.

▶ For maximum effect with colored felt-tip markers, use light off-white or white paper.

▶ Exercise care when using permanent markers. They can be used on fabric if preparing gifts. However, permanent markers do not wash off from upholstery or wallpaper or out of clothing.

▶ Many felt-tip markers may be toxic. Moreover, toxic materials may be inhaled or absorbed through the skin. Exercise care when selecting felt-tip markers by carefully reading the labels.

▶ Encourage hand washing after art activities.

Drawing Activities

The following is a list of drawing activities. Before selecting, observe the child to ensure the choices are developmentally appropriate.

Arm Dancing

Provide the child with two blue crayons and a large sheet of paper. Play music encouraging the child to color, using both arms. Because of the structure of this activity, it should be used with children four years of age and older.

Bubble Prints

Collect the following materials:

- ½ cup water
- ½ cup liquid detergent
- Food coloring
- Straws
- Light-colored construction paper

Mix the water, soap, and food coloring together in a container. Place a straw in the solution and blow until the bubbles reach about 1 to 2 inches over the top of the container. Remove the straw and place a piece of paper over the jar. The bubbles will pop as they touch the paper, leaving a print.

Buttermilk Chalk Picture

Brush a piece of cardboard with 2 to 3 tablespoons of buttermilk or dip chalk in buttermilk. Let the child create designs using the colored chalk as a tool.

Chalk

White chalk and red and pink construction paper can be used to make chalk drawings.

Chalk Drawings

Large pieces of chalk can be used to draw on the sidewalks outdoors. Small plastic berry baskets make handy chalk containers.

Charcoal Drawings

Provide paper and real charcoal to be used as an application tool.

Crayon Melting

Shave crayons and have the child place the shavings on a piece of paper. Place a clean sheet of waxed paper over the picture. Apply a warm iron. Show the child the effect of heat.

 This activity needs to be closely supervised. Only the adult should handle the hot iron.

Crayon Wash

On a table, place paper, light-colored crayons, tempera paint, and brushes. The children can draw on the paper with the light-colored crayons. After this, they can paint over the entire picture.

Creating Christmas Cards

Provide paper, felt-tip colored markers, and crayons. Encourage children to create cards for their favorite people, such as grandparents, aunts, uncles, cousins, child-care provider, neighbors, friends, etc.

Designing Cars

Obtain an appliance-size cardboard box from a television, stove, dishwasher, or refrigerator. Use outdoors (otherwise, to protect the floor surface, place a large sheet of plastic underneath) and provide the child with paint, markers, and collage materials to decorate the box.

Designing Wrapping Paper

Children can design wrapping paper using newsprint and ink stampers, washable felt-tip colored markers, tempera paint, and similar materials. If desired, glitter can also be glued onto the paper to add interest.

Draw to Music

Play various types of music, including jazz, classical, and rock, while the child draws. Different tunes and melodies have different impacts. Over time, observe the variations in the child's work as influenced by the type of music.

Hand Turkey

Collect paper, crayons, or pencils. To make the turkey, begin by having the child place a hand on a piece of paper. Then demonstrate how to spread the fingers open. If possible, have children trace their own fingers. If this is developmentally inappropriate, you need to trace them. After the hand has been drawn, it can be decorated to create a turkey. Eyes, a beak, and a wattle can be added to the outline of the thumb. The fingers can be colored to represent the turkey's feathers. Then, legs can be added by drawing below the outline of the palm.

Household Tracings

Several household items, such as a spatula, wooden spoon, pizza cutter, or cookie cutters, can be placed on a table. These items can be used as outlines for tracing. Also provide paper, scissors, and crayons. You will notice that, depending upon the developmental level of the child, behavior will vary.

Leaf Rubbings

Collect leaves, paper, and crayons and show the child how to place several leaves under a sheet of paper. Using the flat edge of crayon color, rub over the paper. The image of the leaves will appear.

License Plate Rubbings

Place paper on top of a license plate. Using the side of a large crayon, rub across the top of the plate. Observe the image created.

Marker Sets

Children enjoy variety; therefore, using rubber bands, bind two watercolor markers together. Repeat this procedure making several sets. Set the markers, including an unbound set, on a table. The child can use the bound marker sets for creating designs on paper.

Melted Crayon Design

Grate broken crayons. Place the shreddings on one square of waxed paper measuring 6 inches by 6 inches. On top of the shreddings, place another 6-inch by 6-inch piece

> ⏰ *This activity needs to be closely supervised. Only the adult should handle the hot iron.*

of waxed paper. Cover with a dish-towel or old cloth. Apply heat with a warm iron for about 30 seconds. Let the sheets cool, and the child can then trim them with scissors. These melted crayon designs can be used as nice sun catchers on the windows.

Postcards

Postcards can be made to send to family and friends. Provide index cards, magic markers, and crayons. The child can design the postcards.

Pussy Willow Fingerprints

Trace around a tongue depressor with a colored, felt-tip marker. Then, using an inkpad, children can press a finger on the inkpad and transfer the fingerprint to the paper. This will produce pussy willow buds.

Ruler Design

Collect several rulers that are of different colors, sizes, and types. Using a marking tool, paper, and a ruler, the child can create designs.

Shape Mobiles

Trace cookie cutter shapes of various sizes on colored construction paper. If appropriate, encourage the child to cut the shapes from the paper and punch a hole at the top of each shape. Then, put a piece of string through the hole and tie onto a hanger. The mobiles can be hung in the child's bedroom for decoration.

Waxed Paper Rainbow

Collect old crayons. Then prepare red, yellow, green, and blue crayon shavings. Cut wax paper in the shape of large rainbows. After this, have the child sprinkle the crayon shavings on one sheet of waxed paper. Place a second sheet of waxed paper on top of the first, containing the crayon shavings. Finally, place a linen towel over the top of the two waxed paper sheets. Using a warm iron, gently press. The two pieces of paper will become bound together. Let the paper cool and attach a string. Hang from the window or in the child's room.

"⏰ This activity should be carefully and constantly supervised by an adult to prevent accidents. Moreover, only adults should handle the hot iron.

Wet Chalk Drawings

Colored chalk, paper, and water in a shallow pan are needed for this activity. Place ½ inch of lukewarm water into the shallow pan. Demonstrate to the child how to dip chalk into water. Observe the difference between wet and dry chalk with the child. Providing vinegar in addition to water can extend this activity. Encourage the child to observe the difference in the child's marking. The vinegar will intensify the color of the chalk.

Wet Chalk Eggs

Cut egg shapes from pastel-colored construction or wrapping paper. If developmentally appropriate, ask the child to cut out the egg shapes from colored construction paper. Provide two shallow pans, one with water and the other with vinegar. Encourage the child to dip chalk in each and draw. Then ask the child to describe the differences between the two. The vinegar color will be brighter.

Collages, Arts & Crafts, and Gifts

Collage is a French word that means "to paste." A collage can be described as a form of art that is created by introducing different shapes and, sometimes, materials. It involves selecting, organizing, and arranging materials. Then these materials are mounted on a flat surface. Through this process, children learn problem-solving skills. They also learn new ways for using materials and tools.

There are two different types of collages: two-dimensional and three-dimensional. When constructed from flat materials such as fabrics and papers, a collage is called two-dimensional.

Collages are referred to as three-dimensional when they are created from raised or layered materials such as wooden blocks, toothpicks, and Styrofoam.

Children as young as two years of age can create collages. The first collages that children typically prepare are those created from paper. The background should be a heavyweight material. It may be cardboard, construction paper, or manila paper. The collage materials may be cut or torn from gift wrapping, greeting cards, newspaper, magazine advertising, yarn, lace, cloth scraps, calendars, posters, junk mail, and stamps. With the exception of the stamps, the paper pieces are adhered to a larger piece of paper with paste or glue.

Natural materials also make interesting collages. Bark, stones, sticks, seashells, weeds, dried flowers, and wood shavings are examples. All of these items have interesting textures for the children to touch, feel, and smell. New vocabulary words can be introduced. Terms such as "soft," "hard," "long," "short," "sharp," and "smooth" can be used to describe these materials. Familiar terms can be reinforced.

Transparent, cloth, and masking tape may also be used when making collages. These products are much more difficult to handle, particularly for young, preschool children. They lack the necessary small-muscle development to tear these products.

Look around. Many items around the home can be saved and recycled to construct collages. The following chart contains collage materials.

Collage Materials

Aluminum foil	Chalk	Emery board	Macaroni
Ball bearings	Chamois	Eyelets	Masonite
Barrel hoops	Clay	Fabrics	Metal foil
Beads	Clear plastic trays	Feathers	Mirrors
Belts	Cloth	Felt	Muslin
Bottles	Colored pictures	Felt hats	Nails
Bracelets	Confetti	Flannel	Necklaces
Braiding	Containers	Floor covering	Neckties
Brass	Copper foil	Gourds	Oilcloth
Buckles	Cord	Hat boxes	Ornaments
Burlap	Corn husks	Hooks	Pans
Buttons	Corn stalks	Jnner tubes	Paper, cardboard
Candles	Costume jewelry	Jugs	Paper, corrugated
Cartons	Cotton balls	Lacing	Paper, newspaper
Canvas	Crayon pieces	Lampshades	Paper, wrapping
Cellophane	Crystals	Leather remnants	
Cereal boxes		Linoleum	
Chains			

Collage Materials (continued)

Paper bags	Plastic paint	Shoe polish	Twine
Paper boxes	Pocket books	Snaps	Wallpaper books
Paper dishes	Reeds	Soap	Wax
Paper doilies	Ribbon	Sponges	Window blinds
Paper napkins	Rice	Spools	Wire
Paper plates	Rings	Stickers	Wire eyelets
Paper tissue	Rope	Stockings	Wire hooks
Paper towels	Rubber bands	Straws	Wire mesh
Paper tubes	Rug yarn	Sweaters	Wire paper clips
Pebbles	Safety pins	Tacks	Wire screen
Phonograph records	Sand	Tape	Wire staples
	Sandpaper	Thread	Wooden beads
Photographs	Scrap paper	Tiles	Wooden blocks
Picture frames	Seashells	Tin cans	Wooden clothespins
Pine cones	Seeds	Tin foil	
Pins	Sequins	Tongue depressors	Wooden sticks
Pipe cleaners	Sheepskin		Wool
Plastic bags	Shoe boxes	Towels	Yarn
Plastic board	Shoelaces	Tubes	Zippers

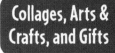

Adhesives

The adhesive used needs to be carefully selected, depending upon the age of the children. For young children, school paste is a good medium. It is easy to handle and inexpensive. Paste can be purchased at a variety of stores, or it can be homemade. The most common paste used with preschool children is called school paste. It can be purchased economically in larger quantities from school specialty stores. School paste is nonpenetrating and slow drying. The texture of paste is generally creamy and smooth. To the hands, it has a slippery feel. When first introduced to paste, often children will experiment with tasting it. Consequently, close supervision is necessary.

Use paste and tape of varying colors and widths for young children two and three years of age. Both of these adhesives will hold lightweight materials together. Observe the children's behavior. They will enjoy taping the pieces. Often, their first experiences are pasting pieces on top of each other. They enjoy smearing and even smelling the paste. Often they will rub their fingers together to explore the texture and stickiness of the paste.

Typically, wait until a child is four or five years old before introducing glue or rubber cement. Both are more difficult media to handle. They also are

more difficult to remove from the child's clothing, furnishings, and countertops. Glue is needed, however, to bond heavier objects such as tinfoil, cardboard, and wood scraps. At this time, a stapler may also be used.

Paste Recipes

Paste can be prepared in the home with a minimum of ingredients. Homemade pastes do not have the storage qualities of school pastes that can be purchased commercially. Bacteria may grow in pastes. If eaten, this could cause a problem. Given its touch and smell, a young child may sample or eat paste.

To avoid the paste drying out, provide young children with a glob on a piece of paper or in a small container. Unused paste can be returned to the container. Moreover, a small piece of wet sponge or a wet piece of paper towel can be placed inside the paste container to help keep it moist. You can prepare your own pastes using the following recipes.

Bookmaker's Paste

1 teaspoon flour	¼ teaspoon powdered alum
2 teaspoons cornstarch	3 ounces water

Mix dry ingredients. Add water slowly, stirring out all lumps. Cook over low heat (preferably in a double boiler), stirring constantly. Remove when paste begins to thicken. It will thicken more as it cools. Keep in covered jars. Thin with water if necessary.

Cooked Flour Paste

1 cup boiling water	1 pint flour
1 tablespoon powdered alum	1 heaping teaspoon oil of cloves
1 pint cold water	Oil of wintergreen (optional)

To 1 cup boiling water, add powdered alum. Mix flour and fold in water until smooth; pour mixture gradually into boiling alum water. Cook until it has a bluish cast, stirring all the time. Remove from heat, add oil of cloves, and stir well. Keep in airtight jars. Thin when necessary by adding water. A drop or two of oil of wintergreen may be added to give the paste a pleasing aroma.

Colored Salt Paste

Mix 2 parts salt to 1 part flour. Add powdered paint and enough water to make a smooth, heavy paste. Keep in an airtight container.

Crepe Paper Paste

Cut or tear 2 tablespoons of crepe paper of a single color. The finer the paper is cut, the smoother the paste will be. Add ½ tablespoon flour, ½ tablespoon salt, and enough water to make a paste. Stir and squash the mixture until it is as smooth as possible. Store in an airtight container.

Storage

Store collage materials in plastic or cardboard boxes. To keep the materials organized, place like materials together.

Helpful Hints!

▶ When constructing collages, children work best on a child-size table.

▶ Paste is an effective medium for adhering paper, cloth, string, yarn, and lace to paper.

▶ Glue is more effective in adhering natural materials such as bark, stones, sticks, and so forth.

▶ To extend glue and keep it from drying out, add a small amount of water.

 Observe children carefully. Given its smell and touch, children may attempt eating adhesives.

▶ To control the amount of paste used, provide a small amount on a paper towel.

▶ Check glue bottles. Children often forget to twist the tops shut. As a result, the glue may dry out.

▶ Purchase the adhesive, paste, or glue in larger quantities, which are more economical.

▶ To add sensory appeal, add coloring to the glue. If desired, you can color the glue according to the holidays. To illustrate, you can use orange for Halloween, red or green for Christmas, red for Valentine's Day, green for St. Patrick's Day, and pastel colors for Easter.

▶ New glue containers with a roller top are available. Some caregivers prefer roll-on glue since there are no drips or mess.

▶ Rubber cement can be purchased as an adhesive for adhering paper together.

 However, it is not advised for young children. This medium often exposes young children to strong, toxic fumes.

▶ Keep your scraps of paper in a box. Children enjoy selecting their own paper.

▶ Keep cleanup materials available. Include a damp sponge and paper toweling.

Collage Activities

Listed below are collage activities. Choose them on the basis of the children's interests, needs, and abilities.

Collages, Arts & Crafts, and Gifts

 Balls

Balls used in various sports come in all different sizes. Using construction paper or wallpaper, cut the paper in various round shapes, as well as football shapes. Encourage the child to paste them on a large piece of construction paper and decorate.

 Birdseed

Birdseed, paper, and white glue are needed for this activity. Apply glue to paper and sprinkle birdseed over the glue. For a variation, use additional types of seeds such as corn and sunflower seeds.

 Camping

Collect leaves, pebbles, twigs, pine cones, and so forth. Provide glue and sturdy tagboard. Encourage the child to create a collage on the tagboard using the materials found while camping.

 Colorful

Use paste, colored sand, and glue to make collages.

 Cotton Snowman

Cut a figure of a snowman from dark construction paper. Provide the children with cotton balls and glue. They can decorate the snowman by gluing on cotton balls.

 Coupons

Collect coupon flyers from the Sunday edition of the paper and magazines for this activity. Place the flyers with scissors on a table in the art area. If interested, the child can cut coupons from the paper.

 Easter

Collect eggshells, straw, and Easter grass or plant seeds for making collages. Place on art table with sheets of paper and glue.

 Easter Eggs

Where did the custom of coloring Easter eggs come from? No one knows for sure. In any case, the Easter holiday centers around eggs for young children. Here are some projects you might like to try.

- To hard cook eggs: Place eggs in a saucepan and add enough cold water to cover at least 1 inch above the eggs. Heat rapidly to boiling and remove from heat. Cover the pan and allow to stand for 22 to 24 minutes. Immediately cool the eggs in cold water.
- Make a vegetable dye solution by adding a teaspoon of vinegar to ½ cup of boiling water. Drop in food coloring and stir. The longer the egg is kept in the dye, the deeper the color will be.
- Add a teaspoonful of salad oil to a dye mixture and mix the oil in well. This results in a dye mixture that produces swirls of color. Immerse the egg in the dye for a few minutes.
- Draw a design on an egg with a crayon before dyeing. The dye will not take to the areas with the crayon marks and the design will show through.
- Wrap rubber bands, string, yarn, or narrow strips of masking tape around an egg to create stripes and other designs. Dip the egg in a dye and allow to dry before removing the wrapping.
- Drip the wax of a lighted birthday candle over an egg or draw a design on the egg using a piece of wax. Place the egg in dye. Repeat the process again, if desired, dipping the egg in another color of dye.

> *The lighted candle is to be used by an adult only.*

- Felt-tip markers can be used to decorate dyed or undyed eggs.
- Small stickers can be used on eggs.
- Craft items such as sequins, glitter, ribbons, lace, and small pom-poms can be adhered with glue to decorate eggs.
- Apply lengths of yarns, string, or thread to the eggs with glue, creating designs, and allow to dry.
- Egg creatures can be created by using markers, construction paper, feathers, ribbon, lace, cotton balls, fabric, and buttons. To make egg holders, make small cardboard or construction paper cylinders. A toilet paper or paper towel tube can be cut to make stands as well.
- Save the shells from the eggs to use for eggshell collages. Crumble the shells and sprinkle over a glue design that has been made on paper or cardboard.

Eggshell

Collect eggshells and crush into pieces. Place the eggshells in the art area for the child to glue on paper. Let dry. If desired, the shells can be painted. If preparation time is available, eggshells can be dyed with food coloring by an adult prior to the activity.

Fall

After taking a walk to collect objects such as grass, twigs, leaves, nuts, and seeds, collages can be made in the art area.

 Family

The child can cut pictures of people from magazines. The pictures can be pasted on a sheet of paper to make a collage.

 Flowers

Collect flowers and weeds. Press the flowers and weeds between paper and books. Dry them for 7 to 10 days. Children can use the pressed foliage to create their own collages on paper plates or construction paper.

 Fruit and Vegetable

Make a fruit and vegetable collage. Have the child draw or cut favorite fruits and vegetables from magazines and paste them on paper.

 Glitter Pictures

The child can make a design using glue on a piece of paper. Then shake red glitter onto glue. Shake the excess glitter into a pan.

 Heart Materials

Cut hearts out of construction paper and decorate them with lace scraps, yarn, and glitter to make original Valentine's Day cards. If developmentally inappropriate (the child has not mastered the cutting skill), precut the hearts. For a child who has developed cutting skills, a heart shape can be traced on paper to cut.

 Homes I Like

Provide magazines from which the child can cut pictures of homes, rooms, appliances, and furniture. These pieces can be glued on large pieces of construction paper. The construction paper pages can be stapled to resemble a book. A cover can also be added and labeled "Things in My Home."

 My Shape Book

Stickers, catalogs, and magazines should be placed on the art table. Also prepare booklets cut into the basic shapes. Encourage the child to find, cut, and glue the round objects in each shape book.

 Nature Collage

- 1 cup water
- 6 tablespoons plaster of Paris
- Assortment of natural items (rocks, leaves, pinecones, shells)
- One heavy-duty paper plate

Mix plaster of Paris and water according to package directions. Pour mixture into heavy-duty paper plate until it is about ½ inch from the top of the plate. Wait for the plaster to set somewhat. Embed natural items in plaster to form a collage. When plaster is dry, peel off the plate. Tip: Never pour unused plaster down a sink or drain.

Paper Plate Meals

Provide magazines from which the child can cut food pictures. The pictures can be pasted on a paper plate to represent a balanced meal—breakfast, lunch, or dinner.

 ## Peanut Shells

Save peanut shells. Then provide the shells, glue, and paper for the child to create a collage.

 ## Popcorn

Place popped popcorn and dried tempera paint into small, sealable bags. Have the child shake the bags to color the popcorn. Then, by gluing the popcorn onto the paper, the child can create designs and pictures.

> *Supervise the activity so that the child does not eat any of the popcorn after it has been mixed with paint.*

 ## Pumpkin Seed

Wash and dry pumpkin seeds and place them on a table or another covered area with glue and paper. The child can make pumpkin seed collages. This is a fun activity to do after carving a pumpkin.

 ## Pumpkin Seed Pictures

Dye pumpkin seeds in many colors. Place the seeds on a table with paste and paper. The child then can create a collage.

 ## Scrapbooks

Provide magazines for the child to cut or tear from. Make a scrapbook of "Things That Go" or "Things I Like to Eat."

 ## Shape

Provide different colored paper shapes and glue for the child to create collages from. The shapes can include a circle, square, rectangle, and/or oval.

 ## Shape Homes

An assortment of construction paper shapes such as squares, triangles, rectangles, and circles should be placed on a table in the art area. Glue and a large piece of paper should also be provided.

 ## Snowflakes

Cut different-size squares out of white construction paper. Fold the squares in half and then in half again. Demonstrate and encourage the children to cut and open their own designs. Hang the snowflakes on your windows for decoration.

Stamps

Collect assorted stamps or stickers. Canceled stamps can be reglued. The child can make a stamp collage.

 Texture

Provide several colors, shapes, and types of fabric for creating a texture collage.

 Thanksgiving

Provide magazines from which children can cut out things for which they are thankful. After the pictures are cut, they can be pasted on paper to form a collage.

Thanksgiving Feast

Provide children with food items cut from magazines and newspaper ads, construction paper, paste, and paper plates. Let the children select the foods they would like to eat for the Thanksgiving feast.

Wheel

Provide magazines from which the child can cut out pictures of wheels. The pictures can be pasted or glued onto sheets of paper.

Yarn and Glue Designs

Provide yarn, glue, and paper for children to use to make their own designs.

Arts and Crafts Activities

Older children who have more refined skills enjoy doing arts and crafts. Many of these activities also may involve cutting and pasting. The following are arts and craft activities that they may enjoy.

Ant Prints

Set out several washable inkpads in black and red and some white paper. To create an ant, have children press their index finger on the inkpad and then make three prints in a row on the paper. Repeat process to make more ants. Provide black and red pens so the children can add six legs and antennae.

Caterpillars

Cut egg cartons vertically in half. Place them on the art table with short pieces of pipe cleaners, markers, and crayons. From these materials, the child can make caterpillars. The pipe cleaners can be an antenna, and eyes and a mouth can be added with a marker or crayon.

Cat Masks

Using paper plates or paper bags, along with paper scraps, yarn, crayons, scissors, and paint, let the child design cat masks.

Christmas Chains

Cut sheets of red, green, and white construction paper into strips. Demonstrate how to form the links.

The links can be pasted, taped, or stapled, depending upon the developmental level of the child.

Clown Face Masks

Provide paper plates and felt-tip markers to make paper plate clown masks. Glue the plate to a tongue depressor. The child can use the masks as puppets.

Drums

Create drums out of empty coffee cans with plastic lids, plastic ice cream pails, or oatmeal boxes. The child can decorate as desired with paper, paint, felt-tip markers, or crayons.

Egg Carton Ants

Cut cardboard egg cartons into three section pieces. The child can paint the sections with "ant color" paints—black, brown, red, and gray. When dry, pipe cleaners or yarn pieces can be added to represent six legs and antennae. Eyes can be made from small pom-poms, pebbles or seeds or can be purchased at a crafts store.

Egg Carton Caterpillars

Collect cardboard egg cartons, pipe cleaners, crayons, markers, and paint. Cut egg cartons in half lengthwise. Help the child fold a pipe cleaner in half and poke it into the top of the first section of the egg carton to represent the antennae. The child can then use the other materials as desired to decorate the caterpillar.

Egg Carton Flowers

Cut apart the individual sections of an egg carton container. Attach pipe cleaners for stems and decorate each section with watercolor markers.

Eggshell Mosaic

Save and clean eggshells. The child can color eggshells with markers or paint. Then have the child spread glue on a piece of cardboard, tagboard, or construction paper. Eggshells can be broken into smaller pieces and placed in the glue to create a design.

Hand and Foot Flowers

Create a flower by tracing the child's hands and feet. Trace and cut two sets of left and right hands and one set of left and right feet. Put one set of hands together to form the top of the flower and the other set (facing down) to form the bottom side. Add a circle to the middle. Cut a stem from green paper and add the green feet as leaves. This makes a cute Mother's Day idea. Mount on white paper.

Kazoos

Kazoos can be made with empty paper towel rolls and waxed paper. The child can decorate the outside of the kazoos with colored felt-tip markers. After this, place a piece of waxed paper over one end of the roll and secure it with a rubber band. Poke two or three small holes into the waxed paper, allowing sound to be produced.

Kites

Provide diamond-shaped construction paper, string, a paper punch, crepe paper, glue, glitter, and markers. For an older child, provide the paper with a diamond already traced but not cut out. This provides an opportunity for practicing finger motor skills. The child can create kites and use them outdoors.

Little Boy Blue's Horn

Collect paper towel tubes. The tubes can be painted with tempera. When the tubes are dry, cover one end with tissue paper and secure with a rubber band. The child can use them as horns.

Making Puppets

Puppets can be made from almost any material. Some suggestions are listed here:

- Cotton covered with cloth attached to a tongue depressor
- Paper sacks stuffed with newspaper
- A cork for a head with a hole in it for a finger
- Socks and gloves
- Cardboard colored with crayon and attached to a tongue depressor
- Fly swatter
- Oatmeal box attached to a dowel
- Nylon pantyhose stretched over a hanger bent into an oval shape
- Empty toilet paper and paper towel rolls

 ## Masks

Provide the child with yarn, paper plates, felt-tip markers, and any other accessories needed to make masks. If desired, yarn can be used as hair on the mask.

 ## Milk Carton Easter Baskets

Cut off the bottom 4 inches of paper milk cartons. Provide precut construction or wallpaper to cover the baskets and yarn. Include small bits of paper or bright cloth to glue on. Make a handle using a plastic strip from a plastic milk carton.

 ## Newspaper Skirt

Depending upon the developmental level of the child, newspaper skirts can be constructed. Begin by stapling about 10 sheets of newspaper across at the top. Draw a bold line about 2 inches from the staples. Then instruct the child to cut vertically from the bottom edge of the paper all the way up to the bold line, creating strips. String pieces can be attached by stapling to the top of both sides to enable the skirt to be tied in the back.

 ## Occupational Vests

Cut a circle out of a large paper grocery bag. Then, from inside the circle, cut a slit down the center of the bag. Cut out arm holes. Provide felt-tip colored markers for your child to use to decorate the vests. Children may elect to be a pilot, police officer, mail carrier, baker, flight attendant, doctor, firefighter, etc.

 ## Officer Hats and Badges

Police officer hats and badges can be constructed out of paper and colored with crayons or felt-tip watercolor markers.

 ## Painting with Feathers

Provide construction paper, feathers (available at craft stores), and paint. The child can use the feathers to apply the paint to the paper.

 Plastic Easter Baskets

Easter baskets can be made from the green plastic baskets used for packaging strawberries and blueberries. Cut thin strips of paper that the child can use to practice weaving through the holes.

Rudolph

Begin the activity by encouraging the child to trace his or her shoe. This will be used for Rudolph's face. Then the child should trace both of his or her hands, to use as the reindeer's antlers. Finally, cut out a red circle to be used as the reindeer's nose. Have the child paste all the pieces together on a sheet of paper and add facial features.

Sailboats

Color Styrofoam meat trays with felt-tip markers. Stick a pipe cleaner in the center of the tray and secure by bending the end underneath the carton. Prepare a sail and glue to the pipe cleaner.

Shakers

Collect a variety of egg-shaped, hard plastic pantyhose containers. Fill each egg with varying amounts of sand, peas, or rice and securely tape or glue it shut. To compare sounds, empty film containers can also be filled.

Tambourines

Two Styrofoam paper plates can be made into a tambourine. Begin by placing bottle caps or small stones between the plates. Staple the paper plates together. Shake to produce sound.

Gifts and/or Decorations

Young children enjoy making gifts for others. Here is a list of gifts and activities that they may enjoy.

Bird's Nest

- 1 can sweetened condensed milk
- 2 teaspoons vanilla
- 3 to 4 cups powdered milk
- 1 cup confectioners' sugar
- Yellow food coloring

Mix all the ingredients together and add food coloring to tint the mixture to a yellow-brown color. Give each child a portion from which to mold a bird's nest. Chill for 2 hours. If so desired, green-tinted coconut may be added to the nest for grass. Add small jelly beans for bird's eggs.

Classroom Valentine

Cut out large, paper hearts. Encourage the child to decorate and sign them. The valentine can be shared with family members, neighbors, and/or friends.

Clay Figures

- 4 cups flour
- 1½ cup water
- 1 cup salt
- Paint
- Paintbrush

Combine flour, water, and salt. Knead for 5 to 10 minutes. Roll and cut dough into figures. (Cookie cutters work well.) Make a hole at the top of the figure. Bake in a 250-degree oven for 2 hours or until hard. When cool, paint to decorate.

Closet Clove Scenter

- Orange
- Cloves
- Netting
- Ribbon

Have the children push the pointed ends of the cloves into an orange. Cover the orange completely. Wrap netting around the orange and tie it with the ribbon. These make good closet or dresser drawer scenters.

Cookie Jar

- Coffee can with lid or oatmeal box
- Construction paper
- Crayons or felt-tip markers
- Glue
- Scissors

Cover the can with construction paper and glue to seal. Let the children decorate their cans with crayons or felt-tip markers. For an added gift, make cookies to put in the jar.

 Decorating Pumpkins

In carving or decorating a pumpkin with the child, you can discuss:

- the physical properties of pumpkins—for example, color, texture, size, and shape (both outside and inside).
- the food category to which pumpkins belong.
- other forms in which the pumpkin meat can be prepared after removal from the shell.
- where pumpkins grow (plant some of the seeds).
- what size and shape to make the features of the pumpkin, including eyes, nose, mouth, and what kind of expression to make.

Accessories:

- 1 bunch parsley (hair)
- 1 carrot (nose)
- 2 string beans (eyebrows)
- 2 radishes (eyes)
- 1 sheet green paper (ears)
- 1 stalk celery (teeth)
- 1 large pumpkin (head)
- Toothpicks for attaching vegetables

Prepare the pumpkin in the usual manner. That is, cut off the cap and scoop out the seeds. If desired, save the seeds for roasting.

Dreidel Top

Collect and wash out ½-pint milk containers. Tape the tops down so that the carton forms a square. Provide construction paper squares for the child to use to paste to the sides of the milk carton. The child may decorate with crayons or felt-tip markers. Upon completion, punch an unsharpened pencil through the milk container so that the child may spin it like a top.

Felt Printing

- Felt
- Glue
- Wood block
- Tempera paint
- Scissors

Let the children cut the felt pieces into any shape. Glue the shape onto the wood block. Dip into a shallow pan of tempera paint. Print on newspaper to test.

Flowerpots

- Plaster of Paris
- ½-pint milk containers
- Straws (3 to 4 for each container)
- Scissors
- Construction paper
- Paint
- Paintbrush
- Stapler

Cut the cartons in half and use the bottom half. Pour 1 to 3 inches of plaster into the containers. Stick 3 or 4 straws into the plaster and let harden. After the plaster has hardened, remove it very carefully from the milk carton. Let the children paint the plaster pot. Then have them make flowers from construction paper and staple the flowers to the straws.

Flowers with Vase

- Styrofoam egg carton
- Pipe cleaner
- Scissors
- Glass jar or bottle
- Liquid starch
- Colored tissue paper (cut into squares)
- Glue
- Yarn
- Paintbrush

Cut individual sections from egg carton and punch a hole in the bottom of each. Insert a pipe cleaner through the hole as a stem. Use the scissors to cut the petals.

For the vase: Using the paintbrush, cover a portion of the jar with liquid starch. Apply the tissue paper squares until the jar is covered. Add another coat of liquid starch. Dip the yarn into the glue and wrap it around the jar. Insert the flower for a decoration.

Glittering Pinecone

Paint pinecones with tempera paint, sprinkle with glitter, and allow the paint to dry. The glittery pinecones can be used for decoration, as presents, or to take home.

Handprint Wreath

- Colored construction paper
- Scissors
- Glue
- Pencil
- Cardboard/tagboard circle

Let the children trace their hand and cut it out. Glue the palm of the hand to the cardboard circle. Using a pencil, roll the fingertips of the hand until curly.

Heart Materials

The child can cut hearts out of construction paper and decorate them with lace scraps, yarn, and glitter to make original Valentine's Day cards. Precut hearts should be available for a child who has not mastered the skill. For a child who has cutting skills, a heart shape can be traced onto paper to be cut.

Holiday Pin

- Outline of a heart, wreath, etc., cut out of tagboard
- Glue
- Sequins, beads, buttons, yarn
- Purchased backing for a pin

Let the children decorate the cardboard figure with glue and other decorating items. Glue onto purchased backing for a pin.

 ## Key Holder

- 8 popsicle sticks
- Construction paper or a cut-out from a greeting card
- Self-adhesive picture hanger
- Yarn

Glue 5 sticks together edge to edge. Cut one ¾-inch piece of stick and glue it across the 5 sticks. Turn the

sticks over. Cut paper or a greeting card to fit between the crossed sticks. Place on the self-adhesive hanger and tie yarn to the top for hanging.

Napkin Holder

- Paper plates
- Scissors
- Yarn
- Paper punch
- Crayons
- Clear shellac

Cut one paper plate in half. Place the inside together and punch holes through the lower half only. Use yarn to lace the plates together. Punch a small hole at the top for hanging. Decorate with crayons or felt-tip markers. Coat with shellac. May be used as a potholder, napkin, or card holder.

Ornaments

- Plaster of Paris
- Any mold
- Glitter
- Yarn
- Straw

Pour the plaster of Paris into the mold. Decorate with glitter and let dry. If so desired, place a straw into the mold and string with yarn or thread.

Paper Plate Flowers

Provide snack-sized paper plates, markers, crayons, and colored construction paper. The child may use these materials to create a flower.

Paper Plate Hand Prints

Either mix finger paint or thick tempera paint. Pour the mixture into a flat container such as a pie plate or cookie sheet. Put out either white or colored dessert-sized paper plates. The child can make hand prints. These prints make a wonderful gift for parents, grandparents, friends, etc.

Paperweights

- Glass furniture glides
- Crepe paper
- Crayons
- Glue
- Plaster of Paris
- Felt piece
- Scissors

Children can decorate a picture and then cut it to fit the glide. Place the picture face down into the recessed part of the glide. Pour plaster of Paris over the top of the picture and let it dry. Glue a felt piece over the plaster.

Paper Wreaths

Purchase green muffin-tin liners. To make the paper wreaths, cut out a large ring from light tagboard or construction paper for the child. The child can glue the green muffin-tin liners to the ring, adding small pieces of red yarn, crayons, or felt-tip marker symbols to represent berries if desired.

Patchwork Flowerpot

- Precut fabric squares
- Glue
- Tins (for glue)
- Flowerpots

Let the children soak the fabric squares one at a time in the glue. Press onto the pot in a patchwork design. Let dry overnight.

 ## Pencil Holder

- Empty soup cans
- Construction paper or contact paper
- Crayons or felt-tip markers
- Glue
- Scissors

Cover the can with construction or contact paper. Decorate with crayons or markers and use as a pencil holder.

Pinecone Ornament

- Pinecones
- Paint
- Paintbrush
- Glue
- Glitter
- Yarn

Paint the pinecones. Next roll the pinecones in the glue and then into a dish filled with glitter. Tie on a loop of yarn for hanging.

 ## Planter Trivets

- 7 popsicle sticks
- Glue

Glue 4 popsicle sticks into a square, with the top 2 overlapping the bottom ones. Fill in the open space with the remaining 3 sticks and glue into place.

 ## Plaster Hand Prints

- Plaster of Paris
- 1-inch deep square container
- Paint
- Paintbrush

Pour plaster of Paris into the container. Have the children place their hand in the plaster to make a mold. Let the mold dry and remove it from the container. Let the children paint the mold and give as a gift with the following poem:

My Hands

Sometimes you get discouraged
Because I am so small
And always have my fingerprints
On furniture and walls.

But every day I'm growing up
And soon I'll be so tall
That all those little handprints
Will be hard for you to recall.

So here's a little handprint
Just for you to see
Exactly how my fingers looked
When I was little me.

 ## Popsicle Stick Picture Frames

- Popsicle sticks (10 per frame)
- Glue
- Picture

Make a background of sticks and glue picture in place. Add additional sticks around the edges, front, and back for the frame and for support. For a free-standing frame, add more popsicle sticks to the bottom of both the front and the back.

 ## Rainbow Mobiles

Precut a rainbow arc. On this arc, the child can paste Styrofoam packing pieces. After this, the pieces can be painted. Display the mobiles in the room.

 ## Refrigerator Clothespin

- Clothespins
- Glue
- Sequins/glitter/beads
- Small magnet

Let the children put glue on one side of the clothespin. Sprinkle this area with glitter, sequins, or beads. Then assist the children in gluing the magnet to the other side.

 ## Refrigerator Magnet

Use small magnets, glue, and any type of decoration (paper cutouts, plaster of Paris molds, yarn, Styrofoam pieces, buttons, etc.) to create a refrigerator magnet. Glue the decorations to the magnet.

 ## Rock Paperweight

- Large rocks
- Paint

Let the children paint a design on a rock they have chosen and give it as a present.

 ## Salt Dough Ornaments

- 1 cup salt
- 2 cups flour
- 1 cup water

Mix salt and flour; add water a little at a time. Knead 7 to 10 minutes until dough is smooth and putty-like. Roll dough about ¼-inch thick. Use cookie cutters in shapes desired. Poke hole in top for thread or yarn. Bake on cookie sheet at 325 degrees until light brown. When cool, varnish or paint.

 ## Service Certificate

- Paper
- Crayons
- Pencils
- Lace
- Ribbon

Have the children write and decorate a certificate that states some service they will do for their parents. (Example: This certificate is good for washing the dishes; sweeping the floor; picking up my toys; etc.)

Snapshot Magnet

- Snapshot
- Plastic lid
- Scissors (preferably pinking shears)
- Glue
- Magnet

Trace the outline of the lid onto the back of the picture. Cut the picture out and glue it onto the lid. Glue the magnet to the underside of the lid.

Soap Balls

- 1 cup Ivory Snow detergent
- ⅛ cup water
- Food coloring
- Colored nylon netting
- Ribbon

Add the food coloring to the water and then add the Ivory Snow detergent. Shape the mixture into balls or any other shape. Wrap in colored netting and tie with ribbon.

Star of David

Provide the child with triangles cut from blue construction paper. Demonstrate to the child how to invert one triangle over the other to form a star. The stars may be glued to construction paper.

Star of David Mobile

Provide the child with two drinking straws. Demonstrate to the child how to bend the straws so that they make triangles. Glue the straw triangles together, inverting one over the other to make a six-pointed star. Tie string to the star and hang from a window or ceiling.

Stationery

Provide the child with various stencils or stamps to make stationery. It can be used for a gift for a parent or a special person. The child can then dictate a letter to a relative or friend.

Twinkle, Twinkle, Little Stars

The child can decorate stars with glitter. The stars can be hung from the ceiling, and during group time you can sing "Twinkle, Twinkle, Little Star."

Wax Paper Placemats

- Wax paper that is heavily waxed
- Crayon shavings
- Paper designs
- Dishtowel
- Scissors

Use at least one of the following:

- Yarn
- Fabric
- Lace
- Dried leaves

Cut the wax paper into 12-inch by 20-inch sheets (two per mat). Place crayon shavings and other items between the wax paper. Place towel on wax paper and press with warm iron until crayon melts. Fringe the edges.

 This activity should be carefully and constantly supervised by an adult to prevent accidents. Moreover, only adults should handle the hot iron.

Dough and Clay

Play dough and clay are satisfying materials for young children. Give a child a handful of play dough and watch. Without encouragement, he will begin to squeeze, pound, pinch, tear, poke, push, and roll it.

It feels good to do so. These materials are helpful in promoting the child's physical development, imagination, and problem-solving skills. Play dough is a softer material than clay and is usually preferred by the young child since it is soft and pliable and thus easier to manipulate. Children can make it do what they want it to do. It also has a likeness to cooking mixtures prepared at home. Clay typically is a firmer or stiffer medium, requiring more refined muscular development to successfully manipulate. As a result, clay is more appropriate for children four years of age and older.

Modeling media such as play dough and clay are valuable materials for young children. They provide many developmental benefits. Manipulating play dough and/or clay stimulates the child's imagination and promotes problem-solving skills. By molding play dough or clay, the child also gains greater control of her hand and finger muscles. Concurrently, the development of hand-eye coordination skills is fostered. These skills are necessary for young children in order to learn how to write and read.

Dough and clay can be purchased commercially on-line through Earlychildhood.com, at toy stores or school supply channels, or in most toy departments at large stores. You can also make a wide variety of types of play dough at home. Preparing play dough is a wonderful opportunity to teach math and science concepts. Children also learn that when you mix different things together, fascinating things happen.

Typical Behavior

Children enjoy the tactile experience that is provided through play dough and clay. Depending on the child's age, the reaction to play dough will vary. Feeling, squeezing, rolling, pounding, pinching, tearing, and pushing it are all typical responses of a two-year-old. By three years of age, a child will enjoy rolling shapes and balls. Forms become more complex for the four-year-old. They may use dishes, rolling pins, and pans to make cookies, bars, pies, bread, and biscuits. They may even add small amounts of water and additional flour to experiment with changing the consistency of the dough. Upon entering kindergarten, at approximately five years of age, the child will tell you what he is going to make. For example, he may say, "I'm going to make a snowman." Other objects he may enjoy making include a ball, car, house, etc.

Texture, Color, Scents, and Accessories

In terms of texture, the younger the child, the softer the medium you should provide. When preparing homemade play dough, if the medium is too sticky, mix it to a consistency that can easily be handled. This can be accomplished by adding additional flour. Otherwise, the child may not enjoy playing for a very long period of time. Some children do not like the feel of residue on their hands. This, too, may prevent them from enjoying the medium for very long. To prevent this from happening, you may want to provide a nonbreakable shaker containing flour. If the play dough appears too sticky, encourage the child to shake some flour on it. After this, encourage her to knead the flour into the dough.

Color. To teach or review color concepts with the child, prepare a colored homemade play dough. There are two ways that you can successfully add color to play dough. Food coloring can be added directly to the liquid ingredient required in the recipe. This is the simplest method. Otherwise, you can add colored tempera paint to the flour. If you choose this method, you will need to knead the dough repeatedly to get a consistent color. You may find that a gallon-size, self-sealing plastic bag is convenient for mixing the tempera. After the dough is formed, add the tempera, close the bag, and then show the child how to knead the dough.

Coloring Play Dough. Food coloring is the preferred coloring medium to add to play dough because it does not rub off on the child's hands or on the table surface. On the other hand, tempera paint can present a challenge. It often will stain the child's hands. Then, too, it may be difficult for you to remove the tempera coloring from the surface where the child manipulated the dough. For this reason, it is recommended that you use a Formica surface or cover the table using an oilcloth or a piece of plastic. These surfaces can be easily washed clean with a damp sponge. Otherwise, you may prefer to have the child work on a work board, which may be a piece of tile, masonite, or plywood. Some caregivers prefer using vinyl placemats, brown paper bags, or a heavy-gauge plastic shopping bag cut to an appropriate size. Avoid, however, using newspaper or wrapping paper. When these materials absorb water from the dough mixture, the paper may mix with the modeling material.

Select a color to denote the holidays. The child will enjoy the variety. As examples, red coloring can be added to play dough for Valentine's Day. Green coloring can be added for St. Patrick's Day. Pink, yellow, light green, and light blue coloring can be added for Easter. Orange and black coloring can be added for Halloween. Red and green coloring can be added during the Christmas holiday season.

Textures and Scents. Children enjoy engaging with play dough of different textures and scents. For variety in textures, add sand or pebbles. Texture can also be added by introducing products found in your kitchen. Cornmeal, coffee grounds, or oats may be added to the play dough to create texture. Scents can also provide variety. For example, oils of wintergreen, lemon, and peppermint can be added. These products can be purchased at a grocery store, drug store, or health food store.

Accessories. Two- to three-year-old children need to process the dough or clay by pushing, squeezing, tearing, etc. Children, especially those aged four, five, or six years, enjoy using accessories with play dough. Plastic knives, cookie cutters, and rolling pins are examples. The first time you introduce these tools, a demonstration may be necessary. Show the child how to roll the dough and use the cookie cutters. If the dough becomes sticky, spread flour on the surface of the table. You can also rub flour on the rolling pin and dip the cookie cutters into an unbreakable bowl filled with flour. The following chart lists accessories that can be used with play dough and clay.

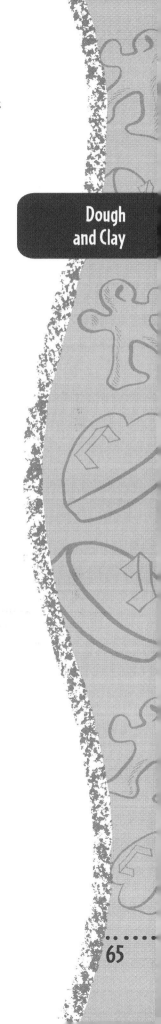

Accessories to Use with Play Dough and Clay

Apple divider for slicing	Melon ball scoop
Cake decorator	Pastry cloth
Cheese slicer	Pie crimper
Cookie cutters, alphabet or holiday	Pizza cutter
Dough press	Plastic knives
Egg slicer	Potato masher
Ice cream scoop	Rolling pins
Meatball scoop	

Storage

Depending on the ingredients, humidity, and storage, some play dough can be used for several weeks. These products may be stored several ways. Some caregivers prefer to keep play dough stored in self-sealing plastic bags. Others prefer to place them in airtight plastic bowls or coffee cans. In either type of container, the play dough can be stored in the refrigerator. However, you may have to let it warm up before giving it to the child, as some children do not like working with cold play dough. Clay, like play dough, can be stored in coffee cans, plastic bowls, or self-sealing plastic bags. There is a difference in the keeping qualities of play dough and clay. Clay, which is available from teacher supply and variety stores, can be stored for many months.

Helpful Hints!

The following are helpful hints when working with play dough or clay:

- Give each child a piece of play dough or clay the size of a small grapefruit.
- With younger children, use play dough as opposed to clay. It is softer and, therefore, easier to mold.
- To reconstitute clay, add a small amount of water and cover with a damp cloth.
- Unless using a Formica, Corian, or granite surface, cover the area with a washable or disposable cover.
- After using a modeling medium, always encourage hand washing.
- Encourage proper storage after use to prevent the medium from drying out.
- Establish rules for using play dough. These might include the following: (1) dough should only be used at the table or other place you designate, and (2) children should not be allowed to interfere with other children's use of the dough.

Gifts

Play dough makes an excellent gift for children. Whether just visiting or attending a special celebration, a gift of play dough is always welcome. Some adults enjoy giving play dough as a birthday present. Often they select colorful tin cans in which to store it. Sometimes they also will add accessories.

Homemade Play Dough and Clay Substitutes

Whenever possible, engage the child in preparing homemade play dough or clay substitutes. Through this process, children can learn measurement, cooking concepts, and how matter changes. Listed below are numerous recipes with which you can experiment. Then watch the children interact with the medium. They may develop a preference for the tactile sensation of one of the recipes. You, too, may develop a preference, based on the keeping qualities of the medium.

Dough and Clay Activities

Dough and Clay

Baker's Clay Ornaments

- 4 cups flour
- 1½ cups water
- 1 cup salt

Combine ingredients. Mix well. Knead 5 to 10 minutes. Roll out to ¼-inch thickness. Cut with decorative cookie cutters or with a knife. Make a hole at the top. Bake at 250 degrees for 2 hours or until hard. When cool, paint with tempera paint and spray with clear varnish or paint with acrylic paint.

Basic Play Dough

- 2 cups flour
- 2 cups water
- 1 cup salt
- 4 tablespoons cream of tartar
- 2 teaspoons vegetable oil
- Food coloring

Mix flour, water, salt, cream of tartar, and oil in a saucepan. Add food coloring to mixture. Cook over medium heat, stirring constantly. Remove from heat when dough forms a ball. Cool 5 minutes before using. For special effects, add glitter, colored pasta, or sand. This dough accepts scents well. Try banana extract, nutmeg, or vanilla. *Tip:* This dough will keep in an airtight container for months, but high-usage dough should be replaced every three weeks.

Bread Clay

- 1 slice of stale, dry white bread
- 1 tablespoon white glue
- Food coloring (optional)

Discard crust and break bread into small pieces. Place bread pieces in bowl. Pour glue over bread and mix. Add food coloring, if desired. Knead until soft and pliable. *Tips:* Dries hard in 12 hours. Keeps several days in the refrigerator if sealed in an airtight container.

Candy Clay

- ⅔ cup margarine
- ⅔ cup light corn syrup
- ½ teaspoon salt
- 2 teaspoon vanilla or peppermint extract
- 2 pounds powdered sugar
- Food coloring, if desired

Melt the margarine. Then add corn syrup, salt, and vanilla. Gradually stir in the powdered sugar. Then knead the mixture until it has a smooth appearance. If the mixture remains sticky, knead in additional powdered sugar. A variety of flavorings can be added, including lemon extract, imitation cherry extract, almond extract, coconut extract, or maple

 Children must wash their hands prior to participating in this activity.

flavoring. When finished kneading, younger children can form the candy into small balls. School-age children may enjoy sculpting the mixture.

Clay

- 3 cups flour
- 3 cups salt
- 3 tablespoons alum

Combine the ingredients and slowly add water, a little at a time. Mix well with a large spoon. As the mixture thickens, continue mixing with your hands until it has the feel of clay. If it feels too dry, add more water. If it is too sticky, add equal parts of flour and salt.

Cloud Dough

- 3 cups flour
- 1 cup oil
- Scent (oil of peppermint, wintergreen, lemon, etc.)
- Food coloring

Combine ingredients. Add water until easily manipulated. Usually, approximately ½ cup of water is required. This will vary depending upon the flour used.

Cooked Clay Dough

- 1 cup flour
- ½ cup cornstarch
- 4 cups water
- 1 cup salt
- 3 to 4 pounds flour
- Food coloring, if desired

Blend the flour and cornstarch with cold water. Add salt to the water and boil. Stir slowly. Pour the boiling salt and water solution into the flour and cornstarch paste and cook over hot water until clear. Continue stirring slowly. Add the flour and coloring to the cooked solution and knead. After the clay has been in use, if it is too moist or sticky, add flour; if too dry, add additional water. Keep in a covered container. Wrap the dough with a damp cloth or towel. This dough has a very nice texture and is very popular with all age groups. May be kept for two to three weeks.

Cooked Dough

- 4 tablespoons cornstarch
- ½ cup boiling water
- ½ cup salt
- Food coloring, if desired

Mix the salt and cornstarch. Then, if desired, add color. Pour the boiling water over the salt and cornstarch. Mix and continue stirring until the mixture becomes smooth. Return to the heat source until the dough forms a ball. Dust hands with cornstarch if the dough is sticky.

Cornstarch and Soda Play Dough

- 2 cups cornstarch
- 4 cups baking soda
- 2½ cups water
- Food coloring, if desired

In a pan, combine the baking soda, cornstarch, and water. While stirring constantly, cook over a medium

heat. When the mixture thickens and forms a ball, remove from heat. Knead when cool and, if desired, add the food coloring. *Note:* If you are preparing the play dough for only one child, divide the recipe in half.

Cornmeal Play Dough

- 2½ cups flour
- 1 cup cornmeal
- 1 tablespoon oil
- 1 cup water

Mix flour with cornmeal. Add oil and water. Additional water may be necessary to create the desired texture. A grainy texture should be evident in the appearance of the dough. Cookie cutters and a rolling pin can be provided to extend this activity.

Cornstarch Play Dough

- ½ cup salt
- ¼ cup water
- ½ cup cornstarch
- Food coloring

Mix ingredients thoroughly and cook over low heat, stirring constantly until the dough forms a lump. Add food coloring in desired color.

Craft Clay

- 1 cup cornstarch
- 2 cups baking soda (1 pound box)
- 1¼ cup water

Combine the cornstarch, baking soda, and water. Then cook until thickened to dough-like consistency. Turn the mixture out on a floured pastry board and knead. After use, cover with damp cloth or store in plastic bag. This recipe is good for plaques and other models, which can be painted when dry.

Cream Cheese Play Dough

- 8 oz. package of cream cheese
- ½ cup nonfat dry milk
- 1 tablespoon honey
- Crackers or bread slices

Combine cream cheese, milk, and honey in bowl. Mix until well blended. Mold sculptures on wax paper, crackers, or bread. *Tip:* Store unused portions in an airtight container and refrigerate. Decorate by pressing fruit pieces, nuts, or seeds into the dough.

Crunchy Clay Dough

- 1 shredded wheat biscuit
- 2 tablespoons white glue
- Food coloring

Crumble shredded wheat biscuit into bowl. Add glue and several drops of food coloring. Mix until shredded wheat is completely coated. *Tips:* This dough does not keep. Use it right away. Projects dry hard in twelve hours.

Edible Dough

- 1 package (or 2½ teaspoons) rapid-rise dry yeast
- 1½ cup warm water
- 1 egg
- ¼ cup honey
- ¼ cup oil
- 5 cups all-purpose flour
- 1 teaspoon salt

Test the water on your wrist. It should be warm but not burning. Mix the yeast with water. Beat the egg. Then add the beaten egg, oil, honey, and salt. Add the flour, slowly stirring until a ball is formed. Knead the dough until blisters of air bubbles appear on the surface. Create flat figures, cover, and let rise in a warm place for 30 to 40 minutes. Preheat oven to 350 degrees and bake until brown for 15 to 20 minutes. After baked, the sculptures can be eaten. If desired, the child can paint them with confectioner's frosting. Moreover, these figures can be preserved by shellacking and either given as gifts or used for decorations.

Favorite Play Dough

Combine and boil until dissolved:

- 2 cups water
- ½ cup salt
- Food coloring or tempera paint, if desired

Mix in while the mixture is very hot:

- 2 tablespoons cooking oil
- 2 tablespoons alum
- 2 cups flour

Knead (approximately 5 minutes) until smooth. Store in covered airtight container.

Goop

- 1 cup cornstarch
- 1 cup water
- Food coloring or tempera (optional)

Mix cornstarch with water in a large bowl. Add color if desired.

Kool-Aid Play Dough

Mix together:

- 2 packages unsweetened Kool-Aid
- 2½ cups flour
- ½ cup salt
- 3 tablespoons vegetable oil
- ½ teaspoon alum

Stir in 2 cups boiling water and knead.

Laundry Lint Modeling Dough

- 1½ cups laundry lint
- 1 cup warm water
- ⅛ cup flour
- 1 drop cinnamon or clove oil

Place lint and water in saucepan and stir. The lint will absorb most of the water. Add flour, stirring constantly. Add oil and cook over medium heat. When small peaks form, remove from heat and pour onto heat-proof working surface or molds and cool for 10 minutes. *Tips:* This dough does not keep well, so you should use it all. Projects dry hard in five days.

Dough and Clay

**Dough
and Clay**

Microwave Play Dough

- 2 cups flour
- ½ cup cornstarch
- 2 cups water
- food coloring
- 1 cup salt
- 1 tablespoon alum
- 1 tablespoon cooking oil

Combine flour, salt, cornstarch, and alum into a 2-quart bowl. Microwave 4½ to 5 minutes until thick, stirring every minute. Cool mixture. Knead in color.

Modeling Goop

- 2 cups table salt
- ⅔ cup water
- 1 cup cornstarch
- ½ cup cold water

Stir salt and ⅔ cup water over heat for 4 to 5 minutes. Remove from heat and add cornstarch and ½ cup cold water. Stir until smooth. Cook until thick. Store in a plastic bag. This may be used for modeling and will not crumble when dry as some modeling clay products tend to do when unfired. Beads, colored macaroni, etc., may be added.

Mud Dough

- 2 cups mud
- 2 cups sand
- ½ cup salt

Combine ingredients and add enough water to make pliable.

Children enjoy working with this mixture. It has a nice texture and is easy to use. You may prefer this as an outdoor activity.

 Remind children that this dough is not meant to be eaten.

Oatmeal Dough

- 2 cups oatmeal
- 1 cup flour
- ½ cup water

Combine ingredients. Knead well. This dough has a very different texture, is easily manipulated, and has an unusual appearance. Finished projects can be painted when dry.

Ornamental Clay

- 1 cup cornstarch
- 2 cups baking soda
- 1½ cups water

Mix all three ingredients together in a double boiler or kettle. Stir consistently until clay is of the desired consistency. Using a rolling pin and floured surface, roll out the clay into ⅛-inch thickness. Then, you can use bell, tree, or Santa cookie cutters as a tool for forming the ornament. While the clay is still moist, make a hole for hanging the ornament.

Peanut Butter Play Dough

- 2½ cups peanut butter
- 2 tablespoons honey
- 2 cups powdered milk

Mix well with very clean hands. Keep adding powdered milk until the dough feels soft, not sticky. This dough is edible.

Play Dough

- 2 cups flour
- 1 cup salt
- 1 cup hot water
- 2 tablespoons cooking oil
- 4 teaspoons cream of tartar
- Food coloring

Mix well. Knead until smooth. This dough may be kept in a plastic bag or covered container and used again. If it gets sticky, more flour may be added.

Play Dough Animals

- 2 cups flour
- 1 cup salt
- 1 cup hot water
- 2 tablespoons oil
- 4 teaspoons cream of tartar
- Food coloring

Mix the ingredients. Then knead the mixture until smooth. This dough may be kept in a plastic bag or covered container. If the dough becomes sticky, add additional flour.

Play Dough Cookies

Using red, green, and white play dough and Christmas cookie cutters, the child can make play dough cookies.

Combine and boil until dissolved:

- 2 cups water
- ½ cup salt
- Food coloring or tempera

Mix while very hot:

- 2 tablespoons salad oil
- 2 tablespoons alum
- 2 cups flour

Knead approximately 5 minutes, until smooth. Store in an airtight covered container. Play dough is a wonderful way to vent feelings. Prepare several types and let the child feel the different textures. Color each type a different color. Add a scent to one and to another add a textured material such as sawdust, rice, or sand.

Quick Modeling Dough

- 1 cup cold water
- 1 cup salt
- 2 teaspoons vegetable oil
- Food coloring or dry tempera powder
- 3 cups flour
- 2 tablespoons cornstarch

Mix water, salt, oil, and enough food coloring or tempera powder to achieve a bright color. Stir for 3 minutes, allowing salt to dissolve slightly. Slowly add flour and cornstarch until mixture resembles bread dough and knead well. *Tips:* Dough

may be dry and crumbly if not kneaded well. Objects will be dry enough to pick up in 48 hours but will retain some moisture. Keeps at least 3 weeks, unrefrigerated, in a plastic bag. Keeps longer when refrigerated.

Salt Dough

- 4 cups salt
- 1 cup cornstarch

Mix salt and cornstarch with sufficient water to form a paste. Cook over medium heat, stirring constantly. This is not sticky like flour dough and will not mold because of its high salt content. Coffee grounds, sand, cornmeal, etc., may be added to add texture and variety when dried. Children may also paint the hardened dough mixture.

Salt Play Dough

- 3 cups flour
- ¼ cup salt
- 1 tablespoon oil
- 1 cup water

Mix flour with salt. Gradually add water with coloring and oil. Add more water if too stiff, or more flour if too sticky. The child should help with mixing and measuring. Alum may be added as a preservative but is not essential in a cool climate.

Sand Dough

- 4 cups sand
- 3 cups flour
- ¼ cup cornstarch
- ¼ cup oil
- 1 cup water

In bowl, mix together sand and flour. Add corn syrup, oil, and water. If needed, add more water for desired texture. This dough does not keep well, so you should use it up quickly.

Sawdust Dough

- 2 cups sawdust
- 3 cups flour
- 1 cup salt

Combine ingredients. Add water as needed. This dough becomes very hard and is not easily broken. It has excellent keeping qualities. Therefore, it is effective for making objects and figures.

Shampoo Dough

- 1 cup flour
- ¼ cup white glue
- ¼ cup shampoo
- Water (for fusing shapes)

Mix ¾ cup flour, glue, and shampoo in a bowl. Add the remaining ¼ cup flour. Lightly flour hands and knead the dough. Reflour hands whenever the dough feels sticky. Shape dough, dipping pieces in water to fuse together. For a sweet smelling dough, try a thick, fruity smelling shampoo. *Tips:* Objects dry hard enough to pick up in three to four days. If dough is too sticky, add more flour. If it is too crumbly, add some water.

Soap and Sawdust Dough

- 1 cup whipped soap flakes
- 1 cup sawdust

Mix all ingredients together. This play dough gives a very different feel and appearance. It is quite easily molded into different shapes by all age groups. If stored in a tightly sealed plastic bag, it may be kept two to three days.

Soap Balls

- 2 cups laundry detergent
- 2 tablespoons water
- Food coloring

Pour detergent in a bowl, add colored water gradually until soap forms a ball with hands.

Soap Modeling

- 2 cups soap flakes

Use any commercial soap flakes. Add enough water to moisten. Then, using a hand or electric mixer, beat to make a molding dough. When ready to be molded, the mixture will have a slightly flaky appearance. This dough is enjoyed by all age groups and is easy to work with. Also, the texture is very different

from other media ordinarily used for molding. The figures the child creates can be dried. Although the drying process is slow, when dried, the soap can be used in the tub.

Space Mud

- 2 cups white glue
- 1½ cups water at room temperature
- 1 cup hot water
- 2½ level tablespoons borax
- Food coloring, if desired

Combine glue and room temperature water; blend thoroughly. Add food coloring if desired. In larger bowl, combine hot water and borax mixture, stirring until borax is completely dissolved. Slowly pour glue mixture into borax mixture, stirring constantly. *Tips:* The final mixing stage may require two to three people to help stir. Space mud will not stick to dry surfaces but may stick to wet or damp clothing and surfaces. Keeps at least five days in an uncovered bowl, longer if the bowl is covered with a damp cloth.

Spiders

Add black tempera paint to a play dough mixture. In addition to the play dough, provide black pipe cleaners or yarn. Using these materials, spiders or other objects can be created.

Toothpaste Putty

- 2 tablespoons cornstarch
- 1 tablespoon white glue
- ½ teaspoon toothpaste (not gel)
- ½ teaspoon water

In bowl, mix cornstarch, glue, and toothpaste. Add water. Stir until mixture is like soft putty. *Tips:* Putty may begin to dry in 20 minutes; to soften, add a drop of water. Projects will dry hard in 24 hours. This mixture does not keep well, so you should use it up quickly.

Used Coffee Grounds

- 2 cups used coffee grounds
- ¼ cup salt
- 1½ cups oatmeal

Combine ingredients and add enough water to moisten. The dough will have an interesting appearance and tactile sense. The child will enjoy rolling, packing, and patting this mixture.

Wheat Flour and Sawdust Play Dough

- 8 cups sawdust
- 2 cups wheat flour
- Water

Slowly add water to the wheat flour until a paste is made. If the mixture is sticky, add additional sawdust.

Yellow Play Dough

Combine two parts flour, one part salt, one part water, and two tablespoons cooking oil. Add yellow food coloring. Mix well. If prepared dough becomes sticky, add more flour.

Painting

Painting is one of the most popular activities for young children. It is a process by which paint is applied to another surface for visual effect. Fascinated by the process, two-year-olds may simply paint lines, and eventually circles. Three-year olds add zigzag lines and large dots, often layering colors. Frequently, this results in the paper becoming soaked. In addition to dots and circles, four-year-old children will begin aking lines that can be thick or thin and long or short. By five years of age, young children are introducing representational symbols into their artwork.

77

The three types of paints most frequently introduced to young children are tempera, watercolor, and finger paint. Tempera, a water-based medium that comes in a variety of hues, is sometimes called poster paint. Tempera paints may be purchased at local art and school supply stores or at select toy stores. A paint that is completely washable is called Bio-Color. It can be ordered on-line through Earlychildhood.com.

Types of Tempera Paint

Tempera paint is water soluble. The consistency can be varied from a sticky paste to a thin, runny fluid. In general, it is recommended that you use a creamy consistency. Otherwise, the amount of cleaning-up time will increase.

Tempera paint can be purchased in a powdered or liquid form. If you purchase the powdered, or less expensive, form, it will need to be mixed. To mix the paint, gradually add enough water to achieve the desired fluidity and opaqueness. The consistency may range from a runny fluid to a sticky paste. The consistency of some tempera paints affects their color.

If you desire to use the powdered tempera paint, only mix a small quantity. Begin by placing a small amount of powder in a container. Then gradually add a small amount of water, stirring until you achieve the desired consistency. If the mixture becomes a thick, sticky mass, continue stirring and slowly add more water.

To save preparation time, tempera paint can be purchased in a ready-to-use form. Before using, always read the directions on the bottle and shake vigorously prior to opening the container. Once opened, you may have to stir the paint. If it is too thick, read the directions on the container. To thin most tempera paints, a small amount of water can be added.

Many people working with young children add three other ingredients to the paint, depending on the desired outcome. Liquid laundry or dish detergent may be added to increase the possibility of stain removal if the paint accidentally gets on the child's clothing. Powdered starch may be added to act as an extender. The extender will thicken the paint, thereby reducing the amount of powdered paint needed to obtain the desired consistency. Liquid glue is also often added to tempera paint to change its texture and appearance. To prevent the mixture from drying out, cover tempera paint when it is not in use. Small, unbreakable plastic cups with lids work well. If the paint does thicken, add a small amount of water.

Introducing Tempera Paint

Use only one color when first introducing tempera paint to young children. Then gradually introduce additional colors. To assist the child in replacing the brush in the appropriate container, attach a strip of colored tape around each handle and container. To prevent dripping, the paint should have a thick, yet fluid, consistency.

Brushes

A brush is a tool for applying paint. There are a variety of different types of brushes that can be used. For young children, good-quality brushes with long wooden handles should be used. The width of the brush will vary depending upon the age of the child. Include a variety of brushes sized ¼, ½, and 1 inch wide. The youngest children need the widest brushes. Brushes with flat bristles and from ½ to ¾ inch wide are best for children up to four years of age. At this stage, they can be introduced to a variety of brush sizes, which will encourage further experimentation.

In addition to brushes, there are many other innovative ways to apply paint using a variety of objects. Use your imagination to provide other interesting tools. Corncobs, cornhusks, vegetable brushes, and orange peels may also be used. The size and shape of the applicators produce unique results. While some applicators are recyclable, others are disposable. The following chart contains other types of brushes that can be used as application tools. The selection of the paint applicators should be based on the child's small-muscle and hand-eye coordination skills.

Paint Applicators

There are many ways to apply paint. The size and shape of the following applicators produce unique results. While some are recyclable, others are disposable.

Recyclable Examples

Aerosol can lids	Marbles and beads	Spools
Bath brushes	Nail brushes	Spray bottles
Bowl brushes	Paint brushes	Straws
Combs	(varying sizes and widths)	String/yarn
Cookie cutters		Styrofoam shapes
Dish-cleaning brushes	Paint rollers	Squeeze bottles
Feet	Pastry brushes	(plastic ketchup bottles)
Fingers and hands	Potato mashers	
Forks and spoons	Roll-on deodorant bottles	Sticks or twigs
Hair brushes		Toilet brushes
Hair rollers	Scrub brushes	Tongue depressors
Household paint brushes	Shaving brushes	(or popsicle sticks)
	Shoe polish applicators	Toothbrushes
Kitchen gadgets		Toothpicks
Makeup brushes	Spatulas	Vegetable brushes
	Sponges	Whisk brooms

Disposable Applicators to Use with Paint

Cardboard tubes	Leaves	Straws
Cloth	Pine cones	String/yarn
Cotton balls	Pipe cleaners	Twigs and sticks
Cotton swabs	Popsicle sticks	
Feathers	Rocks	

Places to Paint

The best surface on which to paint is an easel. The sides of the easel slope outward slightly. Consequently, the paper is held at an angle that helps reduce the amount of paint drippings. The child is also at an advantage when using the easel. Full body movement is permitted when standing at an easel. This position also gives the child a full view of his painting. If you do not have, and do not want to purchase, an easel, the child can paint on a table or the floor.

Easels can be purchased through toy catalogs or at some toy stores. If you are going to purchase an easel, make sure it is sturdy and adjustable. It should also be washable, contain a tray for paint holders, and be collapsible. When selecting an easel, study the design carefully to make sure that it will be easy to clean.

Painting Surfaces

For basic experiences in painting, an inexpensive newsprint can be purchased from art stores, catalogs, and some toy stores for use by preschool children. This paper is large, approximately 18 inches by 24 inches, and allows for the gross movements of the beginning painter. Newsprint is a cream color, smooth, and slightly absorbent. Drawing paper and manila paper can also be used.

Finger painting paper needs to be smooth and shiny. Like newsprint, it can be purchased commercially. Butcher paper or shelf paper can be substituted for the finger painting paper. The following chart contains other types of papers that can be used to paint on.

Painting Surfaces

There are many types of interesting surfaces that children can successfully use for painting. The list of possibilities is only limited by one's imagination.

Air-pocket packing sheets	China	Glass
Bentonite	Clay	Glass windows
Body	Clear/colored acetate	Ice cream pail covers
Bolts	Cloth	Leather scrap
Boxes	Construction paper	Meat trays (plastic, cardboard, Styrofoam)
Bricks	Cookie sheets	
Burlap	Crepe paper	Metal
Canvas	Dried glue	Mirrors
Cardboard	Egg cartons	Netting
Carpet remnants	Felt	Newspaper
Cellophane	Fingernail	Newsprint (plain/printed)
Cement blocks	Floor	

Painting Surfaces (Continued)

Oil cloth	Rubber bands	Tissue paper
Paper	Sand	Toilet paper
Paper bags	Sandpaper	Tracing paper
Paper placemats	Sawdust manila	Transparencies
Paper plates	Sheets	Tree bark
Paper tablecloths	Shelf paper	Typing paper
Paper toweling	Sidewalks	Wallpaper
Plaster board	Smooth stones	Walls
Plaster of Paris	Styrofoam	Waxed paper
Plastic bags	Table surfaces	Wet paper
Plastic wrap	Tagboard	Wood
Plexiglass	Tin cans	Wood blocks
Rocks	Tin foil	Wrapping paper

Adding Textural Interest

Once in a while, it is fun for children to have a painting experience with paint that has some texture or an interesting aroma. Try to think of things to add to the easel or finger paint for texture. Examples are listed in the following chart.

Items for Adding Textural Interest to Painting

Beans	Dried peas	Popped corn
Birdseed	Eggshells	Poppy seeds
Cherry pits	Flour	Potpourri
Chocolate chips	Glitter	Rice
Clean cat litter	Glue	Rice kernels from cereal
Coconut	Grated lemon peels	
Coffee grounds	Grated orange peels	Salt
Confetti	Liquid starch	Sand
Corn flakes	Marshmallows	Sawdust
Cracked corn	Noodles	Shells
Cracked peanut shell	Nuts	Sugar
Crushed crackers	Oatmeal	Water
Crushed leaves	Pebbles	Wax
Dirt	Plastic beads	

Adding Olfactory Interest

Olfactory interest can be enhanced by adding to the paint the ingredients listed in the following chart.

Substances for Adding Olfactory Interest to Painting

Extracts

Almond	Maple	Orange
Lemon	Mint	Vanilla

Spices

Cinnamon	Cloves
Cinnamon sticks	Nutmeg

Other

Coffee grounds	Orange juice	Shampoo
Grape juice	Peanut butter	Soap
Hot chocolate powder	Peppermint sticks	Tea
Jell-O	Perfume	Vinegar
Licorice	Pickles	
Limes	Pine-scented cleaners	

Helpful Hints!

The following are helpful hints while working with painting activities.

▶ Cover the floor if using an easel. A plastic tablecloth, oil cloth, or shower curtain works well.

▶ Plastic aprons should be worn to protect the children's clothing.

▶ Wipe up spills as soon as possible.

▶ Wash brushes as soon as possible after use.

▶ Cover paint containers after use.

▶ Color code brushes and paint containers by taping on a piece of matching colored construction paper or tape. This will help the child return the brush to the matching color of paint container.

▶ Print the child's name on the upper left-hand corner of the paper. Use upper-case (or capital) lettering only for the first letter of the name.

▶ Hang or lay the painting to dry.

▶ If painting outdoors, a portable easel can be constructed from a cardboard television carton. Cut it down to the child's eye level. Clamps can be used to attach the paper.

▶ If desired, using numerals, record the date the child completed the painting under the name.

Painting Activities

There are numerous painting and printing activities that can be introduced to young children. Remember, however, to carefully choose these activities based on the child's needs, abilities, and interests.

Box House

Place a large cardboard box outside. Provide smocks, house painting brushes, and tempera paint for the child to use to decorate the box.

Brush

Display various brushes such as hair, makeup, tooth, and clothes brushes. In addition, thin tempera paint and paper should be provided. Let the child explore the painting process with a variety of brushes.

Candy Cane Marble

Cut red construction paper into candy cane shapes. Paint stripes on the candy canes with white tempera paint.

Car

Provide several small plastic cars and trucks plus large sheets of white paper. Also have available low, flat pans of thin tempera paint. Encourage the child to take the cars and trucks and roll the wheels in the paint. He can then transfer the car to paper and make car or truck tracks on the paper.

Color Mixing

Provide red-, yellow-, and blue-dyed water in shallow pans. Provide the child with medicine droppers and absorbent paper cut in the shape of eggs. The child can also use medicine droppers to apply color to the paper. Observe what happens when the colors blend together.

Color Swab

Place cotton swabs, cotton balls, and tempera paint on a table. The cotton swabs and balls can be used as painting tools.

Corn Cob

Cover the bottom of a shallow pan with thick, yellow tempera paint. Using a corncob as an applicator, apply paint to paper.

Dental Floss

Provide thin tempera paint, paper, and dental floss. The child can spoon a small amount of paint onto the paper and hold onto one end of the dental floss while moving the free end through the paint to make a design.

Eye Dropper

Paint with an eyedropper as an application tool and water colored with food coloring.

Finger

Colored fingerpaint and large sheets of paper can be placed in the art area.

Foot

This may be used as an outdoor activity. The child can dip her feet in a thick tempera paint mixture and make prints by stepping on large sheets of paper. Sponges and pans of soapy water should be available for cleanup.

Footprints

Mix tempera paint. Pour the paint into a shallow jelly roll pan approximately ¼-inch deep. The child can dip his feet into the pan. After this, he can step directly onto paper. Using the feet as an application tool, footsteps can be made. This activity actually could be used to create a mural, which could be hung in the room.

Frosted Pictures

Mix 1 part Epsom salts with 1 part boiling water. Let the mixture cool. Encourage the child to make a crayon design on paper. The mixture can be brushed over the picture. Observe how the crystals form as the mixture dries.

Golf Ball

Place a piece of paper in a shallow tray or pie tin. Spoon two or three teaspoons of thin paint onto the paper. Then, put a golf or ping-pong ball in the tray and tilt the pan in a number of directions, allowing the ball to make designs in the paint.

Ice Cube Art

Place a popsicle stick in each ice compartment of a tray and fill with water. Freeze. Sprinkle dry tempera paint on paper. Then, to make the design, the child can move an ice cube on the paper.

Paint Blots

Fold a piece of paper in half. Open up and place a spoon of red paint on the inside of the paper. Refold paper and press flat. Reopen and observe the design. Add two colors, such as blue and yellow, and repeat the process to show color mixing.

Paint With Celery Leaves

Mix some thin tempera paint. Use celery leaves as a painting tool.

Pine Branch

Collect short pine boughs to use as painting tools. The tools can be placed at the easel or used with a shallow pan of tempera paint on a table.

Shake

Tape a large piece of butcher-block paper on a fence or wall outdoors. Let the child dip the brushes in paint and stand two feet from the paper. Then show her how to shake the brush, allowing the paint to fly onto the paper.

Snow

White chalk and dark construction paper can be placed in the art area.

Sparkly Paint

- ½ cup flour
- ½ cup water
- ½ cup salt
- Dry tempera powder

Mix flour, water, and salt in bowl. Use a funnel to pour the mixture into squeeze bottles. Add tempera to achieve desired color and shake well. Paint can also be used with paintbrushes or other painting gadgets. Try paint rollers, vegetable brushes, old toothbrushes, sponge shapes, eyedroppers, potato mashers, and any other items you may have.

Spider Webs

Cut circles of black paper to fit in the bottom of a pie tin. Mix thin silver or white tempera paint. Place a marble and two teaspoons of paint on the paper. By gently tilting the pie tin, allow the marble to roll through the paint, creating a spider web design.

Sponge

Cut sponges into the four basic shapes. The child can hold the sponges with a clothespin. The sponge can then be dipped in paint and printed on the paper. Make several designs and shapes.

Straw Painting

Paper, straws, thin tempera, and spoons can be placed on the table. Spoon a small amount of paint onto the paper. Using a straw, blow paint on the paper to make a design.

Tile

Ask building companies to donate cracked, chipped, or discontinued tiles. The child can paint these tiles.

Painting

Whipped Soap

Mix 1 cup commercial soap flakes with ½ cup warm water in bowl. The child can beat the mixture with a hand eggbeater until it is fluffy. Apply the mixture to dark construction paper with various tools (toothbrushes, rollers, tongue depressors, brushes, etc.). To create variety, food coloring can be added to the paint mixture.

Painting

Easel Painting Activities

Each day change the type of brushes the child can use while painting at the easel. Variations may include: sponge brushes, discarded toothbrushes, nail polish brushes, vegetable brushes, and makeup brushes.

▷ Feature clothes-shaped easel paper.

▷ Paint using tools created by attaching small sponges to a clothespin.

▷ Paint with discarded toothbrushes.

▷ Paint on tooth-shaped easel paper.

Color Changes

Feature white paint at the easel for snow pictures on colored paper. Or cut easel paper into winter shapes: snowmen, hats, mittens, scarves, snowflakes, etc. Provide orange and black paint at the paint easels. Feature shades of different colors of paint at the easel. Use blue paint on aluminum foil. Add whipped soap flakes to blue paint for variety. Add a container of yellow paint to the easel. Allow the child to mix the yellow and blue paints at the easel. Providing red tempera paint can extend this activity. Provide pastel paints at the easel. To make the paint more interesting, add glitter.

Cutting Vegetable, Fruit, and Flower Shapes

Cut easel paper into a different fruit or vegetable shape each day. Cut basket-shaped paper. Clip to the easel to "hold" the vegetables and fruit. Cut easel paper into different leaves and flowers. Put these into the baskets or easel paper flower pots.

Cutting Sports Shapes

Cut easel paper in various sports shapes.
- Baseball cap
- Baseball diamond
- Baseball glove
- Football
- Football helmet
- Bike
- Tennis racket
- Tennis shoe
- Many different sizes of balls

Printing with Paint Activities

Printing is an extension of painting that requires less whole-arm movement and more hand-eye coordination. It involves placing an object in a pan with thick tempera paint or on a large inkpad and then stamping it on paper. Often this process is referred to as object printing.

Painting

Apple

Cut apples in half. Place them in individual shallow pans of red, yellow, and green tempera paint. Provide paper. The apple can be used as a painting tool. To illustrate, the child can place an apple half in the paint. After wiping off the excess paint, the apple can be placed on paper creating a print.

Bubble

Collect the following materials: ½ cup water, ½ cup liquid soap, food coloring, straws, and light-colored construction paper. Mix together the water, soap, and food coloring in a container. Place a straw in the solution and blow until the bubbles reach 1 to 2 inches over the top of the container. Remove the straw and place a piece of paper over the jar. The bubbles will pop as they touch the paper, leaving a print.

Cookie Cutter

Provide Christmas cookie cutters, paper, and shallow pans containing red and green paint. The child can apply the paint to the paper using the cookie cutters as printing tools.

Heart Prints

Provide white paper and various heart-shaped cookie cutters. Mix pink and red tempera paint and pour into shallow pans. The child can print hearts on white construction paper, using the cookie cutters as a tool, and then paint them.

Popsicle Stick Prints

Cover the bottom of a shallow pan with thick, yellow tempera paint. Apply the paint to paper using a popsicle stick as an applicator.

Potato

Cut potatoes in half. The child can dip them in paint and stamp them on a large sheet of paper.

 Sponge

Cut farm animal shapes out of sponges. If a pattern is needed, cut out of a coloring book. Once cut, the sponge forms can be dipped into a pan of thick tempera paint and used as a tool to apply a design.

Winter Shapes

Cut sponges into various winter shapes such as boots, snowmen, mittens, snowflakes, fir trees, and stars. The child can use the sponges as a tool to print on different pieces of colored construction paper.

Painting

Finger and Hand Painting

Preschool children enjoy finger and hand painting. The direct contact with the painting medium has particular appeal for them. The feel of the paint is cool and the texture is somewhat slimy. In addition, shaving cream may be used for a finger painting medium. However, when selecting shaving cream, avoid the menthol type. Some children are allergic to the smell. Children can also finger paint using pudding, although some people object to having children use food for this experience.

The child's whole arms, hands, and fingers are all tools that can be used for finger painting. To avoid restricting movements, the best place for finger painting is at a table. The following are finger paint recipes that may be used.

Finger and Hand Painting Recipes

Cooked Starch Method

- 1 cup laundry starch dissolved in a small amount of cold water
- 5 cups boiling water added slowly to dissolve starch
- 1 tablespoon glycerin (optional)

Cook the mixture until it is thick and glossy. Add 1 cup mild soap flakes. Add color in separate containers. Cool before using.

Cornstarch Method

- 2 quarts water
- 1 cup cornstarch
- ½ cup soap flakes

Gradually add water to cornstarch. Cook until clear and add soap flakes.

A few drops of glycerin or oil of wintergreen may be added.

Edible Finger Paint

- 1 tablespoon light corn syrup
- Food coloring

Pour a puddle of corn syrup onto the paper plate. Squirt food coloring into the puddle. Mix and paint with fingers. Experiment with other edible additives for flavor and color. Try adding peanut butter, chocolate syrup, fruit jelly, or marshmallow topping. For texture, add candy sprinkles, coconut flakes, or dry cereal. Chocolate or pistachio puddings are other delicious edible finger paints.

Flour and Salt I

- 1 cup flour
- 1½ cups salt
- ¾ cup water
- Food coloring

Combine flour and salt. Add water. This has a grainy quality, unlike the other finger paints, providing a different sensory experience. Some children also enjoy the different touch sensation when 1½ cup salt is added to the other recipes listed here.

Flour and Salt II

- 2 cups flour
- 2 teaspoons salt
- 3 cups cold water
- 2 cups hot water
- Food coloring

Add salt to flour, then pour in cold water gradually and beat mixture with an egg beater until it is smooth. Add hot water and boil until it becomes clear. Beat until smooth, then add coloring to obtain desired color intensity.

Flour Method

- 1 cup flour
- 1 cup cold water
- 3 cups boiling water
- 1 tablespoon alum
- Food coloring

Mix flour and cold water. Add boiling water and bring all to a boil,

stirring constantly. Add alum and coloring. Paintings from this recipe dry flat and do not need to be ironed.

Instantized Flour, Uncooked Method

- 1 pint water (2 cups)
- 1½ cups instantized flour (the kind used to thicken gravy)

Put the water in the bowl and stir the flour into the water. Add color. Regular flour may be lumpy.

Liquid Starch Method

- Liquid starch (put in squeeze bottles)
- Dry tempera paint in shakers

Put about 1 tablespoon of liquid starch on the surface to be painted. Let the child shake the paint onto the starch. Mix and blend the paint. *Note:* If this paint becomes too thick, simply sprinkle a few drops of water onto the painting.

Soap Flake Method

Mix in a small bowl:

- Soap flakes
- A small amount of water

Beat until stiff with an eggbeater. Use white soap on dark paper, or add to the soap and use it on light-colored paper. This gives a slightly three-dimensional effect.

🎨 Uncooked Laundry Starch

A mixture of 1 cup liquid laundry starch, 1 cup cold water, and 3 cups soap flakes will provide a quick finger paint.

🎨 Wheat Flour Paste

- 3 parts water
- 1 part wheat paste flour
- Food coloring

Stir the flour into the water. Then add the coloring and mix. (Wallpaper paste can be bought a low cost in wallpaper stores or department stores.)

Helpful Hints!

The following are helpful hints while working with finger and hand painting activities.

▶ Be sure you have running water and towels nearby or provide a large basin of water where children can rinse off.

▶ Finger paint on a smooth table or on oilcloth or a cafeteria tray. Some children prefer to start finger painting with shaving cream on a sheet of oilcloth.

▶ Food coloring or powdered paint may be added to mixture before using or allow child to choose the colors he wants sprinkled on top of paint.

▶ Sometimes reluctant children are more easily attracted to the paint table if the finger paints are already cooled.

▶ Cover the floor under the table. A plastic tablecloth, oilcloth, or shower curtain works well.

▶ Plastic aprons should be worn to protect the children's clothing.

▶ Wipe up spills as soon as possible.

▶ Hang or lay the painting to dry.

▶ Print the child's name in the upper right-hand corner. If desired, also use numerals to record the date.

Sensory Experiences—
Water and Sand Play

Water and sand play are pleasurable learning activities that serve as sensory experiences. They provide young children with long periods of satisfaction. Watch them. They love to feel, shove, splash, pour, pat, and squirt. For young children, water and sand are basic materials like paint and play dough. Fortunately, these materials are almost always available, and at little expense. Moreover, these activities can occur indoors or outdoors.

Value

Water and sand play are therapeutic. Both mediums offer fluid and unstructured experiences. Children use the satisfying media to explore, imitate, and experiment. They are sensory activities that require no special skills. Nor do they require achievement.

The value of water and sand learning includes:

▶ Experiencing properties of the natural environment.

▶ Observing changes.

▶ Gaining first-hand knowledge of the physical properties of water.

▶ Learning about volume and measurement.

▶ Furthering the development of small muscle control.

▶ Enhancing hand-eye coordination skills.

▶ Learning the use of different tools.

▶ Learning about gravity.

▶ Encountering basic scientific principles.

▶ Gaining feelings of pleasure and satisfaction.

Equipment Needs

Even the equipment needs for water and sand play are minimal. Typically, they can be found around the home. Examples include bathtubs, plastic pools, plastic tubs, and an outdoor sprinkler. Older preschool children may even enjoy using a brush dipped in a bucket of water to paint the sidewalk, swing set, house, or garage.

When choosing the accessories to stimulate water and sand play, exercise caution. To prevent injuries, always select only unbreakable equipment. China, glass, pottery, and other breakable materials need to be avoided. Instead, use sturdy plastic or metal materials. These accessories also need to be chosen in relationship to the maturity of the child.

Two-year-old children will enjoy using floating materials. Three-year-olds will also enjoy these materials. In addition, they will enjoy pouring accessories such as measuring cups, pitchers, and bottles. Three- and four-year-old children will also enjoy the addition of squirting and dribbling and of fantasy toys. The chart on the following page lists accessories that can be used for water play.

For water play, four- and five-year-olds will enjoy the addition of a hose. By washing the sidewalk, a swing set, or the car, they will learn the properties of water. While engaging in hose play, there is also much potential for learning. To illustrate, they can learn that what goes up, will come down. Water in a tub is static, while water from a hose has force. Also, they will learn that some people do not like being sprayed.

Water Play Accessories

Pouring	Floating	Squirting and Dribbling	Fantasy
Bottles	Boats	Hose	Airplanes
Buckets	Corks	Margarine tubs	Bulldozers
Funnel cups	Jar lids	Meat basters	Doll clothes
Ice cube trays	Meat trays	Medicine droppers	Paintbrushes
Ladles	Rubber balls	Plastic bowls	Plastic animals
Measuring cups	Sponges	Plastic tubing	Plastic people
Measuring spoons		Scoops	Toy boats
Pitchers		Sieves	Trucks
Pots and pans		Spray bottles	
Scoops		Strainers	
Sifters		Straws	
		Water pumps	
		Whisks	

Water Activities

Playing with water is an activity that can be described as both relaxing and stimulating. There is a wide variety of activities that you can introduce to young children using water. Usually, the two basic activities that they will engage in involve pouring and washing. However, you can structure their learning by encouraging them to explore other options. These include creating bubbles, rainmaking, and freezing water to make ice.

Creating Bubbles

Young children delight in creating and destroying bubbles. This is an outdoor activity that you can do with children as young as one year of age, providing you create the bubbles. Then they can destroy them by poking, hitting, or batting them.

You can easily create your own bubble mixture by mixing dishwashing detergent and water. If desired, add food coloring to the bubble mixture. Then provide the child with such things as berry baskets, straws, or plastic bubble makers. See the chart below for bubble solutions as tools for creating the bubbles.

Toddlers will enjoy popping the bubbles. They will also learn what causes bubbles to pop. Three-year-old children will enjoy blowing bubbles and learning the effects of air pressure. Four-, five-, and six-year-olds will enjoy preparing the bubble solutions and blowing the bubbles.

Bubble Solutions

Bubble Solution #1	Bubble Solution #2	Bubble Solution #3
1 cup of water	⅔ cup liquid dish detergent	3 cups water
2 tablespoons liquid detergent	1 gallon of water	2 cups liquid detergent
1 tablespoon glycerin	1 tablespoon glycerin (optional)	½ cup corn syrup
½ teaspoon sugar	Allow solution to sit in an open container for at least a day before use.	

 **Moving Water**

Provide the children with a variety of materials that move water. Include the following:

- Sponges
- Basters
- Eye droppers
- Squeeze bottles
- Funnels
- Measuring cups
- Pitchers
- Empty film canisters
- Plastic tubing

Rainmaking

Using a hammer and a nail, pound large holes in the bottom of a plastic, half-gallon milk bottle. Encourage the child to fill the bottle, and she can then sprinkle the grass, sidewalk, and flowers. This definitely is an outdoor activity.

 Ice

Freeze water in large containers such as plastic ice cream containers, milk bottles, or pop bottles with the top cut off. Fill with water and freeze. After the water has frozen, remove the ice block from the container. There are two effective methods. You can place the container outside and let the warm air or sun warm the block of ice enough to remove it from the container. Otherwise, you can place the container in a sink of warm water. Then let the children explore the ice and learn about the process of melting.

Sensory Experiences

Constant supervision is needed whenever water is available. Children should never be left unattended. Adults need to supervise constantly to prevent potential accidents. In addition, water-play rules need to be introduced. These rules may vary depending on whether the water play is indoors or outdoors. For example, rules for indoors may include no splashing, wipe up spills immediately, and keep the water in the containers.

Through water play, children can develop a wide variety of concepts. Included are:

▶ Some foods dissolve in water.

▶ Some items float on water.

▶ Some materials absorb water.

▶ Water takes many forms—ice, snow, liquid.

▶ Water can be used to clean objects.

Variations for Sensory Experiences

To maintain the children's interests and expand their learning, you can introduce variations to both water and sand play. Instead of using water, try providing the children with shaving cream. They will love to play with it in a small tub or on a cookie tray. To add interest to the shaving cream, add oils of wintergreen or peppermint. Tempera paint also makes an interesting addition.

Sand can be dampened to add interest. Indoors, you can sprinkle it with water. Notice the difference in texture. Outdoors, you can use a hose to dampen the sand. Chances are the children will note how much heavier wet sand is than sand that is dry. They will also notice how different it is pouring wet as opposed to dry sand. Then, too, they will learn that it is easier to create forms using wet sand.

The water can be changed. Vary the temperature by using lukewarm water. Otherwise, add ice and snow. You can also make the water different colors by adding food coloring. Then, too, you can add dish detergent, bubble bath, or cornstarch. All of these materials will change the appearance of the water.

Helpful Hints!

The following are helpful hints when providing sensory experiences:

▶ Use only unbreakable equipment.

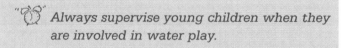
Always supervise young children when they are involved in water play.

▶ For indoor play, make sure the floor covering is water repellent. If not, use a plastic shower curtain or tablecloth to protect it.

▶ Plastic aprons can be worn to protect the child's clothing garments. If unavailable, cut armholes and a place for the head in a large garbage bag.

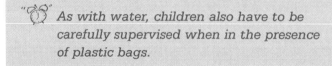
As with water, children also have to be carefully supervised when in the presence of plastic bags.

▶ Rules are needed for sand play. Included should be: (1) sand needs to be kept in the sandbox and (2) throwing sand is prohibited.

▶ Spilled water needs to be wiped up immediately.

Sensory Activities

 **Apple-Tasting Party**

Cut different varieties of apples for a tasting party. This activity can easily be extended. On another day provide the children applesauce, apple pie, apple juice, or apple cider to taste during snack or lunch.

Clay Cutters

Make scented clay. Place on the art table with rabbit, duck, egg, and flower cookie cutters for the children to use during self-directed or self-initiated play.

Goop

Mix together food coloring, 1 cup cornstarch, and 1 cup water in the sensory table—a tub or table in which children can do sensory activities. If a larger quantity is desired, double or triple the recipe.

Sand Play

Sandboxes can be portable such as a washtub or a permanent structure. They also can be located indoors or outdoors. To promote sand play, provide a variety of containers for stirring, sifting, mixing, and molding the sand. Spoons, sifters, strainers, measuring cups, buckets, muffin tins, and cans may also be used. Other accessories to promote sand play include plastic animals, people, cars, trucks, and other transportation toys.

Silly Putty

Mix food coloring, 1 cup liquid starch, and 2 cups of glue together. Stir constantly until the ingredients are well mixed. Add more starch as needed.

Trucks

Small toy fire trucks and police cars can be placed in the sensory table with sand.

Washing Clothes

Fill the sensory table with soapy water and let the children wash doll clothing. After being washed, the clothes can be hung on a low clothesline.

Cooking

Cooking is a "magical" activity for young children. Experimenting in the kitchen can be one of a child's greatest joys. Cooking activities appeal to all of the child's senses—sight, smell, taste, hearing, and feeling. Cooking is a rich experience.

While cooking, the child can explore, discover, and stretch his limits. Experiencing growth opportunities and challenges, the child gains a sense of self-satisfaction. Through cooking, every aspect of the child's life can be enhanced.

Cooking is also an active, purposeful activity. For everyone, food is a staple of life. Therefore, the process is appealing. Do you remember the appeal cooking had for you as a child? Young children today feel the same way. From observing and participating, children learn math concepts, science concepts, and social skills. Participating in food preparation has another appeal. When cooking, children feel grown-up. Through cooking experiences, the child can also develop language concepts, physical skills, problem-solving skills, and creativity.

Value of Cooking Experiences

Cooking is a wonderful way to teach young children a variety of language concepts. It is an experience full of meaning. Through cooking experiences and interaction with you, the child may develop the following conceptual understandings regarding foods.

▷ **Purposes:** We eat food to grow, to be healthy, and to have energy.

▷ **Sources:** Plants and animals are sources of food.

▷ **Groups:** There are six food groups in the Food Pyramid: (1) breads, cereals, rice, and pasta, (2) fruits, (3) milk, yogurt, and cheese, (4) vegetables, (5) poultry, fish, meat, dry beans, and nuts, (6) fats, oils, and sweets.

▷ **Characteristics:** Foods have different names, colors, flavors, sizes, shapes, smells, sounds, and textures.

▷ **Preparation:** Foods can be prepared in different ways. Washing, chopping, cutting, peeling, and mixing are examples.

▷ **Cooking:** Foods can be cooked in different ways. Baking, grilling, broiling, microwaving, steaming, boiling, and frying are examples.

▷ **Celebrating:** Foods are used for celebrations and traditions. Birthdays, holidays, and weddings are examples.

A cooking experience may be as simple as washing fresh fruits or as complex as baking a batch of cookies. Through cooking, children can also learn:

▷ language skills.

▷ math concepts.

▷ science processing skills.

▷ experimenting skills.

▷ physical coordination skills.

▷ social skills.

▷ food concepts.

▷ healthy nutrition.

During the first five years of life, children grow and develop more rapidly than at any other time. Young children need healthy foods that provide the energy they need and help them grow. Care must be taken because eating preferences and habits are formed during these years. As a result, it is important to provide healthy food choices. Depending on the choices, the child could become deficient in some important nutrients. Sugar, candies, syrup, jellies, cookies, and cake are examples of foods that are low in nutrients and high in calories. Consequently, they must be limited in the child's diet.

Remember: A child's daily behavior and learning are impacted by healthy food choices. It is important for you to help them learn how to make healthy food choices. You can do this by including a variety of foods in their daily diets. Make sure to include plenty of vegetables, fruits, and grain products. Then, too, select foods low in fat, cholesterol, and sugar. A child needs these foods only in limited quantities. Moreover, they only need salt in moderation.

Modeling the selection of healthy food choices will impact your child's choices. Food likes are learned, and this learning occurs most rapidly during the first years of life. Therefore, it is important that you carefully select the food choices. Moreover, introduce only nutritious foods and snacks. Encourage your child to participate in food preparation experiences and take him shopping for food. You also need to introduce new foods to children. Generally, they will enjoy tasting new foods.

When observing young children, you will note they have preferences in serving sizes, food sizes, flavors, texture, color, and temperature. Like adults, a child's appetite will vary from day to day. However, there is a rule of thumb that you can use to determine serving size. A child's serving size should be approximately one-half of an adult serving. Then, too, the food sizes need to be controlled. To make eating easier for children, serve bite-size pieces. Lacking the necessary motor coordination to control eating foods, the very young child enjoys eating finger foods that can easily be picked up.

Most children prefer mildly seasoned foods and foods served at almost room temperature. To accommodate their preferences, add only small amounts of sugar, salt, and spices. Also, children are sensitive to extremes. Therefore, it is important to avoid serving foods either too hot or too cold. Rather, serve warm, as opposed to hot, foods. Likewise, serve cold fruits, milks, and salads as opposed to very cold.

Healthy Foods, Healthy Children

Growth and development are closely linked to a child's nutritional status. A child's behavior is also affected. "Active," "attentive," and "alert" are terms that describe the well-nourished child. Poor nutritional status may alter the child's behavior. For example, she may become either quiet and withdrawn or overactive and disruptive. A child's health is put at risk by poor nutrition, making her less resistant to illness.

Having nutritious food choices requires providing variety, balance, and moderation in meal planning. With fewer choices, the child will have a limited food experience. Young growing bodies that are active in play need to have a variety of foods to obtain all the essential nutrients.

Cooking

Balance means serving food from all six groups at mealtimes. Those of us who grew up with the "basic four" might be wondering about this change. The new Food Pyramid's food groups are: (1) bread, cereal, rice, and pasta; (2) vegetables; (3) fruit; (4) milk, yogurt, and cheese; (5) meat, poultry, fish, dry beans, and nuts; and (6) fats, oils, and sweets. Achieving balance includes monitoring calorie intake, while the child's physical activity is another aspect.

Fat intake, especially for saturated fat, should be moderate. (However, parents and caregivers need to remember that fat performs many vital functions for young active children. Severely limiting fat in the diet can be detrimental to a child's growth and development.) Sodium, cholesterol, and sugar in children's diets should also be kept at moderate levels.

Nutrient density is a helpful concept in selecting nutritious foods for children and adults. Foods that are "nutrient dense" provide plenty of nutrients for the calories. Other foods supply plenty of calories but few nutrients. It is easy to label food choices as "good" or "bad." However, parents and caregivers need to avoid this trap, remembering that variety, balance, and moderation are the keys to giving children healthy food choices.

Caregivers' Roles at Mealtimes

Caregivers have many roles at mealtimes. The two primary roles are serving as a role model for healthy eating and providing a positive mealtime environment. Caregivers must realize that their own behaviors and attitudes toward food and eating are powerful influences on children.

Caregivers are responsible for making sure that healthy food is available at the meal. If a variety of food is offered, individual likes and dislikes will be expressed. Young children enjoy exerting some independence and autonomy in food selection. Family-style service allows them a choice of what and how much to eat.

The mealtime environment needs to be positive and supportive. It is important that family members take the time to sit at the table and to eat together. When sitting down at the table, despite the pressures of the day, caregivers should strive to create a relaxed atmosphere that is not rushed and to avoid threatening or nagging over eating. Distractions such as the television and radio should be eliminated. Mealtimes are for sharing, connecting, and focusing attention on each other. They are a time for bonding. For children, having a more quiet activity prior to the mealtime can have a calming influence and provide a transition time. For some children, helping with setting the table can be a sedate activity that also lets them know that mealtime is near.

Establishing some limits for mealtime is important for socializing children; however, being too rigid and inflexible can backfire. On the other hand, being overly permissive at mealtimes does not help the child. There are expectations for behavior at the table, including manners. One important aspect is the timing or scheduling of meals. Children benefit from the routine of regularly scheduled meals. Timing the meals and snacks lets children know when they will next eat and helps to avoid constant requests for food between meals. This ensures, or at least makes it more likely, that when the child sits down to eat, he will be hungry.

Children's Roles at Mealtimes

Children also have clearly defined roles at mealtime, including: (1) selecting the food; (2) eating; and (3) deciding how much to eat. By involving them in food selection at mealtimes, children develop their own food preferences. The caregivers, in their role, will have already provided the healthy food choices.

The introduction of new foods is an aspect of food selection that may be frustrating to caregivers. Experts agree that introducing new foods to children can be tricky. Forcing and rewarding can negatively influence children's reactions to a new food. It is best to be neutral, allowing the children to experience the new food on their own terms. Repeated exposure to the new food will help them be more accepting.

The child is also responsible for the act of eating. This includes deciding how much to eat and sometimes even if the child will eat. There is a difference between hunger and appetite, with hunger being the physical response and appetite the psychological response to food. These responses are highly individual, and caregivers should respect the child's cues regarding hunger and appetite. Children, even very young children, are usually capable of regulating their energy intake over a day's time. Their food intake, when viewed meal by meal, can seem sporadic or even inadequate, but when viewed in a larger context, it is often less alarming. Emotions can influence how much a child eats at a meal, either reducing the appetite or stimulating overeating. Fatigue can also be disrupting to the child's interest in food.

Cultural and Ethnic Food Patterns

Experts have come to realize that the "melting pot" image of culture and ethnicity in the United States is no longer accurate. Preserving family heritage and reinforcing cultural and ethnic diversity are important functions of the family. Religious beliefs frequently influence food choices and invest food with symbolic and ritual meaning. Food patterns are closely tied to culture and ethnicity, with traditional food preferences being passed on for generations. Many of these traditions relate to family celebrations and holidays. Climate and geography have brought about distinct regional food patterns in various areas. Although families today are more mobile, they often carry these regional food preferences to their new location.

Teaching a healthy respect for the family's cultural and ethnic food patterns is important. Yet children should also be taught respect and tolerance for the food patterns of other groups. By exploring the wide variety of ethnic foods that is commonly available, children learn about many different food patterns. This makes eating a fun, adventurous, and educational activity.

Healthy, Active Families

By modeling healthy eating habits for children, caregivers share healthy lifestyle choices. Children are open and perceptive to all that is going on around them. The promotion of positive lifestyle choices is an important gift from caregiver to child. By preschool age, children are developing attitudes and behaviors that will persist through adulthood. Young children are, by nature, active and inquisitive. Families can foster an environment that is conducive to physical activity in areas that are stocked with items that are developmentally appropriate, and caregivers can find ways to share these active times with children.

Cooking

Snacks

Snacks are important for young children. Since young children eat small amounts at one time, three meals a day may be insufficient for meeting their daily nourishment. For many children, snacks help satisfy their hunger. They also help children meet their daily food and calorie requirements.

Serving Schedule

When should snacks be served? They should be scheduled so they do not interfere with the child's appetite at mealtimes. Usually, they are best served an hour and a half before a meal. Typically, serving times are mid-morning, mid-afternoon, and before bedtime if desired.

Choosing Snacks

According to the Food Pyramid, a young child needs six servings of rice, cereals, pasta, and bread daily. They need three servings of vegetables and two servings of fruits. Two servings of poultry, fish, or meat are needed. Two to three servings of dairy products are also needed.

 Safety is important. Therefore, always avoid serving or preparing snacks that could cause choking. Since young children are learning how to chew and swallow, selection is important. In particular, peanut butter, raw carrots, raw celery, whole nuts, popcorn, and grapes should not be served.

Child-Size Servings

When planning snacks, the rule of thumb is that a child-size serving is usually half the size of an adult's. Child-size servings include:

- ½ cup cereal or 3 crackers.
- ¼ cup juice or vegetables.
- ½ apple or banana.
- 1 egg.
- ½ cup milk or yogurt.

The chart on the following pages lists a variety of snack ideas.

Cooking

Snack Ideas

Milk

1. Dips (yogurt, cottage cheese, cream cheese)
2. Cheese (balls, wedges, cutouts, squares, faces, etc.)
3. Yogurt and fruit
4. Milk punches made with fruits and juices
5. Conventional cocoa
6. Cottage cheese (add pineapple, peaches, etc.)
7. Cheese fondues (preheated, no open flames in classroom)
8. Shakes (mix fruit and milk in a blender)

Meat

1. Meat strips, chunks, cubes (beef, pork, chicken, turkey, ham, fish)
2. Meat balls, small kabobs
3. Meat roll-ups (cheese spread, mashed potatoes, spinach, lettuce leaves, or tortillas)
4. Meat salads (tuna, other fish, chicken, turkey, etc.) as spreads for crackers, or rolled in spinach or lettuce
5. Sardines
6. Stuffing for potatoes, tomatoes, squash

Eggs

1. Hard boiled
2. Deviled (use different flavors)
3. Egg salad spread
4. Eggs any style that can be managed
5. Egg as a part of other recipes
6. Eggnog

Fruits

1. Use standard fruits, but be adventurous: pomegranates, cranberries, pears, peaches, apricots, plums, berries, pineapples, melons, grapefruit, tangerines
2. Kabobs and salads
3. Juices and juice blends
4. In muffins, yogurt, milk beverages
5. Fruit "sandwiches"
6. Stuffed dates, prunes, etc.
7. Dried fruits, raisins, currants, prunes, apples, peaches, apricots, dates, figs

Cooking

Snack Ideas (Continued)

Vegetables

1. Variety—Sweet and white potatoes, cherry tomatoes, broccoli, cauliflower, radishes, peppers, mushrooms, zucchini, all squashes, rutabaga, avocados, eggplant, okra, pea pods, turnips, pumpkin, sprouts, spinach
2. Almost any vegetable can be served raw, with or without dip
3. Salads, kabobs, cutouts
4. Juices and juice blends
5. Soup in a cup (hot or cold)
6. Stuffed—cucumbers, zucchini, spinach, lettuce, cabbage, squash, potatoes, tomatoes
7. Vegetable spreads
8. Sandwiches

Dried Peas and Beans

1. Peanuts, kidney beans, garbanzos, limas, lentils, yellow and green peas, pintos, black beans
2. Beans and peas mashed as dips or spreads
3. Bean, pea, or lentil soup in a cup
4. Roasted soybean-peanut mix
5. Three-bean salad

Pastas

1. Different shapes and thickness
2. Pasta with butter and poppy seeds
3. Cold pasta salad
4. Lasagna noodles (cut for small sandwiches)
5. Chow mein noodles (wheat or rice)

Breads

1. Use a variety of grains—whole wheat, cracked wheat, rye, cornmeal, oatmeal, bran, grits, etc.
2. Use a variety of breads—tortillas, pocket breads, crepes, pancakes, muffins, biscuits, bagels, popovers, English muffins
3. Toast—plain, buttered, with spreads, cinnamon
4. Homemade yeast and quick breads
5. Fill and roll up crepes, pancakes
6. Waffle sandwiches

Cooking

Snack Ideas (Continued)

Cereals, Grains, and, Seeds

1. Granola
2. Slices of rice loaf or rice cakes
3. Dry cereal mixes (not presweetened)
4. Seed mixes (pumpkin, sunflower, sesame, poppy, caraway, etc.)
5. Roasted wheat berries, wheat germ, bran as roll-ins, toppings, or as finger mix
6. Popcorn with toppings of grated cheese, flavored butters, mixed nuts
7. Stir into muffins or use as a topping

Language Concepts

While cooking together, you can be adding words and extending the child's vocabulary. While describing the experience, introduce and use words such as *grate, pare, measure, garnish,* and *stir.* Likewise, you can introduce the child to the names of foods, ingredients, and preparation tools. When preparing foods, try using a simple strategy for promoting language called "feeding in." To illustrate, when peeling an apple, you may say, "I am peeling an apple." While mixing flour, eggs, and milk, you can say, "I am blending the pancake batter." Give the words for all of the foods and cooking processes you use. The following chart contains vocabulary words to introduce during cooking experiences.

Cooking Vocabulary Words

The following vocabulary words can be introduced through cooking experiences.

Bake	Drain	Mince	Simmer
Beat	Freeze	Mix	Spread
Boil	Frost	Pare	Sprinkle
Broil	Fry	Peel	Squeeze
Brown	Garnish	Pit	Stir
Chop	Grate	Pour	Strain
Cool	Grease	Roast	Stuff
Core	Grill	Roll	Tear
Cream	Grind	Scrape	Toast
Cube	Heat	Scrub	Whip
Cut	Knead	Shake	
Dice	Marinate	Shred	
Dip	Measure	Sift	

Math Concepts

Simple and complex math skills can also be learned through participating in cooking activities. The kitchen is an ideal place for teaching the child sizes, shapes, numbers, and colors. While cooking, call attention to size. Ask the child, "Which fruit is the biggest?" Likewise, encourage her to identify the smallest fruit.

Science Processing Skills

While learning to cook, the child can also learn many important science processing skills. Observing, comparing, predicting, and experimenting are examples. Through observing, children learn how ingredients change in form and state. They can also develop skills for predicating. Before mixing the ingredients, ask the child, "What do you think will happen?"

Experimenting is provided through cooking activities. By tasting different foods, the child can learn to identify tastes such as sweet, sour, salty, and bitter. He can also identify variation in temperature such as hot, warm, and cold. The child will be continuously learning by exploring different ingredients used in food preparation. Try providing him with different ingredients to taste while you are cooking. Flour, salt, baking powder, brown sugar, and powdered sugar are a few examples.

Comparison skills can be learned through cooking activities. Provide foods in different forms. For example, taste fresh strawberries, strawberry gelatin, and strawberry jam. When you do, ask the child how the foods were similar. When you do this, also talk about the different textures of the foods. Repeat the questions, asking how the foods were different.

Problem-solving skills are important when mixing or applying a heat source to ingredients. Concepts that will need to be addressed are "too much" or "too little." What happens when the pancake batter is too thin? What needs to be done? By adding flour, the child can observe firsthand how the batter changes.

Cooking is also a wonderful **prereading activity**. By observing you read the label or directions, the child will be reminded of the importance of the printed word. Point out the sequence of events, step-by-step, on the back of the muffin or salad mix box or the recipe book. From this, the child will learn necessary prereading skills. As you point out the words, the child will develop left-to-right progression skills. These skills are important for learning how to read and write.

Physical Coordination Skills

The child's physical development will be promoted through cooking experiences. Children enjoy seeing how tools work and using them. From manipulating tools, fine motor and hand-eye coordination skills can be developed. Encourage the child to help in peeling vegetables, beating eggs, or using a can opener (age-appropriate).

The physical ability of preschool children in relationship to cooking varies. Two-year-olds can scrub, dip, and tear. Three-year-olds can serve individual portions, as well as pour juice and milk. They also enjoy spreading, mixing, and shaking.

Four-year-olds are more sophisticated. They can be observed washing, wiping, and setting the table. Food processes enjoyed by this age group include peeling, mashing, and rolling foods. Many five- and six-year-olds have mastered measuring, and they are also capable of assisting in the preparation of simple breakfasts, snacks, and lunches.

Social Skills

Developing social skills is also an outcome of cooking with several people. Through cooking experiences, the child can learn the importance of teamwork. She can learn important concepts such as taking turns. She can also learn to share. Cleanup skills, such as wiping the counter and doing dishes, are also an important part of learning how to cook.

First Experiences

When cooking with the child, providing experiences that ensure success is important. First experiences should include simple, no-fail recipes and tasks.

 While selecting the experience, think of the child's safety in order to promote the sense of security. Choose tools the child can safely use such as unbreakable bowls and strong, serrated plastic knives. Then, too, encourage him to sit when using peelers, knives, and other tools.

Safety Precautions

Before beginning to cook, insist that the children wash their hands. Hand washing is an important control measure for helping prevent communicable and infectious diseases. To help children learn the correct techniques, model correct techniques for them.

Procedures for hand washing include:

- *rinsing hands, fingers, and palms with palms down.*
- *rinsing hands under warm, running water.*
- *applying soap and lathering the palms of hands to create friction. This movement helps remove dirt and microorganisms.*
- *rubbing soap individually over each finger.*
- *turning off water faucet with a paper towel to prevent recontamination.*

 Additional safety hints include the following:

- *Use serrated plastic knives for cutting.*

- *Cut with sawing, as opposed to chopping, movements.*

- *Cut only on a cutting board.*

- *Cut round, slippery vegetables such as carrots and cucumbers in half lengthwise. This provides the child with a flat cutting surface.*

- *Provide a "tasting spoon" for tasting only. If desired, tasting spoons can be color coded using a colored rubber band or colored nail polish.*

- *Provide a damp sponge for wiping up spills.*

Beverages

Apple Banana Frosty

- 1 golden delicious apple, diced
- 1 peeled sliced banana
- ¼ cup milk
- 3 ice cubes

Blend all ingredients in a blender. Makes 4 child-size servings.

Berry Shake

- 1½ cups nonfat dry milk
- 2 cups fresh or frozen berries
- 1 teaspoon vanilla
- 1 cup water
- 1 tray ice cubes

Blend all ingredients in a blender.

Cranberry Freeze

- 16-ounce can (2 cups) whole cranberry sauce
- 8-ounce can (1 cup) crushed pineapple, drained
- 1 cup yogurt

In a medium bowl, combine all ingredients and mix well. Pour the mixture into an 8-inch square pan or an ice cube tray. Freeze 2 hours or until firm. To serve, cut into squares or pop out of the ice cube tray.

Fruit Ice

Mix ½ cup partially thawed juice concentrate with 2 cups of crushed ice in the blender. Liquefy until the contents become snowy. Serve immediately.

Fruit Juice Blend

- 2 cups fat free plain or vanilla yogurt
- 1 can (6 ounces) frozen fruit juice concentrate (any flavor), thawed
- 1 cup cut up fresh or frozen fruit, thawed

Place all ingredients in a blender. Cover and blend on medium-high speed about 30 seconds or until smooth. Makes 4 servings.

Lemonade

- 1 lemon
- 2 to 3 tablespoons sugar
- 1¼ cups water
- 2 ice cubes

Squeeze the juice from the lemon. Add the sugar and water. Stir until sugar is dissolved. This recipe makes 1 serving. Adjust the recipe to accommodate the desired number of servings.

Orange Buttermilk Smoothie

- 1 quart buttermilk
- 3 cups orange juice
- ½ teaspoon cinnamon
- ¼ cup honey

Whip in a blender until the mixture is smooth.

Cooking

113

Peachy Cream Shake

- 1 carton (6 ounces) peach yogurt
- ½ cup drained canned sliced peaches
- ½ teaspoon vanilla
- Dash of ground cinnamon

Place all ingredients in a blender. Cover and blend on medium-high speed about 10 seconds or until smooth. Makes 1 serving.

Purple Cow Drink Mix

- 1 quart milk
- 1 quart grape juice
- 3 ice cubes

Mix the ingredients in a blender for 1 minute. This recipe will make approximately 20 child-size servings.

Raspberry Slush

- 4 10-ounce packages of frozen raspberries
- 1 6-ounce can frozen lemonade concentrate
- 2 quarts chilled gingerale

Thaw and cook raspberries for 10 minutes. Rub the cooked raspberries through a strainer with a wooden spoon. Cool. Add lemonade concentrate, thawed. Just before serving, stir in ginger ale. Makes 24 child-size servings, about ½ cup each.

Vegetable Juice

Prepare individual servings of vegetable juice in a blender by adding ½ cup of cut-up vegetables and ¼ cup water. Salt to taste. Vegetables that can be used include: celery, carrots, beets, tomatoes, cucumbers, and zucchini.

Witch's Brew

- 5 cups cranberry juice, unsweetened
- 5 cups apple cider, unsweetened
- 1 or 2 cinnamon sticks
- ¼ teaspoon ground nutmeg

Place ingredients in a large saucepan. Cover, heat, and simmer for 10 minutes. Serve warm.

Zippy Drink

- 1 ripe banana
- 1 cup orange juice
- 1 cup orange sherbet
- Ice cubes
- Orange slices

Peel the banana, place in a bowl, and mash with a fork. Add the orange juice and sherbet. Beat with a rotary beater until smooth. Pour into pitcher. Add ice cubes and orange slices.

Breads

Banana Bread

- 1¼ cups sugar
- ¼ cup margarine or butter, softened
- 3 egg whites
- 1¼ cups mashed ripe bananas (3 to 4 medium)
- ¾ cup fat free plain or vanilla yogurt
- 1 teaspoon vanilla
- 2¾ cups all-purpose flour
- 1¼ teaspoons baking soda
- 1 teaspoon salt
- 1 teaspoon ground cinnamon
- ¾ cup chopped pecans or walnuts

Place oven rack in lowest position. Heat oven to 350 degrees. Grease bottoms only of two loaf pans, 8½ by 4½ by 2½ inches, or one loaf pan, 9 by 5 by 3 inches. Mix sugar and margarine with spoon in large bowl. Stir in egg whites until well blended. Add bananas, yogurt, and vanilla. Beat until smooth. Stir in remaining ingredients, except pecans, just until moistened. Stir in pecans. Pour into pans.

Bake 3-inch loaves about 1 hour and 9-inch loaf about 1¼ hours, or until a toothpick inserted in the center comes out clean. Cool 5 minutes. Loosen sides of loaves from pans; remove from pans. Cool completely before slicing. Makes 1 or 2 loaves.

Blueberry Muffins

- 1 cup blueberries, fresh or frozen
- 2 tablespoons sugar

Batter:

- 1¾ cups flour
- 2½ teaspoons baking powder
- ¾ teaspoon salt
- 1 egg
- ½ cup milk
- ⅓ cup salad oil

Mix all of the ingredients together. Add sugar to blueberries. Mix slightly and gently add to the batter. Bake at 400 degrees for approximately 25 minutes.

Bran Muffins

- 3 cups whole wheat bran cereal
- 1 cup boiling water
- ½ cup shortening or oil
- 2 eggs
- 2½ cups unbleached flour
- 1½ cups sugar
- 2½ teaspoons baking soda
- 2 cups buttermilk

Preheat oven to 400 degrees. Unless using a non-stick pan, line the muffin tins with paper baking cups. In a large bowl combine the cereal and boiling water. Stir in the shortening and eggs. Add remaining ingredients. Blend well. Spoon batter into cups about ¾ full. Bake at 400 degrees for 18 to 22 minutes or until golden brown.

Cooking

🌿 Corn Bread

- 2 cups cornmeal
- 1 teaspoon salt
- ½ teaspoon baking soda
- 1½ teaspoons baking powder
- 1 tablespoon sugar
- 2 eggs
- 1½ cups buttermilk
- ¼ cup cooking oil

Heat oven to 400 degrees. Sift corn-meal, salt, soda, baking powder, and sugar into a bowl. Stir in unbeaten eggs, buttermilk, and cooking oil until all ingredients are mixed. Pour batter into a greased 9- by 9-inch pan or non-stick pans. Bake for 30 minutes, until lightly browned.

🌿 Cracker Wheels

For this recipe, each child will need:
- 4 round crackers
- ½ hot dog
- ½ piece of cheese

Slice hot dogs and place on a cracker. Cover the top of the hot dog with cheese. Place in oven at 350 degrees for 3 to 5 minutes or microwave for 30 seconds. Let cool and serve.

🌿 Dog Biscuits

- 2½ cups whole wheat flour
- ½ cup powdered dry milk
- ½ teaspoon salt
- ½ teaspoon garlic powder
- 6 tablespoons margarine, shortening, or meat drippings

- 1 egg
- 1 teaspoon brown sugar
- ½ cup ice water

Combine flour, milk, salt, and flour. Cut in shortening. Mix in egg. Add enough water until mixture forms a base. Pat the dough to a ½-inch thickness on a lightly oiled cookie sheet. Cut with cookie cutters and remove scraps. Bake 25 to 30 minutes at 350 degrees. This recipe may be varied by adding pureed soup greens, liver powder, etc.

🌿 French Bread

- ½ cup water
- 2 packages rapid rise yeast
- 1 tablespoon salt
- 2 cups lukewarm water
- 7 to 7½ cups all-purpose flour

Soften yeast in ½ cup lukewarm water. Be careful that the water is not too warm or the activity of the yeast will be destroyed. Add salt to 2 cups of lukewarm water in a large bowl. Gradually add 2 cups of flour and beat well. Add the softened yeast and gradually add the re-maining flour, beating well after each addition. Turn the soft dough out on a lightly floured surface and knead until elastic. Lightly grease a bowl and place the dough into it, turning once to grease surface. Let rise until double. Divide into two portions. Place on a French bread baking pan or a cookie sheet. Bake in a 375 degree oven until light brown, about 35 minutes.

Greek Honey Twists

- 3 eggs beaten
- 2 tablespoons vegetable oil
- ½ teaspoon baking powder
- ¼ teaspoon salt
- 1¾ to 2 cups all-purpose flour
- Vegetable oil
- ¼ cup honey
- 1 tablespoon water
- Ground cinnamon

Mix eggs, 2 tablespoons oil, baking powder, and salt in a large bowl. Gradually stir in enough flour to make a very stiff dough. Knead 5 minutes. Roll half the dough at a time as thin as possible on well-floured surface with a stockinet-covered rolling pin. Cut into wheel shapes. Cover with damp towel to prevent drying.

Pour 2 to 3 inches of oil into a skillet. Heat to 375 degrees. Fry 3 to 5 twists at a time until golden brown, turning once about 45 seconds on each side. Drain on paper towels. Heat honey and water to boiling; boil 1 minute. Cool slightly. Drizzle over twists; sprinkle with cinnamon. Makes 32 twists.

Happy Rolls

- 1 package of rapid-rise dry yeast
- 1 cup warm water
- ⅓ cup sugar
- ⅓ cup cooking oil
- 3 cups flour
- Dash of salt

Measure the warm water and pour it into a bowl. Sprinkle yeast on top of the water. Let the yeast settle into the water. Mix all of the ingredients in a large bowl. Place dough on a floured board to knead it. Demonstrate how to knead and let the child knead the bread. This is a wonderful activity with which to work through emotions. After kneading it for about 10 minutes, put the ball of dough into a greased bowl. If kneaded sufficiently, the top of the dough should have blisters on it. Cover the bowl and put in the sun or near heat. Let it rise for about 1 hour or until doubled. Take dough out of the bowl. Punch it down, knead for several more minutes, and then divide dough into 12 to 15 pieces. Roll each piece of dough into a ball. Place each ball on a greased cookie sheet. Let the dough rise again until doubled. Bake at 450 degrees for 10 to 12 minutes. A happy face can be drawn on the roll with frosting.

Hush Puppies

- Vegetable oil
- 2¼ cups yellow cornmeal
- 1 teaspoon salt
- 2 tablespoons finely chopped onion
- ¾ teaspoon baking soda
- 1½ cups buttermilk

Pour 1 inch oil into skillet. Heat to 375 degrees. Mix cornmeal, salt, onion, and baking soda in a bowl. Add buttermilk. Drop by spoonfuls into hot oil. Fry until brown, about 2 minutes.

Cooking

Individual Pizza

- English muffins
- Pizza sauce
- Grated mozzarella cheese

Spread a tablespoon of sauce on each muffin half. Sprinkle the top with grated cheese. Bake in a pre-heated oven at 375 degrees, until cheese melts.

Muffins

- 1 egg
- ¾ cup milk
- ½ cup vegetable oil
- 2 cups all purpose flour
- ⅓ cup sugar
- 3 tablespoons baking powder
- 1 teaspoon salt

Heat oven to 400 degrees. Grease bottoms only of 12 medium muffin cups. Beat egg. Stir in milk and oil. Stir in remaining ingredients all at once, just until flour is moistened. Batter will be lumpy. Fill muffin cups about ¾ full. Bake until golden brown, about 20 minutes.

For pumpkin muffins: Stir in ½ cup pumpkin and ½ cup raisins with the milk and 2 teaspoons pumpkin pie spice with the flour.

For cranberry-orange muffins: Stir in 1 cup cranberry halves and 1 tablespoon grated orange peel with milk.

Oatmeal Pancakes with Yogurt Toppings

- 1 egg or 2 egg whites
- 1 cup fat free plain yogurt
- ¾ quick-cooking oats or old-fashioned oats
- ½ cup all-purpose flour
- 1 tablespoon sugar
- 2 tablespoons vegetable oil
- 1 teaspoon baking powder
- ½ teaspoon baking soda
- Fruit preserves–yogurt topping, cinnamon-yogurt topping, or maple-yogurt topping

Beat egg in a large bowl with hand beater until foamy; stir in remaining ingredients except topping. Grease heated griddle if necessary. (To test griddle, sprinkle with a few drops of water. If bubbles skitter around and quickly evaporate, heat is just right.) For each pancake, pour about 3 tablespoons batter from tip of large spoon or from pitcher onto hot griddle. Cook pancakes until puffed and dry around edges. Turn and cook other sides until golden brown. Serve with one of the toppings. Refrigerate any remaining topping. Makes about 11 pancakes.

Cooking

Pita or Pocket Bread

- 1 package of yeast
- ¼ cup of lukewarm water
- 3 cups of flour (white, whole wheat, or any combination)
- 2 teaspoons of salt

Dissolve yeast in the water and add the flour and salt. Stir into a rough sticky ball. Knead on a floured board or table until smooth, adding more flour if necessary. Divide dough into 6 balls and knead each ball until smooth and round. Flatten each ball with a rolling pin until ¼-inch thick and about 4 to 5 inches in diameter.

Cover dough with a clean towel and let it rise for 45 minutes. Arrange the rounds upside down on baking sheets. Bake in a 500-degree oven for 10 to 15 minutes or until brown and puffed in the center. The breads will be hard when they are removed from the oven but will soften and flatten as they cool. When cooled, split or cut bread carefully and fill with any combination of sandwich filling.

Pretzels

- 1½ cups lukewarm water
- 1 envelope yeast
- 4 cups flour
- 1 teaspoon salt
- 1 tablespoon sugar
- 1 egg
- Coarse salt (optional)

Mix water, yeast, and sugar. Let stand for 5 minutes. Place salt and flour in a bowl. Add yeast and stir to prepare dough mixture. Shape dough. Beat egg and apply the egg glaze with a pastry brush. Sprinkle with salt, if desired. Bake at 425 degrees for approximately 12 minutes.

Pumpkin Patch Muffins

- 3 cups flour
- 1 cup sugar
- 4 teaspoons baking powder
- 1 teaspoon salt
- 1 teaspoon pumpkin pie spice
- 1 cup milk
- 1 cup canned pumpkin
- ½ cup (1 stick) butter or margarine, melted
- 2 eggs, beaten

Sift flour, sugar, baking powder, salt and pumpkin pie spice into a large mixing bowl. Add milk, pumpkin, melted butter, and eggs. Mix with a wooden spoon just until flour is moist. (Batter will be lumpy.) Place paper liners in the muffin tins and fill ⅔ full with batter. Bake in a preheated 400-degree oven 20 minutes, or until muffins are golden. Cool in muffin tins 10 minutes on a wire rack. Remove muffins from tins and finish cooling on wire racks. Pile into serving baskets and serve warm for a snack.

Cooking

Raisin Bran Muffins

- 4 cups raisin bran cereal
- 2½ cups all purpose flour
- 1 cup sugar
- ½ cup chopped walnuts
- 2½ teaspoons baking soda
- 1 teaspoon salt
- 2 eggs, beaten
- 2 cups buttermilk
- ½ cup cooking oil

Stir cereal, flour, sugar, nuts, baking soda, and salt together in a large mixing bowl. In a separate bowl, beat the eggs, buttermilk, and oil together. Add this mixture to the dry ingredients and stir until moistened. The batter will be thick. Spoon batter into greased or lined muffin cups, filling ¾ full. Bake in a 375-degree oven for 20 to 25 minutes and remove from pans.

Cooking

Candy and Cakes

Fruit Candy

- 1 pound dried figs
- 1 pound dried apricots
- ½ pound dates
- 2 cups walnuts
- ½ cup raisins

Put fruits and 2 cups of walnuts through a food grinder. Mix in the half cup of raisins and press into a buttered, 9- by 13-inch pan. Chill and enjoy!

Pound Cake Brownies

- ¾ cup butter or margarine, softened
- 1 cup sugar
- 3 eggs
- 2 1-ounce squares unsweetened chocolate, melted and cooled
- 1¼ cups all-purpose flour
- ½ teaspoon baking powder
- ¼ teaspoon salt

Cream butter and sugar; beat in eggs. Blend in chocolate and vanilla. Stir flour with baking powder and salt. Add to creamed mixture. Mix well. Spread in a greased 9- by 9- by 2-inch baking pan. Bake at 350 degrees for 25 to 30 minutes. Cool. If desired, sift powdered sugar over the top. Cut into bars. Yields 24 bars.

Cooking

Cookies

Animal

- 1½ cups powdered sugar
- 1 cup butter or margarine
- 1 egg
- 1 teaspoon vanilla extract
- ½ teaspoon almond extract
- 2½ cups flour
- 1 teaspoon baking soda
- 1 teaspoon cream of tartar

Mix powdered sugar, margarine, egg, vanilla, and almond extract. Add flour, baking soda, and cream of tartar. Cover and refrigerate for 2 hours. Preheat oven to 375 degrees. Divide dough into halves. Roll out ¼-inch thick on a lightly floured, cloth-covered board. Cut dough into animal shapes with cookie cutters or let the child cut them. Place on lightly greased cookie sheet. Bake 7 to 10 minutes. Serve for a snack.

Basic Sugar Dough for Cookie Cutters

- ½ cup butter
- 1 cup sugar
- 1 egg
- ½ teaspoon salt
- 2 teaspoons baking powder
- 2 cups flour
- ½ teaspoon vanilla

Mix ingredients. Cut into desired shapes. Place on lightly greased baking sheets. Bake 8 minutes at 400 degrees. This recipe makes approximately 3 to 4 dozen cookies.

Candy Canes

Prepare the basic sugar dough recipe for cookie cutters, dividing recipe in half. Add red food coloring to one half of the dough. Show child how to roll a piece of red dough in a strip about 3 inches long by ½ inch wide. Repeat this process using the white dough. Then twist the two strips together, shaping into a candy cane. Bake cookies in a 350-degree oven for 7 to 10 minutes.

Carrot Cookies

- ½ cup honey
- 1 egg
- ½ cup margarine
- 1 cup whole wheat flour
- 1¼ teaspoons baking powder
- ¼ teaspoon salt
- ½ cup rolled oats
- ½ cup wheat germ
- ½ cup grated raw carrots
- ½ cup raisins
- ½ cup nuts (optional)
- 1 teaspoon vanilla

Mix all ingredients in a bowl. Drop mixture by teaspoons onto a lightly greased cookie sheet. Flatten each ball slightly. Bake in a 350-degree oven for approximately 12 minutes.

Container Cookies

- ½ cup butter or margarine
- ½ cup shortening
- 1 cup sugar
- 1 egg
- 2 tablespoons milk
- ½ teaspoon vanilla
- 2¼ cups flour
- ½ teaspoon baking soda
- ½ teaspoon salt

Filling choices:

- Pie filling—any flavor
- Jam or jelly
- Peanut butter
- Chopped nuts
- Chocolate chips
- Raisins
- Toasted coconut
- Sugar

Beat butter (or shortening) in a large mixing bowl with an electric mixer on medium speed, about 30 seconds. Add sugar and beat until fluffy. Add egg, milk, and vanilla. Beat well. In a medium mixing bowl, combine flour, baking soda, and salt. With electric mixer on low, gradually add the flour mixture to the butter mixture, beating well. Cover and chill dough in the freezer about 20 minutes or until firm to handle. Divide dough in half. Shape each half into a roll 3 inches thick and 3 inches long. Wrap in plastic wrap. Freeze at least 6 hours, or up to 6 months.

When ready to bake the cookies, preheat oven to 375 degrees.

Unwrap one roll of dough. Slice the roll crosswise to make 16 slices about ⅛-inch thick. Repeat with the other roll. Place half of the slices 2 inches apart on ungreased cookie sheets. In the center of the circles, place 2 teaspoons of desired filling(s). Top each with a plain slice of dough. Press a floured fork around the edges to seal well. Sprinkle with a little sugar. Bake for 12 to 15 minutes or until edges are golden brown. Place cookies on rack to cool.

Drop Sugar Cookies

- 2 eggs
- ⅔ cup vegetable oil
- 2 teaspoons vanilla
- ¾ cup sugar
- 2 cups flour
- 2 teaspoons baking powder
- ½ teaspoon salt

Beat eggs with fork. Stir in oil and vanilla. Blend in sugar until mixture thickens. Add flour, baking powder, and salt. Mix well. Drop dough by teaspoons about 2 inches apart on an ungreased baking sheet. Flatten with bottom of a plastic glass dipped in sugar. Bake 8 to 10 minutes or until delicate brown. Remove from baking sheet immediately. Makes about 4 dozen cookies that are 2½ inches in diameter.

Cooking

Favorite Icing

- 1 cup sifted confectioner's sugar
- ¼ teaspoon salt
- ½ teaspoon vanilla
- 1 tablespoon water
- Food coloring

Blend salt, sugar, and vanilla. Add enough water to make frosting easy to spread. Tint with food coloring. Allow the child to spread on cookie with spatula or paintbrush.

Gingerbread Families

- 1½ cups whole wheat pastry flour
- 1 teaspoon baking soda
- ½ teaspoon salt
- ½ teaspoon ginger
- 1 teaspoon cinnamon
- ¼ cup oil
- ¼ cup maple syrup
- ¼ cup honey
- 1 large egg

Preheat oven to 350 degrees. Measure all dry ingredients into a bowl and mix well. Measure all wet ingredients into a second bowl and mix well. Add the two mixtures together. Pour combined mixture into an 8-inch-square pan and bake for 30 to 35 minutes. When cool, roll the gingerbread dough into thin slices and provide cookie cutters for the child to cut their family. Decorate the figures with raisins, peanut butter, wheat germ, etc. Enjoy for snack time.

"Hands-On" Cookies

- 3 cups brown sugar
- 3 cups margarine or butter
- 6 cups oatmeal
- 1 tablespoon baking soda
- 3 cups flour

Place all ingredients in a bowl. Let the child stir and knead. Form into small balls and place on ungreased cookie sheet. Butter the bottom of a glass. Dip bottom of the glass into a saucer with sugar. Use glass to flatten the balls. Bake in an oven preheated to 350 degrees for 10 to 12 minutes. Makes 15 dozen.

Painted Egg Cookies

- ⅓ cup butter or margarine
- ¼ cup sugar
- 1 egg
- ⅔ cup honey
- ¾ teaspoon vanilla
- 2¾ cups flour
- 1 teaspoon baking soda
- ½ teaspoon salt

"Paint":

- 1 egg yolk
- ¼ teaspoon water
- Food coloring

In a large mixing bowl, beat butter and sugar until fluffy. Add egg, honey, and vanilla. Beat well. Combine flour, baking soda, and salt. Gradually add flour mixture to butter mixture. Beat well. Cover and chill 1 hour.

Set oven to 350 degrees. Grease cookie sheets if necessary. Divide dough in half, keeping one half chilled. Roll dough on a lightly floured surface to a ¼-inch thickness. Cut with egg-shaped (oval) cookie cutter. Place 1 inch apart on cookie sheets. Repeat with remaining dough.

Beat egg yolk and water in a small mixing bowl. Divide yolk mixture between 3 or 4 small bowls. Add 2 or 3 drops of different food colors to each bowl and mix well. With a clean small paintbrush or plastic knife, paint cookies as desired. Bake 6 to 8 minutes, or until golden.

Peanut Butter Treats

- ¼ cup margarine
- ¼ cup peanut butter
- 1 cup raisins
- 40 regular-size marshmallows
- 5 cups rice cereal

Melt margarine over low heat. Add marshmallows and melt. Add the peanut butter and stir. Add the rice cereal and raisins; stir until everything is mixed well. Spread the mixture into a buttered pan and press into a firm layer. Cool and cut into squares.

Sugar

- 1½ cups powdered sugar
- 1 cup margarine or butter
- 1 egg
- 1 teaspoon vanilla
- 2½ cups all-purpose flour
- 1 teaspoon baking soda
- 1 teaspoon cream of tartar
- Granulated sugar

Mix powdered sugar, margarine, egg, and vanilla together. Stir in flour, baking soda, and cream of tartar. Chill, to prevent sticking while rolling the dough out. Heat oven to 375 degrees. Roll out dough. Cut into squares, triangles, diamonds, rectangles, and circles. Sprinkle with sugar. Place on lightly greased cookie sheet. Bake until lightly brown, about 7 to 8 minutes.

Cooking

Ethnic Recipes

🥄 Charoses

- 6 medium apples
- ½ cup raisins
- ½ teaspoon cinnamon
- ½ cup chopped nuts
- ¼ cup white grape juice

Chop peeled or unpeeled apples. Add remaining ingredients. Mix well and serve.

🥄 Egg Flower Soup–China

Watch an egg turn into a flower. Chinese cooks say that the cooked shreds of egg afloat in this soup look like flower petals.

- 1 tablespoon cornstarch
- 2 tablespoons cold water
- 1 egg
- 3 cups clear canned chicken broth
- 1 teaspoon salt
- 1 teaspoon chopped scallion or parsley (optional)

Put cornstarch into a small bowl and gradually add water, stirring it with a fork until you no longer see any lumps. Break egg into another small bowl and beat it with the fork. Pour broth into saucepan. Bring it to a boil over high heat. Add salt. Give cornstarch and water mixture a quick stir with the fork. Add it to the soup. Stir soup with a spoon until it thickens and becomes clear (about 1 minute). Slowly pour beaten egg into soup. The egg will cook in the hot soup and form shreds. When all the egg has been added, stir once. Turn off the heat. Pour soup into 4 soup bowls. Top, if desired, with chopped scallion or parsley for decorations.

🥄 Finnish Strawberry Shake

- 20 fresh strawberries
- 4 cups milk
- 3 tablespoons sugar

Wash strawberries and remove stems. Cut strawberries into small pieces. Combine milk, sugar, and strawberries in a large mixing bowl or blender. Beat with an eggbeater or blend for 2 minutes. Pour strawberry shakes into individual glasses. Makes 4 to 8 servings. Variation: Raspberries or other sweet fruit may be used instead.

🥄 Fu-Fu–West Africa

- 3 or 4 yams
- Water
- ½ teaspoon salt
- ⅛ teaspoon pepper
- Optional: 3 tablespoons honey or sugar

Wash and peel yams and cut into ½-inch slices. Place slices in a large saucepan and add water to cover them. Bring to a boil over a hot plate or stove. Reduce heat, cover saucepan, and simmer for 20 to 25 minutes, until yams are soft enough to mash. Remove saucepan from stove and drain off liquid into a small bowl.

Let yams cool for 15 minutes. Place yam slices in a medium-size mixing bowl, mash with a fork or potato masher. Add salt and pepper. Mash again until smooth. Roll mixture into small, walnut-size balls. If mixture is too dry, moisten it with a table-spoon of the reserved yam liquid. For sweeter Fu-Fu, roll yam balls in a dish of honey or sugar. Makes 24 balls.

Ground Nut Soup–Nigeria

- 1 large tomato
- 1 large potato
- 1 onion
- 2 cups water
- 1 beef bullion cube
- 1 cup shelled, unsalted roasted peanuts
- ½ cup milk
- 2 tablespoons rice

Peel potato and onion. Dice potato, tomato, and onion. Place in sauce-pan with the water and bouillon cube. Boil, covered, for 30 minutes. Chop and add peanuts, milk, and rice to the boiling mixture. Stir. Lower heat and simmer 30 minutes. Serves 6 to 8.

Hanukkah Honey and Spice Cookies

- ½ cup (1 stick) margarine, softened
- ½ cup firmly packed dark brown sugar
- ½ cup honey
- 2½ cups unsifted flour

- 2 teaspoons ground ginger
- 1 teaspoon baking soda
- 1 teaspoon ground cinnamon
- 1 teaspoon ground nutmeg
- ½ teaspoon salt
- ¼ teaspoon ground cloves

In a large mixing bowl, cream margarine and sugar. Beat in honey and egg until well combined. In a small bowl, combine flour, ginger, baking soda, cinnamon, nutmeg, salt, and cloves. Add to honey mixture. Beat on low speed until well blended. Cover dough and chill at least 1 hour or up to 3 days. Heat oven to 350 degrees. Grease cookie sheets. Set aside. Working quickly with ¼ of the dough at a time, roll out on floured surface to ¼-inch thickness. Cut into desired shapes, including a dreidel, menorah, or star. Using a spatula, place cookies on prepared cookie sheets 1 inch apart. Reroll scraps. Bake for 7 minutes. Transfer to wire racks to cool. Makes about 4 dozen cookies.

Latkes

- 6 medium-size potatoes (washed, pared, and grated)
- 1 egg
- 3 tablespoons flour
- ½ teaspoon baking powder

In a large bowl, mix egg and the grated potatoes. Add the flour and baking powder. Drop by teaspoons into hot cooking oil in a frying pan. Brown on both sides. Drain on paper towel. Latkes may be served with applesauce or sour cream.

❦ Soft Pumpkin Faces

- 1 cup all-purpose flour
- ½ cup packed dark brown sugar
- ½ cup canned pumpkin
- 1 teaspoon ground cinnamon
- ½ teaspoon baking powder
- ¼ teaspoon salt
- 2 tablespoons vegetable oil
- 1 teaspoon vanilla
- 1 egg

Place 1 paper towel on a microwavable dinner plate; set aside. Mix all ingredients. Make 3 cookies at a time. Drop dough by ¼ cupfuls in a circle on paper towel-lined plate. Flatten dough slightly and smooth it to make a 3-inch circle. Gently press candies and nuts into dough to make fun faces and designs (candy corn, ring-shaped hard candies, peanuts, cashews, etc.). Microwave uncovered on high (100%) 1 minute. Rotate the plate a half-turn. Microwave uncovered 1 to 2 minutes longer, checking every 30 seconds, until cookies are puffed and dry. Slide paper towel with cookies onto cooling rack. Cool 5 minutes. Carefully remove cookies from paper towel and place on cooling rack. Repeat with new paper towel and remaining cookie dough. *Hint:* Microwaving the soft cookies on a paper towel helps keep the bottoms dry, and cooling on a rack helps keep them dry as well. Makes 8 cookies.

❦ Swedish Pancakes

- 3 eggs
- 1 cup milk
- 1½ cups flour
- 1 tablespoon sugar
- ½ teaspoon salt
- 4 tablespoons butter, melted
- 1 cup heavy cream
- 2 tablespoons confectioner's sugar or a 12-ounce jar of fruit jelly

Using a fork or whisk, beat the eggs lightly in a large mixing bowl. Add half the milk. Fold in the flour, sugar, and salt. Add melted butter, cream, and remaining milk to the mixture. Stir well. Lightly grease a frying pan or griddle and place it over medium-high heat on a hot plate or stove. Carefully pour small amounts of the mixture onto frying pan or griddle. Cook until pancakes are golden around the edges and bubbly on top. Turn pancakes over with a spatula and cook until the other sides are golden around the edges. Remove to a covered plate. Repeat until all the mixture is used. Sprinkle pancakes lightly with confectioner's sugar or spread fruit jelly over them. Makes 3 dozen pancakes.

Cooking

Salads

Apple Salad

- 6 medium apples
- ½ cup raisins
- ½ teaspoon cinnamon
- ½ cup chopped nuts
- ¼ cup white grape juice

Peel and chop the apples. Mix well and add the remaining ingredients.

Carrot and Raisin Salad

- 4 cups grated carrots
- 1 cup raisins
- ½ cup mayonnaise or whipped salad dressing

Place ingredients in bowl and mix thoroughly.

Cat Face

- ½ peach (head)
- Almonds (ears)
- Red Hots candy (eyes)
- Raisin (nose)
- Stick pretzels (whiskers)

Show the child how to create a cat face using the ideas above or a variety of other items.

Easy Fruit Salad

- 1 medium banana, mashed (about ⅓ cup)
- 1 tablespoon frozen (thawed) orange juice concentrate
- 1 cup fat free plain or vanilla yogurt
- ⅛ teaspoon ground cinnamon
- ⅛ teaspoon ground nutmeg
- 1 medium peach or nectarine, cut into 1-inch pieces

Mix all ingredients except peach. Cover and refrigerate at least 1 hour. Serve over peach. Refrigerate any remaining dressing. *Note:* If using plain yogurt, add 1 tablespoon honey.

Fruit Tree

Place a lettuce leaf on a plate. On the center of the lettuce, place a pineapple slice. In the hole of the pineapple, place two peeled bananas. Drain 1 small can of fruit cocktail. Spoon fruit cocktail over the bananas.

Lettuce or Spinach Rollups

On clean lettuce or spinach leaves, spread softened cream cheese or cottage cheese. If desired, sprinkle with grated carrots or chopped nuts. Roll them up. Chill and serve.

Cooking

Raspberry-Orange Pops

- 1 can (6 ounces) frozen orange juice concentrate
- 1 can (12 ounces) evaporated skimmed milk
- 3 cartons (6 ounces each) raspberry yogurt
- 1 tablespoon honey
- 15 paper cups (3-ounce size)
- 15 wooden sticks

Place orange juice concentrate, milk, yogurt, and honey in blender. Cover and blend on medium-high speed 5 to 10 seconds. Divide among paper cups. Freeze 30 minutes; insert wooden sticks in centers of cups. Freeze at least 8 hours until firm. Remove paper cups to serve. Makes 15 pops.

Smiling Apples

- Apples, cored and sliced
- Peanut butter
- Mini-marshmallows, raisins, or peanuts

Spread peanut butter on one side of each apple slice. Place 3 to 4 mini-marshmallows, raisins, or peanuts on the peanut butter of one apple slice. Top with another apple slice, peanut butter side down.

Cooking

Sandwiches

Beanito Burritos

- 1 cup finely chopped onion (about 1 large)
- 1 cup finely chopped green bell pepper (about 1 medium)
- 1 teaspoon vegetable oil
- 1 cup refried beans
- 2 teaspoons salt-free herb seasoning
- 4 flour tortillas (9 inches in diameter)
- ½ cup shredded, part-skim mozzarella cheese (2 ounces)
- 1 cup fat-free plain yogurt
- 1¼ cups alfalfa sprouts
- ⅔ cup finely chopped tomato

Heat oven to 350 degrees. Cook onion and bell pepper in oil over medium heat about 5 minutes, stirring frequently, until tender; drain. Mix beans and seasoning. Spread each tortilla with ¼ of the bean mixture, onion, bell pepper, and cheese, 2 tablespoons yogurt, and ¼ cup sprouts. Roll up tortillas; secure with toothpicks. Place in ungreased rectangle pan, 13 by 9 by 2 inches. Bake 12 to 15 minutes, or until it is heated through and the cheese is melted. Top with remaining yogurt, sprouts, and tomato. Makes 4 servings.

Cheese Cat

- English muffins
- Cheese slices

Allow the child to cut out a cat face on a slice of cheese. Put cheese on top of the English muffin and bake long enough to melt the cheese.

Egg Salad

- Eggs
- Bread
- Mayonnaise
- Dry mustard (just a pinch)
- Salt
- Pepper

Boil, shell, and mash eggs, adding enough mayonnaise to provide a consistent texture. Add salt, pepper, and dry mustard to flavor. Spread on bread.

Heart-Shaped Sandwich

- 1 loaf bread
- Heart-shaped cookie cutters
- Strawberry jam or jelly

Give the child 1 or 2 pieces of bread (depending on size of cutter). Cut out 2 heart shapes from bread. Spread jam or jelly on bread to make a sandwich. Eat at snack time.

Cooking

131

Puppet Face

Make open-faced sandwiches using peanut butter or cream cheese spread onto a slice of bread or bun. Carrot curls can be used to represent hair. Raisins and green or purple grape halves can be used for the eyes, nose, and mouth.

Vegetable Patch Pita Sandwiches

- 3 cups bite-size, cut-up fresh vegetables

Choose at least two of the following vegetables:

- Cauliflower
- Broccoli
- Carrots
- Green bell pepper
- Green onion
- Tomatoes
- Zucchini
- ½ cup mayonnaise or salad dressing
- 1 teaspoon prepared mustard
- 4 6-inch pita breads

Mix all ingredients except bread in a medium bowl. Slice pita breads in half. Spoon about ⅓ cup of the vegetable mixture into each pita bread pocket. Makes 8 pita bread pockets.

Warm Turkey Sandwiches

- 4 large round slices whole-grain bread or 8 slices sandwich bread
- 1 carton (6 ounces) plain yogurt
- 1 cup cubed cooked turkey
- 1 cup shredded cheddar cheese (4 ounces)
- 2 tablespoons finely chopped green bell pepper
- 2 tablespoons finely chopped pimento-stuffed olives
- 2 tablespoons finely chopped onion
- 2 tablespoons finely chopped sweet pickle
- 3 hard-cooked eggs, chopped
- 4 to 8 slices tomato
- ½ cup alfalfa sprouts

Heat oven to 400 degrees. Place bread on ungreased cookie sheet. Mix yogurt, turkey, cheese, bell pepper, olives, onion, pickle, and eggs; spoon onto bread. Bake 12 to 15 minutes or until warm. Top with tomato and sprouts; serve immediately. Makes 4 servings.

Snacks

Applesauce

- 6 large apples
- ½ cup water
- ¼ cup sugar
- 1 teaspoon Red Hots candy

Clean apples by peeling, coring, and cutting into small pieces. Place apples in a large kettle containing water. Simmer apples on low heat, stirring occasionally until soft. Add remaining ingredients. Stir and simmer a few minutes. Cool prior to eating.

Banana Bobs

Cut bananas into chunks and dip into honey. Next, roll in wheat germ and use large toothpicks for serving.

Banana Rounds

- 4 medium bananas
- ½ cup yogurt
- 3 tablespoons honey
- ⅛ teaspoon nutmeg
- ⅛ teaspoon cinnamon
- ¼ cup wheat germ

The child can participate by peeling bananas and slicing into "rounds." Measure spices, wheat germ, and honey. Blend this mixture with yogurt and bananas. Chill prior to serving.

Banana Snowman

- 2 cups raisins
- 2 bananas
- Shredded coconut

Chop bananas and raisins in a blender. Then place them in a mixing bowl and refrigerate until mixture is cool enough to be handled. Roll mixture into balls and into shredded coconut. Stack three balls and fasten with toothpicks.

Caramel Apple Slices

Prepare the following recipe for 12 to 14 children:

- 1 pound caramels
- 2 tablespoons water
- Dash of salt
- 5 crisp apples

Melt caramels with water in microwave oven or double boiler, stirring frequently until melted. Stir in salt. Pour melted caramel over sliced apples and cool before serving.

Cheese Balls

- 8 ounces cream cheese, softened
- 1 stick of butter, softened
- 2 cups grated cheddar cheese
- ½ package of onion soup mix

Blend all ingredients together. Shape mixture into small balls. Roll balls in chopped nuts, if desired.

Cooking

Cheese Crunchies

- ½ cup butter or margarine
- 1 cup all-purpose flour
- 1 cup shredded cheddar cheese
- Pinch of salt
- 1 cup rice cereal bits

Cut butter into 6 or 8 slices and mix together with the flour, cheese, and salt. Use fingers or fork to mix. Knead in cereal bits; then roll the dough into small balls or snakes. Press them down flat and place onto ungreased cookie sheet. Bake at 325 degrees for approximately 10 minutes. Cool and serve for snack.

Cottage Cheese

Heat one quart of milk until lukewarm. Dissolve one rennet tablet in a small amount of milk. Stir rennet mixture into remaining milk. Let mixture stand in a warm place until set. Drain mixture through a strainer lined with cheesecloth. Bring corners of the cloth together and squeeze or drain mixture. Rinse mixture with cold water and drain again. Add a small amount of butter and salt.

Dried Apples

- 5 or 6 apples
- 2 tablespoons salt
- Water

Peel, core, and cut apples into slices or rings ⅛-inch thick. Place apple slices in salt-water solution for several minutes. Place in 180-degree oven for 3 to 4 hours, until dry. Turn apples occasionally.

Firehouse Baked Beans

Purchase canned baked beans. To the beans, add cup-up hot dogs and extra catsup. Heat and serve for a snack.

Fruit Leather

- 2 cups applesauce
- Vegetable shortening or oil

Preheat oven to 400 degrees. Pour applesauce onto greased shallow pan. Spread to ⅛-inch in thickness. Place pan in oven and lower temperature to 180 degrees. Cook for approximately 3 hours, until the leather can be peeled from the pan. Cut with scissors to serve.

Hot "Dog" Kebabs on a Stick

- Paper plates and napkins
- Skewers
- ½ package hot dogs
- 1 green pepper, cut up
- Cherry tomatoes

Place 2 pieces of green pepper, 2 cherry tomatoes, and 2 hotdog pieces on the child's plate. Show how to thread the ingredients on skewers. Bake kebobs in a preheated oven for 15 minutes at 350 degrees.

 This activity should be carefully and constantly supervised by an adult to prevent accidents.

Cooking

Mighty Mixture

Mix any of the following:

- A variety of dried fruit (apples, apricots, pineapple, raisins)
- A variety of seeds (pumpkin, sunflower)
- A variety of nuts (almond, walnuts, pecans)

Nachos

- 4 flour tortillas
- ¾ cup grated cheese
- ⅓ cup chopped green pepper (optional)

With clean kitchen scissors, cut each tortilla into 4 or 6 triangle wedges. Place on cookie sheet and sprinkle tortilla wedges with the cheese. Garnish with green pepper, if desired. Bake in a 350-degree oven for 4 to 6 minutes, or until cheese melts. Makes 16 to 20 nachos.

Non-Bake Pumpkin Pie

- 1 can prepared pumpkin pie
- 1 package vanilla instant pudding
- 1 cup milk

Mix and pour into baked pie shell or graham cracker pie shell.

Peanut Butter Log

- ½ cup peanut butter
- ½ cup raisins
- 2½ tablespoons dry milk
- 2 tablespoons honey

Mix together; roll into a log 1 inch by 10 inches long. Chill and slice.

Pizza Rounds

Provide child with one half of an English muffin. Demonstrate how to spread pizza sauce on the muffin. Then lay a few skinny strips of cheese across the top, making the cheese look like wheel spokes. Now let the child prepare her own. Bake in an oven at 350 degrees for 5 to 7 minutes or until cheese melts. Cool slightly before serving.

Popcorn Cake

- Four quarts popped corn
- One pound small gum drops
- ½ pound salted peanuts
- One pound marshmallows
- ½ cup margarine
- ½ cup cooking oil

Mix dry ingredients in a large pan. Melt margarine with oil and marshmallows in top of double boiler. Pour over dry ingredients and mix well. Pack tightly into a greased tube pan. When set, take out of the pan and slice.

 This recipe should only be used with older children, as young children can choke on popcorn and peanuts.

Cooking

Popsicles

- Pineapple juice
- Grape juice
- Cranapple juice
- Popsicle sticks
- Small paper cups

If frozen juice is used, mix according to directions on the can. Fill paper cups ¾ full of juice. Place cups in the freezer. When juice begins to freeze, insert a popsicle stick in the middle of each cup. When frozen, peel paper cup away and serve.

Pumpkin Pie

- 1 unbaked pie shell
- 2 cups (16 to 17 ounces) pumpkin
- 1 can sweetened condensed milk
- 1 egg
- ½ teaspoon salt
- 2 teaspoons pumpkin pie spice

Blend all ingredients in a large mixing bowl. Pour mixture into pie shell. Bake pie in an oven preheated to 375 degrees for 50 to 55 minutes or until a sharp knife blade inserted near center of pie is clean when removed. Cool and refrigerate pie for 1 hour before serving. Top with whipped cream, if desired.

Quick Dip

- 2 cups fat free yogurt
- 1 envelope onion soup mix

Stir the onion soup mix into the yogurt. Refrigerate 1 hour prior to serving.

Roasted Pumpkin Seeds

Soak pumpkin seeds for 24 hours in salt water (¼ cup salt to 1 cup water). Spread on cloth-covered cookie sheet and roast at 100 degrees for 2 hours. Turn oven off and leave seeds overnight.

S'Mores

Place a large marshmallow on a square graham cracker. Next, place a square of sweet chocolate on top of marshmallow. After this, place graham cracker on a baking sheet into a 250-degree oven for about 5 minutes, or until chocolate starts to melt. Remove s'more and press a second graham cracker square on top of chocolate. Let cool for a few minutes and serve while still slightly warm.

Sticks-and-Stones Snack

- 4 cups Cheerios cereal
- 2 cups pretzel twists
- 2 tablespoons margarine, butter, or spread (melted)
- 2 teaspoons Worcestershire sauce
- 1 cup raisins

Mix cereal and pretzel twists in ungreased rectangular pan, 13 by 9 by 2 inches. Stir melted margarine and Worcestershire sauce in small bowl. Pour over cereal mixture, tossing until evenly coated. Bake at 300 degrees, uncovered for 25 minutes, stirring occasionally. Stir in raisins; cool. Store in an airtight container. Makes about 7 cups. For variety, use different pretzel shapes and substitute 1 package (6 ounces) diced dried fruits for the raisins.

Vegetable Dip

- 1 cup plain yogurt
- 1 cup mayonnaise
- 1 tablespoon dill weed
- 1 teaspoon seasoned salt

Mix all the ingredients together and chill. Serve with fresh raw vegetables.

Vegetable Soup

Begin with consommé or soup base. Add whatever vegetables, beans, etc., the child wants to add and can help to prepare. Make soup a day ahead so that all vegetables are cooked thoroughly.

Vegetable-Tasting Party

Prepare raw vegetables for a tasting party. Discuss the color, texture, and flavor of each vegetable.

Watermelon Popsicles

Remove seeds and rind from a watermelon. Puree the melon in a blender or food processor. Pour into small paper cups. Insert popsicle sticks and freeze. These fruit pop-sicles can be served at snack time.

Spread

Butter

Fill baby food jars half full with whipping cream. Allow the children to shake the jars until the cream separates. First it will appear like whipping cream, then like over-whipped cream, and finally an obvious separation will occur. Then pour off liquid and taste. Wash butter in cold water in a bowl several times. Drain off milky liquid each time. Taste and then wash again until nearly clear. Work the butter in the water with a wooden spoon as you wash. Add salt to taste. Let the children spread the butter on crackers or bread.

Music and Movement

Music is a universal language. It is a natural form of expression for people of all ages everywhere. Young children need to have a variety of music experiences that are casual and spontaneous. For example, they need to hear nursery rhymes whose melodies are catchy, simple, and easily remembered.

Lullabies and songs should be introduced to infants and young children. They also need to hear folk and traditional songs. Songs such as "I'm a Little Teapot" and "Where Is Thumbkin?" have been handed down from generation to generation. Likewise, they also need to hear classical music, jazz, rock, and rap, as well as African, South American, and Native American music.

Young children enjoy and respond to music in a variety of forms. They enjoy listening to music even when engaged in other activities. They enjoy singing simple songs. They also enjoy moving and responding to the mood of music. Music can even be played when they lie down to nap or sleep.

Values

Music is a valuable experience for young children. Music:

- ▶ promotes the development of listening skills.

- ▶ builds vocabulary.

- ▶ provides an opportunity for learning new concepts such as loud/soft, heavy/light, fast/slow, up/down.

- ▶ releases tension in young children.

- ▶ promotes the development of auditory memory skills.

- ▶ stimulates the imagination.

Choosing Songs

Choose simple songs that respect the child's age, abilities, and interest. Children like songs that tell a story. They like songs about animals and familiar objects. They enjoy lullabies that are slow, soft, and soothing. They also like songs about families.

A young child will not tire of a well-loved song. The best songs for young children relate to their developmental level. These songs should tell a story with frequent repetition. The vocabulary included in the song should be developmentally appropriate. Moreover, the rhythm or mood should be strongly defined.

Teaching Songs

There are two different methods you can use for teaching songs—the **phrase method** and the **whole song method**. The method you choose will depend on the age of the child and length of the song. Regardless of the method, choose a time when the child is well rested.

Phrase Method. Use the phrase method when teaching longer songs to the young child. To do this, sing the entire song with enthusiasm. When you finish, stop and talk about the song. You can even ask a question such as, "What was the name of the kitten in the song?" Then sing short sections. After each section, have the child repeat the words back to you.

Whole Song Method. When teaching short and simple songs, use the whole song method. After you have sung the song, ask the child to sing the song with you. If the child is interested, repeat the song several times. This should help the child learn the words.

Helpful Hints!

Make music an enjoyable experience for young children. While singing with young children, share an expressive face. Smile and enjoy yourself. Your communication will be contagious. Also, follow these helpful hints listed below:

▶ Expose the child to a wide variety of music types. Nursery rhymes, lullabies, classic music, and folk music should all be included.

▶ Provide music from different ethnic and cultural groups.

▶ Choose songs with a strong melody. Chances are these songs will be more easily remembered.

▶ Encourage the child to sing and show him that singing is fun.

▶ Tape the child's singing voice and play the tape.

▶ Convey enthusiasm when singing. It will be catchy.

▶ Use music in every possible way.

▶ Encourage the child to listen to the sounds of nature such as the wind, leaves blowing and rustling, heavy rain, hail, snow blowing, etc.

▶ While outdoors, encourage the child to listen and identify outdoor sounds. Examples of sounds might include those from an airplane, car, truck, train, and/or streetcar.

▶ Play music for the child during naptime.

▶ Provide rhythm instruments for the child to experiment with sound or accompany the beat of a recording. Examples might include drums, shakers, and bells.

▶ Purchase a compact disc player and compact discs or a cassette player and tapes for your child.

▶ Use travel time for enjoying music.

Music and Movement

Songs

♪ All about Me

Brushing Teeth
(Sing to the tune of "Mulberry Bush.")

This is the way we brush our teeth,
Brush our teeth, brush our teeth.
This is the way we brush our teeth,
So early in the morning.

Catch One If You Can
(Sing to the tune of "Skip to My Lou.")

Butterflies are flying. Won't you try
    and catch one?
Butterflies are flying. Won't you try
    and catch one?
Butterflies are flying. Won't you try
    and catch one?
Catch one if you can.

Raindrops are falling. Won't you try
    and catch one?
Raindrops are falling. Won't you try
    and catch one?
Raindrops are falling. Won't you try
    and catch one?
Catch one if you can.

Clean Teeth
(Sing to the tune of "Row, Row, Row Your Boat.")

Brush, brush, brush your teeth
Brush them everyday.
We put some toothpaste on our
    brush
To help stop tooth decay.

This Is the Way
(Sing to the tune of "Mulberry Bush.")

This is the way we saw our wood,
Saw our wood, saw our wood.
This is the way we saw our wood,
So early in the morning.

Other verses: pound our nails
                drill a hole
                use a screwdriver

♪ Animals

The Animals on the Farm
(Sing to the tune of "The Wheels on the Bus.")

The cows on the farm go moo, moo,
    moo.
Moo, moo, moo, moo, moo, moo.
The cows on the farm go moo, moo,
    moo
all day long.

The horses on the farm go nay, nay,
    nay.
Nay, nay, nay, nay, nay, nay.
The horses on the farm go nay, nay,
    nay
all day long.

Other verses: (pigs—oink)
                (sheep—baa)
                (chicken—cluck)
                (turkeys—gobble)

Bingo

*There was a farmer who had a dog
And Bingo was his name-o.
B-I-N-G-O
B-I-N-G-O
B-I-N-G-O
And Bingo was his name-o.*

Birds

(Sing to the tune of "Mulberry Bush";
The first verse remains the same,
with the children walking around in
a circle holding hands.)

This is the way we scratch for worms.
(children move one foot in a
scratching motion like a chicken)
This is the way we peck our food.
(children peck)
This is the way we sit on our eggs.
(children squat down)
This is the way we flap our wings.
(bend arms at elbows, and put
thumbs under armpit, flap)
This is the way we fly away.
(children can "fly" anywhere they
want and return to the circle at
the end of the verse)

Circus

(Sing to the tune of "Did You Ever
See a Lassie?")

*Let's pretend that we are clowns,
are clowns, are clowns.
Let's pretend that we are clowns.
We'll have so much fun.
We'll put on our makeup and make
people laugh hard.
Let's pretend that we are clowns.
We'll have so much fun.*

*Let's pretend that we are elephants,
are elephants, are elephants.
Let's pretend that we are elephants.
We'll have so much fun.
We'll sway back and forth and stand
on just two legs.
Let's pretend that we are elephants.
We'll have so much fun.*

*Let's pretend that we are on a
trapeze, a trapeze, a trapeze.
Let's pretend that we are on a
trapeze.
We'll have so much fun.
We'll swing high and swoop low
and make people shout "oh!"
Let's pretend that we are on a
trapeze.
We'll have so much fun!*

Did You Ever See a Rabbit?

(Sing to the tune of "Did You Ever
See a Lassie?")

*Did you ever see a rabbit, a rabbit,
a rabbit?
Did you ever see a rabbit, a rabbit
on Easter morn?
He hops around so quietly
And hides all the eggs.
Did you ever see a rabbit, on Easter
morn?*

Easter Bunny

(Sing to the tune of "Ten Little
Indians.")

*Where, oh, where is the Easter
Bunny,
Where, oh, where is the Easter
Bunny,*

*Where, oh, where is the Easter
Bunny,
Early Easter morning?*

*Find all the eggs and put them in a
basket,
Find all the eggs and put them in a
basket,
Find all the eggs and put them in a
basket,
Early Easter morning.*

Easter Eggs

(Sing to the chorus of "Jingle Bells.")

*Easter eggs, Easter eggs,
Hidden all around.
Come my children look about
And see where they are found.*

*Easter eggs, Easter eggs
They're a sight to see.
One for Tom and one for Ann
And a special one for me!*

Kitty

(Sing to the tune of "Bingo.")

*I have a cat. She's very shy.
But she comes when I call K-I-T-T-Y
K-I-T-T-Y
K-I-T-T-Y
K-I-T-T-Y
And Kitty is her name-o.*

Variation: Let children think of other
names.

One Elephant

*One elephant went out to play
On a spider web one day.
He had such enormous fun
That he called for another elephant
to come.*

(Makes a nice flannel story, or
choose one child as an "elephant"
and add another "elephant" with
each verse.)

Pretty Birds

(Sing to the tune of "Ten Little
Indians.")
*One pretty, two pretty,
Three pretty birdies.
Four pretty, five pretty,
Six pretty birdies.
Seven pretty, eight pretty,
Nine pretty birdies,
All sitting in a tree.*

Six Little Pets

(Sing to the tune of "Six Little
Ducks," a traditional early childhood
song.)

*Six little gerbils I once knew,
Fat ones, skinny ones, fair ones too.
But the one little gerbil was so much
fun,
He would play until the day was
done.*

*Six little dogs that I once knew,
Fat ones, skinny ones, fair ones too.
But the one little dog with the brown
curly fur,
He led the others with a grr, grr, grr.*

Six little fish that I once knew,
Fat ones, skinny ones, fair ones too.
But the one little fish who was the
     leader of the crowd,
He led the others around and
     around.

Six little birds that I once knew,
Fat ones, skinny ones, fair ones too.
But the one little bird with the pretty
     little beak,
He led the others with a tweet,
     tweet, tweet.

Six little cats that I once knew,
Fat ones, skinny ones, fair ones too.
But the one little cat who was as
     fluffy as a ball,
He was the prettiest one of all.

Two Little Black Bears
(Sing to the tune of "Two Little
Blackbirds.")

Two little black bears sitting on a hill
One named Jack, one named Jill
Run away Jack
Run away Jill
Come back Jack
Come back Jill.
Two little black bears sitting on a hill
One named Jack, one named Jill.

Two Little Blackbirds
(Traditional)

Two little blackbirds sitting on a hill
One named Jack,
One named Jill.
Fly away Jack,
Fly away Jill.

Come back Jack,
Come back Jill.
Two little blackbirds sitting on a hill
One named Jack,
One named Jill.

Two Little Bluejays
(Sing to the tune of "Two Little
Blackbirds.")

Two little bluejays
Sitting on a hill
One named Sue
One named Bill.
Fly away Sue
Fly away Bill.
Come back Sue
Come back Bill.
Two little bluejays
Sitting on a hill
One named Sue
One named Bill.

(To add interest, you can substitute
names after the song has been sung
several times. The children will enjoy
hearing their names.)

Two Little Kittens
(Sing to the tune of "Two Little
Blackbirds.")

Two little kittens sitting on a hill
One named Jack, one named Jill
Run away Jack, run away Jill
Come back Jack, come back Jill
Two little kittens sitting on a hill
One named Jack, one named Jill.

**Music and
Movement**

♫ Feelings

Feelings

(Sing to the tune of "Twinkle, Twinkle Little Star.")

I have feelings.
You do, too
Let's all sing about a few.

I am happy. (smile)
I am sad. (frown)
I get scared. (wrap arms around
  self)
I get mad. (make a fist and shake it)

I am proud of being me. (hands on
  hips)
That's a feeling too you see.

I have feelings. (point to self)
You do, too. (point to someone else)
We just sang about a few.

If You're Happy and You Know It
(Traditional)

If you're happy and you know it
Clap your hands. (clap twice)
If you're happy and you know it
Clap your hands. (clap twice)
If you're happy and you know it
Then your face will surely show it.
If you're happy and you know it
Clap your hands. (clap twice)

(For additional verses, change the emotions and actions.)

♫ Foods

Little Apples

(Sing to the tune of "Ten Little Indians.")

One little, two little, three little
  apples,
Four little, five little, six little
  apples,
Seven little, eight little, nine little
  apples,
All fell to the ground.

(A variation for older children is to give each child a number card with a numeral from 1 through 9. When that number is sung, that child stands up. At the end of the fingerplay, all the children fall down.)

My Apple Tree
(Sing to the tune of "The Muffin Man.")

Did you see my apple tree,
Did you see my apple tree,
Did you see my apple tree,
Full of apples red?

Music and Movement

♪ Holidays

Christmas Chant

*With a "hey" and a "hi" and a
  "ho-ho-ho,"
Somebody tickled old Santa Claus's
  toe.
Get up ol' Santa, there's work to be
  done,
The children must have their holiday
  fun.
With a "hey" and a "hi" and a
  "ho-ho-ho,"
Santa Claus, Santa Claus,
GO-GO-GO!*

If You're Thankful

(Sing to the tune of "If You're
Happy.")

*If you're thankful and you know it
  clap your hands.
If you're thankful and you know it
  clap your hands.
If you're thankful and you know it,
  then your face will surely show it,
If you're thankful and you know it,
  clap your hands.*

Additional verses: stomp your feet,
tap your head, turn around, shout
hooray, etc.

Have You Made a Jack-O-Lantern?

(Sing to the tune of "Muffin Man.")

*Have you made a jack-o-lantern,
A jack-o-lantern, a jack-o-lantern?
Have you made a jack-o-lantern
For Halloween night?*

Menorah Candles

(Sing to the tune of "Twinkle,
Twinkle, Little Star.")

*Twinkle, twinkle candles in the night,
Standing on the menorah bright,
Burning slow we all know,
Burning bright to give us light.
Twinkle, twinkle candles in the night,
Standing on the menorah bright.*

My Valentine

(Sing to the tune of "The Muffin
Man.")

*Oh, do you know my valentine,
My valentine, my valentine?
Oh, do you know my valentine?
His name is ——.*

Chosen valentine then picks another
child.

One Little, Two Little, Three Little Pumpkins

(Sing to the tune of "Ten Little
Indians.")

*One little two little, three little
  pumpkins,
Four little, five little, six little
  pumpkins,
Seven little, eight little, nine little
  pumpkins,
Ready for Halloween night!*

Popcorn Song

(Sing to the tune of "I'm a Little
Teapot.")

*I'm a little popcorn in a pot.
Heat me up and watch me pop.
When I get all fat and white, then
  I'm done.
Popping corn is lots of fun.*

Music and Movement

S-A-N-T-A

(Sing to the tune of "B-I-N-G-O.")

There was a man on Christmas Day
And Santa was his name-o.
S-A-N-T-A
S-A-N-T-A
S-A-N-T-A
And Santa was his name-o.

Santa in His Shop

(Sing to the tune of "The Farmer in the Dell.")

Santa in his shop
Santa's in his shop
What a scene for Christmas
Santa's in his shop.

Other verses:

Santa takes a drum
The drum takes a doll
The doll takes a train
The train takes a ball
The ball takes a top
They're all in the shop
The top stays in the shop
(Pictures could be constructed for
use during the mention of each toy.)

Ten Little Valentines

(Sing to the tune of "Ten Little Indians.")

One little, two little, three little
valentines.
Four little, five little, six little
valentines.
Seven little, eight little, nine little
valentines.
Ten little valentines here!

Movement

Like music, movement activities are valuable for young children. Movement is an important nonverbal tool. Children can move to music or verbal directions. For example, you may ask the child to crawl like a caterpillar, hop like a bunny, or walk like a heavy horse. However, remember that a child's response to movement will vary depending upon age.

Value

Through movement activities children can learn by:

▶ exploring their bodies as they move.

▶ practicing combining movement and rhythm.

▶ learning vocabulary words such as fast, slow, loud, and soft.

▶ expressing their imaginations.

▶ learning how movement is related to space.

Children's Responses

Two-year-old children respond to rhythm at their own tempo. A big part of a child's life at this stage is moving. Watch. A child at this stage enjoys moving her whole body. While you beat a drum, she may repeat the movement by clapping or jumping for the entire duration of the activity. A child at this stage loves to show off.

As opposed to one steady beat on a drum, for three-year-old children you can vary the rhythm. Make the sounds fast, heavy, loud, slow, light, and soft. Children at this age have a variety of responses. Children between the ages of four and six can make movements to the beat of the music. When the beat is slow, their movements will be slow, and when the beat is fast, their movements will be fast.

Music and Movement

Movement Activities

♪ Listen to the Drum

Accessory: drum

fast

slow

heavy

soft

big

small

♪ Moving Shapes

1. Try to move about like something huge and heavy: elephant, tugboat, bulldozer.
2. Try to move like something small and heavy: a fat frog, a heavy top.
3. Try moving like something big and light: a beach ball, a parachute, a cloud.
4. Try moving like something small and light: a feather, a snowflake, a flea, a butterfly.

♪ Pantomime

1. You're going to get a present. What is the shape of the box? How big is the box? Feel the box. Hold it. Unwrap the present. Take it out. Now put it back in.
2. Think about an occupation. Show me how the worker acts.
3. Show me how you feel when it is cold; hot.
4. Show me how a hungry baby acts. Show me how a tired puppy acts.
5. Show me how you feel very early in the morning; late in the afternoon.
6. Show me what the weather is like.
7. Pretend you are driving, typing, raking leaves.
8. Take a partner. Pretend you're playing ball.

♪ Put Yourself inside Something (bottle, box, barrel)

You're outside something—now get into it.

You're inside something—now get out of it.

You're underneath something.

You're on top of something.

You're beside (or next to) something.

You're surrounded by something.

♪ To Become Aware of Space

Lift your leg up in front of you.

Lift your leg up backwards, sideways.

Lift your leg and step forward, backwards, sideways, and around and around.

Reach up to the ceiling.

Stretch to touch the walls.

Punch down to the floor.

♪ To Become Aware of Time

Run very fast.
Walk very slowly.
Jump all over the floor quickly.
Sit down on the floor slowly.
Slowly grow up as tall as you can.
Slowly curl up on the floor as small
as possible.

♪ To Become Aware of Weight

To feel the difference between heavy
and light, the child should experi-
ment with her own body force:
Punch down to the floor hard.
Lift your arms up slowly and gently
stomp on the floor.
Walk on tip-toe.
Kick out one leg as hard as you can.
Very smoothly and lightly, slide one
foot along the floor.

Music and Movement

Nursery Rhymes

♫ People

Do You Know This Friend of Mine?

(Sing to the tune of "The Muffin Man.")

Do you know this friend of mine,
This friend of mine,
This friend of mine?
Do you know this friend of mine?
His name is ———.

Yes, we know this friend of yours,
This friend of yours,
This friend of yours.
Yes, we know this friend of yours.
His name is ———.

Family Helper

(Sing to the tune of "Here We Are Together.")

It's fun to be a helper, a helper, a
*   helper.*
It's fun to be a helper, just any time.
Oh, I can set the table, the table,
*   the table.*
Oh, I can set the table at dinner
*   time.*
Oh, I can dry the dishes, the dishes,
*   the dishes.*
Oh, I can dry the dishes, and make
*   them shine.*

The Farmer in the Dell

(Traditional)

The farmer in the dell,
The farmer in the dell,
Hi-ho the dairy-o
The farmer in the dell.

The farmer takes a wife/husband,
The farmer takes a wife/husband,
Hi-ho the dairy-o
The farmer in the dell.

Other verses: *The wife/husband*
*   takes the child,*
*   The child takes the nurse,*
*   The nurse takes the dog,*
*   The dog takes the cat,*
*   The cat takes the rat,*
*   The rat takes the cheese,*
Final verse: *The cheese stands*
*   alone,*
*   The cheese stands alone,*
*   Hi-ho the dairy-o*
*   The cheese stands alone.*

The More We Get Together

(Sing to the tune of "Have You Ever Seen a Lassie?")

The more we are together, together,
*   together,*
The more we are together, the
*   happier we'll be.*
For your friends are my friends, and
*   my friends are your friends.*
The more we are together the
*   happier we'll be.*

(Insert names of other children or people you know.)

🎵 Seasons

Flowers
(Sing to the tune of "Pop! Goes the Weasel.")

All around the forest ground
There's flowers everywhere.
There's pink, yellow and purple, too.
Here's one for you.

🎵 Traditional

Hickory Dickory Dock
Hickory dickory dock
The mouse ran up the clock.
The clock struck one, the mouse ran
*   down,*
Hickory dickory dock.

Jack and Jill
Jack and Jill went up a hill
To fetch a pail of water.
Jack fell down and broke his crown
And Jill fell tumbling after.

The Muffin Man
Oh, do you know the muffin man,
The muffin man, the muffin man?
Oh, do you know the muffin man
Who lives on Dreary Lane?
Yes, I know the muffin man . . .

🎵 Transportation

Twinkle, Twinkle, Traffic Light
(Sing to the tune of "Twinkle,
Twinkle, Little Star.")

Twinkle, twinkle, traffic light,
Standing on the corner bright.
When it's green it's time to go.
When it's red it's stop, you know.
Twinkle, twinkle, traffic light,
Standing on the corner bright.

The Wheels on the Bus
The wheels on the bus go round
*   and round,*
Round and round, round and round,
The wheels on the bus go round
*   and round,*
All through the town.

Other verses:
The wipers on the bus go swish,
*   swish, swish,*
The doors on the bus go open and
*   shut,*
The horn on the bus goes beep,
*   beep, beep,*
The driver on the bus says, "Move
*   on back,"*
The people on the bus go up and
*   down,*

Music and Movement

♫ Weather

Snowman
(Sing to the tune of "Twinkle, Twinkle, Little Star.")

*Snowman, snowman, where did you
    go?*
I built you yesterday out of snow.
I built you high and I built you fat.
I put on eyes and a nose and a hat.
Now you're gone all melted away,
*But it's sunny outside so I'll go and
    play.*

The Seed Cycle
(Sing to the tune of "The Farmer in the Dell.")

The farmer sows his seeds,
The farmer sows his seeds,
Hi-ho the dairy-o
The farmer sows his seeds.

Other verses:
The wind begins to blow,
The rain begins to fall,
The sun begins to shine,
The seeds begin to grow,
The plants grow big and tall,
The farmer cuts his corn,
He puts it in his barns,
And now the harvest is in,

(Children can dramatize the parts for each verse.)

Music and Movement

154

Play

For young children, play is a vehicle for learning about living and the world around them. Play is the child's work. During play children experience success in a task that they have defined for themselves. Through interactions with people, materials, and objects, children construct their own knowledge about the world.

Value of Play

Play is a valuable tool for young children. It is the primary way children develop physically. They learn to crawl, walk, run, jump, skip, hop, climb, and throw. An abundance of practice is needed to develop these skills. Young children also develop the skills for social competence and creative expression. Through play, children gain skills in:

- building a useful vocabulary.
- developing fine and large muscle skills.
- developing hand-eye coordination skills.
- learning about cause and effect.
- developing reasoning skills.
- experimenting with people and things.
- exploring their feelings.
- sharing play materials and play things.
- developing independence.
- practicing making predictions and drawing conclusions.
- learning to create, explore, organize, and try out solutions.
- acting out their own feelings.

Types of Play

The beginning of play occurs soon after the birth of an infant. By observing young children, you will note different categories of play, which develop in an orderly sequence. They include solitary, parallel, associative, and cooperative play. These categories may vary depending upon the child's developmental, as opposed to chronological, age.

Solitary Play

Solitary play occurs from infancy to eighteen months of age. During this stage of development, the child uses all of his senses—smelling, listening, feeling, tasting, and touching. During their interaction with toys and objects in their environment, children build their touching and grasping skills. During this stage the child plays independently while gathering information. To illustrate, the child may hit a rattle on the tray of the highchair. Gradually, the child will learn about cause and effect.

A child during this stage of development loves face-to-face talking and peek-a-boo games. Observe. The child manipulates one toy at a time and is learning different characteristics of toys. Initially, a child will explore individual objectives. Then, at approximately nine months of age, multiple objects will be explored. In fact, the child may now hold an object in each hand. Age-appropriate toys include rattles, soft blocks, activity gyms, stuffed toys, water toys, stuffed toys, and balls.

Parallel Play

Parallel play gradually emerges when the child is approximately eighteen months of age. This stage typically lasts until age three. Play during this stage occurs when children with similar toys play side by side. Even though the children may be engaged in similar activities, they play on their own. There is no direct involvement with one another. They may, however, take toys from each other. Children at this stage enjoy wagons, toy telephones, cash registers, cars, trucks, and large, lightweight blocks.

Associative Play

Between three and four years of age, the child will gradually learn to respect property rights. As a result, associative play emerges. This type of play involves the interaction of two or more children in a common play activity. The children now are beginning to exchange toys, and they typically use real objects in their play. They may also, however, incorporate some imaginative objects. To illustrate, they may use a slender building toy to serve as a pencil for a waiter.

The children in the group are engaged in similar activities. Their role-playing is usually based on familiar people, such as their mothers, fathers, siblings, and community helpers. They drive cars, take care of the baby, clean, cook, and may act out the role of a mother or father. When observing children at this age, you will note that sharing is still a difficult concept for them to master. Often their conflict will be over the roles, as well as the props, used in the play activity. Then, too, children at this age lack the ability to separate the real world from make-believe.

Play

Cooperative Play

Cooperative play occurs between three and four years of age. Now three or four children can play together, and sharing typically is a common behavior. When observing children at this age, you will note that they are able to distinguish the real from the imaginary.

Children at this stage are playing together for a purpose, and their play is often aggressive. One of the favorite themes is to play a monster, a ghost, or a television character. True interaction can be observed as the children accept and assign roles. They now share materials and equipment. For example, one child will be a cashier in a fast food restaurant, and another child will play the role of the cook or customer. During the process, the children will search for the right objects to serve as play tools.

Helpful Hints!

These helpful hints provide valuable tools in encouraging play:

▶ Provide space that will minimize interruptions for the child to play.

▶ Provide age-appropriate, real-life tools and props to encourage play.

▶ Take part in play scenarios that the child creates. However, the child should be the star by retaining the lead and control unless safety is an issue.

▶ Watch for times when you are needed to add props or participate.

▶ Arrange to have the child spend time with other children of her own age. Moreover, provide opportunities for her to engage in play with children of other ages.

▶ Provide opportunities for constructive play that include the manipulation of objects for the purpose of creating and building. Open-ended building materials such as blocks and Legos should always be available.

Play

Dramatic Play Themes

The following are dramatic play themes that young children enjoy.

Animals

Animal Clinic

Provide children with stuffed animals and doctor instruments.

Barn

A barn and plastic animals can be provided. The child can use blocks as accessories to make pens, cages, etc.

Birdhouse

Construct a large birdhouse out of cardboard. Allow the child to imitate a bird. (Unless adequate room is available, this may be more appropriate for an outdoor activity.) Bird accessories such as homemade beaks and wings may be supplied to stimulate interest.

Bird Nest

Place several hay bales in the corner of a play yard, confining the materials to one area. Let the child rearrange the straw to simulate a bird nest. Also provide bird masks, a perch, and other bird-related items for use during self-initiated play.

Cat/Dog Grooming

Provide the child with empty shampoo and conditioner bottles, brushes, combs, ribbons, collars, a plastic bathtub, towels, and stuffed toy cats and dogs. A grooming area can be set up with stuffed animals, brushes, and combs. If available, cut the cord off an electric dog shaver and provide it for the child's use.

Circus

Lions, cheetahs, panthers, leopards, and tigers are also cats. Use large boxes for cages. Set up a circus by making a circle out of masking tape on the floor. The child can perform in the ring. The addition of hula hoops, animal and clown costumes, tickets, and chairs may extend the child's interest.

Play

Dog House

Construct a doghouse from a large cardboard box. Provide dog ears and tails for the child to wear as he imitates the pet.

Hatching

Here is a general idea of what you can say to create the hatching experience with a young child. Say:

Close your eyes. Curl up very small, as small as you can. Lie on your side. Think of how dark it is inside your egg. Yes, you're in an egg! You're tiny and curled up and quiet. It's very dark. Very warm. But now, try to wiggle a little—just a little! Remember, your eggshell is all around you. You can wiggle your wingtips a little, and maybe your toes. You can shake your head just a little. Hey! Your beak is touching something. I think your beak is touching the eggshell. Tap the shell gently with your beak. Hear that? Yes, that's you making that noise. Keep tapping. A little harder. Something is happening. The shell has cracked—oh, close your eyes. It's bright out there. Now you can wiggle a little more. The shell is falling away. You can stretch out, stretch to be as long as you can make yourself. Stretch your feet. Stretch your wings. Doesn't that feel good, after being in that little egg? Stretch! You're brand new—can you stand up slowly? Can you see other new baby birds?

Pet Store

Using stuffed animals, simulate a pet store. Include a counter complete with cash register, play money, and empty pet food containers. Post a large sign that says "Pet Store." Set out many stuffed dogs with collars and leashes. The child will enjoy pretending to have a new pet. Cages and many small stuffed animals can be added.

Saddle

A horse saddle can be placed on a bench. The child can sit on it, pretending he is riding a horse.

Spider Web

Tie together a big piece of rope to resemble a spider web. Have the child pretend to be a spider playing on its web.

Veterinarian's Office

Use some toy medical equipment and stuffed animals to create a veterinarian's office. Stuffed animals can also be used as patients. Collect materials for a veterinarian prop box. Include a stethoscope, empty pill bottles, fabric cut as bandages, splints, and stuffed animals.

Zoo

Lions, cheetahs, panthers, leopards, and tigers are also cats. Use large boxes for cages. Collect large appliance boxes. Cut slits to resemble cages. Old fur coats or blankets can be added. The child may use the fur pieces to pretend to be different animals in the zoo.

Home and Family

Baby Clothing

Arrange the play area for washing baby dolls. Include a tub with soapy water, washcloths, drying towels, play clothes, brush, and comb.

Cardboard Houses

Collect large cardboard boxes. Place outdoors or in a large open room. The child may build and construct her own home. If desired, tempera paint can be used for painting the home. Wallpaper may also be provided.

Cleaning House

Housecleaning tools such as a vacuum cleaner, dusting cloth, sponges, mops, and brooms can be provided.

Doll Baths

Fill a play sink or plastic tub with water. The child can wash dishes or give a doll a bath.

Dollhouse

Set up a large dollhouse. The house can be constructed from cardboard. Include dolls to represent several members of a family.

Dress-Up Clothes

Provide clothing for the child to dress up in. Suits, dresses, hats, purses, gloves, and dress-up shoes should be included. See the chart on the following page for more examples.

Dress-Up for Winter

If available, put outdoor winter clothing such as coats, boots, hats, mittens, scarves, and ear muffs in a room with a large mirror. The child may enjoy trying on a variety of clothing items.

Play

Dramatic Play Clothes

The following list contains names of clothing articles to save for use in the dramatic play area.

Aprons	Leotards	Slacks
Belts	Pajamas	Slippers
Billfolds	Purses	Snow pants
Boots	Raincoats	Socks
Coats	Robes	Suspenders
Dresses	Scarves	Sweaters
Ear muffs	Shirts	Sweatsuits
Gloves/mittens	Shoes	Swimsuits
Hats	Shorts	Ties
Jewelry: rings; bracelets; necklaces; clip-on earrings	Skirts	

Family Celebration

Collect materials for a special family meal. This may include dresses, hats, coats, plates, cups, plastic food, napkins, etc. The child can have a holiday meal.

Gift Wrapping

Collect various-sized boxes, wrapping paper, scissors, tape, and ribbon. Also collect newspaper comic pages, wallpaper books, and paper scraps. The child can wrap presents for a special holiday.

Hanging Clothes

String a low clothesline in the room or outdoors. Provide clothespins and doll clothes for the child to hang up.

Party Clothes

Provide dressy clothes, jewelry, shoes, hats, and purses.

Picnic

Collect items to make a picnic basket. Include paper napkins, cups, plates, plastic eating utensils, plastic food, etc. A purse and a small cooler can also be placed in the room to stimulate play.

Tea Party

Provide dress-up clothes, play dishes, and water to have a tea party.

Telephone Booth/Telephones

Provide telephones, real or toy, to encourage the child to talk to others. Also, make your own telephones by using two large, empty orange juice concentrate cans, removing one end for the removal of content. After washing the cans, connect with a long string. The child can pull the string taut. Then he can talk and listen to others. Prepare a telephone book with names and telephone numbers. The child can practice dialing these numbers.

Our Community

Art Gallery/Store

Mount pictures from magazines on sheets of tagboard. Let the child hang the pictures. A cash register and play money for buying and selling the paintings can extend the play. Set up an art supply store. Include paints, crayons, markers, paper, chalk, brushes, play money, and cash register.

Artist

Artist's hats, smocks, easels, and paint tables can be provided. The child can use the materials to pretend to be an artist.

Baker/Bake Shop

Collect and provide baking props such as hats, aprons, cookie cutters, baking pans, rolling pins, mixers, spoons, and bowls. Play dough, as well as scissors and cooking tools, can be placed on a table. If desired, make paper baker hats and a sign.

Band

Collect materials for a band prop box, which may include band uniforms, a baton, music stand, cassette player, and tapes with marching music. The child can also experiment with musical instruments.

Buildings

Collect large cardboard boxes from an appliance dealer. The child can construct buildings and paint them with tempera paint.

Card Shop

Stencils, paper, markers, scraps, stickers, etc., can be provided to make a card making shop.

Carpenter

Place a carpentry box with scissors, rulers, and masking tape in a woodworking area. Also provide large cardboard boxes and paint, if desired.

Classroom Café

Cover the table with a tablecloth. Provide menus, a pad for the waitress to write on, a space for a cook, etc. A cash register and play money may also be added to encourage play.

Clock Shop

Collect a variety of clocks for the child to explore. Using discarded clocks with the glass face removed is an interesting way to let the child explore numerals and the internal mechanisms.

Clothing Store

Place dress-up clothing on hangers and a rack. A cash register, play money, bags, and small shopping carts can also be provided to extend the play.

Construction Site

Place cardboard boxes, blocks, plastic pipes, wheelbarrows, hard hats, paper, and pencils to represent a construction site. Provide the child with toy tools and blocks. Scrap wood can also be provided for outdoor play. Cardboard boxes and masking tape should be available.

Costume Shop

Provide costumes for a bunny, Easter baskets, and Easter eggs in the play area. The child can hide the eggs and go on Easter egg hunts. Also add Halloween costumes. (These may be purchased at thrift stores or garage sales and stored in a Halloween prop box from year to year.)

Disc Jockey

Provide a tape recorder and cassettes for the child.

Doctors and Nurses

Make a prop box for a doctor and nurse. Include a white coat, plastic gloves, a thermometer, gauze, tape, masks, eye droppers, tweezers, tongue depressors, eye chart, cots, blankets, pencil and paper, empty and washed medicine bottles, a stethoscope, a scale, and syringes without needles. A first-aid kit including gauze and tape, bandages, butterflies, a sling, and ace bandages can be placed in this box.

Eye Doctor Clinic

Ask a local eye doctor for discontinued eyeglass frames. Place the frames, with a wall chart of letters to read, in the play area.

Farmer

Clothes and props for a farmer can be provided. Include items such as hats, scarves, overalls, boots, etc.

Play

Firefighters/Fire Station

Provide firefighter clothing such as hats, boots, and coats for the child to wear. Also provide a bell to use as an alarm. To extend play, a vacuum cleaner hose or a length of garden hose can be included to represent a water hose.

Grocery Store

Plan a grocery store containing many plastic fruits and vegetables, a cash register, grocery bags, and play money if available. The child can pretend to be a produce clerk, cashier, or price tagger. Collect a variety of empty boxes, paper bags, sales receipts, etc. Removable stickers can be used to indicate the grocery prices.

Hair Stylist

Collect empty hair spray bottles, brushes, empty shampoo bottles, chairs, mirrors, hair dryers, and curling irons and place in the play area. (If possible, cut the cords off the electrical appliances.) Also provide combs, brushes, barrettes, wigs, ribbons, and magazines. Include a chair, plastic covering, and beauty shop sign. A cash register and play money can be added to encourage play.

Hat Shop

Make a hat shop. Place hats with ribbons, flowers, netting, and other decorations in the play area. The child can decorate the hats. If the child is interested, plan an Easter Parade. Firefighter hats, bonnets, top hats, hard hats, bridesmaids' hats, baby hats, etc., can all be available in the hat store. Encourage the child to buy and sell hats using a cash register and play money. The following chart lists additional types of hats to use.

Hats

A variety of hats can be collected for use in the dramatic play area. Some examples are listed here.

Beret	Motorcycle helmet	Sports:
Bicycle helmet	Nurse's cap	football
Chef	Party (birthday)	baseball
Cloche	Pillbox	Stocking cap
Cowboy	Police officer	Straw hat
Firefighter	Railroad engineer	Sun bonnet
Hard hat	Sailor	Top hat
Headband	Scarf	Visor
Mantilla	Ski cap	
Mail carrier	Sombrero	

Ice Cream Stand

Trace and cut ice cream cones from brown construction paper. Cotton-balls or small yarn pompoms can be used to represent ice cream. The addition of ice cream buckets and scoops can make this activity more inviting during self-selected play periods.

Juice Stand

Set up a lemonade or orange juice stand. To prepare, use real oranges and lemons and let the child squeeze them and make the juice. The juice can be served at snack time.

Laundromat

Collect two large appliance boxes. Cut a hole in the top of one to represent a washing machine and cut a front door in the other to represent a dryer. To extend the play, a laundry basket, empty soap box, and play clothing may be welcome additions.

Library

Rearrange the play area to resemble a library. Include books, library cards, bookmarkers, tables, and chairs for the child's use. Books on a shelf, a desk for the librarian, and a stamper and inkpad to check out books should be provided. A small table where the child can sit and look at the books will also add interest.

Mailboxes

Construct an individual mailbox for the child using a shoebox, empty milk carton, paper bag, or partitioned box. Print the child's name on the box or encourage her to do so. The child can sort letters and small packages into the partitioned mailbox.

Paint Store

Provide paintbrushes, buckets, and paint sample books. Set up a paint store by including paint caps, pans, rollers, drop cloths, and painting clothes. The addition of a cash register, play money and pads of paper will extend the child's play.

Post Office

Develop the play area into a post office. Provide a mailbox, envelopes, old cards, paper, pens, old stampers, ink pads, hats, mailbags, a cash register, and a letter scale. During self-selected or self-initiated play periods, the child may enjoy acting out the role of a mail carrier or a post office worker.

Radio Station

Place an old microphone, or one made from a styrofoam ball and cardboard, with records in the play area.

Restaurant

Tables, tablecloths, menus, and tablets for taking orders can be provided. Paste pictures of food on the menus. A sign for the area could read, "Eating for Health." Collect bags, containers, and hats to set up a take-out restaurant.

Scientist

The child can dress up in a white lab coat and observe spiders and insects with magnifying glasses.

Shining Shoes

Gather clear shoe polish, shoes, brushes, and shining cloths for the child to use to polish shoes.

 Constantly observe and supervise the child while using shoe polish.

Shoemaker Store

Set up a shoemaker's store. Provide the child with shoes, toy hammers, smocks, cash registers, and play money. The child can act out mending, buying, and selling shoes.

Television

Obtain an old, discarded television console to use for a puppetry or storytelling experience. Remove the back and set, retaining just the wooden frame. If desired, make curtains.

Uniforms

Collect occupational clothing and hats, such as police officer shirts and hats, a firefighter's hat, nurse and doctor lab coats, and artist smocks. High school athletic uniforms can also be provided.

Plants

Flower Arranging

Artificial flowers and containers can be used to make centerpieces or flower arrangements.

Flower Shop

Set up a flower shop complete with plastic flowers, boxes, containers, vases, watering cans, misting bottle, and a cash register, and play money. Artificial corsages would also be a fun addition. Include spring plants, baskets, and Easter lilies. To extend

the child's interest, provide wrapping paper. Make a sign that reads "Flower Shop." The child may want to arrange, sell, deliver, and receive flowers. (If desired, flowers can be made from tissue paper and pipe cleaners.) Collect different kinds of vases and also Styrofoam or sponge blocks so the child can make flower arrangements. Aprons, play money, and sacks can be provided to encourage play. Seed packages and catalogs can also be used.

Fruit/Vegetable Stand

Prepare an apple stand by providing the child with bags, plastic fruits and vegetables, a cash register, play money, a stand, and bushel baskets. Encourage him to play at buying, selling, and packaging. To encourage play, aprons, market baskets, or bags can also be used. Provide a balance scale for the child to use to weigh the produce. He can pretend to be either the owner or a shopper.

Garden

Aprons, small garden tools, a tin of soil, seeds, watering cans, pots, and vases can be provided. Also gather gloves, hats, and plastic flowers or plants. Pictures of flowers with their names written on them can be hung in the room. The child can pretend to plant and grow seeds. Provide seed catalogs and order blanks to use to shop for seeds.

Greenhouse

Provide materials for a greenhouse. Include window space, pots, soil, water, watering cans, seeds, plants, posters, work aprons, garden gloves, a terrarium, and empty seed packages to mount on sticks.

"Jack and the Beanstalk"

Act out the story "Jack and the Beanstalk." The child can dramatize a beanstalk growing.

Seasons and Weather

Beach

Set up lawn chairs, beach towels, buckets, shovels, sunglasses, etc. Weather permitting, these items can be placed outdoors. Also use beach toys, beach balls, magazines, and books. If the activity is done outdoors, a sun umbrella can be added to stimulate interest in play.

Fall Wear

Set out warm clothes such as sweaters, coats, hats, and blankets to indicate cold weather coming on. The child can use the clothes for dressing up.

Hats

After reading *Caps for Sale* (1987) by Ersphyr Slobodykina, set out colored hats for the child to use to retell the story.

Rainy Day Clothing

Umbrellas, raincoats, hats, galoshes, and a tape containing rain sounds should be provided.

> *Use caution when selecting umbrellas for this activity. Some open quickly and can be dangerous.*

Weather Station

A map, pointer, adult clothing, and a pretend map can be used. The child can play a television weather person. Pictures depicting different weather conditions can be included.

Sports and Hobbies

Baseball

Baseball caps, plastic balls, uniforms, a catcher's mask, and gloves can be placed in the play area.

Block Play

Set out a big selection of blocks and rubber, plastic, or wooden models of zoo animals.

Canoeing

Bring a canoe into the room or onto the play yard. Provide paddles and a life vest for the child to wear.

Camping

Collect various types of clothing and camping equipment and place them in the play area or outdoors. Include items such as hiking boots, sweatshirts, raincoats, sleeping bags, backpacks, cooking tools, and a tent. A small, freestanding tent can be set up indoors, if room permits, or else outdoors, and blocks or logs can represent a campfire.

Play

Clown Makeup

Prepare clown makeup by mixing 1 part facial cream with 1 drop food coloring. Place the makeup by a large mirror. The child can apply the face makeup. Clown suits can also be provided if available.

Dance Studio

Utilize tap shoes, tutus, ballet shoes, tights, leotards, and either a compact disc player with CDs or cassette player with tapes to simulate a dance studio.

Dramatizing

Provide a cassette recorder and a small microphone. The child may enjoy using it for singing and recording voices.

Fishing

Set up a rocking boat or a large box in the room or outdoors. Prepare paper fish with metal paper clips attached to them. Include a fishing pole made from a wooden dowel and a long string with a magnet attached to the end. The magnet will attract the paper clip, allowing the children to catch the fish. Add a tackle box, canteen, hats, and life jackets for interest.

Fitness Gym

Provide a small mat, headbands, wristbands, sweatshirts, sweat pants, leotards, and music.

Football

Balls, shoulder pads, uniforms, and helmets can be provided for the child to use outdoors.

Health Club

Mats, fake weights (made from large Tinker Toys), headbands, and recorded music can be provided to represent a health club.

Ice Skating

Make a masking tape border on a carpeted floor. Give the child two pieces of waxed paper. Show her how to fasten the waxed paper to her ankles with large rubber bands. Play instrumental music and encourage the child to skate around on the carpeted floor.

Letters

Provide a variety of writing materials. Include different colors of paper, writing tools, and envelopes. The child can dictate a letter to a friend or family member. Apply stamps and walk to the nearest mailbox or post office. (Contact a local printer, office supply store, or card shop and ask for discontinued samples or misprinted envelopes.)

Puppets

Develop a puppet corner and include various animal and people puppets. If available, a puppet stage should be added. Otherwise, a puppet stage can be made from cardboard. The child can use puppets to act out friendships in various situations. To add variety, each day a different set of puppets can be added.

Skiing

Ski boots and skis can be provided for the child to try on.

Tennis

Tennis rackets, balls, visors, and sunglasses can be placed outdoors. A variation would be to use balloons for balls and rackets made from plastic hangers covered with nylon pantyhose.

Tent Living

A small tent can be set up either indoors or outdoors, depending upon weather and space. Accessories such as sleeping bags, flashlights, rope, cooking utensils, and backpacks should also be provided, if available.

Water Painting

As an outdoor activity, provide the child with a bucket of water and a house paintbrush. He can pretend to "paint" buildings, sidewalks, equipment, or fences.

Workbench

A hammer, nails, saws, vices, a carpenter's apron, etc., should be added to the workbench. Eye goggles for the child's safety should also be included.

 Constant supervision is needed for this activity.

Transportation

Airplane

Create an airplane out of a large cardboard refrigerator box. If desired, the child can paint the airplane. To extend the child's interest, also provide a telephone, tickets, travel brochures, and suitcases.

Bus

Set up a bus situation by lining up chairs in one or two long rows. Provide a steering wheel for the driver. A money bucket and play money can also be provided. If a steering wheel is unavailable, improvise using a heavy, round, cardboard pizza-box liner.

Car Mechanic

Place various wheels, tires, tools, overalls, and broken bicycles outside. The child can experiment with using tools.

> ⏰ *To avoid introducing a safety hazard, this activity needs to be developmentally appropriate for the child.*

Filling Station

Provide cardboard boxes for cars and hoses for the gas pumps. Also make available play money and pretend steering wheels.

Fire Truck/Engine

Contact the local fire chief and ask to use old hoses, fire hats, and firefighter clothing. A fire truck can be cut from a cardboard refrigerator box. The child may want to paint the box yellow or red. A steering wheel and chairs may be added. These props could also be placed outdoors, weather permitting. See the chart on the following page for ideas on assembling prop boxes.

Floats

Paper, tape, crepe paper, and balloons can be provided to decorate the wheels on tricycles, wagons, and scooters.

Seat Belts

Collect child-sized car seats. Place them in the play area, letting the child adjust them for a doll.

Taxi

Set up two rows of chairs side by side to represent a taxi. Use a pizza cardboard, or other round objects, as the steering wheel. Provide a telephone, dress-up clothes for the passengers, and a hat for the driver. To invite play, a "TAXI" sign can also be placed by the chairs.

Play

Prop Boxes

The following is a list of prop boxes that can be made by collecting the related materials. These boxes can be made available for the child's use at any time.

Police Officer
- Badge
- Hat
- Uniforms
- Whistle
- Walkie-talkie
- Handcuffs
- Stop sign (to hold)

Mail Carrier
- Letter bag
- Letters and stamps
- Uniforms
- Mailbox
- Envelopes
- Paper
- Pencil
- Rubber stamp
- Ink pad
- Wrapped cardboard boxes

Firefighter
- Boots
- Helmet
- Hose
- Jacket/uniform
- Gloves
- Raincoat
- Suspenders
- Goggles
- Bell
- Whistle
- Oxygen mask
- Hats

Doctor/Nurse
- Stethoscope
- Medicine bottles
- Adhesive tape
- Cotton balls
- Red Cross armband
- Chart holder

Games

Children enjoy games. Throughout history, children have enjoyed a wide variety of games. Included have been hiding, guessing, aiming, board games, playing cards, ball games, and games involving verbal commands.

Think about it. You too, probably have fond memories of playing games with siblings, family members, friends, and neighbors.

Typically children will learn the basic rules for play through training. That is, you will need to remind the child with comments such as, "It is my turn now," or "Tommy is waiting patiently for his turn." In addition to learning to understand rules, there are many other values to game playing for young children.

Values

Through game playing the young child gains by:

- learning to take turns.
- developing social awareness.
- building social, personal, intellectual, and physical skills.
- developing verbal skills.
- developing a conscience.
- developing fine and large muscle coordination.
- developing moral conduct and codes.
- developing sensory discrimination.
- developing visual skills (hiding games).
- developing auditory skills (for example, hide the egg timer).
- developing tactile skills ("duck, duck, goose").

Selecting Games

Games should be selected on the basis of a child's abilities, needs, and interests. Typical preschool games include Hide and Seek, Drop the Hanky, Lotto, memory games, concentration, and color recognition games. A child's first games, however, will generally include Hide and Seek and color matching. The following chart lists games for preschool children and their purpose.

Preschool Games and Skills Developed	
Candy Land	Color recognition, turn taking, visual discrimination
Chutes and Ladders	Understanding mathematics, problem solving, turn taking
Go Fish, Lotto	Improving reading skills, visual discrimination skills, turn taking
Ring Toss	Counting skills, motor coordination, hand-eye coordination
Who Has the Button?	Learning strategies, problem solving, turn taking
Checkers	Problem solving, turn taking, counting skills
Old Maid	Visual memory, visual discrimination, turn taking
Simon Says	Auditory memory, problem solving
Musical Chairs	Listening skills, problem solving
Bean Bag Toss	Hand-eye coordination, counting skills, large motor skills

Games

Helpful Hints!

The following are hints for selecting, supervising, and/or playing games with young children:

▶ Match the games to the child's growing skills and abilities to ensure that they are developmentally appropriate.

▶ Remember that children develop confidence through achieving one success at a time.

▶ Teach the child to take turns.

▶ Encourage cooperative play and avoid competitive play. It is unhealthy for children to identify themselves as winners and losers.

▶ Be patient and provide sufficient time for children to make choices, decisions, etc.

▶ Be willing to play a game over and over again. As with storytelling, children have their favorite games.

▶ Remember that older children are learning to think logically. Encourage this type of thinking. You may ask the child why she made a specific decision.

Game Activities

♣ Bear Hunt

This is a chant. Tell the child to listen and watch carefully so that he can echo back each phrase and imitate the motions as they accompany the story. Begin by patting your hands on your thighs to make footstep sounds.

Let's go on a bear hunt . . . (echo)
We're going to find a bear . . . (echo)
I've got my camera . . . (echo)
Open the door, squeak . . . (echo)
Walk down the walk . . . (echo)
Open the gate, creak . . . (echo)
Walk down the road . . . (echo)
Coming to a wheat field . . . (echo)
Can't go under it . . . (echo)
Can't go over it . . . (echo)
Have to walk through it . . . (echo)
   (stop patting your thighs and now rub your hands together to make a swishing sound)
Got through the wheat field . . . (echo)
Coming to a bridge . . . (echo)
Can't go under it . . . (echo)
Can't go around it . . . (echo)
Have to walk over it . . . (echo)
   (stop patting your thighs and now pound your fists on your chest)
Over the bridge . . . (echo)
Coming to a tree . . . (echo)
Can't go under it . . . (echo)
Can't go around it . . . (echo)
We'll have to climb it . . . (echo)
   (stop patting your thighs and now place one fist on top of the other repeatedly in a climbing motion)

All the way to the top . . . (echo)
   (look from one side to the other)
Do you see a bear? . . . (echo)
No (shaking head) . . . (echo)
We'll have to climb down . . . (echo)
   (place one fist under the other to climb down)
Coming to a river . . . (echo)
We can't go under it . . . (echo)
We can't fly over it . . . (echo)
Can't go around it . . . (echo)
We'll have to cross it . . . (echo)
Let's get in the boat . . . (echo)
And row, row, row . . .
   (all sing "Row, Row, Row Your Boat," accompanied by rowing motions)
We got across the river . . . (echo)
We're coming to a cave . . . (echo)
We can't go under it . . . (echo)
We can't go over it . . . (echo)
Can't go around it . . . (echo)
We'll have to go in it . . . (echo)
Let's tip-toe
   (use fingertips to pat thighs and whisper)
It's dark inside . . . (echo)
It's very dark inside . . . (echo)
I can see two eyes . . . (echo)
And a big furry body . . . (echo)
And I feel a wet nose . . . (echo)
   (yell)
It's a BEAR—RUN . . . (echo)
   (patting hands very quickly)
Run back to the river . . . (echo)
Row the boat across the river . . .
   (echo)
   (rowing motion)
Run to the tree . . . (echo)

Climb up and climb down . . . (echo)
  (make the climbing motion)
Run to the bridge and cross it . . .
  (echo)
  (pat chest)
Run through the wheat field . . .
  (echo)
  (swish hands together)
Run up the road . . . (echo)
Open the gate—it creaks . . . (echo)
  (open gate)
Run up the walk . . . (echo)
Open the door—it squeaks (echo)
  (open door)
SLAM IT!
  (clap hands together)

Source: Wirth, Marion, Stassevitch, Verna, Shotwell, Rita, & Stemmler, Patricia. (1983). *Musical Games, Fingerplays and Rhythmic Activities for Early Childhood.* Old Tappan, NJ: Parker Publishing.

 Child-Created Stories

Show the child a picture of a stuffed dog and encourage her to tell you a story about it.

"Cookie Jar"

This activity requires several children. Sit the children in a circle formation on the floor with their legs crossed. Together they repeat a rhythmic chant while using an alternating leg clap–hand clap to emphasize the rhythm. The chant is as follows.

Someone took the cookies from the
  cookie jar.
Who took the cookies from the
  cookie jar?
Mary took the cookies from the
  cookie jar.
Mary took the cookies from the
  cookie jar?
Who, me? (Mary)
Yes, you. (all the children)
Then who? (all the children)
—— *took the cookies from the*
  cookie jar.
Mary then names another child.
Make sure to use each child's name.

Doctor, Doctor, Nurse

Play Duck, Duck, Goose but instead use the words, "doctor, doctor, nurse."

Dog Catcher

Hide stuffed dogs or dogs cut from construction paper around the room and have the child find them.

Duck, Duck, Goose

This activity requires several children and could be played at a birthday party. Ask the children to squat in a circle. Then ask one child to walk around the outside of the circle, lightly touching each child's head and saying "Duck, Duck." When he touches a child and says "Goose," that child chases him around the circle. If the child who

was "it" returns to the "goose's" place without being tapped, he remains there. When this happens, the tapped child becomes "it." This game is appropriate for older (four-, five-, six-, and seven-year-old) children.

Guess What's Inside

Place a familiar object inside a box. Let the child shake, feel, and try to identify the object. After this, open the box and show the child the object.

Hide the Ball

Ask the child to cover her eyes. Then hide a small ball or other object in an accessible place. Ask the child to uncover her eyes and try to find the ball.

If This is Red–Nod Your Head

Point to an object in the room and say: "If this is green, shake your hand. If this is yellow, touch your nose." If the object is not of the color stated, the child should not imitate the requested action.

I Spy

Say, "I spy something blue that is sitting on the piano bench," or other such statements. The child will look around and try to figure out what you have spied. An older child may enjoy taking turns repeating, "I spy something on the ——."

"Little Red Wagon Painted Red"

As a prop for this game, cut a red wagon with wheels out of construction paper. Then cut rectangles the same size as the box of the red wagon. Include rectangles of purple, blue, yellow, green, orange, brown, black, and pink.

Sing this song to the tune of "Skip to My Lou."

Little red wagon painted red.
Little red wagon painted red.
Little red wagon painted red.
What color would it be?

Give the child a turn to pick and name a color. As the song is sung, let the child change the wagon color.

Memory Game

Collect common household items, a towel, and a tray. Place the items on the tray. Show the child the tray containing the items and then cover the items with a towel. Now ask the child to recall the names of the items on the tray. To ensure success for young children, begin the activity with only two or three objects. Additional objects can be added depending upon the developmental maturity of the child.

Near or Far?

The purpose of this game is to locate sound. First, tell the child to close his eyes. Then play a sound recorded on a cassette tape. Ask the child to identify the sound as being near or far.

Nice Kitty

This activity requires several children and could be played at a birthday party. One child is chosen to be the kitty. The rest of the children sit in a circle. As the kitty goes to each child in the circle, he or she pets the kitty and says, "Nice kitty," but the kitty makes no reply. Finally, the kitty meows in response to a child. That child must run around the outside of the circle as the kitty chases her. If the child returns to her original place before the kitty can catch her, the child becomes the new kitty. This activity is appropriate for four-, five-, and six-year-old children.

What Is It?

Collect a variety of fruits such as apples, bananas, and oranges. Begin by placing one fruit in a bag. Ask the child to touch the fruit, describe it, and name it. Repeat with each fruit, discussing the characteristics.

What Sound Is That?

The purpose of this game is to promote the development of listening skills. Begin by asking the child to close his eyes. Make a familiar sound. Then ask the child to identify it. Sources of sound may include:

- tearing paper
- sharpening a pencil
- walking, running, or shuffling feet
- clapping hands
- sneezing or coughing
- tapping on glass, wood, or metal
- jingling money
- opening a window
- pouring water
- shuffling cards
- blowing a whistle
- banging blocks
- bouncing a ball
- shaking a rattle
- turning the lights on
- knocking on a door
- blowing a pitch pipe
- dropping an object
- moving a desk or chair
- snapping one's fingers
- blowing one's nose
- opening or closing a drawer
- stirring paint in a jar
- clearing the throat
- splashing water
- rubbing pieces of sandpaper together
- chattering teeth
- making a sweeping sound, such as with a broom
- raising or lowering window shades
- leafing through book pages
- cutting with scissors

Games

- snapping rubber bands
- ringing a bell
- clicking the tongue
- crumpling paper
- opening a box
- sighing
- stamping feet
- rubbing palms together
- rattling keys

A variation of this game could be played by having the child make a sound while you close your eyes and attempt to identify it. For older children this game can be varied with the production of two sounds. Begin by asking the child if the sounds are the same or different. Then have her identify the sounds.

Games

Math

Mathematics is everywhere, all around us. Mathematics is sometimes defined as the science of numbers and shapes. It relates to things we do everyday. In the home, mathematics is used while cooking, filling a cup of milk, stacking cups, sorting clothes, and counting things. Likewise, mathematical terms, such as "some," "none," and "all," are used daily.

Helping your child learn math is simple. Skills involving colors, shapes, patterns and relationships, numbers, and measurements are all considered mathematical skills. The secret is providing the child with hands-on, informal, everyday experiences. Young children learn best by touching and manipulating objects such as boxes, blocks, cooking tools, containers, puzzles, and shape sorters.

If you think about it, you can see that science and math have many commonalities. Classifying, measuring, and comparing are fundamental mathematical concepts. When applied to science problems, they are referred to as process skills. Thus, in order to solve science problems, a child needs mathematical concepts. Mathematics is about connections. It helps children see relationships in everything they do.

Before a child can learn the more abstract concepts of arithmetic, he must be visually, physically, and kinesthetically aware of basic quantitative concepts. The following chart contains vocabulary you can use to teach math concepts.

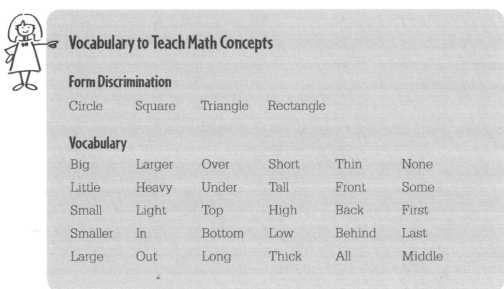

Vocabulary to Teach Math Concepts

Form Discrimination

Circle	Square	Triangle	Rectangle

Vocabulary

Big	Larger	Over	Short	Thin	None
Little	Heavy	Under	Tall	Front	Some
Small	Light	Top	High	Back	First
Smaller	In	Bottom	Low	Behind	Last
Large	Out	Long	Thick	All	Middle

Color Concepts

Color is one of the first mathematical concepts children learn: They learn to discriminate among objects by color. Beginning as toddlers, children often become interested in color. An example is eighteen-month-old Jeffrey. When you ask him, "What color is this?" he will respond by saying "Green" to every color. Gradually Jeffrey's cognitive and language skills will grow and he will learn the names of other colors. By two years of age, Jeffrey should be able to match color to a sample. To illustrate, when shown a sample and asked to find a block of the same color, he should be able to choose the correct block.

Shape Concepts

When observing preschool-aged children, you will find that after color concepts develop, they will start to learn basic shape concepts. The shapes are called geometric. They include the circle, triangle, square, and rectangle. The circle is usually the first shape a child learns to identify. After this, she will typically learn to recognize the square, followed by the triangle. Finally, the rectangle shape can be identified. During the school-age years, the rhombus and ellipse will be learned. The following chart contains geometric shapes. Learning the geometric shapes helps young children note similarities and differences.

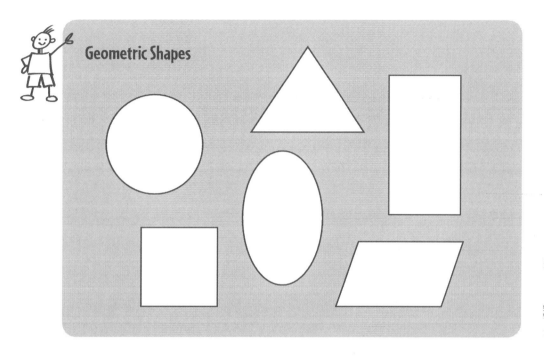

Geometric Shapes

Numbers

Numbers can be defined as the means to understand quantity. Young children need to learn the different uses of numbers in their world. Children will come to understand other aspects of mathematics if they can count. Therefore, it is important to have them count real objects. To do this, use your finger as a tool and touch each item. As you do so, recite the number name. Encourage the child to recite the numbers after you. Gradually he will learn to count with you, and then to count independently.

Point out numbers to children. Show them numbers on license plates, in phonebooks, storybook pages, and street signs. You can also print these numbers on paper and review them with the child. Young children first recognize quantities between one and four to five years of age.

Rote Counting

There are two types of counting, rote and rational. **Rote counting** is a process that involves reciting numbers in order from memory. How often have you heard a young child recite, "One, two, three, four, five . . ." Often the young learner will reverse the numbers. Gradually, with experience and maturity, the child will say the numbers in order. Four- and five-year-olds can count from 1 to 10 relatively easily. However, this does not mean that they understand the quantities.

Rational Counting

Rational counting involves attaching a numeral to each in a series of objects. To illustrate, a child may have five toy trucks in a small box. Taking them out of the box, one at a time, she places them on the floor. As she places each one on the floor, she gives them a number in sequence. Often a beginning learner will count an object twice or skip numbers. If this occurs, you should help the child.

Rational counting is complicated to do rationally. Most two- and three-year-old children will struggle with the task. To be successful, the child must have developed the necessary hand-eye coordination and auditory memory skills. However, by four or five years of age, a child's rational counting skills typically catch up with his rote counting skills.

Before a child can learn the more abstract concepts of arithmetic, she must be visually, physically, and kinesthetically aware of the basic quantitative concepts. The following chart contains manipulatives that you can use to introduce math activities.

Manipulatives for Math Activities

Buttons	Checkers	Small toy cars
Beads	Crayons	Plastic bread ties
Bobbins	Golf tees	Marbles
Craft pompoms	Plastic caps from markers	Cotton balls
Spools	Plastic milk containers	Bottle caps
Shells	Bottles	Poker chips
Seeds (corn, soybeans)	Stickers	Paper clips
Shelled peanuts	Fishing bobbers	Clothespins
Toothpicks	Keys	Erasers
Pennies	Magnetic numbers	

 Constantly observe and supervise children using small manipulatives. If placed in the mouth, small manipulatives can become a safety hazard.

Math

One-to-One Correspondence Skills

Preschool children need to develop one-to-one correspondence skills. This involves the ability to match each number with a single item while counting. To illustrate, a child may be counting five pennies. He could count the same item twice and, thus, end up with six items. Likewise, the young child who has not yet developed one-to-one correspondence skills may skip a penny and end up by calling the last penny "four."

At this stage, children's reasoning is dominated by their perception. To illustrate, place five pennies in a row, next to each other. Then, in a second row, place five pennies with a half-inch space between each one. Now ask the child, "Are there more pennies in one row than the other?" Chances are the child will respond by saying yes and point to the second row. Because the pennies in the second row are spread out, to the child it looks like there are more in that row.

Patterns and Relationships

Help your child look for patterns and relationships in his environment. Patterns are things that repeat, whereas relationships are things that are connected. By listening, children can find patterns in music. By observing and/or feeling, children can see relationships in art and in clothing. Children can learn patterns by stringing beads according to size and shape. Encourage your child to sort by looking for similarities in either color, size, or shape. You can have the child sort chips or blocks by color. She can also sort crayons by size, or blocks by size or shape. Then, too, have the child look for differences. Ask questions such as:

▶ Which box is bigger?

▶ Which glass has the most milk?

▶ Whose shoe is smallest?

▶ What chair is the largest?

▶ What stuffed animal is the largest?

▶ Which shoes look alike?

Children also learn patterns through music, fingerplays, and listening to stories. One activity that is helpful in teaching children patterns is playing Head, Shoulders, Knees, and Toes.

Geometry and Spatial Sense

The area of mathematics that involves size, space, shape, position, and direction of movement is called geometry. Geometry describes the physical world in which we live. Children need to learn the different shapes, sizes, and positions. Manipulating blocks, boxes, and containers is a helpful way of learning geometry for young children. Spatial concepts help them learn directions. They can crawl in, over, through, around, out of, and on top of boxes. While they engage in this activity, provide them with the language to understand the directions. Other groups of words you can use to stress spatial concepts are included in the following chart.

Words Stressing Spatial Concepts

Up, down	Over, under	High, low	Above, below
On, off	In front of, in back of	Here, there	Near, far away
Far, near	Before, after	Inside, outside	Top, bottom

Measurement

Methods of finding the weight, height, and length of a unit are forms of measurement. Many activities occur during daily activities that involve measurement. Cooking, grocery shopping, and wrapping packages all require skills in measurement. Time is another form of measurement. Involve the child in assisting with grocery shopping and cooking activities. Call attention to, and point out, numbers.

Time

Time is another form of measurement, using seconds, minutes, and hours. Time, however, is a difficult concept for children to comprehend. This is because they cannot feel, see, or manipulate it. Until about the age of seven, young children cannot read a clock to tell time. However, five-year-olds typically know the difference between morning and afternoon. Up until that time there are two kinds of time, sequence and duration.

Young children thrive on predictability and consistency. They know time as a sequence of events. To illustrate, ask a four-and-a-half-year-old to tell you what he did with his time each day. He may reply by saying:

> I get up. Then I get dressed and eat. Then I go to child care. We play, have snack, listen to stories, go outside, eat lunch, nap, and play again. After this, my dad comes to get me. At home I play with my dog. Then I eat dinner, take a bath, and listen to stories, and then I go to bed.

You should begin talking about time. Milestones for children involve talking about "before breakfast" and "after breakfast." You can begin to stress more abstract concepts when talking with four- and five-year-olds. Introduce terms such as *yesterday, today,* and *tomorrow.*

Math

Helpful Hints!

The following are helpful hints to help the child learn mathematical concepts.

▶ Provide the child with repeated practice in counting objects. You can use a variety of items, including silverware, cards, shoes, books, blocks, toy cars, trucks, etc.

▶ Provide and encourage your child to practice one-to-one correspondence with movable objects. Again, this is an activity that can be repeated throughout the day.

▶ Integrate math concepts into daily routines by asking, "Are there enough plates on the table?," "Do we have enough apples for everyone?," or "Do we have a napkin by each plate?"

▶ Select simple fingerplays in this book that include numerals and shapes. Introduce these fingerplays to the children.

▶ Select and share with the child books that rhyme, repeat, and include color, shape, and number concepts.

▶ Label foods and utensils during mealtime. For instance, you can say: "We have round crackers today for snack. Our napkins are square. Our plates are round like a circle. The bun is a circle shape like our plates. The potatoes are cut in triangles."

▶ Cut pictures from catalogs, magazines, and newspapers for the child to sort.

▶ Call attention to the days of the week.

▶ Help your child to reason by asking her a question. Then give her time to think about the answer.

▶ At mealtime, cut sandwiches into shapes and then encourage your child to rearrange them.

▶ Set time limits in order to teach measurement. For example, say, "We only have five minutes and then we need to clean up." You may want to set an egg timer.

Math

Math Activities

Animal Sets

Cut and mount pictures of zoo animals. The children can classify the pictures by sorting. Examples might include birds, four-legged animals, furry animals, etc.

Animal Sort

Collect pictures of elephants, lions, giraffes, monkeys, and other zoo animals from magazines, calendars, or coloring books. Encourage the children to sort the pictures into labeled baskets. For example, one basket might be for large animals and another for small animals.

Apple Shapes

Cut apple shapes of various sizes from construction paper. Let the children sequence the shapes from smallest to largest.

Ball Sort

Sort various balls by size, texture, and color.

Blocks

Set out blocks of various shapes, including triangles, rectangles, and squares, for the child to build with.

Breadstick Seriation

Provide breadsticks or pictures of breadsticks of varying lengths. The child can place the breadsticks in order from shortest to longest.

Broken Hearts

Cut heart shapes out of red and pink tagboard. Then cut each heart shape in half using a different cutting pattern. Using a felt-tip marker, print a numeral on one side of the heart cutout. On the other half, paste the corresponding number of small heart stickers, or draw the hearts. The children can match the puzzle pieces.

Bubble Count

If appropriate, encourage the child to blow a certain number of bubbles, which you specify. For example, if you say the number "three," the child would try to blow three bubbles.

Bubble Wand Sort

Collect small, commercially manufactured bubble wands and place them in a small basket. These wands can be sorted by size or color. They could also be counted or placed in order by size.

Camping Scavenger Hunt

Before going outdoors, instruct the child to find things outside that you would see while camping. Sort these items and count them when they are brought inside (five twigs, three rocks, etc.).

Car and Truck Sequencing

Collect a variety of cars and trucks. Children can sequence them from largest to smallest and vice versa.

Cars and Garages

Car garages can be constructed out of empty, half-pint milk cartons. Collect and carefully wash the milk cartons. Cut out one side and write a numeral, starting with 1, on each carton. Next, collect a corresponding number of small matchbox cars. Attach a strip of paper with a numeral from 1 to the appropriate number on each car's top. The children can drive each car into the garage with the corresponding numeral.

Classifying Dog Biscuits

If you have a pet, purchase three sizes of dog biscuits. Using dog dishes, have the children sort the biscuits according to size and type.

Clothes Seriation

Provide a basketful of clothes for the children to line up, from largest to smallest. Include hats, sweatshirts, shoes, and pants. Use clothing items whose sizes are easily distinguishable.

Colored Bags

Place three bags labeled red, yellow, and blue and a variety of blocks on a table. The children can sort the blocks by placing them in the matching colored bag. *Hint:* Use a yellow coloring tool to print the word *yellow,* a blue tool to print the word *blue,* and a red tool to print the word *red.*

Colored Corn Sort

After the children have removed field corn and Indian corn from the cob, place a bowl of the mixed corn on a table with egg cartons cut in half. Encourage the children to sort the mixed corn kernels by color: white, yellow, orange, red, brown, and black.

Colored Popcorn

Provide the children with unpopped colored popcorn kernels. Place corresponding colored circles in the bottom of muffin tins or egg cartons. Encourage the children to sort the kernels by color.

Math

Constructing Numerals

Provide the child with a ball of play dough. Instruct her to form some numerals randomly. Then the child can add the proper corresponding number of dots for the numerals just formed. In this activity, it is important to monitor the child's work and correct reversals. In the early stages of writing, children often have difficulty learning the directions that numbers and letters face. As a result, children may reverse them or write them backwards. For example, a child may print the letter *d* when she intends to write *b,* or a *J* may have the tail reversed.

Counting Pumpkin Seeds

Cut circles from construction paper. The number needed will depend upon the developmental level of the children. Write a numeral on each paper circle and place each into a pie tin. The children should be encouraged to count enough pumpkin seeds into each tin to match the numeral on the circle.

Dot-to-Dot Pictures

Make a dot-to-dot snowperson. The children connect the dots in numerical order. You can also make dot-to-dot patterns of other winter objects such as hats, snowflakes, mittens, etc. This activity requires numeral recognition and an understanding of order.

Egg Carton Math

Using a permanent marker, randomly number the egg cups in an egg carton from 1 to 12 (or use fewer numerals or sets of dots, if appropriate). Put a button or bread tag in the carton and close the lid. The children can shake the carton, open the lid, and try to identify the number the piece landed on.

Egg Match

Using brightly colored plastic eggs, hobby paint, and a fine paintbrush, paint a numeral on the top half of each egg. Paint the corresponding number of dots on the bottom half of each egg. When dry, place the top and bottom of each egg together and put them into an egg carton. Provide the child with a bowl of dry cereal or grapes. Encourage the child to place the correct number of pieces from the bowl into each egg. When completed correctly—eat and enjoy.

Examine a Puppet

With the children, examine a puppet and count all of its various parts. Count its eyes, legs, arms, stripes on its shirt, etc. Discuss how the puppet is constructed.

Face Match

Collect two small shoeboxes. On one shoebox, draw a happy face. On the other box, draw a sad face. Cut faces of people from magazines. The children can sort the pictures accordingly.

Family Size–Biggest to Smallest

Cut from magazines pictures of several members of a family. The children can place the family groups from largest to smallest and then smallest to largest. They can also identify each family member as the tallest and the shortest.

Grouping and Sorting

Collect plastic farm animals. Place in a basket and let the children sort them according to size, color, where they live, how they move, etc.

Growing Chart

Make a growing chart in the shape of a giraffe. (If desired, another animal can be substituted.) Record the child's height on the chart at various times during the year.

Hat Seriation

Collect a variety of hats. The children can arrange them from smallest to largest and largest to smallest. Also, they can classify the hats by colors and uses.

Holiday Card Puzzles

Collect two sets of identical Christmas cards. Cut the covers off the cards. Cut one of each of the identical sets of cards into puzzle pieces. The matching card can be used as a form for the child to match the pieces on.

Holiday or Greeting Card Sort

Place a variety of Christmas cards on a table. The child can sort by color, pictures, size, etc.

How Many?

Place a number of small objects (such as paper clips, dice, marbles, buttons) in a clear plastic bag or jar. Let children guess how many of the objects are in the bag. Count the objects together. Repeat with a different number of objects.

Line 'em Up

Print numerals on wooden clothespins. The children can attach the clothespins on a low clothesline and sequence them in numerical order.

Mitten Match

Collect several matching pairs of mittens. Mix them up and have children match the pairs.

Math

⊛ Muffin Tin Math

Muffin tins can be used for counting and sorting activities, based on the child's developmental level. For example, numerals can be printed in each cup, and the child can place the corresponding set of corn kernels or toy pieces in each cup. Likewise, colored circles can be cut out of construction paper and glued to the bottom of the muffin cups. The child then can place objects of matching colors in the corresponding muffin cups.

⊛ "My House"

Construct a book titled "My House." On the pages write things like:

My house has —— steps.
My house is the color ——.
My house has —— windows.
There are —— doors in my house.
My house has —— keyholes.

Other ideas could include the number of beds, people, pets, etc.

⊛ Number Chain

Cut enough strips of paper to make a number chain for the days of the month. Each day, add a link to represent the passage of time. Another option is to use the chain to count down by removing a link every day up until an anticipated event. This makes an interesting approach to an upcoming holiday.

⊛ Number Rhyme

Say the following song to reinforce numbers:

One, two, three, four
Come right in and shut the door.
Five, six, seven, eight
Come right in. It's getting late.
Nine, ten, eleven, twelve
Put your books upon the shelves.
Will you count along with me?
It's as easy as can be!

⊛ Numeral Caterpillar

From an egg carton, make a caterpillar with ten body segments and a head. Have the children put the numbers in order to complete the caterpillar's body.

⊛ Parts and Wholes

To introduce the concepts of parts and whole, cut apples in halves at snack time.

⊛ Phone Numbers

Make a list of people's names and phone numbers. Place the list by a toy telephone.

⊛ Pocket Count

Have the child take note of the pockets on his clothes. Assist in counting the number of pockets the child has. If appropriate, the information could be recorded and put on a graph to be displayed. Repeat the activity on a different day and compare the results.

Pot and Pan Sort

Collect various pots and pans and place in a laundry basket. Encourage the child to find ways to sort them. Pots and pans can be sorted by type, size, construction material, etc.

Pretzel Sort and Count

Provide the child with a cup containing various sizes and shapes of pretzels. Encourage her to empty the cup onto a clean napkin or plate and sort the pretzels by size or shape. If appropriate, the child can count how many pretzels there are of each shape. Upon completion of this activity, the child can eat the pretzels.

Purple Chain

Provide 8½-by-11-inch strips of purple, lilac, and white construction paper. If necessary, demonstrate to the child how to create a paper chain by using tape or glue to fasten the strips. Encourage the child to create a pattern with the colored strips. Display the chains in the room.

Rote Counting

Say or sing the "One, Two, Buckle My Shoe" nursery rhyme to help children with rote counting.

One, two, buckle my shoe
Three, four, shut the door
Five, six, pick up sticks
Seven, eight, lay them straight
Nine, ten, a big fat hen.

Sand Numbers and Shapes

During outdoor play, informally make shapes and numbers in the sand and let the children identify them.

Sectioning Fruit

Section oranges or tangerines for a snack. Count the sections, then discuss the whole and the parts of the whole.

Seed Match

Collect a variety of seeds such as corn, pumpkin, orange, apple, lima bean, watermelon, pea, and peach. Cut several rectangles out of white tagboard. On the top half of each rectangle, glue one of the seed types you have collected. Encourage the children to sort the seeds, matching them to the seeds glued on the cards.

Math

Shape Sequence

Cut three different-sized white circles from construction paper with which the child can make a snow-person. Which is the largest? Which is the smallest? How many pieces do you have? What shape are they? Then have the child sequence the circles from largest to smallest and smallest to largest.

Shape Sort

Cut out shapes of different colors and sizes. Place the shapes on a table for the children to sort by color, shape, and size.

Sock Matching

Collect pairs of different colors, patterns, and sizes of socks. Place them in a box or laundry basket. Encourage the children to match and fold the socks. If desired, the children can sort by color, size, and patterns.

Sorting and Counting Activities

The following items can be collected and used for various sorting and counting activities: acorns, small pinecones, walnuts, pecans, almonds, apple seeds, citrus fruit seeds.

"Ten in the Bed"

Chant the following words to reinforce numbers:

There were ten monkeys in the bed and the little one said,
"Roll over, roll over."
So they all rolled over and one fell out.
There were nine monkeys in the bed and the little one said,
"Roll over, roll over."
So they all rolled over and one fell out.

Continue until there is only one monkey left. The last line will be ". . . and the little one said, Good night!"

Trace Walk

Record the number of trees observed on a walk. If appropriate, the trees might also be classified as broadleaf or evergreen or by the type, such as maple, oak, pine, etc.

Use of Rulers

Discuss how rulers are used. Provide the child with a ruler so he may measure various objects. Allow him to compare the lengths. Also, measure the child and construct a chart showing his height.

Math

Science

Look around. Science is everywhere. It is a way of thinking that offers children powerful ways to understand their world. Science involves seeing patterns and connections.

To learn science, young children need to be able to hear and use language, observe, predict, and experiment. The best way to learn these science skills is to have hands-on learning experiences.

The ideal environment stimulates the child's curiosity. It also encourages the child's active participation and exploration of her surroundings to gather information. For the young child, this includes daily opportunities to explore by feeling, seeing, hearing, tasting, and touching. Through these processes and with a science-rich environment, the young child will construct her own knowledge. The ideal environment encourages active participation and exploration of the child's natural surroundings. For the child, this includes many opportunities to feel, see, hear, taste, and touch as a basis for constructing knowledge.

Observing, comparing, classifying, measuring, communicating, inferring, predicting, and hypothesizing are thinking, or process, skills needed to learn science. Children learn science through process skills. By observing, they gather information through their senses. By looking at similarities and differences, they learn comparison skills. By sorting and grouping according to color, shape, and size, they learn classification skills. By using quantitative descriptions, such as "two cups," or terms, such as "longer," they learn measurement.

Communication skills are learned through verbal descriptions, photographs, and pictures. Gradually children will learn ***inferring skills***. This includes recognizing patterns. By making guesses based upon observation and/or data, they learn ***predicting skills***. ***Hypothesizing skills*** involve being able to make formal conditional statements. For example, trying to answer the question, "What would happen if we placed the chocolate bar in the sun?"

The Value of Science

Science provides children with hands-on opportunities for exploring and, thus, understanding their world. Through science, they develop an understanding of their environment by observing, exploring, discovering, measuring, comparing, classifying, and predicting. Other values of science include:

- learning to live in a changing world.
- learning to think critically.
- experiencing properties in the natural environment.
- observing changes in substances.
- developing new vocabulary words.
- classifying objects by color, size, shape, and use.
- communicating directions, descriptions, and ideas.
- recognizing patterns.
- identifying similarities and differences.
- classifying objects into subsets that contain common characteristics.
- predicting what would happen if . . .

The Importance of Play

A natural way for children to learn to understand science and their environment is through spontaneous play. Many science concepts start to grow and develop as early as infancy. Think about it. When the young child is born into this world, he begins to learn sense concepts. The beginning of this process for the child involves discovering the environment through his senses.

During play, children learn basic concepts. Observe: Even newborn babies are learning about their environment. They begin to recognize faces. Gradually, they learn about cause and effect. If they cry, they are changed and fed. With their developing abilities, they begin showing interest in their surroundings. Watch as they learn to crawl and creep. They can creep into, under, through, and over things. In the process, they are discovering space and developing a spatial sense.

As the young preschool child grows and develops, you will observe that some of the important science experiences are unplanned. For instance, observe the bird nest in the tree outside of the breakfast nook window. This can be a starting point to discuss birds, eggs, and the construction of a nest. Likewise, when a baby toad moves across the front lawn, you can observe, study, and discuss it.

The Adult's Role

Your role is to encourage the child's exploration and discovery of people and the world around her. In doing so, you will foster her curiosity and interest in science. Observe: By manipulating objects, most children will engage, and satisfy, their curiosity. To encourage science concepts, this curiosity needs to be valued and rewarded by the adults in the child's world.

Providing Science Materials and Equipment

The adult's role also is to provide an environment that stimulates the child's curiosity. This entails having science materials readily available. The following chart contains a list of science materials and equipment to collect and provide that can be used to promote the development of science concepts.

Science Materials and Equipment

Materials that can be collected to promote science concepts include:

Acorns and other nuts	Bowls and cups	Eggbeaters
Aluminum foil	Cocoon	Egg cartons
Ball bearings	Corks	Eyedroppers and basters
Balloons	Clock (wind-up)	
Binoculars	Dishpans	Fabric scraps
Bird nests	Drinking straws	Filter paper
Bones	Drums	Flashlight

Science Materials and Equipment (Continued)

Flowers	Nails, screws, bolts	Screen wire
Gears	Paper bags	Sieves, sifters, and funnels
Insect nests	Paper of various types	
Insects	Paper rolls and spools	Seeds
Jacks	Plants	Spatulas
Kaleidoscope	Plastic bags	Sponges
Locks and keys	Plastic containers with lids	Stones
Magnets of varying sizes		String
	Plastic tubing	Styrofoam
Marbles	Pots, pans, and trays	Tape
Measuring cups	Prisms	Thermometers
Measuring spoons	Pulleys	Tongs and tweezers
Microscope	Rocks	Tools—hammer, pliers
Milk cartons	Rubber tubing	
Mirrors of all sizes	Ruler	Tuning forks
Moths	Safety goggles	Waxed paper
Muffin tins	Sandpaper	Weeds
Musical instruments	Scales	Wheels
Newspapers	Scissors of assorted sizes	Wood/building materials

Questioning

Questioning is one way to help a child understand science concepts. Basically, there are two types of questions. **Divergent questions** help the child create information. Only the child's thoughts and experiences limit these questions. These questions include the why's and how's of science concepts. Convergent questions have limited responses, as they are designed to seek specific answers. Through questioning, children develop important skills for learning science concepts.

Divergent Questions. *Divergent questions* are often referred to as "open-ended" questions. These questions require decision-making skills on the part of the child and promote discussion. Divergent questions are excellent tools to stimulate language and problem solving and to tap into the child's imagination. These questions also promote the development of critical-thinking skills. Seeing interrelationships, making hypotheses, and drawing conclusions are all important skills for learning science concepts.

Convergent Questions. *Convergent questions* are called "closed-ended" questions. Basically, these questions require a single answer. Convergent questions are used to recall or review prior information; consequently, they are limited in their use. For young learners, particularly two- and some three-year-old children, such questions are necessary since they demand fewer decision-making skills. However, to move to higher-level thinking skills, "open-ended" questions are necessary. The following chart contains examples of both types of questions.

Convergent and Divergent Questions

Convergent: "Closed-Ended" Questions	Divergent: "Open-Ended" Questions
Does a guinea pig have a tail?	Why does a guinea pig have a tail?
What is ice made of?	How is ice made?
Has the popcorn popped?	Why did the popcorn pop?
What animal is this?	How does the rabbit look?

Questioning is an art. Try to ask a variety of questions. Ask the child questions that require him to recall simple information, such as, "What did you see at the farm?", "What did we do at the apple orchard?", or "What do you want to do on your birthday?" Ask the child questions that require reasoning skills. Examples of reasoning questions may include:

"*Why* does the ice freeze?"

"*How* do flowers grow?"

"*Tell* me about the story."

"*Why* do you brush your teeth?"

"*What* would happen if you didn't water the flowers?"

"*Why* did the ice cream melt?"

Science Concepts

Introduce your child to science concepts every day. Colors, water, gardening, air, magnets, and pets are all means of teaching science concepts that you should include.

Colors

Colors, water, food, gardening, air, magnets, animals, and pets all teach science concepts. When teaching colors, begin by introducing one primary color (red, yellow, or blue) at a time. Keep highlighting the color through your interactions since one way young children learn is through repetition. Once the child can easily recognize the color, introduce a second color and repeat the same procedure. However, at this time you also need to continue reinforcing the first color that was introduced. During the preschool years, continue this process until the child can recognize all of the primary and secondary colors.

Water

Children delight in water play. Through water, they can learn the following concepts:

▶ When poured, water flows.

▶ Water dissolves some foods.

▶ Some matter absorbs water.

▶ Water freezes.

▶ Frozen water is cold and slippery.

▶ Water can be warmed.

▶ Some objects float on water.

▶ Some objects sink when placed on water.

Gardening

Through gardening, children can learn about plant life. Concepts you can foster include:

▶ Plants need water and sun to grow.

▶ There are many kinds of seeds in foods.

▶ Some foods that we eat have seeds.

▶ Plants with roots, stems, leaves, and flowers grow seeds.

▶ There are likenesses and differences among plants.

Growing plant seeds in your home or garden can be rewarding. Therefore, plant seeds with the child. Then observe what happens. Questions that might be asked include:

▶ "How deep do you plant the seed?"

▶ "How long will it take to grow?"

▶ "Why does the plant have green leaves?"

▶ "Why are seeds different shapes and colors?"

▶ "What seeds can be eaten?"

There are a variety of different vegetable plants that can be started in the home and later transplanted—cabbage, cucumber, melons, onions, parsley, squash, pumpkins, tomatoes, beans, corn, etc.

Science

Air

By watching flying kites, birds, airplanes, and balloons, children can learn about air. Concepts that you can reinforce with the children include:

- Air is all around us.
- Air takes up space.
- Air moves some objects.
- Moving air pushes objects.

Magnets

In addition to colors, gardening, air, and cooking, science concepts can be learned through playing with magnets. Magnets captivate the attention of young children because they provide an invisible force. This invisible force makes them interesting because the effects can be seen and felt. When provided with magnets, and with your guidance, the young child can learn that:

- Magnets have the strongest force at each end.
- Magnets can pull some materials, but not others.
- Magnets pick up objects made with iron.
- Some magnets are big; others are small.

To teach these concepts, purchase some magnets at a toy store or e-commerce site, or through a toy catalog. Then provide the child with materials that the magnet will not pick up, such as paper, plastic blocks, pencils, puzzle pieces, etc. In addition, provide materials that are made with iron, such as paper clips, screws, nails, bolts, and other objects.

Pets

Pets are another way in which children can learn about science. Having a family pet provides an opportunity for learning. Children can observe how animals look and act. They can feel them to find out how their coat feels. Specific concepts they can learn include:

- Animals are fun to watch.
- Animals need water, food, and shelter.
- Animals have different types of body covers.
- Animals move in different ways.
- Animals behave in different ways.

Science

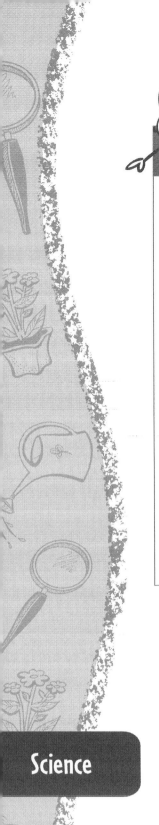

Helpful Hints!

▶ Share your appreciation and curiosity in relationship to science. Your continuous and supportive interest will motivate the child and encourage observation and experimentation.

▶ Listen carefully to the child. Listening will strengthen the child's desire to participate.

▶ Respond positively to all of the child's answers.

▶ Whenever possible, and if developmentally appropriate, ask divergent or "open-ended" questions.

▶ Begin by asking simple questions and then gradually move to more complex ones.

▶ After asking questions, allow the child time to think and respond without answering for her.

▶ When a child does not know the answer, show him how to use resources such as books to obtain information. Likewise, when you do not know an answer, show the child how to find it.

▶ Help the child by pointing out likenesses and differences.

▶ Provide books and toys containing science concepts.

Science

Science Activities

Growing Experiences

Beanstalk Window Gardens

Soak bean seeds overnight. (You can use a variety of bean seeds, such as lima, green, adzuki, pinto, navy, or sugar snap pea seeds.) Place a slightly damp paper towel inside a self-sealing, transparent plastic bag. Place one or more seeds on the paper towel. Seal the bag and tape on the window. Encourage children to observe and compare the sprouting of their seeds, adding a few drops of water as needed. Allow the children to plant their sprouted seeds when ready.

Growing Grass

Germinate grass seeds by placing a damp sponge in a pie tin of water and sprinkling seeds on the sponge. The child will notice tiny sprouts after a few days. Experiment by putting one sponge in the freezer, one near a heat source, and one in a dark closet. Discuss what happens to each group of seeds.

Growing Seeds

Give the child a plastic sealable bag, a moistened paper towel, and a lima bean. Demonstrate how to place the bean in the paper towel and close the bag. After planting the bean in the bag, place the bag on a bulletin board. Check the bulletin board on a daily basis to see when the seed sprouts.

Planting Pumpkin Seeds

Purchase a packet of pumpkin seeds. Plant the pumpkin seeds in small paper cups. Set the paper cups with the pumpkin seeds in a sunny place. Water as needed. Observe on a daily basis to see if there is growth.

Planting Seeds

Plant flower, bean, or radish seeds in a Styrofoam or paper cup. Save the seed packages and mount on a piece of tagboard. Place this directly behind the containers. Otherwise, tape the seed package to the Styrofoam or paper cup. Encourage the child to compare the plants. When the plant starts growing, compare the seed package picture to the actual plant.

Science

Plants Contain Water

Cut off a quarter inch from the bottom of a celery stalk. Fill a clear vase with water containing food coloring. Place the celery stalk in the vase. Encourage the child to observe color changes in the celery stalk. This activity can be repeated using a white carnation.

Potato Sprouts

Provide the child with a clear plastic cup. Fill the plastic cup halfway full with water. Place a potato partially in the water, supported by toothpicks to keep it from dropping into the jar. Put the end with tubers into the water, and leave the other end sticking out. Refill with fresh water as the water in the cup evaporates and watch the roots begin to grow and leaves start to sprout.

Rooting a Sweet Potato

To root a sweet potato in water, push toothpicks halfway into the potato. Then place the potato in a glass of water with the toothpicks resting on the top rim. Make sure the end of the potato is immersed in water. Place the glass where it will receive adequate light. Maintain the water level so that the bottom of the potato is always immersed. Note that in a few weeks roots will grow out of the sides and bottom of the potato and leaves will grow out of the top. The plant can be left in the water or

replanted in soil. This activity provides the child an opportunity to observe root growth.

Sprout Gardens

Obtain seeds for sprouting from a grocery or natural food store and soak overnight. Radish, bean, and alfalfa seeds work well for sprout gardens. Drain well and place in a large jar. Cover the jar with several layers of cheesecloth and secure the cheesecloth with a rubber band. Rinse and drain the sprouts in cool water several times each day. Eat the sprouts and enjoy.

> *Sprouts need to be carefully washed prior to being eaten or handled by children.*

Sprouting Carrots

Cut the large end off a fresh carrot and place it in a small cup of water. In a few days, a green top will begin to sprout.

Start with a Seed

Lemon, orange, tangerine, and grapefruit seeds are easily started and can be grown into beautiful plants. Select seeds from a ripe fruit. They need to be planted immediately so they will not dry out. Label a small pot with the child's name. Let the child fill her pot two-thirds full with potting soil. Place two or three seeds in the pot and cover the seeds with about one-half inch of soil. Help child place the pot into a plastic bag. Keep the soil evenly moist and out of direct sunlight for several weeks. When the seeds begin to sprout, remove the plants from the bags and put the seedlings in a sunny, warm window.

Tops Off

Both pineapple tops and carrot tops yield plants. Select a pineapple with fresh-looking, green leaves. Cut the top off where it meets the fruit, leaving no fruit on the crown. Strip away two layers of leaves and place the crown in a narrow, water-filled jar so that the bottom of the crown is in the water. After several weeks,

roots will appear. Now the children may plant the pineapple top in soil, covering only one inch of the crown. This soil should be kept moist and the plants should be kept in a sunny place.

Watch Seeds Grow

Two identical plastic transparent plates and blotting paper are needed for this activity. Moisten the blotting paper. Then lay the wet paper on one of the plates. On the top of the paper plate, place various seeds— corn, peas, squash, beans, etc. Place the other plate over the seeds to serve as a cover. Tie the plates together tightly. Stand the plates on edge in a pan containing a half inch of water. Watch the seeds sprout and grow.

Nature Recipes

Cattails

For decoration, use cattails in their natural color or tint them by shaking on metallic powder. Handle carefully. The cattail is dry and feels crumbly. It will fall apart easily.

Crystal Garden

Place broken pieces of brick or terra cotta clay in a glass bowl or jar. Pour the following solution over this:

- 4 teaspoons water
- 1 teaspoon ammonia
- 4 teaspoons bluing solution
- 1 teaspoon Mercurochrome
- 4 teaspoons salt

Add more solution each day until the crystal garden has grown to the desired size.

 Adult supervision is required.

Drying Plants for Winter Bouquets

Strip leaves from the flowers immediately. Tie flowers by their stems with string and hang them with heads down in a cool, dry place, away from light. Darkness is essential for preserving their color. Thorough drying takes about two weeks.

Preserving Fall Leaves

Place alternate layers of powdered borax and leaves in a box. The leaves must be completely covered. Allow them to stand for four days. Shake off the borax and wipe each leaf with liquid floor wax. Rub a warm iron over a cake of paraffin and then press the iron over the front and back of the leaves.

An adult should constantly observe and supervise this activity. Moreover, only an adult should handle the hot iron.

Preserving Magnolia Leaves

Mix two parts of water with one part of glycerin. Place stems of magnolia leaves in the mixture and let them stand for several days. The leaves will turn brown and last several years. Their surface may be painted or sprayed with silver or gold paint.

Pressing Wild Flowers

When gathering specimens, include roots, leaves, flowers, and seed pods. Place between newspapers, laying two layers of blotters underneath the newspaper and two on top to absorb moisture. Change the newspapers three times during the week. Place specimens between two sheets of corrugated cardboard and press. It usually takes seven to ten days to press them completely. Cardboard covered with cotton batting can be used as the mounting base. Lay flower on the cotton and cover with cellophane or plastic wrap to preserve the color.

Treating Gourds

Soak gourds in water for two hours. Then scrape them clean with a knife and rub them with fine sandpaper. While still damp, cut an opening to remove seeds.

Science

Sensory Experiences

Cheese Types

Observe, taste, and compare different kinds of cheese. Examples include Swiss, cheddar, colby, cottage cheese, and cheese curds.

Eggs

Taste different kinds of cooked eggs. Let the child choose from scrambled, poached, deviled, hard-boiled, and fried. This could also be integrated as part of the breakfast menu.

Feely Box

Prepare a feely box, which includes such things as tape cassette, pen, pencil, plastic or wooden letters, an envelope, and anything else that is related to communication. The child can place a hand in the box and identify objects using his sense of touch. For older children, fill the box with different parts of a plant, such as root, stem, leaves, flowers, fruit, and buds. The children can feel and verbally identify each part of the plant before looking at it.

Milk Tasting

Plan a milk-tasting party. To do this, taste and compare the following types of milk products: cow's milk versus goat's milk, cream, skimmed milk versus whole milk, cottage cheese, sour cream, butter, margarine, and buttermilk.

Smelling Party

Thoroughly wash and dry several empty yogurt containers. Into each container, place a familiar food. Cover each container with aluminum foil. Put several holes in the aluminum foil. The children can smell each container and identify the food by its smell. Oranges, onions, bananas, coffee, strawberries, ketchup, peas, and chocolate all work well for this activity.

Tasting Parties

Place a festive tablecloth on a table and provide food cut into small pieces for children to taste. Discuss colors, smells, flavors, and textures of the foods. Suggestions for various types of tasting parties include fruits, vegetables, cheeses, bagels, pickles, breads, yogurts, ice creams, crackers, juices, muffins, etc. This is a fun way for children to try new and unusual foods (e.g., pomegranates, persimmons, mangoes).

Tasting Water

Collect tap water, soda water, mineral water, and distilled water. Pour the different types of water into paper cups and let child taste them. Discuss the differences.

Science

Sound Experiences

Bells

Collect bells of various shapes and sizes. Listen for differences in sounds in relationship to the sizes of the bells.

Matching Sounds

Collect twelve containers, such as film canisters, milk cartons, or covered baby food jars, that are unbreakable and safe to use. Fill two containers with rice, two with beans, two with pebbles, two with water, and the remaining two with dry pasta. Coins, such as pennies, could be substituted. Color code each pair of containers on the bottom. Let the child shake the containers, listening to the sounds, in an attempt to find the matching pairs.

Pop Bottle Music

Fill six 12-ounce pop bottles, each with a different amount of water. For effect, place a drop of food coloring in each bottle, providing six different colors. A younger child can tap the bottles with a spoon as she listens for the sound. An older child may try blowing directly into the opening for sound production.

Sounds

Tape different sounds from around the house that children hear daily,

such as a crying baby, brushing teeth, telephone ringing, toilet flushing, doorbell ringing, water running, electric shaver, alarm clock, etc. Play the tape and have the child identify the sounds.

Sound Shakers

Using small, identical orange juice cans, pudding cups, or empty film containers, fill pairs of the containers with different objects. Included may be sand, coins, rocks, rice, salt, etc. Replace the lids. Make sure to secure the lids with glue or heavy tape to avoid spilling. To make the activity self-correcting, place numbers or like colors on the bottoms of the matching containers.

Vibrations

Encourage the child to gently place a hand on the side of a piano, guitar, record player, radio, television, etc., in order to feel the vibrations. Then have the child feel his throat vibrate as he speaks. A tuning fork can also be used as a teaching aid when talking about vibrations.

Voices

Tape the child's voice throughout the course of the day. The following day, leave the tape recorder at the science table so that the child can listen to the sounds of her voice.

Substance Changes

Dyeing Eggs

Use natural products to make egg dye. Beets produce deep red colors, onions produce yellow (add baking soda to make bright yellow), cranberries produce light red, spinach leaves produce green, and blackberries produce blue colors. To make dyed eggs, pick two or three colors from the list. Make the dye by boiling the fruit or vegetable in small amounts of water. Let the child put a cool hard-boiled egg in a nylon stocking and dip it into the dye. Keep the egg in the dye for several minutes. Pull out the nylon and check the color. If it is dark enough, place the egg on a paper towel to dry. If the child wants to color the eggs with crayons before dyeing, you can show how the wax keeps liquid from getting on the egg.

Making Candles

Candles can be made for gifts. This experience provides an opportunity for the child to see how a substance can change from solid to liquid and back to a solid form. The child can place pieces of paraffin in a tin can that is bent at the top, forming a spout. A piece of crayon can be used to add color. The bottom of the tin cans should be placed in a pan of water and heated on the stove until the paraffin is melted. Meanwhile, the child can prepare small paper cups. Place a wick in the bottom of each paper cup mold. Wicks can be made by tying a piece of string to a paper clip and a pencil. Then lay the pencil horizontally across the cup, allowing the string to hang vertically into the cup. When the wax is melted, an adult should carefully pour the wax into the cup. After the wax hardens, the candles can be used as decorations or presents.

This activity should be restricted to children at least four years old. Constant supervision is required.

Making Toothpaste

In individual plastic bags, place 4 teaspoons of baking soda, 1 teaspoon salt, and 1 teaspoon water. Add a drop of food flavoring extract such as peppermint, mint, or orange. The child can now mix her own toothpaste.

One Food or Many?

With an adult's assistance, select one food and prepare it in many different ways: for apples, fresh apple slices, dried apples, applesauce, apple cider, apple crisp, etc. Discuss with the children other foods they eat that are prepared in many different ways (e.g., for beef, roast beef, hamburger, beef jerky, etc.).

Science

Roasting Pumpkin Seeds

Wash and dry pumpkin seeds. Then spread the seeds out on a cookie sheet to dry. Bake the seeds in a preheated oven at 350 degrees until brown. Salt, cool, and eat at snack time.

Temperature Experiences

Outdoor and Indoor Temperatures

Place an outdoor thermometer in the yard. Encourage the child to examine the thermometer. Record the temperature by marking it on the thermometer with masking tape. Bring the thermometer inside. Check the thermometer again in half an hour. Show the child the change in temperature.

Thermometer

Experiment with a thermometer. Begin introducing the concept by observing and discussing what happens when the thermometer is placed in a bowl of warm water and a bowl of cold water. Demonstrate and encourage experimentation under supervision during a self-selected activity period.

Tool Experiences

Gears

Collect gears and place them on the science table. The child can experiment, observing how the gears move. When appropriate, discuss their similar and different characteristics.

Pulley

Set up a pulley. Provide the child with blocks so he may lift a heavy load with the help of a wheel. Supervision may be necessary for this activity.

Magnifying Glasses

Provide magnifying glasses for looking at objects seen on a camping or outside field trip.

Science

Water Experiences

Bubble Solution Recipe

- ¾ cup liquid soap
- ¼ cup glycerin (obtain at a drugstore)
- 2 quarts water

Place the mixed solution in a shallow pan and let the child insert the bubble makers. Bubble makers can be successfully made from the following:

- Plastic six-pack holders from beverages
- Straws
- Bent wire with no sharp edges
- Funnels

Chase the Pepper

Collect the following materials: water, pepper, shallow pan, piece of soap, and sugar. Fill the pan with water and shake the pepper on the water. Then take a piece of wet soap and dip it into the water. What happens? (The pepper moves away from the soapy water to the clear water.) The skin on water pulls, and on soapy water the pull is weak. On clear water, it is strong and pulls the pepper along. Now take some sugar and shake it into the soapy water. What happens? Sugar gives the skin a stronger pull.

Coloring Snow

Provide spray bottles containing colored water, preferably red, yellow, and blue. Allow the child to spray on snow and mix the colors.

Evaporation

The child can pour water into a jar. Mark a line at the water level. Place the jar on a window ledge and check it every day. The disappearance of water is called evaporation.

Fabric Sink and Float

Provide various kinds of clothing and fabric on the science table along with a large tub of water. The child can test the different types of clothing to see which will sink and which will float. Some clothing articles will only float until they become saturated with water. After a test has been made, the clothes can be hung to dry.

Freezing Water

Freeze a container of water. Periodically observe the changes. In colder climates, water can be frozen outdoors. The addition of food coloring may add interest.

Science

Making Frost

Changes in temperature cause dew. When dew freezes, it is called frost. The materials needed are a tin can with no lid, rock salt, and crushed ice. Measure and pour 2 cups of crushed ice and ½ cup rock salt in the can. Stir rapidly. Let the mixture sit for 30 minutes. The outside of the can will now have dew on it. Wait longer and the dew will change to frost. To hasten the process, place in a freezer.

Making Rainbows

If you have a hose available, the child can spray the hose into the sun. The rays of sunlight contain all the colors mixed together. The water acts as a prism and separates the water into colors, creating a rainbow.

Measuring Rainfall

During spring, place a bucket outside with a plastic ruler set vertically by securing to the bottom. Check the height of the water after each rainfall. With an older child, make a chart to record rainfalls.

Painting Sidewalks

On a sunny day, allow the child to paint sidewalks with water. To do this, provide various paintbrushes and buckets of water. Call attention to the water's evaporation.

Testing Volume

Containers that hold the same amounts of liquid are needed. Try to include containers that are tall, skinny, short, and flat. Ask the child, "Do they hold the same amount?" Encourage experimenting by pouring liquids from one container to another.

Water and Vinegar Fun

Collect the following materials: two small jars with lids, water, and white vinegar. Pour water into one jar and an equal amount of vinegar into the other jar. Replace caps. Then let the child explore the jars of liquids and discuss the similarities. Then let the child smell each jar.

Wave Machine

Collect the following materials: mineral oil, water, food coloring, and a transparent jar. Fill the jar half to two-thirds full with water. Add a few drops of food coloring. Then add mineral oil to completely fill the jar. Secure the lid. Then tilt jar slowly from side to side to make waves. Notice that the oil and water move into separate layers and will not stay mixed after the jar is shaken.

Weather Experiences

Signs and Sounds of Winter

On a winter walk (in colder climates) have the child watch and listen for signs and sounds of winter. The signs of winter are:

Weather: cold, ice, snow, the day is shorter, darkness comes earlier.

Plants: all but evergreen trees are bare.

People: we wear warmer clothes, we play inside more, we shovel snow, we play in the snow.

Some of the sounds of winter are: boots crunching in the snow, rain splashing, wind howling, etc. (Adapt this activity to the signs of winter in your climate.)

Weather Calendar

Construct a calendar for the month. Record changes of weather each day by attaching a symbol to the calendar. Symbols should include clouds, sun, snow, rain, etc.

Weather Chart

A weather chart can be constructed that depicts weather conditions, such as sunny, rainy, warm, cold, windy, etc. Attach at least two arrows to the center of the chart so that the child can point the arrow at the appropriate weather conditions.

Other Interesting Science Activities

1. Observe food forms, such as potatoes, in the raw, shredded, or sliced form. Fruits can be juiced, sliced, or sectioned.

2. Prepare tomatoes in several ways, such as sliced, juiced, stewed, baked, and pureed.

3. Show corn in all forms, including on the cob, popcorn, freshly cooked, and canned.

4. Sort picture cards into piles, such as living versus inanimate.

5. Take the children on a sensory walk. Prepare by filling dishpan-sized containers with different items. Foam, sand, leaves, pebbles, mud, cold and warm water, and grains can be used. Have the children remove their shoes and socks to walk through the filled containers.

6. Enjoy a nature walk. Provide each child with a grocery bag and instructions to collect leaves, rocks, soil, insects, etc.

7. Show the children how to feel their heartbeat following vigorous activity.

8. Observe popcorn popping.

9. Record body weight and height.

10. Prepare hair- and eye-color charts. This information can be made into bar graphs that show the number of children with particular hair/eye colors.

11. Introduce the concept of water absorption by providing containers with water. Allow the children to experiment with coffee filters, paper towels, newspaper, sponges, dishcloths, waxed paper, aluminum foil, and plastic wrap.

12. Plan a seed party. Provide the children with peanuts, walnuts, pecans, and coconuts. Observe the different sizes, shapes, textures, and flavors.

13. Make a desk garden. Cut carrots, turnips, and a pineapple 1½ inches from the stem. Place the stems in a shallow pan of water.

14. Create a worm farm. Place gravel and soil in a clear, large-mouth jar. Add worms and keep soil moist. Place lettuce, corn, or cereal on top of the soil. Tape black construction paper around the outside of the jar. Remove the paper temporarily to see the tunnels.

15. Make shadows. In a darkened room, turn on a flashlight. Place a hand or object in front of the light source, making a shadow.

16. Produce static electricity by rubbing wool fabric over inflated balloons.

17. Install a bird feeder outside the window.

18. Play the What's Missing game. Provide children with a variety of small, familiar items. Tell them to cover their eyes or put their heads down. Remove one item. Then tell the children to uncover their eyes and ask them what is missing. As the children gain skill, remove a second and a third item.

19. Notice how seeds are scattered: milkweed pods, dandelion.

20. Care for potted plants.

21. Collect pictures of different kinds of fruits and vegetables.

22. Visit the grocery store or farmers' market and see fruits and vegetables that were grown locally.

23. Collect pictures of farm animals, pets, or animals that are wild.

24. Visit a farm and see how animals work and how they are cared for.

25. Watch how goldfish swim.

26. Keep a turtle and watch how it crawls and swims.

27. Take a walk and look for caterpillars, crickets, grasshoppers, and other insects.

28. Listen to the noise of insects on a hot day.

29. Provide pictures of babies that look like their parents and those that look different; e.g., cats and kittens, tadpoles and frogs.

30. Make a feeding station for birds.

31. Use a prism to show rainbow colors.

32. Watch shadows at different times of the day.

33. Slide a box of blocks across the floor. Then put the box in a wagon and move it. Discuss how the wheels help to move the blocks.

34. Grow radish plants in two containers for about a week. Stop watering one container. Observe that the plants in that container soon die.

35. Compare the size of the child's hand with your own. Draw around the hands and name the fingers, thumb, wrist, fingernails, etc. Then draw around the child's shoes and your own. Compare sizes.

36. Fill a glass or other container with soil. Pour water over it and watch the bubbles come out. Discuss why worms come to the top of the soil after a heavy rain.

37. Take a trip to the produce department of a grocery store. Call attention to the arrangement of vegetables and fruits in the display bins. Some are in stacks, and others are in bags or bunches.

38. Cut pictures from seed catalogs or magazines.

39. Plan an animal cracker party. Identify and discuss the animals represented.

40. Observe how animals can move by running, galloping, swimming, walking, flying, crawling, jumping, and hopping.

41. Place a small piece of milk chocolate or butter on a dish in the sun and some on a dish in the shade. What happens after a while to the dish in the sun? Put the melted chocolate or butter

Science

in the refrigerator. Now discuss what heat does and what cold does.

42. Raise the shades in the room. Then lower all of the shades. Ask the child, "What happened?" Observe that the sun gives light and heat.

43. At the zoo, discuss the different places in which animals find or build homes. Then take a walk and look for some animal homes.

44. Give the child an opportunity to feel various objects and tell whether they feel sticky, dry, wet, soft, hard, smooth, etc.

Science

Storytelling and Fingerplays

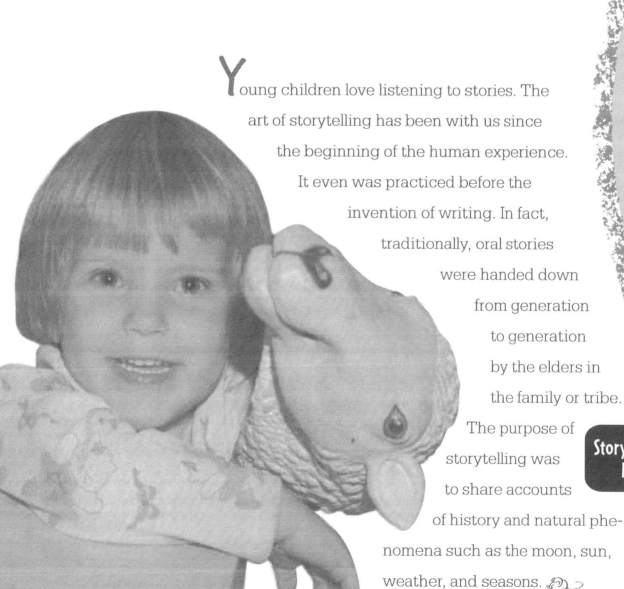

Young children love listening to stories. The art of storytelling has been with us since the beginning of the human experience. It even was practiced before the invention of writing. In fact, traditionally, oral stories were handed down from generation to generation by the elders in the family or tribe. The purpose of storytelling was to share accounts of history and natural phenomena such as the moon, sun, weather, and seasons.

As they are today, stories were also a powerful tool for molding a child's interests, self-esteem, and behavior.

Studies show that it is important for the adults in a child's life to value books and to promote a love of reading. To do this, books need to be available in the home and the child needs to be read to on a daily basis. Model the love of reading and value of the book for the child. She will also enjoy owning her own books. Give books for birthday gifts, special surprise gifts, Valentine's Day, and any other opportunity that presents itself. Books are a present young children can open over and over again, so it is important take the child to the bookstore and library to look at, discuss, and choose books.

Value of Books and Storytelling

The magic of using books as a tool for storytelling is endless. Young children find books captivating, entertaining, and inviting. They enjoy the visual and auditory stimulation of having books read to them over and over again. How often have you heard a young child say, "Read the story again." To young children, listening to a book is a wonderful and highly valued activity. Language development is prompted by asking what, where, and how questions. Then, too, the more young children listen to stories, the more they learn about themselves. Books also help young children by:

- developing listening and auditory memory skills.
- developing an appreciation of the printed word.
- adding to and enriching children's first-hand ideas.
- developing visual memory skills.
- developing the capacity to empathize with others.
- developing critical-thinking skills.
- develop listening skills.
- fostering social relationships.
- presenting information.
- understanding family roles—mothers, fathers, brothers, sisters, grandparents, as well as other types that are aligned differently.
- learning to become independent and accomplishing things on their own.
- viewing situations from perspectives other than their own.
- stimulating new ideas.
- helping children learn left-to-right progression skills (because we read from left to right across the page).

Choosing Books

When choosing books for young children, look for award winners. The American Association for Library Services to Children and the American Library Association recognize, with the Caldecot medal and Honor awards, respectively, the artist producing the most distinguished picturebook for children. Other awards include the Newbery Medal, Coretta Scott King Award, and book awards given by the American Library Association.

You can ask the librarian at your local library to give you a list of these picture books; likewise, you can ask the salesperson at a local bookstore to provide this information. Chances are they will have a list of these award-winning books or can complete a computer search to obtain this information for you.

Illustrations

Carefully review the illustrations of picture books. Look carefully: You will note a wide variety of illustration types in books for young children. There are photographs, watercolors, line drawing, and collages. During this review process, remember that the younger the child, the more realistic these illustrations need to be. Illustrations will help the children develop concept formation and maintain their interest in the book.

The illustrations in a good picture book for young children should tell a story without the use of words. After listening to a story several times, the child with verbal skills should be able to retell the story through the pictures. Kindergarten and some older preschool children will prefer more details in the illustrations, as well as fantasy.

Vocabulary Words

Consider the vocabulary words when choosing a book. The majority of words in a good book will be understandable to the child. The book should contain only a few new words. When introducing a book with new words, provide the child with definitions. The following chart lists definitions of terms that can be used especially with three-, four-, and five-year-old children.

Storytelling and Fingerplays

Vocabulary Words and Definitions

Vocabulary Word	Definition
Add	to put things together
Afraid	the feeling of being unsure of or frightened about something
Airport	a place where airplanes take off and land
Alphabet	letter symbols that are used to write a language
Angry	you are angry when you are upset and unhappy
Ant	a small insect that lives in the ground; ants live in small groups
Antennae	feelers on an insect that stick out from the head
Apartment	a group of rooms to live in
Apartment building	a building including many homes
Apple	a fruit that is grown on a tree; apples can be red, yellow, or green
Apple blossom	a flower on the apple tree
Apple butter	a spread for bread made from apples
Architect	a person who designs homes
Art	a form of beauty; paintings and drawings are a form of art
Artist	a person who creates art; an artist makes paintings and drawings
Aunt	sister of a parent; an aunt can be your mother's sister or your father's sister
Automobile	a machine that we ride in; *car* is another word for an automobile
Backpack	a zippered bag worn on one's back to carry objects

Vocabulary Words and Definitions (Continued)

Vocabulary Word	Definition
Bake	to cook something; we can bake in an oven or on a grill
Baker	makes breads, rolls, cookies, and pies
Ball	is usually round; it is used to play games
Ballet	a form of dance that usually tells a story
Bank	a place where people keep their money
Bark	(1) the tough, outer covering of a tree; or (2) a sound that puppies and dogs make
Barn	building to house animals and store grain; it is usually on a farm
Basket	a woven container used to hold things; baskets can also be used for decoration
Beach	a sandy place used for sunbathing and playing; it is next to water
Beak	the part around a bird's mouth
Bean	a vegetable that grows on vines; there are many kinds of beans
Bear	a large animal with thick black, brown, or white fur
Bed	something to sleep on
Bedroom	a room for sleeping
Bee	a flying insect; bees make honey
Bell	makes a sound when shaken
Berry	small fruits with seeds that are juicy; raspberries and strawberries are berries
Bicycle	a two-wheeled vehicle; you move it by pushing the pedals
Bird	an animal that has a head, two legs, wings, and feathers; birds usually can fly

Storytelling and Fingerplays

Vocabulary Words and Definitions (Continued)

Vocabulary Word	Definition
Bird feeder	a container that has food for birds
Bird watching	watching birds
Birthday	the day on which someone is born; people often have parties to celebrate their birthdays
Bite	to cut something with your teeth
Blade	cutting edge of scissors
Blanket	a cloth made to keep you warm
Blended family	people from two or more families living together
Blow	to quickly move air
Blue	a primary color
Boat	designed to ride in on water
Body sounds	sounds made by moving one or more body parts
Bone	people and animals have bones in their bodies; an object a dog uses to chew on
Bonnet	a kind of hat
Book	sheets of paper inside two covers
Boots	clothing worn on the feet to keep them warm and dry
Bowl	a deep dish; soup and cereal can be eaten from a bowl
Box	usually has sides, a top, and a bottom; boxes are made to hold things
Braille	a system of bumpy printing for people who are blind
Bread	a food prepared by mixing flour or grain meal with water or milk and shortening; bread needs to be baked in an oven

Storytelling and Fingerplays

Vocabulary Words and Definitions (Continued)

Vocabulary Word	Definition
Breakfast	a meal eaten in the morning; it is the first meal of the day
Bristle	a short, stiff hair- or thread-like object
Brother	a boy or man having the same parents as another person
Brown	is a color; chocolate is brown
Brush	a tool made of bristles or wires attached to a handle; brushes can be used to paint
Bubble	a round circle that has a skin and contains air
Bubble skin	the outside of a bubble
Bubble solution	a mixture of water and liquid soap
Bubble wand	a tool used to make bubbles
Bug	insects that fly or crawl; flies, ants, and spiders are bugs
Build	to put things together
Building	has walls and a roof; houses are buildings
Bulb	a type of seed
Bunny	a baby rabbit
Bus	a vehicle that carries many people; buses take people to work; they also take children to school
Butterfly	insect with wings
Button	holds clothes together; shirts, coats, and dresses may have buttons
Cab	a car that has a driver; cabs take people places
Cage	a home for animals
Calendar	a chart that shows days, months, and weeks

Storytelling and Fingerplays

Vocabulary Words and Definitions (Continued)

Vocabulary Word	Definition
Campfire	a controlled fire that is made at a campground
Camping	living outdoors in sleeping bags, tents, cabins, or campers
Campsite	a place for tents and campers to park
Can	used to hold something; soup, paint, and juice comes in cans
Car	machine used for moving people; *automobile* is another word for car
Card	a piece of folded paper with a design; cards are sent to people on special occasions: birthdays, holidays, celebrations, or when ill
Carol	a Christmas song
Carrot	orange vegetable that grows in the ground
Carton	a box or container to hold food or other objects
Caterpillar	insect that is bright and furry; caterpillars may change to butterflies
Cavity	a hole; people may have cavities in their teeth
Cereal	a food usually eaten at breakfast; it can be made from rice, wheat, corn, or other grains
Chalk	a soft stone used for writing or drawing
Checkup	a visit to a doctor to make sure you are healthy
Cheek	part of the face below the eye
Cheese	food made from milk; pizza usually has cheese on it
Cheese factory	a place where cheese is made or sold
Cherry	small, round, red fruit grown on a tree

Vocabulary Words and Definitions (Continued)

Vocabulary Word	Definition
Chick	a baby chicken
Children	young boys or girls; when children grow up, they are called men and women
Circle	a shape that is a round line
Circus	traveling show with clowns, horses, and other animals
Circus parade	a march of people and animals at the beginning of the circus performance
City	a large town where many people live
Clamp	a tool used to join or hold things
Clean	means that there is no dirt
Climb	means to go up something; we can climb stairs, trees, and ladders
Clock	a tool that shows what time it is
Clothespin	a clip used to hang clothes on a clothesline or a hanger
Clothing	a covering for the body; shirts, dresses, and pants are clothes
Cloud	water droplets formed in the sky; clouds can be gray or white
Clowns	people who wear makeup and dress in silly clothes; clowns paint their faces; they do tricks and act silly to make people laugh
Coat	clothing worn over other clothes; it is often used for warmth
Cold	(1) means not warm; or (2) a kind of sickness; when people have a cold, they cough and sneeze
Collar	a band worn around an animal's neck
Color	red, blue, yellow, and green are examples of colors

Storytelling and Fingerplays

Vocabulary Words and Definitions (Continued)

Vocabulary Word	Definition
Communication	sharing information
Computer	machine that can do many things; you can play games on a computer; computers also give you information
Construction worker	a person who builds
Cook	means to make food ready
Cooked	food prepared by heating
Cooperating	working together to help someone
Core	the part of the apple that contains seeds
Corn	a white or yellow vegetable; both animals and people eat corn
Costume	clothing worn to pretend something
Cousin	the son or daughter of an uncle or aunt
Crayon	an art tool made of colored wax; crayons are used for coloring and drawing pictures
Cream	the yellowish part of milk
Crib	a small bed with high sides for babies to sleep in
Cricket	a small, leaping insect known for its chirping
Crow	a large, black bird that has a loud cry
Crust	the outside part of the bread
Cry	(1) to call loudly; or (2) to have tears coming from the eyes
Cupid	a symbol of Valentine's Day, usually a baby boy with a bow and arrows
Cut	to divide something in pieces
Dairy product	a product made from milk

Vocabulary Words and Definitions (Continued)

Vocabulary Word	Definition
Dance	a pattern of body movements
Daughter	a girl child of a father or mother
Dental floss	a string used to clean between the teeth
Dentist	a person who helps keep our teeth healthy
Diet	the food we eat
Dig	to make a hole; we can dig in the ground, snow, or sand
Dish	something used to place food on
Doctor	a man or woman who helps keep our bodies healthy
Dog	an animal; dogs may be small or large; they are kept as pets
Dog brush	a brush used to clean a dog's hair
Doghouse	a place where dogs can sleep and keep warm and dry
Doll	a toy that looks like a person
Dreidel	a four-sided toy that spins like a top
Dress	clothing that a girl or woman wears
Drill	a tool that cuts holes
Driver	someone who operates a machine and makes it go
Duckling	a baby duck; ducklings like to swim; they live near lakes, rivers, or streams
Duplex	a house divided into two separate homes
Dye	to change the color of something using a colored liquid
Ear	body part that helps you hear
Easter	a holiday in spring

Storytelling and Fingerplays

Vocabulary Words and Definitions (Continued)

Vocabulary Word	Definition
Egg	food that is laid by chickens
Elf	Santa's helper; fairy tales may include stories about elves
Entertainment	things we enjoy seeing, doing, and listening to
Envelope	a cover for a letter
Exercise	moving our body parts; running, playing ball, and swimming are types of exercise
Eye	a part of the body that help you see; eyes are located on the face
Face	the part of the head that has the eyes, nose, and mouth
Fairy	a tiny, make-believe person in stories
Fall	the season between summer and winter
Family	people living together
Farmer	a person who works on a farm; some farmers care for farm animals; some farmers grow food for animals and people
Father	a male parent
Feathers	soft and light, feathers cover the skin of birds
Feelings	expressed emotions; love and happiness are feelings, as are anger and sadness
Fin	the part that fish move to help themselves swim
Fire alarm	a sound warning people about fire
Fire drill	practice for teaching people what to do in case of a fire
Fire engine	trucks carrying tools and equipment needed to fight fires

Vocabulary Words and Definitions (Continued)

Vocabulary Word	Definition
Fire extinguisher	equipment that puts out fires
Fire station	a building that provides housing for fire-fighters and fire trucks
Fish	an animal that lives in the water
Fish farm	a place to raise fish for food
Float	to rest on top of a liquid
Flour	wheat that has been ground to a soft powder
Flower	a colored plant part that contains seeds or has colored petals; flowers are pretty and usually smell nice
Folk tale	a story that has been told by many people for a long time
Food	what we eat; it helps us grow; milk, fruits, vegetables, breads, and meats are all foods
Fork	a tool used for eating; it usually has sharp points
Freeze	hardened liquid
Friend	a person we enjoy
Frost	very small ice pieces
Frozen	chilled or refrigerated to make a solid
Fruit	usually a sweet-tasting part of a plant; strawberries, apples, and oranges are fruits
Fuel	gas, diesel, or other material used to produce power
Fur	hairy coating of some animals; it is thick and usually soft
Gallery	a place to display works of art
Game	something you can play

Storytelling and Fingerplays

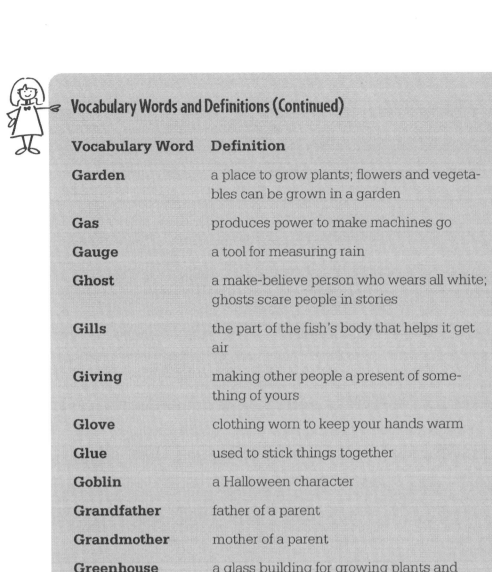

Vocabulary Words and Definitions (Continued)

Vocabulary Word	Definition
Garden	a place to grow plants; flowers and vegetables can be grown in a garden
Gas	produces power to make machines go
Gauge	a tool for measuring rain
Ghost	a make-believe person who wears all white; ghosts scare people in stories
Gills	the part of the fish's body that helps it get air
Giving	making other people a present of something of yours
Glove	clothing worn to keep your hands warm
Glue	used to stick things together
Goblin	a Halloween character
Grandfather	father of a parent
Grandmother	mother of a parent
Greenhouse	a glass building for growing plants and flowers
Grocery	a store that sells food
Groom	to clean
Guide dog	a dog trained to help people who are blind
Halloween	holiday when people wear costumes and go trick-or-treating
Hammer	a tool used to insert or remove objects such as nails
Hamster	a furry animal that looks like a mouse and is kept as a pet
Handle	the part of a brush or other tool that is held

Vocabulary Words and Definitions (Continued)

Vocabulary Word	Definition
Hanukkah	eight-day Jewish festival of lights; a celebration of the Jewish people's fight long ago to keep the right to practice their religion; one candle is lighted on the menorah each day (see *menorah*)
Happy	a feeling of being glad; when you feel good about things, you are happy
Hat	clothing that covers our head
Hatch	to break out of a shell
Health	feeling good; not sick
Heart	(1) a part of the body; or (2) a symbol of love
Helmet	a protective hat
Herd	a group of animals
Hibernate	to sleep during the winter
Hiking	taking a long walk
Holiday	a special day; it is a day on which we celebrate
Hose	a tube that water flows through
Hot	a warm temperature experienced during the summer months
House	a place to live
Hue	variations in lightness and brightness created by adding black to a color
Hug	to put your arms around some person or animal in a friendly way
Hygienist	the dentist's assistant
Ice	water that has frozen
Icicle	a hanging piece of frozen ice

Storytelling and Fingerplays

Vocabulary Words and Definitions (Continued)

Vocabulary Word	Definition
Imaginary	something that is not real
Insect	a small animal with six legs; a fly is an insect
Instrument	a tool for making musical sounds
Jack-o-lantern	a pumpkin cut to look like a face
Job	a type of work
Kitchen	a room for cooking
Kitten	a baby cat
Labor Day	holiday to honor working people
Lake	a large body of water surrounded by land
Lamb	a baby sheep
Lantern	a covered light used for camping
Latkes	potato pancakes eaten during Hanukkah (*see* Hanukkah)
Laundromat	a place where we can wash and dry clothes
Leaf	part of the plant or tree that grows on the stem; leaves are usually green
Leash	a rope, chain, or cord that attaches to a collar
Leaven	a food that makes the bread dough rise
Leaves	growth from the stem
Letter	paper with a written or typed message
Library	a place where books are kept
Like	feeling good about someone or something
Line	a mark made with a pencil, crayon, etc., to make a shape
Liquid	substance that can be poured
Love	feeling of warmth toward another

Vocabulary Words and Definitions (Continued)

Vocabulary Word	Definition
Machine	has moving parts; they help people to do things faster; cars and dishwashers are machines
Mail	letters, cards, postcards, and packages
Mail bag	bag that holds letters and postcards
Mailbox	a place to mail letters or hold letters
Mail carrier	person who delivers mail
Makeup	colored face paint
Mallets	special sticks used to play the xylophone and bells
Marionette	a puppet with strings for movement
Mask	face covering worn when pretending
Meal	food that is eaten at one time
Melt	to change from a solid to a liquid
Menorah	eight-branched candlestick; the middle or ninth candle is taller than the other eight and is called the shammash (*see* Hannukah)
Money	used to buy something; pennies, nickels, dimes, quarters, and dollars are money
Moth	a night-flying insect with four wings related to the butterfly
Mother	a female parent; a person who has a child or children
Mouse	a small, furry animal that has a head, ears, eyes, mouth, whiskers, four legs, body, and tail
Mouth	part of the face that helps you talk and eat
Movement	change in position by our body or by an animal or thing

Storytelling and Fingerplays

235

Vocabulary Words and Definitions (Continued)

Vocabulary Word	Definition
Music	sounds made by instruments or voices; a way of expressing ideas and feelings
Native Americans	people who lived in America when the Pilgrims first arrived
Nephew	son of a brother or sister
Nest	bed or home prepared by a bird
Newspaper	words printed on paper
Niece	daughter of a brother or sister
Nose	lets you smell things; it is in the middle of your face
Number	a symbol used to represent an amount; it tells you how many
Numeral	a symbol that represents a number
Nurse	a man or woman who usually assists the doctor
Nursery rhyme	short, simple poem or rhyme
Nutrition	eating foods that are good for our body
Obedience school	a school where dogs are taught to obey
Occupation	the job a person performs to earn money
Ocean	a large body of salt water
One-parent family	a child or children who lives with only one parent, either a father or mother
Ophthalmologist	an eye doctor
Orange	a fruit that grows on a tree
Ornament	decoration for the home or tree
Oval	shaped like an egg
Owl	a bird with a big head and big eyes that hoots and flies around at night

Vocabulary Words and Definitions (Continued)

Vocabulary Word	Definition
Paint	a colored liquid used to color things
Paintbrush	a tool for applying paint
Pal	another word for *friend* or *buddy*
Passenger	the rider in a car or cab
Patient	a person who goes to see a doctor
Paw	the dog's foot
Pediatrician	a children's doctor
Perch	a pole for a bird to stand on
Pet	an animal kept for pleasure
Petal	colored part of a flower
Picnic	a party where people eat outside
Pilgrims	early settlers who sailed to America
Piñata	brightly colored papier-maché figure that is filled with candy and gifts
Pine tree	the tree we decorate for the Christmas holidays
Pinking shears	special kind of sewing scissors
Plane	(1) a machine that flies; or (2) a tool used for shaving wood
Plant	a living thing, usually green, that grows and changes; flowers, bushes, and trees are plants
Play	to have fun
Pliers	a tool used for holding things
Pollinate	the way insects help flowers grow
Pool	a place to swim
Post office	the place where mail is sorted to be delivered

Storytelling and Fingerplays

Vocabulary Words and Definitions (Continued)

Vocabulary Word	Definition
Powder brush	a brush that is used to apply facial powder
Present	a gift that you give someone; you may also receive a gift from someone
Pretending	acting like someone or something else
Primary colors	red, yellow, and blue
Prince	the son of a king or a queen
Produce	agricultural products such as fruits and vegetables
Puddle	rain collection on the ground
Pulley	a wheel that can be connected to a rope to move things
Pupa	the intermediate stage of an insect; chrysalis
Puppet show	a story told with puppets
Puppet stage	a place on which puppets are moved
Puppet	a toy that is moved by the hand or finger
Puppeteer	a person who makes a puppet move and speak
Puppy	a baby dog
Purple	a color made by mixing red and blue
Rabbit	an animal with long legs and long ears; rabbits can hop very fast
Rain	water that falls from clouds
Rainbow	a colorful arc formed when the sun shines after it has rained
Rake	a tool with teeth or prongs
Recreational vehicle	a living and sleeping area on wheels
Rectangle	a shape with four sides

Vocabulary Words and Definitions (Continued)

Vocabulary Word	Definition
Red	a primary color
Reindeer	an animal used to pull Santa's sleigh
Ringmaster	person in charge of the circus performance
Roots	part of a plant that grows downward into the soil and is edible in some plants (potatoes, turnips, radishes, onions, and carrots)
Rule	the way we are to act
Ruler	a measuring tool
Sad	the feeling of being hurt or unhappy
Safety	freedom from danger
Santa Claus	an imaginary jolly man who wears a red suit and is associated with Christmas
Sap	the fluid part of a tree
Saw	a cutting tool with sharp edges
Scales	skin covering of fish and other reptiles
School of fish	a group of fish
Scissors	tool used for cutting things
Scratching	a noise like the sound a mouse makes by rubbing its nails against a surface; people can scratch with their nails or a tool
Screwdriver	a tool that turns screws
Season	a time of the year
Seat belt	the strap that holds a person safely in a vehicle
Seed	part of a plant that can grow into another plant; in some plants, seeds are edible (sunflower, pumpkin)
Service	helping people
Shade	being in the shadow of something

Vocabulary Words and Definitions (Continued)

Vocabulary Word	Definition
Shake	to quickly move something in any direction
Sharing	giving and taking turns
Shears	large scissors
Shirt	clothing that covers the chest and sometimes the arms
Shiver	to shake from cold or fear
Shoes	clothing worn on the feet
Shorts	short pants worn in warm weather
Sign	a lettered board
Sign language	symbols we make with our hands to communicate
Signs	symbols
Sink	(1) to drop to the bottom of a liquid; or (2) a place to wash things
Sister	a girl having the same parents as another person
Size	how small or big something is
Ski	runners fit on the feet and move over snow and ice
Skirt	clothing that hangs from the waist
Sled	transportation for moving over snow and ice
Sleep	to rest your body
Sleeping bag	a zippered blanket
Sleet	a mixture of rain and snow
Smile	a facial expression of pleasure or happiness
Snow	frozen drops of water that fall from the sky
Snow person	snow shaped in the form of a person
Socks	clothing that covers your feet

Vocabulary Words and Definitions (Continued)

Vocabulary Word	Definition
Soil	portion of earth; dirt used for growing plants
Spider	very small animal with four pairs of legs
Spiderling	a baby spider
Spoon	a tool used to eat food
Sport	an activity played for fun
Spring	the season of the year when plants begin to grow; it comes after winter and before summer
Sprout	first sign of growth
Square	a shape with four sides of equal length
Squeaking	a clear, sharp sound made by a mouse or other animal or thing
Stable	a building for horses and cattle
Stamp	a sticker put on mail so that it will be delivered
Star	(1) something that shines in the sky at night; or (2) an object that can be used as a decoration
Star of David	a six-sided star-shaped figure that is a Jewish symbol
Stems	part of a plant; stems support the leaves and grow upward; the part of the plant used for transporting food and water; stems are edible in some plants (e.g., celery)
Stethoscope	a tool used for checking the heartbeat and breathing
Stilts	long sticks a performer stands on to be taller
Stocking	a large Christmas sock in which treats are put
Store	a place to buy things

Storytelling and Fingerplays

Vocabulary Words and Definitions (Continued)

Vocabulary Word	Definition
Stranger	a person you have not seen before, or you have seen but not met
Surprise	a feeling from something unexpected
Sweater	clothing that keeps you warm
Swimming	moving yourself through water with body movements
Tail	the end body part that helps fish move
Team	a group of people who play together
Teeth	used to chew food
Temperature	how hot or cold something is
Tempo	the speed of music
Tent	a movable shelter made out of material
Texture	how something feels
Thankful	feeling and expressing thanks
Thanksgiving	a holiday in November when we express thanks
Thermometer	a tool for checking temperature
Tints	changes in brightness and lightness created by adding white to a color
Togetherness	being with one another and sharing a good feeling
Tongue	the part of your mouth that helps you talk and taste
Tool	an object to help us
Toothbrush	a small brush used to clean teeth
Toothpaste	a paste used to clean teeth
Toothpick	a stick-like tool used for removing food parts from between our teeth

Vocabulary Words and Definitions (Continued)

Vocabulary Word	Definition
Toy	something to play with; balls are toys
Trapeze	a short bar on a rope used for swinging
Tree	a large plant with a thick trunk
Triangle	a shape with three sides
Trick-or-treat	walking from house to house on Halloween to ask for candy or treats
Truck	a wheeled vehicle used to move people and big objects
Trunk	the main stem and largest part of a tree (see *tree*)
Turkey	a large bird that is cooked for Thanksgiving
Typewriter	a machine that prints letters
Umbrella	a shade for protection against rain
Uncle	the brother of a parent
Unicycle	a vehicle with one wheel
Uniform	clothing worn for some sports and jobs
Valentine	a card designed for someone special
Vegetable	a plant that can be eaten
Vegetable brush	a stiff brush used to clean vegetables
Veterinarian	an animal doctor
Vine	a plant with long, slender stem (*see* stems)
Washing machine	an appliance used to clean clothes
Wasp	a winged insect with a poisonous sting
Water	a clear, colorless, odorless, tasteless liquid; it fills lakes, oceans, rivers, and swimming pools; all living things need water
Wedge	a tool used for splitting something

Vocabulary Words and Definitions (Continued)

Vocabulary Word	Definition
Weed	plant that is not needed
Wheel	a form in the shape of a circle used to move people and things
Wheelbarrow	a vehicle used for moving small loads; a wheelbarrow must be pushed
Wheelchair	a chair on wheels used by someone who cannot walk
Whiskers	stiff hair growing around a dog or other animal's nose, mouth, and eyes
Wing	a movable body part that helps most birds fly
Witch	a make-believe person who wears black and can do magic
Woods	an area with many trees
Wreath	a decoration made from pine tree branches (*see* pine tree)
Wrench	a tool that holds things
Yellow	a primary color
Yogurt	a milk product that can be flavored with fruit
Zip code	the last numbers on a mailing address
Zipper	used to hold clothing together
Zoo	a place to look at animals
Zookeeper	a person who feeds and cares for zoo animals

Storytelling and Fingerplays

Books for Infants and Toddlers

When selecting books for young children, careful consideration needs to be given to choosing age-appropriate books. Special care needs to be taken when choosing books for infants and toddlers. There are a wide variety of developmentally appropriate books for infants. Such books are concept oriented. They focus on familiar items in the child's environment, such as toys, pets, baby animals, colors, shapes, and routines. For toddlers, concept development is still the primary orientation. However, now the child is capable of taking an interactive role. For example, he may be able to lift or add cling-on features.

For ease in manipulating, books for infants and toddlers need to have thick pages. They should have large, clearly defined pictures, which should be brightly colored. Toddlers enjoy pointing at and touching the pictures. Infant and toddler books can be purchased in a variety of formats.

Toddlers love books that focus on favorite activities. They enjoy familiar actions such as eating, dressing, and interacting with family members or animals. Since these children are developing basic concepts, the colors of the illustrations should be realistic. Then, too, the sounds and actions represented in the pictures need to be familiar. Think about it. "Doggies" is one of the first words spoken. When choosing books on animals for the preschool level, consider the child's stage of development. Toddlers are just beginning to identify animals. The books need to be simple. They may focus on zoo animals, farm animals, or pets. A different animal can be placed on each page. You can help the child identify the animals and their sounds.

The following list of books by material type was included in *Creative Resources for Infants and Toddlers* (Herr, J., & Swim, T. (1998). Albany, NY: Delmar). These books were carefully selected by a children's literature specialist.

Cloth Books

Animal Play. (1996). New York: Dorling Kindersley.

Briggs, Raymond. (1993). *The Snowman.* New York: Random House.

Cousins, Lucy. My First Cloth Books series. Cambridge, MA: Candlewick Press. *Flower in the Garden* (1992); *Hen on the Farm* (1992); *Kite in the Park* (1992); *Teddy in the House* (1992).

Good Night, Moon. (1995). New York: Dutton. (Has detachable pieces. Ages 3+)

Harte, Cheryl. (1989a). *Bunny Rattle.* New York: Random House.

Harte, Cheryl. (1989b). *Ducky Squeak.* New York: Random House.

Hill, Eric. (1993a). *Clothes-Spot Cloth Book.* New York: G. P. Putnam.

Hill, Eric. (1993b). *Play-Spot Cloth Book.* New York: G. P. Putnam.

Pienkowski, Jan. (1995). *Bronto's Brunch.* New York: Dutton. (Has detachable pieces. Ages 3+)

Pienkowski, Jan. (1995). Jan Pienkowski's First Cloth Book series. New York: Little Simon. *Animals* (1995); *Friends* (1995); *Fun* (1996); *Play* (1995).

Potter, Beatrix. (1994). Beatrix Potter Cloth Books. New York: Frederick Warne & Co. *My Peter Rabbit Cloth Book; My Tom Kitten Cloth Book.*

Pudgy Pillow Books. (1989). New York: Grosset & Dunlap. *Baby's Animal Sounds; Baby's Little Engine That Could; Baby's Mother Goose; Baby's Peek a Boo.*

Tong, Willabel L. Cuddly Cloth Books. Kansas City: Andrews & McMeel Pub. *Farm Faces.* (1996); *My Pets.* (1997); *My Toys.* (1997); *Zoo Faces.* (1997).

Tucker, Sian. (1994). My First Cloth Book series. New York: Simon & Schuster. *Quack, Quack; Rat-a-Tat-Tat; Toot Toot; Yum Yum.*

Vinyl Cover and Bath Books

Bracken, Carolyn. (1984). *Baby's First Rattle: A Busy Bubble Book.* New York: Simon & Schuster.

De Brunhoff, Laurent. (1992). *Babar's Bath Book.* New York: Random House.

Hill, Eric. (1984a). *Spot's Friends.* New York: G. P. Putnam.

Hill, Eric. (1984b). *Spot's Toys.* New York: G. P. Putnam.

Hill, Eric. (1984c). *Sweet Dreams, Spot.* New York: G. P. Putnam.

Hoban, Tana. (1994a). *Tana Hoban's Red, Blue, Yellow Shoe.* New York: Greenwillow.

Hoban, Tana. (1994b). *Tana Hoban's What Is It?* New York: Greenwillow.

My First Duck. (1996). New York: Dutton. (Shape book)

Nicklaus, Carol. (1992). *Grover's Tubby.* New York: Random House/Children's Television Workshop.

Potter, Beatrix. Beatrix Potter Bath Books series. New York: Frederick Warne & Co. *Benjamin Bunny* (1994); *Jemima Puddle-Duck* (1988); *Mr. Jeremy Fisher* (1989); *Peter Rabbit* (1989); *Tom Kitten, Mittens, and Moppet* (1989).

Reichmeier, Betty. (1988). *Potty Time.* New York: Random House.

Smollin, Michael J. (1982). *Ernie's Bath Book.* New York: Random House/Children's Television Workshop.

Tubby, I. M. Shape books. New York: Simon & Schuster. *I'm a Little Airplane* (1982); *I'm a Little Choo Choo* (1982); *I'm a Little Fish* (1981).

Tucker, Sian. (1995). Sian Tucker Bath Books series. New York: Simon & Schuster. *Animal Splash; Splish Splash.*

Touch and Feel Books

Carter, David A. (1995). *Feely Bugs.* New York: Little Simon.

Chang, Cindy. (1994a). *Good Morning Puppy.* New York: Price Stern Sloan.

Chang, Cindy. (1994b). *Good Night Kitty!* New York: Price Stern Sloan.

Demi, Hitz. (1987). *Fluffy Bunny.* New York: Grosset & Dunlap.

Demi, Hitz. (1988). *Downy Duckling.* New York: Grosset & Dunlap.

Hanna, Jack. (1992). *Let's Go to the Petting Zoo with Jungle Jack.* New York: Doubleday.

Hill, Eric. (1997). *Spot's Touch and Feel Day.* New York: G. P. Putnam.

Kunhardt, Dorothy. (1968). *Pat the Bunny.* New York: Western Publishing.

Kunhardt, Dorothy, & Kunhardt, Edith. (1984). *Pat the Cat.* New York: Golden Books.

Kunhardt, Dorothy, & Kunhardt, Edith. (1993). *Pat the Puppy.* New York: Golden Books.

Lodge, J. (1996a). *Patch and His Favorite Things.* Orlando, FL: Harcourt Brace.

Lodge, J. (1996b). *Patch in the Garden.* Orlando: Harcourt Brace.

Offerman, Lynn. (1998). *Puppy Dog's Special Friends.* Kearney, NE: Joshua Morris Publishing.

Scarry, Richard. (1997). *Richard Scarry's Egg in the Hole Book.* New York: Golden Books.

Chunky and Chubby Books

Barton, Byron. (1994a). *Boats.* New York: HarperCollins.

Barton, Byron. (1994b). *Planes.* New York: HarperCollins.

Barton, Byron. (1994c). *Trains.* New York: HarperCollins.

Bond, Michael. (1992). *Paddington at the Seashore.* New York: HarperCollins.

Brown, Marc. Chunky Flap Book series. New York: Random House. *Arthur Counts* (1998); *Arthur's Farm Tales* (1998); *D.W.'s Color Book* (1997); *Where Is My Frog?* (1991); *Where's Arthur's Gerbil?* (1997); *Where's My Sneaker?* (1991).

Cowley, Rich. (1996). *Snap! Snap! Buzz Buzz.* Buffalo, NY: Firefly Books.

Dunn, Phoebe. (1984). *Farm Animals.* New York: Random House.

Dunn, Phoebe. (1988). *Baby's Animal Friends.* New York: Random House.

Freeman, Don. (1985). *Corduroy's Toys.* New York: Viking.

Fujikawa, Gyo. (1990). *Good Night, Sleep Tight! Shhh . . .* New York: Random House. (Chunky shape)

Hill, Eric. (1997). Spot Block Book series. New York: G. P. Putnam. *Spot's Favorite Baby Animals; Spot's Favorite Numbers; Spot's Favorite Words.*

Hirashima, Jean. (1994). *ABC.* New York: Random House. (Chunky shape)

Ingle, Annie. (1992). *Zoo Animals.* New York: Random House.

Loehr, Mallory. (1992). *Trucks.* New York: Random House. (Chunky shape)

McCue, Lisa. (1995). *Little Fuzzytail.* New York: Random House. (Chunky Peek a Board book)

Miller, Margaret. Super Chubby Book series. New York: Simon & Schuster. *At the Shore.* (1996); *Family Time.* (1996); *Happy Days.* (1996); *Let's Play.* (1997); *My Best Friends.* (1996); *Water Play.* (1996); *Wheels Go Round.* (1997).

Oxenbury, Helen. (1996). *Helen Oxenbury's Little Baby Books.* Cambridge, MA: Candlewick Press. Boxed set includes: *I Can; I Hear; I See; I Touch.*

Pienkowski, Jan. Nursery Board Book series. New York: Simon & Schuster. *Colors.* (1987); *Faces.* (1991); *Food.* (1991); *Homes.* (1990); *Sizes.* (1991); *Stop Go.* (1992); *Time.* (1991); *Yes No.* (1992).

Ricklen, Neil. Super Chubby Book series. New York: Simon & Schuster. *Baby Outside.* (1996); *Baby's ABC.* (1997); *Baby's Big and Little.* (1996); *Baby's Clothes.* (1997); *Baby's Friends.* (1997); *Baby's Good Morning.* (1992). *Baby's Good Night.* (1992); *Baby's Home.* (1997); *Baby's Neighborhood.* (1994); *Baby's 1 2 3.* (1990); *Baby's Playtime.* (1994); *Baby's Toys.* (1997); *Baby's Zoo.* (1992); *Daddy and Me.* (1997); *Mommy and Me.* (1997).

Ross, Anna. (1994). *Knock Knock, Who's There?* New York: Random House/ Children's Television Workshop. (Chunky flap book)

Ross, Katharine. (1989). *The Little Quiet Book.* New York: Random House.

Santoro, Christopher. (1993). *Open the Barn Door.* New York: Random House. (Chunky flap book)

Scarry, Richard. (1981). *Richard Scarry's Lowly Worm Word Book.* New York: Random House.

Scarry, Richard. (1990). *Richard Scarry's Cars and Trucks from A–Z.* New York: Random House. (Chunky shape)

Smollin, Michael. (1982a). *Ernie & Bert Can . . . Can You?* New York: Random House/Children's Television Network.

Smollin, Michael. (1982b). *In & Out, Up & Down.* New York: Random House/Children's Television Network.

Snapshot Chubby Book series. New York: Dorling Kindersley. *ABC* (1994); *Colors* (1994); *My Home* (1995); *My Toys* (1995); *Shapes* (1994).

Wik, Lars. (1985). *Baby's First Words.* New York: Random House.

Board Books

Bang, Molly. (1998). *Ten, Nine, Eight.* First Tupelo Board Book edition. New York: Tupelo Books.

Boynton, Sandra. Boynton Board Book series. New York: Simon & Schuster. *Blue Hat, Green Hat.* (1995); *Doggies: A Counting and Barking Book.* (1995); *Going to Bed Book.* (1995); *Moo, Baa, La La La.* (1995); *Opposites.* (1995).

Brett, Jan. (1996). *The Mitten: A Ukrainian Folktale.* New York: G. P. Putnam.

Brown, Margaret Wise. First Board Book editions. New York: HarperCollins. *Child's Good Night Book.* Pictures by Jean Charlot (1996); *Goodnight Moon.* Pictures by Clement Hurd (1991); *Runaway Bunny.* Pictures by Clement Hurd (1991).

Carle, Eric. (1994–98). First Board Book editions. New York: HarperCollins. *Do You Want to Be My Friend?* (1995); *The Mixed-Up Chameleon* (1998); *The Secret Birthday Message* (1998); *The Very Quiet Cricket* (1997); *Have You Seen My Cat?* First Little Simon Board Book edition (1996). New York: Simon & Schuster; *The Very Hungry Caterpillar.* First Board Book edition (1994). New York: Philomel Books.

Carle, Eric. (1998). Play-and-Read Books. St. Paul, MN: Cartwheel Books. *Catch the Ball.* (1998); *Let's Paint a Rainbow.* (1998); *What's for Lunch?* (1998).

Carlstrom, Nancy White. Illus. by Bruce Degen. New York: Simon & Schuster. *Bizz Buzz Chug-A-Chug: Jesse Bear's Sounds.* (1997); *Hooray for Blue: Jesse Bear's Colors.* (1997); *I Love You, Mama, Any Time of Year.* (Jesse Bear Board Book). (1997); *I Love You, Papa, In All Kinds of Weather.* (Jesse Bear Board Book). (1997); *Jesse Bear, What Will You Wear?* (1996).

Choosing Colors. (1995). Photos by Sandra Lousada. New York: Dutton Children's Books/Playskool.

Cousins, Lucy. New York: Dutton Children's Books. *"Humpty Dumpty" and Other Nursery Rhymes.* (1996); *"Jack and Jill" and Other Nursery Rhymes.* (1996); *"Little Miss Muffet" and Other Nursery Rhymes.* (1997); *"Wee Willie Winkie" and Other Nursery Rhymes.* (1997). (Board books)

Day, Alexandra. (1996). *Good Dog, Carl.* First Little Simon Board Book edition. New York: Simon & Schuster.

Degen, Bruce. (1995). *Jamberry.* First Board Book edition. New York: Harper-Collins.

De Paola, Tomie. (1997). *Strega Nona.* First Little Simon Board Book edition. New York: Simon & Schuster.

Ehlert, Lois. (1996). *Eating the Alphabet.* First Red Wagon Books. Orlando, FL: Harcourt Brace.

Ehlert, Lois. (1997a). *Color Farm.* First Board Book edition. New York: Harper-Collins.

Ehlert, Lois. (1997b). *Color Zoo*. First Board Book edition. New York: Harper-Collins.

Fleming, Denise. (1997). *Count!* First Board Book edition. New York: Holt.

Hooker, Yvonne. (1989). Poke and Look books. Illus. by Carlo A. Michelini. New York: Grosset & Dunlap. *One Green Frog* (1989); *Wheels Go Round* (1989).

Hopp, Lisa. (1997). *Circus of Colors*. Illus. by Chiara Bordoni. Poke and Look book. New York: Grosset & Dunlap.

Isadora, Rachel. (1991). *I Touch*. New York: Greenwillow.

Keats, Ezra Jack. (1996). *The Snowy Day*. New York: Viking.

Kirk, David. (1997). *Miss Spider's Tea Party: The Counting Book*. First Board Book edition. New York: Callaway & Kirk/Scholastic Press.

Lewison, Wendy. (1992). *Nighty Night*. Illus. by Giulia Orecchia. Poke and Look book. New York: Grosset & Dunlap.

Lundell, Margaretta. (1989). *Land of Colors*. Illus. by Nadia Pazzaglia. Poke and Look book. New York: Grosset & Dunlap.

Lundell, Margo. (1990). *What Does Baby See?* Illus. by Roberta Pagnoni. Poke and Look book. New York: Putnam & Grosset.

Martin, Bill. Illus. by Eric Carle. First Board Book editions. New York: Holt. *Brown Bear, Brown Bear, What Do You See?* (1996); *Polar Bear, Polar Bear, What Do You Hear?* (1997).

Martin, Bill, & Archambault, John. (1993). *Chicka Chicka ABC*. Illus. by Lois Ehlert. First Little Simon Board Book edition. New York: Simon & Schuster.

Marzollo, Jean. (1997). *I Spy Little Book*. Illus. by Walter Wick. New York: Scholastic.

Marzollo, Jean. (1998). *I Spy Little Animals*. Photos by Walter Wick. New York: Scholastic.

McBratney, Sam. (1996). *Guess How Much I Love You*. First Board Book edition. Cambridge, MA: Candlewick Press.

McMullan, Kate. (1998). *If You Were My Bunny*. Illus. by David McPhail. First Board Book edition. St. Paul, MN: Cartwheel Books.

Ogden, Betina, illus. (1995). *Busy Farmyard*. So Tall board book. New York: Grosset & Dunlap.

Opie, Iona Archibald. Illus. by Rosemary Wells. Mother Goose Board Book series. Cambridge, MA: Candlewick Press. *Humpty Dumpty and Other Rhymes* (1997); *Little Boy Blue and Other Rhymes* (1997); *Pussycat, Pussycat and Other Rhymes* (1997); *Wee Willie Winkie and Other Rhymes* (1997).

Piper, Watty. (1991). *The Little Engine That Could*. Illus. by Christina Ong. New York: Platt & Munk.

Pfister, Marcus. (1998a). *Hopper*. New York: North-South Books.

Pfister, Marcus. (1998b). *Hopper Hunts for Spring.* New York: North-South Books.

Pfister, Marcus. (1998c). *The Rainbow Fish.* New York: North-South Books.

Pfister, Marcus. (1998d). *Rainbow Fish to the Rescue.* New York: North-South Books.

Potter, Beatrix. (1996). *The Tale of Peter Rabbit.* Illus. by Florence Graham. Pudgy Pal Board Book. New York: Grosset & Dunlap.

Pragoff, Fiona. Fiona Pragoff Board Books. New York: Simon & Schuster. *Baby Days* (1995); *Baby Plays* (1995); *Baby Ways* (1994); *It's Fun to Be One* (1994); *It's Fun to Be Two* (1994).

Raffi. First Board Book editions. New York: Crown Publishers. *Baby Beluga.* Illus. by Ashley Wolff (1997); *Wheels on the Bus.* Illus. by Sylvie Kantorovitz Wickstrom (1998).

Rathmann, Peggy. (1996). *Good Night, Gorilla.* New York: G. P. Putnam.

Reasoner, Charles & Hardt, Vicky. (1989). *Alphabite! A Funny Feast from A to Z.* New York: Price Stern Sloan.

Rey, H. A., & Rey, Margret. (1998). Boston: Houghton Mifflin. *Curious George and the Bunny; Curious George's ABC's; Curious George's Are You Curious?; Curious George's Opposites.* (Board books)

Rosen, Michael. (1997). *We're Going on a Bear Hunt.* Illus. by Helen Oxenbury. First Little Simon Board Book edition. New York: Simon & Schuster.

Seuss, Dr. Bright and Early Board Book series. New York: Random House. *Dr. Seuss's ABC* (1996); *The Foot Book* (1997); *Mr. Brown Can Moo, Can You?* (1996); *The Shape of Me and Other Stuff* (1997); *There's a Wocket in My Pocket* (1996).

Snapshot Board Book series. (1994). New York: Dorling Kindersley. *All about Baby* by Stephen Shott; *Baby and Friends* by Paul Bricknell; *Good Morning, Baby* by Jo Foord et al.; *Good Night, Baby* by Mike Good & Stephen Shott.

Waddell, Martin. (1992). *Owl Babies.* Illus. by Patrick Benson. First Board Book edition. Cambridge, MA: Candlewick Press.

Wells, Rosemary. (1998a). *Max's Birthday.* Max Board Book. New York: Dial Books for Young Readers.

Wells, Rosemary. (1998b). *Old MacDonald.* Bunny Reads Back Board Book. New York: Scholastic.

Wilkes, Angela. (1997). *My First Word Board Book.* New York: Dorling Kindersley.

Williams, Sue. (1996). *I Went Walking.* Illus. by Julie Vivas. First Red Wagon Books edition. Orlando, FL: Harcourt Brace.

Williams, Vera B. (1997). *More, More, More Said the Baby.* First Tupelo Board Book edition. New York: William Morrow.

Wood, Jakki. (1996). *Moo Moo, Brown Cow.* Illus. by Rog Bonner. First Red Wagon Board book. Orlando, FL: Harcourt Brace.

Ziefert, Harriet. (1996a). *Food!* New York: Dorling Kindersley.

Ziefert, Harriet. (1996b). *My Clothes.* New York: Dorling Kindersley.

Ziefert, Harriet. (1997). *Let's Get Dressed.* Illus. by Susan Baum. New York: Dorling Kindersley.

Books for Three- and Four-Year-Olds

By three years of age, children will listen to books for six to ten minutes. They enjoy books that include things outside of the home. Community helpers are appealing to them. They want to know what mail carriers, police officers, bakers, doctors, nurses, and garbage collectors do, and how and why they do these things.

Like three-year-olds, four-year-old children like books that explain the "hows" and "whys." However, their attention span is now longer. Typically, they can listen to a book for eight to twelve minutes. You will find that these children are becoming increasingly curious about the world around them. After you finish reading the book, they may enjoy looking at the picture. The chart on the following page contains selection criteria for children's books by age.

Three-, four-, and five-year-olds enjoy books where animals display human characteristics. These animals often think, talk, and act like humans. Examples include "The Three Little Pigs," "Little Red Riding Hood," and "The Tale of Peter Rabbit." They also enjoy books on dogs as pets, such as "Harry, the Dirty Dog."

Books for Five-Year-Olds

Five-year-olds are delightful. They can listen to a book for ten to fifteen minutes. Moreover, they will share their likes and dislikes. Children at this age enjoy books that take them beyond the here and now, adding to their knowledge. They also enjoy stories containing fantasy, such as "The Three Little Pigs."

Changing Interests of Preschoolers

Choose books that complement the child's changing interests. Children are more motivated to look at and listen to books that interest them. Books also need to be chosen on the basis of a child's developmental level. Consequently, books that appeal to infants and toddlers will differ from those for older preschoolers. The following is a list of books that have been carefully selected by a children's literature specialist to represent the interests of preschool children.

Storytelling and Fingerplays

Selection Criteria for Children's Books by Age

Age	Criteria for Books
Infant/Toddler	• Thick pages • Pictures of simple objects • Large, clearly outlined pictures
Two-Year-Old	• Imitate familiar sounds • Repeat their own experiences—daily lives, families, and living problems, including fear, appearance, stress • Contain large pages with big pictures • Include the familiar
Three-Year-Old	• Include things and people outside the home • Explain the "whos" and "whys" • Interpret the child's own experiences • Contain words like *surprise* and *secret*
Four-Year-Old	• Include humor in reality • Contain new words • Explain the "hows" and "whys" • Include exaggeration
Five-Year-Old	• Add something to their knowledge • Take them beyond the here and now • Contain new information and relationships between familiar facts

Source: Herr, J. (1998). *Working with Young Children.* Finley, IL: Goodheart, Wilcox.

Books for Preschoolers, by Subject

Ants

Chinery, Michael. (1991). *Ant.* Mahwah, NJ: Troll. (Paperback)

Climo, Shirley. (1995). *The Little Red Ant and the Great Big Crumb: A Mexican Fable.* New York: Clarion Books.

Cole, Joanna. (1996). *The Magic School Bus Gets Ants in Its Pants: A Book about Ants.* New York: Scholastic.

Demuth, Patricia Brennan. (1994). *Those Amazing Ants.* Illus. by S. D. Schindler. New York: Simon & Schuster.

Dorros, Arthur. (1987). *Ant Cities.* Bellevue, WA: Ty Crowell.

Fowler, Allan. (1998). *Inside an Ant Colony.* Chicago: Children's Press.

Hepworth, Catherine. (1992). *Antics! An Alphabetical Anthology.* New York: G. P. Putnam.

Pinczes, Elinor. (1993). *One Hundred Hungry Ants.* Illus. by Bonnie MacKain. Boston: Houghton Mifflin.

Savage, Stephen. (1995). *Ant.* Illus. by Clive Pritchard. Cincinnati, OH: Thomson Learning.

Ants, Multimedia

Ants: Hunters and Gardeners [video]. (1986). Washington, DC: National Geographic Society.

The Ants Go Marching [book and cassette]. (1992). Bothell, WA: Wright Group.

"Ants on Parade" (1993). On *Songs about Insects, Bugs and Squiggly Things* [compact disc]. Long Branch, NJ: Kimbo Educational.

Magic School Bus Gets Ants in Its Pants [video]. (1997). New York: Distributed by Kidvision.

Scruggs, Joe. *Ants* [cassette or compact disc]. (1994). Shadow Play Records and Video/Educational Graphics Press.

Apples

Aliki. (1991). *The Story of Johnny Appleseed.* New York: Simon & Schuster.

Early, Margaret. (1991). *William Tell.* New York: Abrams.

Fisher, Leonard Everett. (1996). *William Tell.* New York: Farrar, Straus & Giroux.

Hall, Zoe. (1996). *The Apple Pie Tree.* Illus. by Shari Halpern. New York: Scholastic.

Hodges, Margaret. (1997). *The True Tale of Johnny Appleseed.* New York: Holiday House.

Lindbergh, Reeve. (1990). *Johnny Appleseed.* Illus. by Kathy Jakobsen. Boston: Little, Brown.

Maestro, Betsy. (1992). *How Do Apples Grow?* New York: HarperCollins, 1992.

Marzollo, Jean. (1997). *I Am an Apple.* Illus. by Judith Moffatt. St. Paul, MN: Cartwheel Books. (Paperback)

Micucci, Charles. (1992). *The Life and Times of the Apple.* New York: Orchard Books.

Patent, Dorothy Hinshaw. (1998). *Apple Trees.* Photos by William Munoz. Minneapolis: Lerner Publications.

Priceman, Marjorie. (1994). *How to Make an Apple Pie and See the World.* New York: Knopf.

Rockwell, Anne. (1991). *Apples and Pumpkins.* New York: Simon & Schuster.

Slawson, Michele Benoit. (1994). *Apple Picking Time.* Illus. by Deborah Kogan Ray. New York: Crown Publishers.

Tryon, Leslie. (1993). *Albert's Field Trip.* New York: Simon & Schuster.

Apples, Multimedia

Apples [video]. (1996). DeBeck Educational Video.

Kunstler, James Howard. (1992). *Johnny Appleseed* [video]. Told by Garrison Keillor. Rabbit Ears.

Art

Anholt, Laurence. (1994). *Camille and the Sunflowers: A Story about Vincent Van Gogh.* Hauppauge, NY: Barron's Educational Series.

Auch, Mary Jane. (1996). *Eggs Mark the Spot.* New York: Holiday House.

Blizzard, Gladys. Come Look with Me series. West Palm Beach, FL: Lickle Publishing. *Animals in Art* (1992); *Enjoying Art with Children* (1991); *Exploring Landscape Art with Children* (1992); *World of Play* (1993).

Catalanotto, Peter. (1995). *The Painter.* New York: Orchard Books.

Cooney, Barbara. (1990). *Hattie and the Wild Waves.* New York: Viking.

Crespi, Francesca. (1995). *A Walk in Monet's Garden: Full Color Pop-Up with Guided Tour.* Boston: Little, Brown.

De Paola, Tomie. (1989). *Art Lesson.* New York: G. P. Putnam.

Dixon, Annabelle. (1990). *Clay.* Photos by Ed Barber. Ada, OK: Garrett.

Dunrea, Olivier. (1995). *The Painter Who Loved Chickens.* New York: Farrar, Straus & Giroux.

Florian, Douglas. (1993). *Painter.* New York: Greenwillow.

Folk Art Counting Book. (1992). Developed by Amy Watson and the staff of the Abby Aldrich Rockefeller Folk Art Center. New York: Abrams.

Hest, Amy. (1996). *Jamaica Louise James.* Illus. by Sheila White Samton. Cambridge, MA: Candlewick Press.

Hurd, Thacher. (1996). *Art Dog.* New York: HarperCollins.

Jeunesse, Gallimard. (1991). *Colors.* Illus. by P.M. Valet. New York: Scholastic.

Le Tord, Bijou. (1995). *Blue Butterfly: A Story about Claude Monet.* New York: Bantam.

Lynn, Sara. (1993). *Play with Paint.* Minneapolis: Carolrhoda Books.

Moon, Nicola. (1997). *Lucy's Picture.* Illus. by Lynn Munsinger. New York: Dial Books.

Porte, Barbara Ann. (1995). *Chickens Chickens.* Illus. by Greg Henry. New York: Orchard Books.

Richardson, Joy. (1993). *Inside the Museum: A Children's Guide to the Metropolitan Museum of Art.* New York: Abrams.

Rockwell, Anne F. (1993). *Mr. Panda's Painting.* New York: Simon & Schuster.

Stanley, Diane. (1994). *The Gentleman and the Kitchen Maid.* Illus. by Dennis Nolan. New York: Dial Books.

Venezia, Mike. (1988–97). Getting to Know the World's Greatest Artists series. Chicago: Children's Press. (23+ titles)

Winter, Jeanette. (1996). *Josefina.* Orlando, FL: Harcourt Brace.

Wolestein, Diane. (1992). *Little Mouse's Painting.* Illus. by Jaryjane Begin. New York: William Morrow.

Yenawine, Philip. (1991). *Colors.* The Museum of Modern Art, New York. New York: Delacorte Press.

Art, Multimedia

I Want to Be an Artist [video]. (1993). Glenview, IL: Crystal Productions.

Kid Pix Studio [CD-ROM]. (1994). Broderbund.

New Kid Pix [CD-ROM]. (1996). Broderbund.

Paint, Write and Play [CD-ROM]. (1996). Fremont, CA: Learning Company.

Polisar, Barry Louis. (1994). *Barry's Scrapbook: A Window Into Art* [video]. ALA Video/Library Video Network.

Rylant, Cynthia. (1990). *All I See* [video]. Hightstown, NJ: McGraw-Hill Media.

Birds

Arnosky, Jim. (1992). *Crinkleroot's Guide to Knowing the Birds.* New York: Simon & Schuster.

Arnosky, Jim. (1993). *Crinkleroot's 25 Birds Every Child Should Know.* New York: Bradbury Press.

Arnosky, Jim. (1997). *Watching Water Birds.* Washington, DC: National Geographic Society.

Bennett, Penelope. (1995). *Town Parrot.* Illus. by Sue Heap. Cambridge, MA: Candlewick Press.

Berger, Bruce. (1995). *A Dazzle of Hummingbirds.* Illus. by John Chellman. Morristown, NJ: Silver Burdett.

Bernhard, Emery. (1994). *Eagles: Lions of the Sky.* Illus. by Durga Bernhard. New York: Holiday House.

Brenner, Barbara, & Takaya, Julia. (1996). *Chibi: A True Story from Japan.* Illus. by June Otani. New York: Clarion Books.

Cannon, Janell. (1993). *Stellaluna.* Orlando, FL: Harcourt Brace.

Cherry, Lynne. (1997). *Flute's Journey: The Life of a Wood Thrush.* San Diego, CA: Gulliver Books.

Demuth, Patricia. (1994). *Cradles in the Trees: The Story of Bird Nests.* Illus. by Suzanne Barnes. New York: Simon & Schuster.

Ehlert, Lois. (1997). *Cuckoo: A Mexican Folktale.* Orlando, FL: Harcourt Brace.

Esbensen, Barbara Juster. (1991). *Tiger with Wings: The Great Horned Owl.* Illus. by Mary Barrett Brown. New York: Orchard Books.

Ezra, Mark. (1997). *The Frightened Little Owl.* Illus. by Gavin Rowe. New York: Crocodile Books.

Flanagan, Alice K. (1996). New True Book series. Chicago: Children's Press. *Desert Birds; Night Birds; Seabirds; Songbirds; Talking Birds.*

Fontanel, Beatrice. (1992). *The Penguin.* Illus. by Valerie Tracqui. Watertown, MA: Charlesbridge Publishers. (Paperback)

Foster, Joanna. (1995). *The Magpies' Nest.* Illus. by Julie Downing. New York: Clarion Books.

Gans, Roma, and Paul Mirocha. (1996). *How Do Birds Find Their Way?* New York: HarperCollins.

Gibbons, Gail. (1997). *Gulls—Gulls—Gulls.* New York: Holiday House.

Gibbons, Gail. (1998). *Soaring with the Wind: The Bald Eagle.* New York: William Morrow.

Jenkins, Priscilla Belz. (1995). *Nest Full of Eggs.* Illus. by Lizzy Rockwell. New York: HarperCollins.

Kalbacken, Joan. (1997). *Peacocks and Peahens.* Chicago: Children's Press.

Lewin, Betsy. (1995). *Booby Hatch.* New York: Clarion Books.

Maynard, Thane. (1997). *Ostriches.* Mankato, MN: Child's World.

Storytelling and Fingerplays

Mazzola, Frank. (1997). *Counting Is for the Birds*. Watertown, MA: Charlesbridge Publishers.

McMillan, Bruce. (1995). *Nights of the Pufflings*. Boston: Houghton Mifflin.

Morrison, Gordon. (1998). *Bald Eagle*. Boston: Houghton Mifflin.

Neitzel, Shirley. (1997). *The House I'll Build for the Wrens*. New York: Greenwillow.

Owens, Mary Beth. (1993). *Counting Cranes*. Boston: Little, Brown.

Parry-Jones, Jemima. (1992). *Amazing Birds of Prey*. Illus. by Mike Dunning. New York: Knopf.

Pfeffer, Wendy. (1996). *Mute Swans*. Morristown, NJ: Silver Burdett Press.

Rau, Dana Meachen. (1995). *Robin at Hickory Street*. Illus. by Joel Snyder. Norwalk, CT: Soundprints/Smithsonian Institution.

Rockwell, Anne. (1992). *Our Yard Is Full of Birds*. New York: Macmillan.

Royston, Angela. (1992). *Birds*. New York: Alladin Books.

Savage, Stephen. (1995a). *Duck*. Illus. by Steve Lings. Cincinatti, OH: Thomson Learning.

Savage, Stephen. (1995b). *Seagull*. Illus. by Andre Boos. Cincinnati, OH: Thomson Learning.

Sill, Cathryn P. (1991). *About Birds: A Guide for Children*. Illus. by John Sill. Atlanta: Peachtree Publishers.

Swinburne, Stephen R. (1996). *Swallows in the Birdhouse*. Illus. by Robin Brickman. Brookfield, CT: Millbrook Press.

Torres, Leyla. (1993). *Subway Sparrow*. New York: Farrar, Straus & Giroux.

Willis, Nancy Carol. (1996). *The Robins in Your Backyard*. Montchanin, DE: Cucumber Island Storytellers.

Birds, Multimedia

"Birds and How They Grow." (1993) On *Animals and How They Grow* [CD-ROM]. Washington, DC: National Geographic Society.

Eastman, P.D. (1991). *Are You My Mother? Plus Two More P. D. Eastman Classics* [video]. New York: Random House Video.

Flying, Trying, and Honking Around [video]. (1994). Washington, DC: National Geographic Kids Video.

Blue

Bogacki, Tomek, & Bogacki, Tomasz. (1998). *Story of a Blue Bird.* New York: Farrar, Straus & Giroux.

Campilonga, Margaret S. (1996). *Blue Frogs.* Illus. by Carl Lindahl. Circleville, NY: Chicken Soup Press.

Childress, Mark. (1996). *Joshua and the Big Bad Blue Crabs.* Illus. by Mary B. Brown. Boston: Little, Brown.

Davies, Nicola. (1997). *Big Blue Whale.* Illus. by Nick Maland. Cambridge, MA: Candlewick Press.

Demarest, Chris L. (1995). *My Blue Boat.* Orlando, FL: Harcourt Brace.

Hausman, Gerald. (1998). *The Story of Blue Elk.* Illus. by Kristina Rodanas. Boston: Houghton Mifflin.

Inkpen, Mick. (1996). *The Blue Balloon* (Vol. 1). Boston: Little, Brown.

Jensen, Patsy. (1993). *Paul Bunyan and His Blue Ox.* Illus. by Jean Pidgeon. Mahwah, NJ: Troll.

Lewin, Betsy. (1995). *Booby Hatch.* New York: Clarion Books.

Lionni, Leo. (1995). *Little Blue and Little Yellow.* New York: Mulberry Books. (Paperback)

Onyefulu, Ifeoma. (1997). *Chidi Only Likes Blue: An African Book of Colors.* New York: Cobblehill Books.

Oram, Hiawyn. (1993). *Out of the Blue: Poems about Color.* Illus. by David McKee. New York: Hyperion.

Ostheeren, Ingrid, et al. (1996). *The Blue Monster.* New York: North-South Books.

Pulver, Robin. (1994). *Mrs. Toggle's Beautiful Blue Shoe.* Illus. by R. W. Alley. New York: Simon & Schuster.

Whitman, Candaceaut. (1998). *Bring on the Blue.* New York: Abbeville Press.

Woolfitt, Gabrielle. (1992). *Blue (Colors).* Minneapolis: Carolrhoda Books.

Blue, Multimedia

"The Big Piece of Blue Corn." (1991). On *Tall Tales, Yarns and Whoppers* [video]. Atlas Video.

"Look Blue." (1976). On *There's Music in the Colors* [cassette]. Long Branch, NJ: Kimbo Educational.

Storytelling and Fingerplays

Breads

Barton, Byron. (1993). *The Little Red Hen.* New York: HarperCollins.

Carle, Eric. (1995). *Walter the Baker.* New York: Simon & Schuster.

Curtis, Neil, & Greenland, Peter. (1992). *How Bread Is Made (I Wonder).* Minneapolis: Lerner Publications.

Czernecky, Stefan, et al. (1992). *The Sleeping Bread.* New York: Hyperion.

De Paola, Tomie. (1997). *Antonio the Bread Boy.* New York: G. P. Putnam.

Dooley, Norah. (1995). *Everybody Bakes Bread.* Illus. by Peter J. Thornton. Minneapolis: Carolrhoda Books.

Dragonwagon, Crescent. (1991). *This Is the Bread I Baked for Ned.* Illus. by Isadore Seltzer. New York: Simon & Schuster.

Flanagan, Romie, & Flanagan, Alice K. (1998). *Mr. Santizo's Tasty Treats.* Chicago: Children's Press.

Gershator, David, et al. (1995). *Bread Is for Eating.* New York: Holt.

Granowsky, Alvin. (1996). *Help Yourself, Little Red Hen! (Another Side to the Story).* Illus. by Wendy Edelson & Jane K. Manning. Austin, TX: Raintree/Steck Vaughn.

Heath, Amy. (1992). *Sophie's Role.* Illus. by Sheila Hamanaka. New York: Simon & Schuster.

Hoban, Russell. (1993). *Bread and Jam for Frances.* Illus. by Lillian Hoban. New York: HarperCollins.

Hoopes, Lyn Littlefield. (1996). *The Unbeatable Bread.* Illus. by Brad Sneed. New York: Dial Books.

Pellam, David. (1991). *Sam's Sandwich.* New York: Dutton. (Flap book)

Wolff, Ferida. (1993). *Seven Loaves of Bread.* Illus. by Katie Keller. New York: William Morrow.

Breads, Multimedia

Greg and Steve. (1986) "Muffin Man." On *We All Live Together* (Vol. 2) [compact disc]. Los Angeles: Youngheart Records.

"The Muffin Man." (1995). On *Toddler Tunes: Twenty-Six Classic Songs for Toddlers* [compact disc]. (1995). Franklin, TN: Cedarmont Music; Distributed by Benson Music Group.

Brushes

Bang, Molly Garrett. (1992). *Tye May and the Magic Brush*. New York: Mulberry Books. (Paperback)

De Paola, Tomie. (1988). *The Legend of the Indian Paintbrush*. New York: G. P. Putnam.

Demi. (1988). *Liang and the Magic Paintbrush*. New York: Holt. (Paperback)

Florian, Douglas. (1993). *A Painter (How He Works)*. New York: Greenwillow.

Grohmann, Almute, et al. (1998). *Dragon Teeth and Parrot Beaks: Even Creatures Brush Their Teeth*. Carol Stream, IL: Edition Q.

Hurd, Thacher. (1996). *Art Dog*. New York: HarperCollins.

Kleven, Elisa. (1992). *The Lion and the Little Red Bird*. New York: Dutton.

Langreuter, Jutta. (1997). *Little Bear Brushes His Teeth*. Illus. by Vera Sobat. Brookfield, CT: Millbrook Press.

Buildings

Ackerman, Karen. (1995). *The Sleeping Porch*. Illus. by Elizabeth Sayles. New York: William Morrow.

Barton, Byron. (1997). *Machines at Work*. New York: HarperCollins.

Dorros, Arthur. (1992). *This Is My House*. New York: Scholastic.

Gibbons, Gail. (1986). *Up Goes the Skyscraper!* New York: Macmillan.

Gibbons, Gail. (1990). *How a House Is Built*. New York: Holiday House.

Hautzig, David. (1994). *At the Supermarket*. New York: Orchard Books.

Hoban, Tana. (1997). *Construction Zone*. New York: Greenwillow.

James, Alan. (1989). *Homes on Water*. Minneapolis: Lerner Publications.

Jaspersohn, William. (1994). *My Hometown Library*. Boston: Houghton Mifflin.

Kalman, Bobbie. (1994). *Homes around the World*. New York: Crabtree Publishing.

McDonald, Megan. (1996). *My House Has Stars*. Illus. by Peter Catalanotto. New York: Orchard Books.

Miller, Marilyn. (1996). *Behind the Scenes at the Shopping Mall*. Illus. by Ingo Fast. Austin, TX: Raintree/Steck Vaughn.

Morris, Ann. (1992). *Houses and Homes*. Photos by Ken Heyman. New York: Lothrop, Lee & Shepard.

Novak, Matt. (1996). *Elmer Blunt's Open House*. New York: Orchard Books. (Paperback)

Storytelling and Fingerplays

Richardson, Joy. (1994). *Skyscrapers.* New York: Franklin Watts.

Rounds, Glen. (1995). *Sod Houses on the Great Plains.* New York: Holiday House.

Seltzer, Isadore. (1992). *The House I Live In: At Home in America.* Colchester, CT: Atheneum.

Shelby, Anne. (1996). *The Someday House.* Illus. by Rosanne Litzinger. New York: Orchard Books.

Shemie, Bonnie. (1990). *Houses of Bark.* San Francisco: Children's Book Press.

Yeoman, John. (1995). *The Do-It-Yourself House That Jack Built.* Illus. by Quentin Blake. Colchester, CT: Atheneum.

Buildings, Multimedia

Building Skyscrapers [video]. (1994). New York: David Alpert Associates.

Community Construction Kit [CD-ROM]. (1998). Watertown, MA: Tom Snyder Productions.

Dig Hole, Build House [video]. (1994). Gig Harbor, WA: Real World Video.

The Fire Station [video]. (1990). Washington, D.C: National Geographic Society.

Gryphon Bricks [CD-ROM]. (1996). San Diego, CA: Gryphon Software Corp.

Let's Build a House [video]. (1996). San Diego, CA: Video Connections.

Camping

Bauer, Marion Dane. (1995). *When I Go Camping with Grandma.* Illus. by Allen Garns. Mankato, MN: Bridgewater Books.

Brillhart, Julie. (1997). *When Daddy Took Us Camping.* Niles, IL: Albert Whitman & Co.

Brown, M. K. (1995). *Let's Go Camping with Mr. Sillypants.* New York: Crown Publishers.

Brown, Marc Tolon. (1984). *Arthur Goes to Camp.* Madison, WI: Demco Media.

Christelow, Eileen. (1998). *Jerome Camps Out.* New York: Clarion Books.

Duffey, Betsy. (1996). *Camp Knock Knock.* Illus. by Fiona Dunbar. New York: Delacorte Press.

Hoff, Syd. (1996). *Danny and the Dinosaur Go to Camp.* New York: Harper-Collins.

Howe, James. (1995). *Pinky and Rex and the Double-Dad Weekend.* Illus. by Melissa Sweet. Colchester, CT: Atheneum.

Kalman, Bobbie D. (1995). *Summer Camp.* New York: Crabtree Publishing.

Locker, Thomas. (1984). *Where the River Begins.* New York: Dial Books.

Rand, Gloria. (1996). *Willie Takes a Hike.* Illus. by Ted Rand. Orlando, FL: Harcourt Brace.

Say, Allen. (1989). *The Lost Lake.* Boston: Houghton Mifflin.

Shaw, Nancy E. (1994). *Sheep Take a Hike.* Illus. by Margot Apple. Boston: Houghton Mifflin.

Tafuri, Nancy. (1987). *Do Not Disturb.* New York: William Morrow.

Williams, Vera B. (1983). *Three Days on a River in a Red Canoe.* New York: Greenwillow.

Camping, Multimedia

Barney's Campfire Sing-Along [video]. (1990). Allen, TX: Lyons Group.

Let's Go Camping [video]. (1995). Burlington, VT: Vermont Story Works.

Mercer Mayer's Just Me and My Dad [CD-ROM]. (1996). New York: GT Interactive Software.

Cars, Trucks, and Buses

Bingham, Caroline. Mighty Machines series. New York: Dorling Kindersley. *Big Rig.* Illus. by Mary Ling (1996); *Fire Truck: And Other Emergency Machines* (1995); *Monster Machines* (1998); *Race Car* (1996).

Blanchard, Arlene. (1995). *The Dump Truck.* Illus. by Tony Wells. Cambridge, MA: Candlewick Press.

Crews, Donald. (1984). *School Bus.* New York: William Morrow.

Eick, Jean. (1997). *Giant Dump Trucks.* Illus. by Michael Sellner. Minneapolis: Abdo & Daughters.

Gibbons, Gail. (1987). *Fill It Up: All about Service Stations.* New York: HarperCollins.

Gray, Libba Moore. (1994). *The Little Black Truck.* Illus. by Elizabeth Sayles. New York: Simon & Schuster.

Howland, Naomi. (1994). *ABC Drive!: A Car Trip Alphabet.* New York: Clarion Books.

Katz, Bobbi. (1997). *Truck Talk: Rhymes on Wheels.* St. Paul, MN: Cartwheel Books.

Kirk, Daniel. (1997). *Trash Trucks.* New York: G. P. Putnam.

Storytelling and Fingerplays

Oxlade, Chris. (1997). *Car (Take It Apart).* Morristown, NJ: Silver Burdett.

Mahy, Margaret. (1994). *The Rattlebang Picnic.* Illus. by Steven Kellogg. New York: Dial Books.

Marston, Hope Irvin. (1993). *Big Rigs.* New York: Cobblehill Books.

Patrick, Denise Lewis. (1993). *The Car Washing Street.* Illus. by John Ward. New York: William Morrow.

Radford, Derek. (1997). *Harry at the Garage.* Cambridge, MA: Candlewick Press.

Ready, Dee. (1998). *School Bus Driver.* New York: Capstone.

Richardson, Joy. (1994). *Cars.* New York: Franklin Watts.

Rockwell, Anne F. (1992). *Cars.* New York: Dutton.

Royston, Angela. (1991). *Cars.* Photos by Tim Ridley. New York: Macmillan.

Wilkins, Verna Allette, et al. (1993). *Mum Can Fix It.* Lawrenceville, NJ: Red Sea Press.

Cars, Trucks, and Buses, Multimedia

Big Red [video]. (1993). Mill Valley, CA: Fire Dog Pictures.

Firefighter [CD-ROM]. (1994). New York: Simon & Schuster Interactive.

How a Car Is Built [video]. (1995). Think Media.

K.C.'s First Bus Ride [video]. (1994). KidSafety of America.

Murphy, Jane Lawliss. (1997). *Cars, Trucks and Trains* [compact disc]. Long Branch, NJ: Kimbo Educational.

Snowplows at Work [video]. (1994). Truckee, CA: Bill Aaron Productions.

Cats

Allen, Sarah. (1996). *Cats.* Illus. by Charlotte Hard. Hauppauge, NY: Barron's Educational Series.

Bare, Colleen Stanley. (1995). *Toby the Tabby Kitten.* New York: Cobblehill.

Buck, Nola. (1997). *Oh, Cats.* Illus. Nadine Bernard Westcott. New York: HarperCollins.

Casey, Patricia. (1996). *My Cat Jack.* Cambridge, MA: Candlewick Press.

Cole, Joanna. (1995). *My New Kitten.* Photos by Margaret Miller. New York: William Morrow.

Farjeon, Eleanor. (1996). *Cats Sleep Anywhere*. Illus. by Anne Mortimer. New York: HarperCollins.

Gibbons, Gail. (1996). *Cats*. New York: Holiday House.

Hall, Donald. (1994). *I Am the Dog, I Am the Cat*. Illus. by Barry Moser. New York: Dial Books.

Harper, Isabelle. (1995). *My Cats Nick and Nora*. Illus. by Barry Moser. New York: Scholastic.

Hirschi, Ron. (1991). *What Is a Cat?* New York: Walker & Co.

Hoban, Julia. (1992). *Buzby*. Illus. by John Himmelman. New York: Harper-Collins.

Kallan, Stuart A. (1996). Cats series. Minneapolis: Abdo & Daughters. *Abyssinian Cats; Siamese Cats; Tabby Cats*.

Kuklin, Susan. (1988). *Taking My Cat to the Vet*. New York: Bradbury Press.

Newberry, Clare Turlay. (1993). *April's Kittens*. New York: HarperCollins.

Petersen-Fleming et al. (1994). *Kitten Care and Critters, Too!* New York: William Morrow.

Say, Allen. (1997). *Allison*. Illus. by Susan Guevara. Boston: Houghton Mifflin.

Scott, Carey. (1997). *Kittens*. New York: Dorling Kindersley.

Simon, Seymour. (1991). *Big Cats*. New York: HarperCollins.

Soto, Gary. (1995). *Chato's Kitchen*. Illus. by Susan Guevara. New York: G. P. Putnam.

Sykes, Julie. (1996). *This and That*. Illus. by Tanya Linch. New York: Farrar, Straus & Giroux.

Wheeler, Cindy. (1994). *Bookstore Cat*. New York: Random House.

Wilson, Gina. (1995). *Prowlpuss*. Illus. by David Parkins. Cambridge, MA: Candlewick Press.

Cats, Multimedia

The Adventures of Milo and Otis [video]. (1989). Culver City, CA: Columbia TriStar Home Video.

Archambault, John. (1997). *Counting Kittens* [cassette and book]. Parsippany, NJ: Silver Press.

Brand, Oscar. (1994). *I Love Cats* [cassette]. Waterbury, VT: Alacazam!

Cat [video]. (1995). Eyewitness Video.

Cats in the Cradle [video]. (1997). Bethesda, MD: Discovery Communications.

Storytelling and Fingerplays

Christmas

Ammon, Richard. (1996). *An Amish Christmas.* Illus. by Pamela Patrick. Colchester, CT: Atheneum.

Barracca, Debra, et al. (1994). *A Taxi Dog Christmas.* Illus. by Alan Ayers. New York: Dial Books.

Brett, Jan. (1990). *Christmas Reindeer.* New York: G. P. Putnam.

Brimmer, Larry Dane. (1995). *Merry Christmas Old Armadillo.* Illus. by Dominic Catalano. Honesdale, PA: Boyds Mills Press.

Brown, Margaret Wise. (1994). *A Pussycat's Christmas.* Newly illus. by Anne Mortimer. New York: HarperCollins.

Brown, Margaret Wise. (1996). *On Christmas Eve.* Newly illus. by Nancy Edwards Calder. New York: HarperCollins.

Burningham, John. (1993). *Harvey Slumfenburger's Christmas Present.* Cambridge, MA: Candlewick Press.

Carlstrom, Nancy White. (1995). *I Am Christmas.* Illus. by Lori McElrath-Eslick. Grand Rapids, MI: Wm. B. Eerdmans Publishing.

Ciavonne, Jean. (1995). *Carlos, Light the Farolito.* Illus. by Donna Clair. New York: Clarion Books.

Davis, Rebecca. (1995). *The 12 Days of Christmas.* Illus. by Linnea Asplind Riley. New York: Simon & Schuster.

Day, Alexandra. (1994). *Carl's Christmas.* Orlando, FL: Harcourt Brace.

De Paola, Tomie. (1994). *Legend of the Poinsettia.* New York: G. P. Putnam.

Fearrington, Ann. (1996). *Christmas Lights.* Boston: Houghton Mifflin.

Francisco, X. Mora. (1993). *La Gran Fiesta.* Fort Atkinson, WI: Highsmith Co.

George, William T. (1992). *Christmas at Long Pond.* Illus. by Lindsay Barrett George. New York: Greenwillow.

Hoffman, Mary. (1997). *An Angel Just Like Me.* Illus. by Cornelius Van Wright. New York: Dial Books.

Jordan, Sandra. (1993). *Christmas Tree Farm.* New York: Orchard Books.

Moore, Clement C. (1994). *The Night before Christmas: Told in Signed English.* Washington, DC: Gallaudet University Press.

Moore, Clement C. (1995). *Twas the Night before Christmas.* Illus. by Ted Rand. New York: North-South Books.

Moore, Clement C. (1996). *Twas the Night b'fore Christmas: An African-American Version.* Illus. by Melodye Rosales. New York: Scholastic.

Packard, Mary. (1997). *Christmas Kitten.* Illus. by Jenny Williams. San Francisco: Children's Book Press.

Rahaman, Vashanti. (1996). *O Christmas Tree*. Illus. by Frane Lessac. Honesdale, PA: Boyds Mills Press.

Rylant, Cynthia. (1997). *Silver Packages: An Appalachian Christmas Story*. Illus. by Chris K. Soentpiet. New York: Orchard Books.

Say, Allen. (1991). *Tree of Cranes*. Boston: Houghton Mifflin.

Stevenson, James. (1996). *The Oldest Elf*. New York: William Morrow.

Tompert, Ann. (1994). *A Carol for Christmas*. Illus. by Laura Kelly. New York: Simon & Schuster.

Waldron, Jan L. (1997). *Angel Pig and the Hidden Christmas*. Illus. by David M. McPhail. New York: Dutton.

Christmas, Multimedia

De Paola, Tomie. (1991). *Merry Christmas, Strega Nona* [cassette]. Read by Celeste Holm. Old Greenwich, CT: Listening Library.

A Multicultural Christmas [video]. (1993). Niles, IL: United Learning.

The Night before Christmas [CD-ROM]. (1991). Toronto.: Discis Knowledge Research.

Palmer, Hap. (1997). *Holiday Songs and Rhythms* [compact disc]. Educational Activities.

Raffi. (1983). *Raffi's Christmas Album* [cassette]. Long Branch, NJ: Kimbo Educational.

Circus

Bond, Michael. (1992). *Paddington at the Circus*. Illus. by John Lobban. New York: HarperCollins.

Burmingham, John. (1994). *Cannonball Simp*. Cambridge, MA: Candlewick Press.

Chwast, Seymour. (1993). *The Twelve Circus Rings*. Orlando, FL: Harcourt Brace.

De Paola, Tomie. (1992). *Jingle, the Christmas Clown*. New York: G. P. Putnam.

Duncan, Lois. (1993). *The Circus Comes Home: When the Greatest Show on Earth Rode the Rails*. Illus. by Joseph Janney Steinmetz. New York: Doubleday.

Ehlert, Lois. (1992). *Circus*. New York: HarperCollins.

Ernst, Lisa Campbell. (1996). *Ginger Jumps.* Madison, WI: Demco Media.

Johnson, Neil. (1995). *Big-Top Circus.* New York: Dial Books.

McCully, Emily Arnold. (1992). *Mirette on the Highwire.* New York: G. P. Putnam.

Paxton, Tom. (1997). *Engelbert Joins the Circus.* Illus. by Roberta Wilson. New York: William Morrow.

Schumaker, Ward. (1997). *Sing a Song of Circus.* Orlando, FL: Harcourt Brace.

Spier, Peter. (1992). *Peter Spier's Circus.* New York: Delacorte Press.

Vincent, Gabrielle. (1989). *Ernest and Celestine at the Circus.* New York: Greenwillow.

Ziefert, Harriet M. (1992). *Clown Games.* Illus. by Larry Stevens. New York: Viking.

Circus, Multimedia

Circus [video]. (1984). Edited by Steven Rosofsky. Chicago: Encyclopedia Britannica Educational Corporation.

Hanna, Jack. (1994). *A Day with the Greatest Show on Earth* [video]. Glastonbury, CT: VideoTours.

Petersham, Maud, & Petersham, Miska. "Circus Baby." On *Max's Chocolate Chicken and Other Stories for Young Children* [video]. (1993). Weston, CT: Children's Circle Home Video; Los Angeles, CA: Wood Knapp Video, distributors.

Rogers, Fred. (1995). *Circus Fun* [video]. Beverly Hills, CA: CBS/Fox Video.

Seuss, Dr. (1992). *Horton Hatches the Egg/If I Ran the Circus* [video]. Narrated by Billy Crystal. New York: Random House.

Clothing

Burton, Marilee Robin. (1994). *My Best Shoes.* Illus. by James E. Ransome. New York: William Morrow.

Havill, Juanita. (1993). *Jamaica and Brianna.* Illus. by Anne Sibley O'Brien. Boston: Houghton Mifflin.

Hilton, Nette. (1991). *The Long Red Scarf.* Illus. by Margaret Power. Minneapolis: Carolrhoda Books.

Howard, Elizabeth Fitzgerald. (1991). *Aunt Flossie's Hats and Crab Cakes Later.* Illus. by James Ransome. New York: Clarion Books.

Hurwitz, Johanna. (1993). *New Shoes for Silvia.* Illus. by Jerry Pinkney. New York: William Morrow.

Keller, Holly. (1995). *Rosata.* New York: Greenwillow.

London, Jonathan. (1992). *Froggy Gets Dressed.* Illus. by Frank Remkiewicz. New York: Viking.

Mendel, Lydia J. (1993). *All Dressed Up and Nowhere to Go.* Illus. by Normand Chartier. Boston: Houghton Mifflin.

Miller, Margaret. (1988). *Whose Hat?* New York: William Morrow.

Morris, Ann. (1989). *Hats, Hats, Hats.* Photos by Ken Heyman. New York: Lothrop, Lee & Shepard.

Morris, Ann. (1995). *Shoes, Shoes, Shoes.* New York: Lothrop, Lee & Shepard.

Murphy, Stuart. (1996). *A Pair of Socks.* Illus. by Lois Ehlert. New York: Harper-Collins.

Neitzel, Shirley. (1989). *The Jacket I Wear in the Snow.* Illus. by Nancy Winslow Parker. New York: Greenwillow.

Neitzel, Shirley. (1992). *The Dress I'll Wear to the Party.* Illus. by Nancy Winslow Parker. New York: Greenwillow.

O'Brien, Claire. (1997). *Sam's Sneaker Search.* Illus. by Charles Fuge. New York: Simon & Schuster.

Patrick, Denise Lewis. (1993). *Red Dancing Shoes.* Illus. by James Ransome. New York: William Morrow.

Pearson, Tracey Campbell. (1997). *The Purple Hat.* New York: Farrar, Straus & Giroux.

Serfozo, Mary. (1993). *Benjamin Bigfoot.* Illus. by Joseph A. Smith. New York: Margaret McElderry.

Small, David. (1996). *Fenwick's Suit.* New York: Farrar, Straus & Giroux.

Stoeke, Janet Morgan. (1994). *A Hat for Minerva Louise.* New York: Dutton.

Clothing, Multimedia

Jenkins, Ella. (1991). "One Two Buckle My Shoe." On *Ella Jenkins Live at the Smithsonian* [video]. Washington, DC: Smithsonian/Folkways.

London, Jonathan. (1997). *Froggy Gets Dressed* [cassette and book]. New York: Penguin Books.

Parker, Dan. (1988). *Teach Me about Getting Dressed* [cassette and book]. Fallbrook, CA: Living Skills Music.

Scullard, Sue. (1992). *The Flyaway Pantaloons* [video]. Pine Plains, NY: Live Oak Media.

Storytelling and Fingerplays

Communication

Aliki. (1993). *Communication*. New York: Greenwillow.

Aliki. (1996). *Hello! Good-Bye*. New York: Greenwillow.

Bornstein, Harry. (1992). *Nursery Rhymes from Mother Goose: Told in Signed English*. Washington, DC: Kendall Green Publications.

Brown, Marc Tolon. (1997). *Arthur's TV Trouble*. Boston: Little, Brown. (Paperback)

Brown, Ruth. (1991). *Alphabet Times Four: An International ABC*. New York: Dutton.

Buck, Nola. (1996). *Sid and Sam*. Illus. by G. Brian Karas. New York: HarperCollins.

Coffelt, Nancy. (1995). *The Dog Who Cried Woof*. Orlando, FL: Harcourt Brace.

Gibbons, Gail. (1993). *Puff—Flash—Bang: A Book about Signals*. New York: William Morrow.

King, Mary Ellen. (1997). *A Good Day for Listening*. Harrisburg, PA: Morehouse Publishing.

Klove, Lars. (1996). *I See a Sign*. New York: Aladdin Paperbacks.

Leedy, Loreen. (1990). *The Furry News: How to Make a Newspaper*. New York: Holiday House.

Lester, Helen. (1995). *Listen, Buddy*. Illus. by Lynn Munsinger. Boston: Houghton Mifflin.

Nelson, Nigel. (1994a). *Codes*. Illus. by Tony De Saulles. Cincinnati, OH: Thomson Learning.

Nelson, Nigel. (1994b). *Writing and Numbers*. Illus. by Tony De Saulles. Cincinnati, OH: Thomson Learning.

Oxlade, Chris. (1997). *Electronic Communication*. Illus. by Colin Mier. New York: Franklin Watts.

Peterson, Jeanne Whitehouse. (1994). *My Mama Sings*. Illus. by Sandra Speidel. New York: HarperCollins.

Rankin, Laura. (1991). *The Handmade Alphabet*. New York: Dial Books.

Shapiro, Arnold. (1997). *Mice Squeak, We Speak*. Illus. by Tomie De Paola. New York: G. P. Putnam.

Showers, Paul. (1991). *Listening Walk* (Rev. ed.). New York: HarperCollins.

Weller, Janet. (1997). *The Written Word*. Illus. by Colin Mier. New York: Franklin Watts.

Wheeler, Cindy. (1998). *More Simple Signs*. New York: Viking.

Storytelling and Fingerplays

Communication, Multimedia

Bailey's Book House [CD-ROM]. (1995). Redmond, WA: Edmark.

Be a Better Listener [video]. (1995). Pleasantville, NY: Sunburst Communications.

Exciting People, Places and Things [video]. (1989). Washington, DC: Gallaudet University Press.

Lonnquist, Ken, et al. (1994). *Sign Songs: Fun Songs to Sign and Sing* [video]. Madison, WI: Aylmer Press.

Reader Rabbit's Ready for Letters [computer program]. (1994). Learning Company.

Tossing, Gaia. (1995). *Sing 'n Sign for Fun!* [compact disc]. Glenview, IL: Heartsong.

Construction Tools

Barton, Byron. (1995). *Tools.* New York: HarperCollins. (Board book)

Brady, Peter. (1996). *Bulldozers.* Mankato, MN: Bridgestone Books.

Gibbons, Gail. (1982). *Tool Book.* New York: Holiday House.

Gibbons, Gail. (1990). *How a House Is Built.* New York: Holiday House.

Hoban, Tana. (1997). *Construction Zone.* New York: Greenwillow.

Klinting, Lars. (1996). *Bruno the Carpenter.* New York: Holt.

Miller, Margaret. (1990). *Who Uses This?* New York: Greenwillow.

Morris, Ann. (1992). *Tools.* Photos by Ken Heyman. New York: Lothrop, Lee & Shepard.

Neitzel, Shirley. (1997). *The House I'll Build for the Wren.* Illus. by Nancy Winslow Parker. New York: Greenwillow.

Radford, Derek. (1994). *Building Machines and What They Do* (Reprint). Cambridge, MA: Candlewick Press.

Robbins, Ken. (1993). *Power Machines.* New York: Holt.

Rockwell, Anne F. (1990). *Toolbox.* New York: Aladdin.

Wallace, John. (1997). *Building a House with Mr. Bumble.* Cambridge, MA: Candlewick Press.

Construction Tools, Multimedia

Big Job [CD-ROM]. (1995). Bethesda, MD: Discovery Communications.

Let's Build a House [video]. (1996). San Diego, CA: Video Connections.

Macaulay, David. (1994). *The Way Things Work* [CD-ROM]. New York: Dorling Kindersley Multimedia.

There Goes a Bulldozer [video]. (1993). Van Nuys, CA: Live Action Video for Kids.

Containers

Boivin, Kelly. (1991). *What's in a Box?* Illus. by Janice Skivington. Chicago: Children's Press.

Carter, David A. (1990). *More Bugs in Boxes Pop-Up Book: A Pop-Up Book about Color.* New York: Simon & Schuster.

King, Stephen Michael. (1996). *A Special Kind of Love.* New York: Scholastic.

Lillegard, Dee. (1992). *Sitting in My Box.* Illus. by Jon Agee. New York: Puffin. (Paperback)

Rau, Dana Meachen. (1997). *A Box Can Be Many Things.* Illus. by Paige Bellin-Frye. Chicago: Children's Press.

Stevenson, James. (1997). *The Mud Flat Mystery.* New York: Greenwillow.

Stock, Catherine. (1994). *Sophie's Bucket.* Orlando, FL: Harcourt Brace. (Paperback)

Tibo, Gilles. (1995). *Simon and His Boxes.* Plattsburgh, NY: Tundra Books.

Westcott, Nadine. (1990). *There's a Hole in the Bucket.* New York: Harper & Row.

Containers, Multimedia

Carter, David A. (1996). *How Many Bugs in a Box?* [CD-ROM]. New York: Simon & Schuster Interactive.

Storytelling and Fingerplays

Creative Movement

Auch, Mary Jane. (1995). *Hen Lake*. New York: Holiday House.

Duvall, Jill D. (1997). *Meet Rory Hohenstein, a Professional Dancer*. Photos by Lili S. Duvall. Chicago: Children's Press.

Esbensen, Barbara Juster. (1995). *Dance with Me*. Illus. by Megan Lloyd. New York: HarperCollins.

Gauch, Patricia Lee. (1992). *Bravo, Tanya*. Illus. by Satomi Ichikawa. New York: Philomel Books.

Gauch, Patricia Lee. (1994). *Tanya and Emily in a Dance for Two*. Illus. by Satomi Ichikawa. New York: Philomel Books.

Gray, Libba Moore. (1995). *My Mama Had a Dancing Heart*. Illus. by Raul Colon. New York: Orchard Books.

Grimm, Jakob. (1996). *The Twelve Dancing Princesses*. Retold by Jane Ray. New York: Dutton.

Isadora, Rachel. (1993). *Lili at Ballet*. New York: G. P. Putnam.

Isadora, Rachel. (1997). *Lili Backstage*. New York: G. P. Putnam.

King, Sandra. (1993). *Shannon: An Ojibway Dancer*. Minneapolis: Lerner Publications.

Kroll, Virginia L. (1996). *Can You Dance, Dalila?* Illus. by Nancy Carpenter. New York: Simon & Schuster.

Lee, Jeanne M. (1991). *Silent Lotus*. New York: Farrar, Straus & Giroux.

Loredo, Elizabeth. (1997). *Boogie Bones*. Illus. by Kevin Hawkes. New York: G. P. Putnam.

Lowery, Linda. (1995). *Twist with a Burger, Jitter with a Bug*. Boston: Houghton Mifflin.

O'Connor, Jane. (1993). *Nina, Nina Ballerina*. Illus. by DyAnne DiSalvo-Ryan. New York: Grosset & Dunlap.

Patrick, Denise Lewis. (1993). *Red Dancing Shoes*. Illus. by James E. Ransome. New York: Tambourine Books.

Schomp, Virginia. (1997). *If You Were a . . . Ballet Dancer*. Tarrytown, NY: Marshall Cavendish.

Thomassie, Tynia. (1996). *Mimi's Tutu*. Illus. by Jan Spivey Gilchrist. New York: Scholastic.

Walsh, Ellen Stoll. (1993). *Hop Jump*. Orlando, FL: Harcourt Brace.

Waters, Kate. (1990). *Lion Dancer: Ernie Wan's Chinese New Year*. New York: Scholastic.

Wilder, Laura Ingalls. (1994). *Dance at Grandpa's: Adapted from the Little House Books*. New York: HarperCollins.

Storytelling and Fingerplays

Creative Movement, Multimedia

All-Time Favorite Dances [cassette or compact disc]. (1991). Long Branch, NJ: Kimbo Educational.

Dance with Us: A Creative Movement Video [video]. (1994). Pleasantville, NY: Sunburst.

Jack, David. *Gotta Hop* [cassette]. (1990). Leucadia, CA: Ta-Dum Productions.

Jack, David. (1991). *David Jack . . . Live!: Makin' Music, Makin' Friends* [video]. Leucadia, CA: Ta-Dum Productions.

Jenkins, Ella. (1990). *Growing Up with Ella Jenkins: Rhythms, Songs and Rhymes* [cassette]. Rockville, MD: Smithsonian/Folkways.

Stewart, Georgiana Liccione. (1991). *Children of the World: Multi-Cultural Rhythmic Activities* [cassette]. Long Branch, NJ: Kimbo Educational.

Dairy Products

Aliki. (1992). *Milk: From Cow to Carton* (Rev. ed.). New York: HarperCollins.

Asch, Frank. (1992). *Milk and Cookies*. Milwaukee, WI: Gareth Stevens.

Barton, Byron. (1995). *Wee Little Woman*. New York: HarperCollins.

Brady, Peter. (1996). *Cows*. Illus. by William Munoz. Mankato, MN: Bridgestone Books.

Ericsson, Jennifer A. (1993). *No Milk*. Illus. by Ora Eitan. New York: Tambourine Books.

Fowler, Allan. (1992). *Thanks to Cows*. Chicago: Children's Press.

Gibbons, Gail. (1985). *The Milk Makers*. New York: Simon & Schuster.

Godfrey, Neale S. (1995). *Here's the Scoop: Follow an Ice-Cream Cone around the World*. Illus. by Randy Verougstraete. Morristown, NJ: Silver Burdett Press.

Grossman, Bill, & Chess, Victoria. (1991). *Tommy at the Grocery Store*. New York: HarperCollins. (Paperback)

Jackson, Ellen. (1995). *Brown Cow, Green Grass, Yellow Mellow Sun*. Illus. by Victoria Raymond. New York: Hyperion.

Keillor, Garrison. (1996). *The Old Man Who Loved Cheese*. Illus. by Anne Wilsdorf. Boston: Little, Brown.

Keller, Stella, & Holm, John. (1990). *Ice Cream*. Austin, TX: Raintree/Steck Vaughn.

Mazen, Barbara S. (1994). *Pass the Cheese Please*. Illus. by Paul Harvey. Delran, NJ: Newbridge. (Paperback)

Older, Jules. (1997). *Cow.* Illus. by Lyn Severance. Watertown, MA: Charlesbridge Publishers.

Peterson, Cris. (1994). *Extra Cheese, Please! Mozzarella's Journey from Cow to Pizza.* Illus. by Alvis Upitis. Honesdale, PA: Boyds Mills Press.

Reid, Mary Ebeltoft. (1997). *Let's Find Out about Ice Cream.* New York: Scholastic. (Paperback)

Schertle, Alice. (1994). *How Now Brown Cow?* Illus. by Amanda Schaffer. San Diego, CA: Browndeer Press.

Seymour, Tres. (1993). *Hunting the White Cow.* Illus. by Wendy Anderson Halperin. New York: Orchard Books.

Van Laan, Nancy. (1993). *The Tiny, Tiny Boy and the Big, Big Cow: A Scottish Folk Tale.* Illus. by Marjorie Priceman. New York: Knopf.

Dairy Products, Multimedia

From Moo to You [CD-ROM]. (1996). Westmont, IL: Dairy Council of Wisconsin.

Let's Go to the Ice Cream and Yogurt Factory [video]. (1996). Burlington, VT: Vermont Story Works.

Milk Cow, Eat Cheese [video]. (1995). Gig Harbor, WA: Real World Video.

Paterson, Katherine. (1996). *Smallest Cow in the World* [book and cassette]. Scranton, PA: Harper Audio.

Dentist

Adler, David A. (1997). *Young Cam Jansen and the Lost Tooth.* Illus. by Susanna Natti. New York: Viking.

Falwell, Cathryn. (1996). *Dragon Tooth.* New York: Clarion Books.

Finnegan, Evelyn M. (1995). *My Little Friend Goes to the Dentist.* Illus. by Diane R. Houghton. Scituate, MA: Little Friend Press.

Gomi, Taro. (1994). *The Crocodile and the Dentist.* Brookfield, CT: Millbrook Press.

Hall, Kirsten. (1994). *The Tooth Fairy.* Illus. by Nan Brooks. Chicago: Children's Press.

Hoban, Lillian. (1987). *Arthur's Loose Tooth: Story and Pictures.* New York: HarperCollins.

Luttrell, Ida. (1997). *Milo's Toothache.* Illus. by Enzo Giannini. New York: Puffin. (Paperback)

Storytelling and Fingerplays

MacDonald, Amy. (1996). *Cousin Ruth's Tooth.* Illus. by Marjorie Priceman. Boston: Houghton Mifflin.

Paxton, Tom. (1996). *The Story of the Tooth Fairy.* Illus. by Rob Sauber. New York: William Morrow.

Ready, Dee. (1997). *Dentists.* Chicago: Children's Press.

Rockwell, Harlow. (1987). *My Dentist.* New York: William Morrow. (Paperback)

Showers, Paul. (1991). *How Many Teeth?* New York: HarperCollins. (Paperback)

Dentist, Multimedia

Goofy over Dental Health [video]. (1991). Newton, PA: Disney Educational Productions.

McPhail, David M. (1986). *The Bear's Toothache* [book and cassette]. Pine Plains, NY: Live Oak Media.

Parker, Dan. (1988). *Teach Me about the Dentist* [book and cassette]. Fallbrook, CA: Living Skills Music.

Doctors and Nurses

Brazelton, T. Berry. (1996). *Going to the Doctor.* Photos by Alfred Womack. Portland, OR: Perseus Press.

Dooley, Virginia. (1996). *Tubes in My Ears: My Trip to the Hospital.* Illus. by Miriam Katin. Greenvale, NY: Mondo Publications. (Paperback)

Fine, Anne. (1992). *Poor Monty.* Illus. by Clara Vulliamy. New York: Clarion Books.

Flanagan, Alice K. (1997). *Ask Nurse Pfaff, She'll Help You.* Photos by Christine Osinski. Chicago: Children's Press.

Howe, James. (1994). *The Hospital Book.* Photos by Mal Warshaw. New York: William Morrow.

Kuklin, Susan. (1988). *Taking My Cat to the Vet.* Minneapolis: Bradbury Press.

Miller, Marilyn. (1996). *Behind the Scenes at the Hospital.* Illus. by Ingo Fast. Austin, TX: Raintree/Steck Vaughn.

Moses, Amy. (1997). *Doctors Help People.* Mankato, MN: Child's World, Inc.

Ready, Dee. (1997a). *Doctors.* Chicago: Children's Press.

Ready, Dee. (1997b). *Nurses.* Chicago: Children's Press.

Redberg, Rita F., et al. (1996). *You Can Be a Woman Cardiologist.* Culver City, CA: Cascade Pass. (Paperback)

Rogers, Fred. (1997). *Going to the Hospital.* Illus. by Jim Judkis. New York: G. P. Putnam.

Rosenberg, Maxine B. (1997). *Mommy's in the Hospital Having a Baby.* Photos by Robert Maass. New York: Clarion Books.

Schomp, Virginia. (1998). *If You Were a Veterinarian.* Tarrytown, NY: Marshall Cavendish.

Doctors and Nurses, Multimedia

Come See What the Doctor Sees [video]. (1994). Half Moon Bay, CA: Visual Mentor.

Emergency 911 [video]. (1994). Washington, DC: National Geographic.

Hospital [video]. (1990). Washington, DC: National Geographic.

Rogers, Fred. (1996). *Mister Rogers' Neighborhood: Doctor* [video]. Beverly Hills, CA: CBS/Fox Home Video.

Ronno. (1996). "Doctor Doctor." On *People in Our Neighborhood* [cassette]. Long Branch, NJ: Kimbo Educational.

When I Grow Up I Wanta Be [video]. (1994). Birmingham, AL: Five Points South.

Dogs

Boland, Janice D. (1996). *A Dog Named Sam.* Illus. by G. Brian Karas. New York: Dial Books.

Coffelt, Nancy. (1995). *Dog Who Cried Woof.* Orlando, FL: Harcourt Brace.

Cole, Joanna. (1991). *My Puppy Is Born.* Revised and newly illustrated. Photos by Margaret Miller. New York: William Morrow.

Copeland, Eric. (1994). *Milton, My Father's Dog.* Plattsburgh, NY: Tundra.

Ernst, Lisa Campbell. (1992). *Walter's Tail.* New York: Simon & Schuster.

Gibbons, Gail. (1996). *Dogs.* New York: Holiday House.

Gliori, Debi. (1996). *The Snow Lambs.* New York: Scholastic.

Gregory, Nan. (1995). *How Smudge Came.* Illus. by Ron Lightburn. New York: Red Deer College Press.

Hall, Donald. (1994). *I Am the Dog, I Am the Cat.* Illus. by Barry Moser. New York: Dial Books.

Harper, Isabelle. (1994). *My Dog Rosie.* Illus. by Barry Moser. New York: Scholastic.

Storytelling and Fingerplays

Harper, Isabelle. (1996). *Our New Puppy.* Illus. by Barry Moser. New York: Scholastic.

Hesse, Karen. (1993). *Lester's Dog.* Illus. by Nancy Carpenter. New York: Crown Publishers.

Masurel, Claire. (1997). *No, No, Titus!* Illus. by Shari Halpern. New York: North-South Books.

McGeorge, Constance W. (1994). *Boomer's Big Day.* Illus. by Mary Whyte. San Francisco: Chronicle.

Moore, Eva. (1996). *Buddy: The First Seeing Eye Dog.* Illus. by Don Bolognese. New York: Scholastic.

Osofsky, Audrey. (1992). *My Buddy.* Illus. by Ted Rand. New York: Holt.

Robertus, Polly M. (1991). *The Dog Who Had Kittens.* Illus. by Janet Stevens. New York: Holiday House.

Rylant, Cynthia. (1991). *Bookshop Dog.* New York: Scholastic.

Rylant, Cynthia. (1994). *Mr. Putter and Tabby Walk the Dog.* Illus. by Arthur Howard. Orlando, FL: Harcourt Brace.

Siracusa. Catherine. (1991). *Bingo, the Best Dog in the World.* Illus. by Sidney Levitt. New York: HarperCollins.

Wells, Rosemary. (1997). *McDuff Moves In.* Illus. by Susan Jeffers. New York: Hyperion.

Wild, Margaret. (1994). *Toby.* Illus. by Noela Young. New York: Ticknor & Fields.

Zolotow, Charlotte. (1995). *Old Dog.* (Rev. ed.). Newly illus. by James Ransome. New York: HarperCollins.

Dogs, Multimedia

"Bingo." (1997). On *Six Little Ducks: Classic Children's Songs* [cassette or compact disc]. Long Branch, NJ: Kimbo Educational.

Pets: See How They Grow [video]. Sony. Long Branch, NJ: Kimbo Educational.

"Puppy Dog." (1976). On *Walk Like the Animals* by Georgiana Liccione Stewart [cassette]. Long Branch, NJ: Kimbo Educational.

Robertus, Polly M. (1992). *The Dog Who Had Kittens* [video]. Pine Plains, NY: Live Oak Media.

Wagging Tails: The Dog and Puppy Music Video [video]. (1994). Forney Miller Film & Video; distributed by New Market Sales.

World of Pets: Dogs [video]. (1985). Washington, DC: National Geographic Society.

Easter

Adams, Adrienne. (1991). *Easter Egg Artists.* Madison, WI: Demco Media.

Auch, Mary Jane. (1992). *The Easter Egg Farm.* New York: Holiday House.

Auch, Mary Jane. (1996). *Eggs Mark the Spot.* New York: Holiday House.

Barth, Edna. (1981). *Lilies, Rabbits, and Painted Eggs: The Story of the Easter Symbols.* Boston: Houghton Mifflin. (Paperback)

Fisher Aileen Lucia. (1997). *The Story of Easter.* Illus. by Stefano Vitale. New York: HarperCollins.

Gibbons, Gail. (1989). *Easter.* New York: Holiday House.

Hallinan, P. K. (1993). *Today Is Easter!* Nashville, TN: Ideals Children's Books. (Paperback)

Hopkins, Lee Bennett. (1993). *Easter Buds Are Springing: Poems for Easter.* Illus. by Tomie De Paola. Honesdale, PA: Boyds Mills Press.

Kennedy, Pamela. (1991). *An Easter Celebration: Traditions and Customs from around the World.* Nashville, TN: Ideals Children's Books.

McDonnell, Janet. (1993). *The Easter Surprise.* Illus. by Linda Hohag. Chicago: Children's Press.

Milich, Mellissa. (1997). *Miz Fannie Mae's Fine New Easter Hat.* Illus. by Yong Chen. Boston: Little, Brown.

Nielsen, Shelly. (1992). *Celebrating Easter.* Minneapolis: Abdo & Daughters.

Polacco, Patricia. (1988). *Rechenka's Eggs.* New York: G. P. Putnam.

Polacco, Patricia. (1992). *Chicken Sunday.* New York: Philomel Books.

Zolotow, Charlotte. (1998). *The Bunny Who Found Easter.* Boston: Houghton Mifflin.

Easter, Multimedia

Auch, Mary Jane. (1995). *Easter Egg Farm* [book and cassette]. Pine Plains, NY: Live Oaks Media.

"Easter Egg Hunt." (1978). On *Holiday Songs for All Occasions* [cassette]. Long Branch, NJ: Kimbo Educational.

"Easter Time Is Here Again." (1997). On *Holiday Songs and Rhythms* [compact disc]. Freeport, NY: Educational Activities.

Max's Chocolate Chicken and Other Stories for Young Children [video]. (1993). Weston, CT: Children's Circle Home Video.

"Peter Cottontail." (1989). On *Holidays and Special Times* [cassette]. Sung by Greg Scelsa and Steve Millang. Los Angeles, CA: Youngheart Records.

Storytelling and Fingerplays

Eggs

Burton, Robert. (1994). *Egg: A Photographic Story of Hatching.* Photos by Kim Taylor. New York: Dorling Kindersley.

Butrum, Ray. (1998). *I'm Sorry You Can't Hatch an Egg.* Sisters, OR: Multnomah Press.

De Bourgoing, Pascale. (1992). *The Egg.* Illus. by RenGe Mettle. New York: Scholastic.

Ernst, Lisa Campbell. (1992). *Zinnia and Dot.* New York: Viking.

Fowler, Allan. (1993). *The Chicken or the Egg!* Chicago: Children's Press.

Heller, Ruth. (1981). *Chickens Aren't the Only Ones.* New York: G. P. Putnam.

Humphrey, Paul. (1996). *Frog's Eggs.* Austin, TX: Raintree/Steck Vaughn. (Paperback)

Jenkins, Priscilla Belz. (1995). *A Nest Full of Eggs.* Illus. by Lizzy Rockwell. New York: HarperCollins.

Johnson, Sylvia A. (1992). *Inside an Egg.* Photos by Kiyoshi Shimizu. Minneapolis: Lerner Publishing. (Paperback)

Joyce, William. (1992). *Bently and Egg.* New York: HarperCollins.

Lionni, Leo. (1994). *An Extraordinary Egg.* New York: Knopf.

Polacco, Patricia. (1988). *Rechenka's Eggs.* New York: G. P. Putnam.

Reasoner, Charles. (1994). *Who's Hatching? (A Sliding Surprise Book).* New York: Price Stern Sloan.

Ruurs, Margriet. (1997). *Emma's Eggs.* Illus. by Barbara Spurll. New York: Stoddart Kids.

Seuss, Dr. (1992). *Scrambled Eggs Super!* New York: Random House.

Eggs, Multimedia

Kids Get Cooking: The Egg [video]. (1987). Newton, MA: Kidviz.

Palmer, Hap. (1991). "Humpty Dumpty." On *Hap Palmer Sings Classic Nursery Rhymes* [cassette]. Freeport, NY: Educational Activities.

Polacco, Patricia. (1992). *Rechenka's Eggs* [video]. Lincoln, NE: GNP.

Fall

Arnosky, Jim. (1993). *Every Autumn Comes the Bear.* New York: G. P. Putnam.

Bunting, Eve. (1997). *The Pumpkin Fair.* Illus. by Eileen Christelow. New York: Clarion Books.

Ehlert, Lois. (1991). *Red Leaf, Yellow Leaf.* Orlando, FL: Harcourt Brace.

Fowler, Allan. (1992). *How Do You Know It's Fall?* Chicago: Children's Press.

Fowler, Allan. (1993). *It Could Still Be a Leaf.* Chicago: Children's Press.

George, Lindsay Barrett. (1995). *In the Woods: Who's Been Here?* New York: Greenwillow.

Hall, Zoe. (1994). *It's Pumpkin Time!* Illus. by Shari Halpern. New York: Scholastic.

Hoban, Lillian. (1996). *Arthur's Back to School Day.* New York: HarperCollins.

Hunter, Anne. (1996). *Possum's Harvest Moon.* Boston: Houghton Mifflin.

Hutchings, Amy. (1994). *Picking Apples and Pumpkins.* Illus. by Richard Hutchings. St. Paul, MN: Cartwheel Books. (Paperback)

Lotz, Karen E. (1993). *Snowsong Whistling.* Illus. by Elisa Kleven. New York: Dutton.

Maestro, Betsy C. (1994). *Why Do Leaves Change Color?* Illus. by Loretta Krupinski. New York: HarperCollins.

Moore, Elaine. (1995). *Grandma's Smile.* Illus. by Dan Andreasen. New York: Lothrop, Lee & Shepard.

Robbins, Ken. (1998). *Fall Leaves.* New York: Scholastic.

Rockwell, Anne F. (1989). *Apples and Pumpkins.* Illus. by Lizzy Rockwell. New York: Simon & Schuster.

Russo, Marisabina. (1994). *I Don't Want to Go Back to School.* New York: Greenwillow.

Saunders-Smith, Gail. (1997). *Autumn Leaves.* Mankato, MN: Pebble Books.

Schweninger, Ann. (1993). *Autumn Days.* New York: Puffin. (Paperback)

Simon, Seymour. (1993). *Autumn across America.* New York: Hyperion.

White, Linda. (1996). *Too Many Pumpkins.* Illus. by Megan Lloyd. New York: Holiday House.

Zagwyn, Deborah Turney. (1997). *The Pumpkin Blanket.* Berkeley, CA: Tricycle Press.

Storytelling and Fingerplays

Fall, Multimedia

Bingham, Bing. (1988). "The First Day of School." On *A Rainbow of Songs* [cassette]. Long Branch, NJ: Kimbo Educational.

James, Dixie, & Becht, Linda. *The Singing Calendar* [cassette]. Long Branch, NJ: Kimbo Educational.

Maestro, Betsy C. (1996). *Why Do Leaves Change Color?* [book and cassette]. Illus. by Loretta Krupinski. New York: Harper Audio.

What Is a Leaf? [video]. (1991). Washington, DC: National Geographic.

White, Linda. (1997). *Too Many Pumpkins* [video]. Pine Plains, NY: Live Oak Productions.

Families

Buckley, Helen E. (1994a). *Grandfather and I.* Illus. by Jan Ormerod. New York: Lothrop, Lee & Shepard.

Buckley, Helen E. (1994b). *Grandmother and I.* Illus. by Jan Ormerod. New York: Lothrop, Lee & Shepard.

DePaola, Tomie. (1996). *The Baby Sister.* New York: G. P. Putnam.

Flournoy, Valerie. (1995). *Tanya's Reunion.* Illus. by Jerry Pinkney. New York: Dial Books.

Hausherr, Rosmarie. (1997). *Celebrating Families.* New York: Scholastic.

Johnson, Angela. (1990). *When I Am Old with You.* Illus. by David Soman. New York: Orchard Books.

Johnson, Angela. (1991). *One of Three.* Illus. by David Soman. New York: Orchard Books.

Jones, Rebecca C. (1995). *Great Aunt Martha.* Illus. by Shelley Jackson. New York: Dutton.

Knight, Margy Burns. (1994). *Welcoming Babies.* Illus. by Anne Sibley O'Brien. Gardner, ME: Tilbury House.

Kroll, Virginia L. (1994). *Beginnings: How Families Came to Be.* Illus. by Stacey Schuett. Niles, IL: Albert Whitman & Co.

Kuklin, Susan. (1992). *How My Family Lives in America.* Minneapolis: Bradbury Press.

Lakin, Patricia. (1994). *Dad and Me in the Morning.* Illus. by Robert G. Steele. Niles, IL: Albert Whitman & Co.

Leedy, Loreen. (1995). *Who's Who in My Family.* New York: Holiday House.

Maynard, Christopher. (1997). *Why Are All Families Different?: Questions Children Ask about Families.* New York: Dorling Kindersley.

Storytelling and Fingerplays

Morris, Ann. (1995a). *The Daddy Book.* Photos by Ken Heyman. Englewood Cliffs, NJ: Silver Press.

Morris, Ann. (1995b). *The Mommy Book.* Photos by Ken Heyman. Englewood Cliffs, NJ: Silver Press.

Pellegrini, Nina. (1991). *Families Are Different.* New York: Holiday House.

Rosenberg, Maxine B. (1991). *Brothers and Sisters.* Photos by George Ancona. New York: Clarion Books.

Rotner, Shelley, & Kelly, Sheila M. (1996). *Lots of Moms.* New York: Dial Books.

Rotner, Shelley, & Kelly, Sheila M. (1997). *Lots of Dads.* New York: Dial Books.

Russo, Marisabina. (1998). *When Mama Gets Home.* New York: Greenwillow.

Schindel, John. (1995). *Dear Daddy.* Illus. by Dorothy Donohue. Niles, IL: Albert Whitman & Co.

Schwartz, Amy. (1994). *A Teeny Tiny Baby.* New York: Orchard Books.

Stevenson, Harvey. (1994). *Grandpa's House.* New York: Hyperion.

Vigna, Judith. (1997). *I Live with Daddy.* Niles, IL: Albert Whitman & Co.

Wild, Margaret. (1994). *Our Granny.* Illus. by Julie Vivas. New York: Ticknor & Fields.

Williams, Vera B. (1990). *More More More Said the Baby.* New York: Greenwillow.

Zamorano, Ana. (1997). *Let's Eat!* Illus. by Julie Vivas. New York: Scholastic.

Families, Multimedia

Byars, Betsy. (1998). *My Brother Ant* [book and cassette]. Prince Frederick, MD: Recorded Books.

Daddy Doesn't Live with Us [video]. (1994). Pleasantville, NY: Sunburst.

My Family, Your Family [video]. (1994). Pleasantville, NY: Sunburst.

We're a Family [video]. (1992). Pleasantville, NY: Sunburst.

Farm Animals

Aliki. (1992). *Milk from Cow to Carton* (Rev. ed.). New York: HarperCollins.

Brown, Craig. (1994). *In the Spring.* New York: Greenwillow.

Edwards, Pamela Duncan. (1998). *The Grumpy Morning.* Illus. by Loretta Krupinski. New York: Hyperion.

Ehrlich, Amy. (1993). *Parents in the Pigpen, Pigs in the Tub.* Illus. by Steven Kellogg. New York: Dial Books.

Fleming, Denise. (1994). *Barnyard Banter.* New York: Holt.

Fowler, Allan. (1992). *Thanks to Cows.* San Francisco: Children's Book Press.

Storytelling and Fingerplays

Gibbons, Gail. (1988). *Farming*. New York: Holiday House.

Gray, Libba Moore. (1997). *Is There Room on the Feather Bed?* Illus. by Nadine Bernard Westcott. New York: Orchard Books.

Hutchins, Pat. (1994). *Little Pink Pig*. New York: Greenwillow.

Jackson, Ellen. (1995). *Brown Cow, Green Grass, Yellow Mellow Sun*. Illus. by Victoria Raymond. New York: Hyperion.

Lesser, Carolyn. (1995). *What a Wonderful Day to Be a Cow*. Illus. by Melissa Bay Mathis. New York: Knopf.

MacLachlan, Patricia. (1994). *All the Places to Love*. Illus. by Mike Wimmer. New York: HarperCollins.

Masurel, Claire. (1997). *No, No, Titus!* Illus. by Shari Halpern. New York: North-South Books.

McDonnell, Flora. (1994). *I Love Animals*. Cambridge, MA: Candlewick Press.

Older, Jules. (1997). *Cow*. Illus. by Lyn Severance. Watertown, MA: Charlesbridge Publishers.

Plourde, Lynn. (1997). *Pigs in the Mud in the Middle of the Rud*. Illus. by John Schoenherr. New York: Scholastic.

Sykes, Julie. (1996). *This and That*. Illus. by Tanya Linch. New York: Farrar, Straus & Giroux.

Tafuri, Nancy. (1994). *This Is the Farmer*. New York: Greenwillow.

Tresselt, Alvin. (1991). *Wake Up, Farm*. Newly illus. by Carolyn Ewing. New York: Lothrop, Lee & Shepard.

Waddell, Martin. (1992). *Farmer Duck*. Illus. by Helen Oxenbury. Cambridge, MA: Candlewick Press.

Wallace, Karen. (1994). *My Hen Is Dancing*. Illus. by Anita Jeram. Cambridge, MA: Candlewick Press.

Wormell, Christopher. (1995). *A Number of Animals*. Mankato, MN: Creative Education.

Ziefert, Harriet. (1996). *Who Said Moo?* Illus. by Simms Taback. New York: HarperCollins.

Storytelling and Fingerplays

Farm Animals, Multimedia

Cows [video]. (1995). Churchill Media.

Let's Go to the Farm [video]. (1994). With Mac Parker. Burlington, VT: Vermont Story Works.

Rosenthal, Phil. (1996). "Little White Duck." On *Animal Songs* [compact disc]. Guilford, CT: American Melody.

See How They Grow: Farm Animals [video]. (1993). New York: Sony Music Entertainment.

We're Goin' to the Farm [video]. (1994). Minneapolis, MN: Shortstuff Entertainment.

Feelings

Berry, Joy. (1996). Let's Talk About series. Illus. by Maggie Smith. New York: Scholastic. (Paperback). *Feeling Afraid; Feeling Angry; Feeling Sad.*

Brown, Laurie Krasny. (1996). *When Dinosaurs Die: A Guide to Understanding Death.* Illus. by Marc Tolon Brown. Boston: Little, Brown.

Carle, Eric. (1995). *The Very Lonely Firefly.* New York: Philomel Books.

Carlson, Nancy L. (1997). *ABC, I Like Me.* New York: Viking.

Conlin, Susan, et al. (1991). *All My Feelings at Preschool: Nathan's Day.* Seattle, WA: Parenting Press.

Crary, Elizabeth. Dealing with Feelings series. Illus. by Jean Whitney. Seattle, WA: Parenting Press. *I'm Excited* (1996); *I'm Frustrated* (1992); *I'm Furious* (1996); *I'm Mad* (1992); *I'm Proud* (1992); *I'm Scared* (1996).

Curtis, Munzee. (1997). *When the Big Dog Barks.* Illus. by Susan Ayishai. New York: Greenwillow.

Egan, Tim. (1996). *Metropolitan Cow.* Boston: Houghton Mifflin.

Emberley, Ed. (1993). *Go Away, Big Green Monster!* Boston: Little, Brown.

Emberley, Ed. (1997). *Glad Monster, Sad Monster: A Book about Feelings.* Illus. by Anne Miranda. Boston: Little, Brown.

Hamilton, Dewitt. (1995). *Sad Days, Glad Days: A Story about Depression.* Illus. by Gail Owens. Beaver Dam, WI: Concept Books.

Krueger, David. (1996). *What Is a Feeling?* Seattle, WA: Parenting Press.

Lachner, Dorothea. (1995). *Andrew's Angry Words.* Illus. by Tjong-Khing The. New York: North-South Books.

Havill, Juanita. (1993). *Jamaica and Brianna.* Illus. by Anne Sibley O'Brien. Boston: Houghton Mifflin.

Joosse, Barbara M. (1991). *Mama, Do You Love Me?* Illus. by Barbara Lavalle. San Francisco: Chronicle Books.

Roth, Susan L. (1997). *My Love for You.* New York: Dial Books.

Seuss, Dr. (1996). *My Many Colored Days.* Edited by Lou Fancher; illus. by Steve Johnson. New York: Knopf.

Waddell, Martin. (1993). *Let's Go Home, Little Bear.* Illus. by Barbara Firth. Cambridge, MA: Candlewick Press.

Ward, Heather P. (1994). *I Promise I'll Find You.* Illus. by Sheila McGraw. Buffalo, NY: Firefly Books.

Storytelling and Fingerplays

Feelings, Multimedia

Berenstain, Stan. (1996). *Berenstain Bears in the Dark* [CD-ROM]. New York: Random House/Broderbund.

Groark Learns about Prejudice [video]. (1996). Featuring Randel McGee. Elkind & Sweet Communications/distributed by Live Wire Media.

I Get So Mad! [video]. (1993). Pleasantville, NY: Sunburst Communications.

Murphy, Jane. *Songs for You and Me: Kids Learn about Feelings and Emotions* [cassette]. Long Branch, NJ: Kimbo Educational.

Firefighters

Flanagan, Alice K. (1997). *Ms. Murphy Fights Fires*. Photos by Christine Osinski. Chicago: Children's Press.

Hines, Gary. (1993). *Flying Firefighters*. Illus. by Anna Grossnickle Hines. New York: Clarion Books.

Kallen, Stuart A. (1997). *The Fire Station*. Minneapolis: Abdo & Daughters.

Kuklin, Susan. (1993). *Fighting Fires*. New York: Simon & Schuster.

Kunhardt, Edith. (1995). *I'm Going to Be a Fire Fighter*. St. Paul, MN: Cartwheel Books. (Paperback)

Lakin, Pat. (1995). *The Fire Fighter: Where There's Smoke*. Austin, TX: Raintree/Steck Vaughn.

Packard, Mary. (1995). *I'm a Fire Fighter*. Illus. by Julie Durrell. Madison, WI: Demco Media.

Ready, Dee. (1997). *Fire Fighters*. Danbury, CT: Grolier Pub.

Simon, Norma. (1995). *Fire Fighters*. Illus. by Pam Paparone. New York: Simon & Schuster.

Winkleman, Katherine. (1994). *Firehouse*. Illus. by John S. Winkleman. New York: Walker & Co.

Firefighters, Multimedia

Big Job [CD-ROM]. (1995). Bethesda, MD: Discovery Communications, Inc.

Big Red [video]. (1993). Mill Valley, CA: Fire Dog Pictures.

Fire and Rescue [video]. (1993). Montpelier, VT: Focus Video Productions.

Firefighter [CD-ROM]. (1994). New York: Simon & Schuster Interactive.

Fire Safety for Kids [video]. (1995). South Burlington, VT: Children's Video Development.

Fire Station [video]. (1990). Washington, DC: National Geographic.

Sound the Alarm: Firefighters at Work [video]. (1994). Bohemia, NY: Rainbow Educational Media.

Fish

Adams, Georgie. (1993). *Fish, Fish, Fish.* New York: Dial Books.

Aliki. (1993). *My Visit to the Aquarium.* New York: HarperCollins.

Arnosky, Jim. (1993). *Crinkleroot's 25 Fish Every Child Should Know.* New York: Simon & Schuster.

Bailey, Donna. (1990). *Fishing.* Austin, TX: Raintree/Steck Vaughn.

Boyle, Doe. (1997). *Coral Reef Hideaway: The Story of a Clown Anemonefish.* Illus. by Steven James Petruccio. Norwalk, CT: Soundprints Corp.

Clark, Elizaabeth. (1990). *Fish.* Illus. by John Yates. Minneapolis: Carolrhoda Books.

Cole, Joanna. (1997). *Magic School Bus Goes Upstream: A Book about Salmon on Migration.* Illus. by Bruce Degen. New York: Scholastic. (Paperback)

Dunphy, Madeleine. (1998). *Here Is the Coral Reef.* Illus. by Tom Leonard. New York: Hyperion.

Ehlert, Lois. (1990). *Fish Eyes: A Book You Can Count On.* Orlando, FL: Harcourt Brace.

Evans, Mark. (1993). *Fish: Practical Guide to Caring for Your Fish.* New York: Dorling Kindersley.

Fowler, Allan. (1995). *The Best Way to See a Shark.* Chicago: Children's Press.

Gibbons, Gail. (1992). *Sharks.* New York: Holiday House.

Holmes, Kevin J. (1998). *Sharks.* Chicago: Children's Press.

Johnston, Tony. (1996). *Fishing Sunday.* Illus. by Barry Root. New York: William Morrow.

Jonas, Ann. (1995). *Splash!* New York: Greenwillow.

Ling, Mary. (1991). *Amazing Fish.* Photos by Jerry Young. New York: Knopf.

McKissack, Patricia. (1992). *A Million Fish—More or Less.* Illus. by Dena Schutzer. New York: Knopf.

Morley, Christine et al. (1997). *Me and My Pet Fish.* Chicago: World Book.

Pfeffer, Wendy. (1996). *What's It Like to Be a Fish?* Illus. by Holly Keller. New York: HarperCollins.

Storytelling and Fingerplays

Pfister, Marcus. (1992). *The Rainbow Fish*. Translated by J. Alison James. New York: North-South Books.

Pfister, Marcus. (1995). *Rainbow Fish to the Rescue*. Illus. by J. Alison James. New York: North-South Books.

Ryder, Joanne. (1997). *Shark in the Sea*. Illus. by Michael Rothman. New York: William Morrow.

Samson, Suzanne. (1995). *Sea Dragons and Rainbow Runners: Exploring Fish with Children*. Illus. by Preston Neel. Niwot, CO: Roberts Rinehart Publishers.

Sharp, N. L. (1993). *Today I'm Going Fishing with My Dad*. Illus. by Chris L. Demarest. Honesdale, PA: Boyds Mills Press.

Van Laan, Nancy. (1998). *Little Fish, Lost*. Illus. by Jane Conteh-Morgan. New York: Simon & Schuster.

Wallace, Karen. (1993). *Think of an Eel*. Illus. by Mike Bostock. Cambridge, MA: Candlewick Press.

Wood, Jakki. (1998). *Across the Big Blue Sea: An Ocean Wildlife Book*. Washington, DC: National Geographic.

Fish, Multimedia

Eastman, David. (1993). *What Is a Fish?* [video]. Northbrook, IL: Film Ideas.

Exploring the World of Fish [video]. (1992). Troy, MI: Anchor Bay Entertainment.

Fish [video]. Eyewitness Videos. Long Branch, NJ: Kimbo Educational.

Tell Me Why: Fish, Shellfish, Underwater Life [video]. (1987). Marina del Rey, CA: Tell Me Why.

Wet and Wild: Under the Sea with OWL/TV [video]. (1994). Toronto: Children's Group Inc.

World of Pets: Fish [video]. (1985). Washington, DC: National Geographic.

Flowers

Barker, Cicely Mary. (1996). *Flower Fairies: The Meaning of Flowers*. New York: Frederick Warne.

Barker, Cicely Mary. (1998). *Flower Fairies of the Spring: A Celebration*. New York: Frederick Warne.

Bryant-Mole, Karen. (1996). *Flowers*. Austin, TX: Raintree/Steck Vaughn.

Bunting, Eve. (1994). *Flower Garden*. Illus. by Kathryn Hewitt. Orlando, FL: Harcourt Brace.

Burnie, David. (1992). *Flowers*. New York: Dorling Kindersley.

Cole, Henry. (1995). *Jack's Garden*. New York: Greenwillow.

Cole, Joanna. (1995). *The Magic School Bus Plants Seeds: A Book about How Living Things Grow*. Illus. by Bruce Degen. New York: Scholastic. (Paperback)

De Paola, Tomie. (1994). *The Legend of the Poinsettia*. New York: G. P. Putnam.

Ford, Miela. (1995). *Sunflower*. Illus. by Sally Noll. New York: Greenwillow.

King, Elizabeth. (1993). *Backyard Sunflower*. New York: Dutton.

Lobel, Anita. (1990). *Alison's Zinnia*. New York: Greenwillow.

Lucht, Irmgard. (1995). *The Red Poppy*. Illus. by Frank Jacoby-Nelson. New York: Hyperion.

Marzollo, Jean. (1996). *I'm a Seed*. Madison, WI: Demco Media.

Pallotta, Jerry. (1990). *Flower Alphabet Book*. Illus. by Leslie Evans. Watertown, MA: Charlesbridge Publishers.

Pomeroy, Diana. (1997). *Wildflower ABC: An Alphabet of Potato Prints*. Orlando, FL: Harcourt Brace.

Robbins, Ken. (1990). *A Flower Grows*. New York: Dial Books.

Samson, Suzanne. (1994). *Fairy Dusters and Blazing Stars: Exploring Wildflowers with Children*. Illus. by Neel Preston. Niwot, CO: Roberts Rinehart Publishers.

Sun, Chyng-Feng. (1996). *Cat and Cat-Face*. Illus. by Lesley Liu. Boston: Houghton Mifflin.

Flowers, Multimedia

Flowers and Seeds [video]. (1994). Princeton, NJ: Films for the Humanities.

Flowers, Plants and Trees [video]. (1987). Tell Me Why series. Marina Del Rey, CA: Penguin Productions.

Raffi. (1994). "Spring Flowers" on *Bananaphone* [compact disc]. Cambridge, MA: Shoreline. Long Branch, NJ: Kimbo Educational.

Friends

Aliki. (1995). *Best Friends Together Again*. New York: Greenwillow.

Carlson, Nancy L. (1994). *How to Lose All Your Friends*. New York: Viking.

Caseley, Judith. (1991). *Harry and Willy and Carrothead*. New York: Greenwillow.

Champion, Joyce. (1993). *Emily and Alice*. Illus. by Sucie Stevenson. Orlando, FL: Harcourt Brace.

Cote, Nancy. (1993). *Palm Trees*. New York: Four Winds.

Dugan, Barbara. (1992). *Loop the Loop.* Illus. by James Stevenson. New York: Greenwillow.

Egan, Tim. (1996). *Metropolitan Cow.* Boston: Houghton Mifflin.

Fuchs, Diane Marcial. (1995). *A Bear for All Seasons.* Illus. by Kathryn Brown. New York: Holt.

Havill, Juanita. (1993). *Jamaica and Brianna.* Illus. by Anne Sibley O'Brien. Boston: Houghton Mifflin.

Hoban, Russell. (1994). *Best Friends for Frances.* Illus. by Lillian Hoban. New York: HarperCollins.

Hutchins, Pat. (1993). *My Best Friend.* New York: Greenwillow.

Hutchins, Pat. (1996). *Titch and Daisy.* New York: Greenwillow.

Leedy, Loreen. (1996). *How Humans Make Friends.* New York: Holiday House.

Mavor, Salley. (1997). *You and Me: Poems of Friendship.* New York: Orchard Books.

Monson, A. M. (1997). *Wanted: Best Friend.* Illus. by Lynn Munsinger. New York: Dial Books.

Morris, Ann. (1990). *Loving.* Photos by Ken Heyman. New York: Lothrop, Lee & Shepard.

Naylor, Phyllis Reynolds. (1991). *King of the Playground.* Illus. by Nola Langner Malone. Colchester, CT: Atheneum.

Polacco, Patricia. (1992a). *Chicken Sunday.* New York: Philomel Books.

Polacco, Patricia. (1992b). *Mrs. Katz and Tush.* New York: Bantam.

Raschka, Chris. (1993). *Yo! Yes?* New York: Orchard Books.

Reiser, Lynn. (1993). *Margaret and Margarita/Margarita Y Margaret.* New York: Greenwillow.

Reiser, Lynn. (1997). *Best Friends Think Alike.* New York: Greenwillow.

Spohn, Kate. (1996). *Dog and Cat Shake a Leg.* New York: Viking.

Waber, Bernard. (1995). *Gina.* Boston: Houghton Mifflin.

Friends, Multimedia

Berenstain, Stan. (1995). *Berenstain Bears Get in a Fight* [CD-ROM]. New York: Random House/Broderbund.

Brown, Marc. (1994). *Arthur's Birthday* [CD-ROM]. New York: Random House/Broderbund.

Hartmann, Jack. (1990). *Make a Friend, Be a Friend: Songs for Growing Up and Growing Together with Friends* [cassette]. Freeport, NY: Educational Activities.

Fruits and Vegetables

Brown, Laurene Krasny. (1995). *The Vegetable Show*. Boston: Little, Brown.

Caseley, Judith. (1990). *Grandpa's Garden Lunch*. New York: Greenwillow.

Charles, N. N. (1994). *What Am I? Looking through Shapes at Apples and Grapes*. Illus. by Leo and Diane Dillon. New York: Scholastic.

Ehlert, Lois. (1994). *Eating the Alphabet: Fruits and Vegetables from A to Z*. Orlando, FL: Harcourt Brace.

Fowler, Allan. (1995). *Corn—On and Off the Cob*. Chicago: Children's Press. (Paperback)

Fowler, Allan. (1996). *It's a Fruit, It's a Vegetable, It's a Pumpkin*. Illus. by Robert L. Hillerich. Chicago: Children's Press.

French, Vivian. (1995). *Oliver's Vegetables*. Illus. by Alison Bartlett. New York: Orchard Books.

Gershator, Phillis. (1996). *Sweet, Sweet Fig Banana*. Illus. by Fritz Millvoix. Niles, IL: Albert Whitman & Co.

Greenstein, Elaine. (1996). *Mrs. Rose's Garden*. New York: Simon & Schuster.

Hall, Zoe. (1996). *The Apple Pie Tree*. Illus. by Shari Halpern. New York: Scholastic.

Hoban, Tana. (1995). *Animal, Vegetable, or Mineral?* New York: Greenwillow.

Maestro, Betsy C. (1992). *How Do Apples Grow?* Illus. by Giulio Maestro. New York: HarperCollins.

Patent, Dorothy Hinshaw. (1991). *Where Food Comes From*. Illus. by William Munoz. New York: Holiday House.

Powell, Jillian. (1997). *Fruit*. Austin, TX: Raintree/Steck Vaughn.

Robinson, Fay. (1994). *Vegetables, Vegetables*. Chicago: Children's Press.

Robson, Pam. (1998a). *Banana*. Chicago: Children's Press.

Robson, Pam. (1998b). *Corn*. Chicago: Children's Press.

Rylant, Cynthia. (1995). *Mr. Putter and Tabby Pick the Pears*. Orlando, FL: Harcourt Brace.

Seabrook, Elizabeth. (1997). *Cabbages and Kings*. Illus. by Jamie Wyeth. New York: Viking.

Sekido, Isamu. (1993). *Fruits, Roots, and Fungi: Plants We Eat*. Minneapolis: Lerner Publications.

Wiesner, David. (1992). *June 29, 1999*. New York: Clarion Books.

Storytelling and Fingerplays

Fruits and Vegetables, Multimedia

Bingham, Bing. (1988). "Goober Peas." On *A Rainbow of Songs* [cassette]. Long Branch, NJ: Kimbo Educational.

Cranberry Bounce [video]. (1991). DeBeck Educational Video.

Fruit: Close Up and Very Personal [video]. (1995). Geneva, IL: Stage Fright Productions.

Scelsa, Greg, & Milang, Steve. (1986). "I Like Potatoes." On *We All Live Together* (Vol. 5) [cassette or compact disc]. Long Branch, NJ: Kimbo Educational.

Gardens

Bunting, Eve. (1994). *Flower Garden.* Illus. by Kathryn Hewitt. Orlando, FL: Harcourt Brace.

Cole, Henry. (1995). *Jack's Garden.* New York: Greenwillow.

Cutler, Jane. (1996). *Mr. Carey's Garden.* Illus. by G. Brian Karas. Boston: Houghton Mifflin.

Delaney, A. (1997). *Pearl's First Prize Plant.* New York: HarperCollins.

Dyjak, Elisabeth. (1995). *Bertha's Garden.* Illus. by Janet Wilkins. Boston: Houghton Mifflin.

Florian, Douglas. (1991). *Vegetable Garden.* Orlando, FL: Harcourt Brace.

Glaser, Linda. (1996). *Compost! Growing Gardens from Your Garbage.* Illus. by Anca Hariton. Brookfield, CT: Millbrook Press.

Godkin, Celia. (1998). *What about Ladybugs?* Boston: Little, Brown. (Paperback)

Greenstein, Elaine. (1996). *Mrs. Rose's Garden.* New York: Simon & Schuster.

Hall, Zoe. (1994). *It's Pumpkin Time!* Illus. by Shari Halpern. New York: Scholastic.

Hines, Anna Grossnickle. (1997). *Miss Emma's Wild Garden.* New York: Greenwillow.

Llewellyn, Claire. (1991). *First Look at Growing Food.* Milwaukee, WI: Gareth Stevens.

Moore, Elaine. (1994). *Grandma's Garden.* Illus. by Dan Andreasen. New York: Lothrop, Lee & Shepard.

Perkins, Lynne Rae. (1995). *Home Lovely.* New York: Greenwillow.

Ryder, Joanne. (1994). *My Father's Hands.* New York: William Morrow.

Rylant, Cynthia. (1993). *Everyday Garden.* New York: Simon & Schuster. (Board book)

Seabrook, Elizabeth. (1997). *Cabbages and Kings*. Illus. by Jamie Wyeth. New York: Viking.

Shannon, George. (1994). *Seeds*. Illus. by Steve Bjorkman. Boston: Houghton Mifflin.

Shories, Pat. (1994). *Over Under in the Garden: An Alphabet Book*. New York: Farrar, Straus & Giroux.

Stewart, Sarah. (1997). *The Gardener*. Illus. by David Small. New York: Farrar, Straus & Giroux.

Tamar, Erika. (1996). *The Garden of Happiness*. Illus. by Barbara Lambase. Orlando, FL: Harcourt Brace.

Gardens, Multimedia

Get Ready, Get Set, Grow [video]. (1987). Brooklyn Botanic Garden Children's Garden. Oley, PA: Bullfrog Films.

"I'm Going to Plant a Garden." On *Science in a Nutshell* [cassette]. Long Branch, NJ: Kimbo Educational.

Palmer, Hap. *Walter the Waltzing Worm* [cassette or compact disc]. Long Branch, NJ: Kimbo Educational.

Halloween

Andrews, Sylvia. (1995). *Rattlebone Rock*. Illus. by Jennifer Plecas. New York: HarperCollins.

Carlstrom, Nancy White. (1995). *Who Said Boo? Halloween Poems for the Very Young*. Illus. by R. W. Alley. New York: Simon & Schuster.

Caseley, Judith. (1996). *Witch Mama*. New York: Greenwillow.

Dillon, Jana. (1992). *Jeb Scarecrow's Pumpkin Patch*. Boston: Houghton Mifflin.

Enderle, Judith Ross. (1992). *Six Creepy Sheep*. Illus. by John O'Brien. Honesdale, PA: Boyds Mills Press.

Hall, Zoe. (1994). *It's Pumpkin Time!* Illus. by Shari Halpern. New York: Scholastic.

Heinz, Brian J. (1996). *The Monsters' Test*. Illus. by Sal Murdocca. Brookfield, CT: Millbrook Press.

Johnston, Tony. (1990). *The Soup Bone*. Illus. by Margot Tomes. Orlando, FL: Harcourt Brace.

Johnston, Tony. (1995). *Very Scary*. Illus. by Douglas Florian. Orlando, FL: Harcourt Brace.

Storytelling and Fingerplays

Lachner, Dorothea. (1997). *Meredith: The Witch Who Wasn't.* Illus. by Christa Unzner. New York: North-South Books.

Levine, Abby. (1997). *This Is the Pumpkin.* Niles, IL: Albert Whitman & Co.

Martin, Bill. (1993). *Old Devil Wind.* Illus. by Barry Root. Orlando, FL: Harcourt Brace.

Meddaugh, Susan. (1994). *Witches Supermarket.* Madison, WI: Demco Media.

Nikola-Lisa, W. (1997). *Shake Dem Halloween Bones.* Boston: Houghton Mifflin.

Pilkey, Dav. (1995). *Hallo-Wiener.* New York: Scholastic.

Roberts, Bethany. (1995). *Halloween Mice!* Illus. by Doug Cushman. New York: Clarion Books.

Shaw, Nancy. (1997). *Sheep Trick or Treat.* Boston: Houghton Mifflin.

Sierra, Judy. (1995). *The House That Drac Built.* Illus. by Will Hillenbrand. Orlando, FL: Harcourt Brace.

Silverman, Erica. (1992). *Big Pumpkin.* Illus. by S. D. Schindler. New York: Macmillan.

Stock, Catherine. (1990). *Halloween Monster.* New York: Simon & Schuster.

Stutson, Caroline. (1993). *By the Light of the Halloween Moon.* Illus. by Kevin Hawkes. New York: Lothrop, Lee & Shepard.

Van Rynbach, Iris. (1995). *Five Little Pumpkins.* Honesdale, PA: Boyds Mills Press.

Wolff, Ferida. (1994). *On Halloween Night.* Illus. by Dolores Avendano. New York: Tambourine Books.

Halloween, Multimedia

Gold, Andrew. (1996). *Andrew Gold's Halloween Howls* [compact disc]. Redway, CA: Music for Little People.

Halloween [video]. (1993). Niles, IL: United Learning.

Lavender, Cheryl. (1993). *Moans, Groans and Skeleton Bones* [compact disc]. Milwaukee, WI: Hal Leonard.

Palmer, Hap. (1997). "Have a Good Halloween Night." On *Holiday Songs and Rhythms* [compact disc]. Freeport, NY: Educational Activities.

Skiera-Zucek, Lois. (1989). *Halloween Fun* [cassette]. Long Branch, NJ: Kimbo Educational.

Storytelling and Fingerplays

Hanukkah

Adler, David A. (1995). *One Yellow Daffodil: A Hanukkah Story.* Illus. by Lloyd Bloom. San Diego: Gulliver Books.

Adler, David A. (1997). *Chanukah in Chelm.* Illus. by Kevin O'Malley. New York: Lothrop, Lee & Shepard.

Conway, Diana Cohen. (1994). *Northern Lights: A Hanukkah Story.* Rockville, MD: Kar-Ben Copies.

Jaffe, Nina. (1992). *In the Month of Kislev: A Story for Hanukkah.* Illus. by Louise August. New York: Viking.

Kimmel, Eric A. (1996). *The Magic Dreidels: A Hanukkah Story.* Illus. by Katya Krenina. New York: Holiday House.

Kuskin, Karla. (1995). *A Great Miracle Happened There: A Chanukah Story.* Madison, WI: Demco Media.

Oberman, Sheldon. (1997). *By the Hanukkah Light.* Illus. by Neil Waldman. Honesdale, PA: Boyds Mills Press.

Penn, Malka. (1994). *The Miracle of the Potato Latkes: A Hanukkah Story.* Illus. by Giora Carmi. New York: Holiday House.

Polacco, Patricia. (1996). *Trees of the Dancing Goats.* New York: Simon & Schuster.

Rosen, Michael J. (1992). *Elijah's Angel: A Story for Chanukah and Christmas.* Illus. by Aminah B. L. Robinson. Orlando, FL: Harcourt Brace.

Schnur, Steven. (1995). *The Tie Man's Miracle: A Chanukah Story.* Illus. by Stephen Johnson. New York: William Morrow.

Schotter, Roni. (1993). *Hanukkah!* Illus. by Marylin Hafner. Madison, WI: Demco Media.

Wax, Wendy, ed. (1993). *Hanukkah, Oh Hanukkah!: A Treasury of Stories, Songs, and Games to Share.* Illus. by John Speirs. New York: Bantam Doubleday.

Hanukkah, Multimedia

Chanukah at Home [cassette]. (1988). Cambridge, MA: Rounder Records.

Holidays for Children: Hanukkah/Passover [video]. Schlessinger Media.

Lewis, Shari. (1995). *Lamb Chop's Special Chanukah!* [video]. Cypress, CA: Youngheart Music.

Palmer, Hap. (1997). "Hanukkah." On *Holiday Songs and Rhythms* [compact disc]. Baldwin, NY: Educational Activities.

Rosenthal, Margie. (1987). *Just in Time for Chanukah!* [compact disc]. Portland, OR: Sheera Recordings.

Storytelling and Fingerplays

Hats

Bancroft, Catherine. (1993). *Felix's Hat*. Illus. by Hannah Coale Gruenberg. New York: Simon & Schuster.

Brett, Jan. (1997). *The Hat*. New York: G. P. Putnam.

Carlson, Laurie. (1998). *Boss of the Plains: The Hat That Won the West*. Illus. by Holly Meade. New York: Dorling Kindersley.

Gardella, Tricia. (1997). *Casey's New Hat*. Illus. by Margot Apple. Boston: Houghton Mifflin.

Geringer, Laura. (1987). *A Three Hat Day*. Illus. by Arnold Lobel. New York: HarperCollins.

Hanel, Wolfram. (1995). *The Extraordinary Adventures of an Ordinary Hat*. Illus. by Christa Unzner-Fischer. New York: North-South Books. (Paperback)

Howard, Elizabeth Fitzgerald. (1991). *Aunt Flossie's Hats (and Crab Cakes Later)*. Illus. by James Ransome. New York: Clarion Books.

Kalman, Bobbie. (1998). *Bandanas, Chaps, and Ten-Gallon Hats*. New York: Crabtree Publishing.

Keller, Holly. (1995). *Rosata*. New York: Greenwillow.

Malka, Lucy. (1995). *Fun with Hats*. Illus. by Melinda Levine. Greenvale, NY: Mondo Pub. (Paperback)

Milich, Melissa. (1997). *Miz Fannie Mae's Fine New Easter Hat*. Illus. by Yong Chen. Boston: Little, Brown.

Miller, Margaret. (1988). *Whose Hat?* New York: William Morrow.

Morris, Ann. (1989). *Hats, Hats, Hats*. Photos by Ken Heyman. New York: Lothrop, Lee & Shepard.

Oborne, Martine. (1997). *Juice the Pig*. Illus. by Axel Scheffler. New York: Holt.

Pearson, Tracey Campbell. (1997). *The Purple Hat*. New York: Farrar, Straus & Giroux.

Reed, Lynn Rowe. (1995). *Pedro, His Perro, and the Alphabet Sombrero*. New York: Hyperion.

Smath, Jerry. (1995). *A Hat So Simple*. Mahwah, NJ: Troll. (Paperback)

Stoeke, Janet Morgan. (1994). *A Hat for Minerva Louise*. New York: Dutton.

Storytelling and Fingerplays

Health

Aliki. (1992). *I'm Growing*. New York: HarperCollins.

Barner, Bob. (1996). *Dem Bones*. San Francisco: Chronicle Books.

Berger, Melvin. (1995). *Germs Make Me Sick* (Rev. ed.). Illus. by Marylin Hafner. New York: HarperCollins.

Brown, Laurene Krasny, & Brown, Marc Tolon. (1990). *Dinosaurs Alive and Well! A Guide to Good Health.* Boston: Little, Brown.

Caffey, Donna. (1998). *Yikes—Lice!* Illus. by Patrick Girouard. Niles, IL: Albert Whitman & Co.

Dooley, Virginia. (1996). *Tubes in My Ears: My Trip to the Hospital.* Illus. by Miriam Katin. Greenvale, NY: Mondo Publications.

Gosselin, Kim. (1998). *Taking Diabetes to School* (2nd ed.). Illus. by Moss Freedman. Valley Park, MO: JayJo Books.

Janovitz, Marilyn. (1994). *Is It Time?* New York: North-South Books.

Leedy, Loreen. (1994). *The Edible Pyramid: Good Eating Every Day.* New York: Holiday House.

London, Jonathan. (1992). *The Lion Who Had Asthma.* Illus. by Nadine B. Westcott. Beaver Dam, WI: Concept Books.

Newcome, Zita. (1997). *Toddlerobics.* Cambridge, MA: Candlewick Press.

Powell, Jillian. (1997). Health Matters series. Austin, TX: Raintree/Steck Vaughn. *Exercise and Your Health; Food and Your Health; Hygiene and Your Health.*

Rockwell, Harlow. (1987). *My Dentist.* New York: William Morrow. (Paperback)

Rockwell, Harlow. (1992). *My Doctor.* New York: Macmillan.

Showers, Paul. (1991). *How Many Teeth?* Newly illus. by True Kelley. New York: HarperCollins.

Showers, Paul. (1997). *Sleep Is for Everyone.* Illus. by Wendy Watson. New York: HarperCollins.

Teague, Mark. (1994). *Pigsty.* New York: Scholastic.

Thompson, Carol. (1997). *Piggy Washes Up.* Cambridge, MA: Candlewick Press.

Van Cleave, Janice. (1998). *Janice Van Cleave's Play and Find Out about the Human Body.* Somerset, NY: Wiley.

Health, Multimedia

Chef Combo's Fantastic Adventures in Tasting and Nutrition [kit]. (1996). Rosemont, IL: National Dairy Council.

Come See What the Doctor Sees [video]. (1994). Half Moon Bay, CA: Visual Mentor.

Goofy over Dental Health [video]. (1991). Disney Educational Productions.

Storytelling and Fingerplays

A Kid's Guide to Personal Grooming [video]. (1989). Englewood, CO: Learning Tree Publishing.

K–6 Classroom Gallery [CD-ROM]. (1997). Lancaster, PA: Classroom Connect.

Leokum, Arkady. (1988). *Tell Me Why: A Healthy Body* [video]. Marina del Rey, CA: Tell Me Why.

Preschool Power! Jacket Flips and Other Tips [video]. (1991). Concept Associates.

Raffi. (1988). "Bathtime." On *Raffi in Concert with the Rise and Shine Band* [video]. Hollywood, CA: Troubadour Records.

Rock 'N Roll Fitness Fun [cassette or compact disc]. (1989). Long Branch, NJ: Kimbo Educational.

Stewart, Georgiana. (1987). *Good Morning Exercises for Kids* [cassette]. Long Branch, NJ: Kimbo Educational.

Homes

Ackerman, Karen. (1992). *I Know a Place*. Illus. by Deborah Kogan Ray. Boston: Houghton Mifflin.

Ackerman, Karen. (1995). *The Sleeping Porch*. Illus. by Elizabeth Sayles. New York: William Morrow.

Arnold, Ted. (1987). *No Jumping on the Bed*. New York: Dutton.

Ballard, Robin. (1994). *Good-Bye House*. New York: Greenwillow.

Brown, Richard Eric. (1988). *100 Words about My House*. Orlando, FL: Harcourt Brace.

Bunting, Eve. (1991). *Fly Away Home*. Illus. by Ronald Himler. New York: Clarion Books.

Delafosse, Claude. (Ed.). (1998). *Houses*. New York: Scholastic.

Dorros, Arthur. (1992). *This Is My House*. New York: Scholastic.

Gibbons, Gail. (1990). *How a House Is Built*. New York: Holiday House.

Hill, Elizabeth Starr. (1991). *Evan's Corner*. Revised and newly illus. by D. Brodie. New York: Viking.

Hoberman, Mary Ann. (1978). *A House Is a House for Me*. Illus. by Betty Fraser. New York: Viking.

Kalman, Bobbie. (1994). *Homes around the World*. New York: Crabtree Publishing.

Kuklin, Susan. (1992). *How My Family Lives in America*. New York: Bradbury Press.

McDonald, Megan. (1996). *My House Has Stars.* Illus. by Peter Catalanotto. New York: Orchard Books.

McGovern, Ann. (1997). *The Lady in the Box.* Illus. by Marni Backer. New York: Turtle Books.

Morris, Ann. (1992). *Houses and Homes.* Photos by Ken Heyman. New York: Lothrop, Lee & Shepard.

Rosen, Michael. (Ed.). (1992). *Home.* New York: HarperCollins.

Rosen, Michael. (1996). *This Is Our House.* Illus. by Bob Graham. Cambridge, MA: Candlewick Press.

Rounds, Glen. (1996). *Sod Houses on the Great Plains.* New York: Holiday House.

Rylant, Cynthia. (1993). *Everyday House.* New York: Simon & Schuster. (Board book)

Saul, Carol P. (1995). *Someplace Else.* Illus. by Barry Root. New York: Simon & Schuster.

Shelby, Anne. (1996). *The Someday House.* Illus. by Rosanne Litzinger. New York: Orchard Books.

Williams, John. (1997). *Houses and Homes.* Austin, TX: Raintree/Steck Vaughn.

Homes, Multimedia

Community Construction Kit [CD-ROM]. (1998). Watertown, MA: Tom Snyder Productions.

Dig Hole, Build House [video]. (1994). Gig Harbor, WA: Real World Video.

Gryphon Bricks [CD-ROM]. (1996). San Diego, CA: Gryphon Software Corp.

Let's Build a House [video]. (1996). San Diego, CA: Video Connections.

A Silly, Noisy House [CD-ROM]. (1991). Santa Monica, CA: Voyager Company.

Insects and Spiders

Arnosky, Jim. (1996). *Crinkleroot's Guide to Knowing Butterflies and Moths.* New York: Simon & Schuster.

Banks, Kate. (1997). *Spider, Spider.* Illus. by Georg Hallensleben. New York: Farrar, Straus & Giroux.

Cassie, Brian and Jerry Pallotta. (1995). *The Butterfly Alphabet Book.* Illus. by Mark Astrella. Watertown, MA: Charlesbridge Publishers.

Storytelling and Fingerplays

Cole, Joanna. (1995). *Spider's Lunch: All about Garden Spiders*. Illus. by Ron Broda. New York: Grosset & Dunlap. (Paperback)

Cole, Joanna. (1996). *The Magic School Bus inside a Beehive*. Illus. by Bruce Degen. New York: Scholastic.

Cole, Joanna. (1997). *The Magic School Bus Spins a Web: A Book about Spiders*. Illus. by Bruce Degen. New York: Scholastic. (Paperback)

Crewe, Sabrina. (1997). *The Bee*. Austin, TX: Raintree/Steck Vaughn.

Dallinger, Jane. (1990). *Grasshoppers*. Illus. by Yuko Sato. Minneapolis: First Avenue Editions. (Paperback)

Fowler, Allan. (1996). *Spiders Are Not Insects*. Chicago: Children's Press.

Fowler, Allan. (1997). *It Could Still Be a Butterfly*. Chicago: Children's Press.

Gerholdt, James E. (1996a). *Black Widow Spiders*. Minneapolis: Abdo & Daughters.

Gerholdt, James E. (1996b). *Jumping Spider*. Austin, TX: Raintree/Steck Vaughn.

Gerholdt, James E. (1996c). *Trapdoor Spiders*. Minneapolis: Abdo & Daughters.

Gerholdt, James E. (1996d). *Wolf Spiders*. Minneapolis: Abdo & Daughters.

Gibbons, Gail. (1993). *Spiders*. New York: Holiday House.

Gibbons, Gail. (1997). *The Honey Makers*. New York: William Morrow.

Greenberg, David T. (1997). *Bugs!* Illus. by Lynn Munsinger. Boston: Little, Brown.

Hariton, Anca. (1995). *Butterfly Story*. New York: Dutton.

Heiligman, Deborah. (1996). *From Caterpillar to Butterfly*. Illus. by Bari Weissman. New York: HarperCollins.

Hillyard, P. D. (1993). *Insects and Spiders*. New York: Dorling Kindersley.

Jeunesse, Gallimard. (1997a). *Bees*. New York: Scholastic.

Jeunesse, Gallimard. (1997b). *Butterflies*. New York: Scholastic.

Krulik, Nancy E., & Cole, Joanna. (1996). *The Magic School Bus: Butterfly and the Bog Beast: A Book about Butterfly Camouflage*. Illus. by Dana and Del Thompson. New York: Scholastic. (Paperback)

Laughlin, Robin Kittrell. (1996). *Backyard Bugs*. Illus. by Sue Hubbell. San Francisco: Chronicle Books.

Ling, Mary. (1992). *Butterfly*. Photos by Kim Taylor. New York: Dorling Kindersley.

MacDonald, Amy. (1996). *The Spider Who Created the World*. Illus. by G. Brian Karas. New York: Orchard Books.

MacQuitty, Miranda. (1996). *Amazing Bugs*. New York: Dorling Kindersley.

McDonald, Megan. (1995). *Insects Are My Life.* Illus. by Paul Brett Johnson. New York: Orchard Books.

Oppenheim, Joanne. (1998). *Have You Seen Bugs?* Illus. by Ron Broda. New York: Scholastic.

Pallotta, Jerry. (1993). *The Icky Bug Alphabet Book.* Illus. by Ralph Masiello. Watertown, MA: Charlesbridge Books.

Pinczes, Elinor. (1995). *A Remainder of One.* Illus. by Bonnie MacKain. Boston: Houghton Mifflin.

Polacco, Patricia. (1993). *The Bee Tree.* New York: Philomel Books.

Porte, Barbara Ann. (1993). *"Leave That Cricket Be, Alan Lee."* Illus. by Donna Ruff. New York: Greenwillow.

Ring, Elizabeth. (1994). *Night Flier.* Photos by Dwight Kuhn. Brookfield, CT: Millbrook Press.

Ryden, Hope. (1996). *ABC of Crawlers and Flyers.* New York: Clarion Books.

Ryder, Joanne. (1994). *My Father's Hands.* Illus. by Mark Graham. New York: William Morrow.

Savage, Stephen. (1995a). *Butterfly.* Cincinnati, OH: Thomson Learning.

Savage, Stephen. (1995b). *Spider.* Illus. by Phil Weare. Cincinnati, OH: Thomson Learning.

Thompson, Mary. (1996). *Gran's Bees.* Illus. by Donna Peterson. Brookfield, CT: Millbrook Press.

Trapani, Iza. (1993). *The Itsy Bitsy Spider.* Dallas, TX: Whispering Coyote Press.

Wechsler, Doug. (1995). *Bizarre Bugs.* New York: Cobblehill.

Insects and Spiders, Multimedia

Griffith, Joelene. (1993). *We Like Bugs* [cassette and book]. East Wenatchee, WA: Learning Workshop.

Insects and Spiders [video]. (1993). New York: Sony Kids' Video.

The Multimedia Bug Book [CD-ROM]. (1995). New York: Workman Publishing Co.

Murphy, Jane Lawliss. (1993). *Songs about Insects, Bugs and Squiggly Things* [cassette]. Long Branch, NJ: Kimbo Educational.

Tell Me Why: Insects [video]. (1987). Marina del Rey, CA: Tell Me Why.

Storytelling and Fingerplays

Mail Carrier

Gibbons, Gail. (1987). *The Post Office Book: Mail and How It Moves*. New York: HarperCollins.

Henkes, Kevin. (1995). *Good-Bye, Curtis*. Illus. by Marisabina Russo. New York: Greenwillow.

Keats, Ezra Jack. (1998). *A Letter to Amy* (Reprint). San Francisco: Children's Books.

Lakin, Pat. (1995). *Red-Letter Day*. Illus. by Doug Cushman. Austin, TX: Raintree/Steck Vaughn.

Landstrom, Olof, & Landstrum, Lena. (1994). *Will Goes to the Post Office*. New York: Farrar, Straus & Giroux.

Levinson, Nancy Smiler. (1992). *Snowshoe Thompson*. Illus. by Joan Sandin. New York: HarperCollins.

Lillegard, Dee. (1997). *Tortoise Brings the Mail*. Illus. by Jillian Lund. New York: Dutton.

Miller, Robert H. (1994). *The Story of "Stagecoach" Mary Fields*. Illus. by Cheryl Hanna. Englewood Cliffs, NJ: Silver Press.

Rylant, Cynthia. (1993). *Mr. Griggs' Work*. Illus. by Julie Downing. New York: Orchard Books.

Scott, Ann Herbert. (1994). *Hi*. Illus. by Glo Coalson. New York: Philomel Books.

Skurzynksi, Gloria. (1992). *Here Comes the Mail*. New York: Macmillan.

Mail Carrier, Multimedia

At the Post Office [video]. (1995). Tallahassee, FL: Dogwood Video.

Postal Station [video]. (1991). TV Ontario/distributed by Films for the Humanities.

Post Office [video]. (1991). Washington, DC: National Geographic.

There Goes the Mail [video]. (1997). New York: KidVision.

Mice

Brett, Jan. (1994). *Town Mouse, Country Mouse*. New York: G. P. Putnam.

Cowley, Joy. (1995). *Mouse Bride*. Illus. by David Christiana. New York: Scholastic.

Duke, Kate. (1992). *Isabelle Tells a Good One*. New York: Dutton.

Edwards, Pamela Duncan. (1996). *Livingstone Mouse*. Illus. by Henry Cole. New York: HarperCollins.

Farris, Pamela J. (1996). *Young Mouse and Elephant: An East African Folktale*. Illus. by Valeri Gorbachev. Boston: Houghton Mifflin.

Fleming, Denise. (1992). *Lunch*. New York: Holt.

Galvin, Laura Gates et al. (1998). *Deer Mouse at Old Farm Road*. Illus. Katy Bratun. Norwalk, CT: Soundprints Corp.

Holabird, Katharine. (1993). *Angelina Ice Skates*. Illus. by Helen Craig. New York: C. N. Potter Publishers.

Krensky, Stephen. (1995). *Three Blind Mice Mystery*. Illus. by Lynn Munsinger. New York: Delacorte.

McBratney, Sam. (1996). *The Dark at the Top of the Stairs*. Illus. by Ivan Bates. Cambridge, MA: Candlewick Press.

McMillan, Bruce. (1993). *Mouse Views: What the Class Pet Saw*. New York: Holiday House.

Monson, A. M. (1997). *Wanted: Best Friend*. Illus. by Lynn Munsinger. New York: Dial Books.

Palazzo-Craig, Janet. (1995). *Max and Maggie in Spring*. Illus. by Paul Meisel. Mahwah, NJ: Troll.

Reiser, Lynn. (1995). *Two Mice in Three Fables*. New York: Greenwillow.

Riley, Linnea Asplind. (1997). *Mouse Mess*. New York: Blue Sky Press.

Ring, Elizabeth. (1995). *Lucky Mouse*. Illus. by Dwight Kuhn. Brookfield, CT: Millbrook Press.

Roth, Susan. (1997). *My Love for You*. New York: Dial Books.

Sathre, Vivian. (1995). *Mouse Chase*. Illus. by Ward Schumaker. Orlando, FL: Harcourt Brace.

Schindel, John. (1994). *What's for Lunch?* Illus. by Kevin O'Malley. New York: Lothrop, Lee & Shepard.

Summers, Kate. (1997). *Milly and Tilly: The Story of a Town Mouse and a Country Mouse*. Illus. by Maggie Kneen. New York: Dutton.

Waber, Bernard. (1995). *Do You See a Mouse?* Boston: Houghton Mifflin.

Walsh, Ellen Stoll. (1996). *Samantha*. Orlando, FL: Harcourt Brace.

Young, Ed. (1992). *Seven Blind Mice*. New York: Philomel Books.

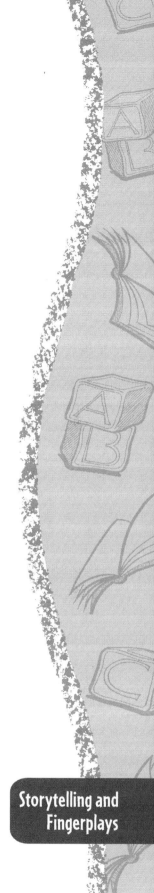

Storytelling and Fingerplays

Mice, Multimedia

If You Give a Mouse a Cookie [CD-ROM]. (1995). New York: HarperCollins Interactive.

Lionni, Leo. (1987). "Frederick." On *Five Lionni Classics* [video]. New York: Random House Home Video.

Palmer, Hap. (1995). "The Mice Go Marching." On *Rhythms on Parade* [compact disc]. Baldwin, NY: Educational Activities.

Sharon, Lois, & Sharon, Bram. (1984). "Three Blind Mice" and "Hickory, Dickory, Dock." On *Mainly Mother Goose* [compact disc]. Toronto.: Elephant Records.

Milk

Aliki. (1992). *Milk: From Cow to Carton*. New York: HarperCollins.

Asch, Frank. (1992). *Milk and Cookies*. Milwaukee, WI: Gareth Stevens.

Barton, Byron. (1995). *Wee Little Woman*. New York: HarperCollins.

Brady, Peter and William Munoz. (1996). *Cows*. Mankato, MN: Bridgestone Books.

Ericsson, Jennifer A. (1993). *No Milk*. Illus. by Ora Eitan. New York: Tambourine Books.

Fowler, Allan. (1992). *Thanks to Cows*. Chicago: Children's Press.

Gibbons, Gail. (1985). *The Milk Makers*. New York: Simon & Schuster.

Godfrey, Neale S. (1995). *Here's the Scoop: Follow an Ice Cream Cone around the World*. Illus. by Randy Verougstraete. Morristown, NJ: Silver Burdett Press.

Grossman, Bill, & Chess, Victoria. (1991). *Tommy at the Grocery Store*. New York: Harper Collins. (Paperback)

Keillor, Garrison. (1996). *The Old Man Who Loved Cheese*. Illus. by Anne Wilsdorf. Boston: Little, Brown.

Keller, Stella, & Holm, John. (1990). *Ice Cream*. Austin, TX: Raintree/Steck Vaughn.

Mazen, Barbara S. (1994). *Pass the Cheese Please*. Illus. by Paul Harvey. Delran, NJ: Newbridge. (Paperback)

Older, Jules. (1997). *Cow*. Illus. by Lyn Severance. Watertown, MA: Charlesbridge Publishers.

Peterson, Cris. (1994). *Extra Cheese, Please! Mozzarella's Journey from Cow to Pizza*. Illus. by Alvis Upitis. Honesdale, PA: Boyds Mills Press.

Reid, Mary Ebeltoft. (1997). *Let's Find Out about Ice Cream.* New York: Scholastic. (Paperback)

Schertle, Alice. (1994). *How Now Brown Cow?* Illus. by Amanda Schaffer. San Diego, CA: Browndeer Press.

Seymour, Tres. (1993). *Hunting the White Cow.* Illus. by Wendy Anderson Halperin. New York: Orchard Books.

Van Laan, Nancy. (1993). *The Tiny, Tiny Boy and the Big, Big Cow: A Scottish Folk Tale.* Illus. by Marjorie Priceman. New York: Knopf.

Milk, Multimedia

From Moo to You [CD-ROM]. (1996). Westmont, IL: Dairy Council of Wisconsin.

Let's Go to the Ice Cream and Yogurt Factory [video]. (1996). Burlington, VT: Vermont Story Works.

Milk Cow, Eat Cheese [video]. (1995). Gig Harbor, WA: Real World Video.

Paterson, Katherine. (1996). *Smallest Cow in the World* [book and cassette]. Scranton, PA: Harper Audio.

Music

Bartlett, T. C. (1997). *Tuba Lessons.* Illus. by Monique Felix. Orlando, FL: Harcourt Brace.

Brett, Jan. (1991). *Berlioz the Bear.* New York: G. P. Putnam.

Buck, Nola. (1996). *Sid and Sam.* Illus. by G. Brian Karas. New York: HarperCollins.

Davis, Wendy. (1997). *From Metal to Music: A Photo Essay.* Chicago: Children's Press.

Drew, Helen. (1993). *My First Music Book.* New York: Dorling Kindersley.

Eversole, Robyn. (1995). *Flute Player / La Flautista.* Illus. by G. Brian Karas. New York: Orchard Books.

Fleming, Candace. (1997). *Gabriella's Song.* Illus. by Giselle Potter. Colchester, CT: Atheneum.

Hayes, Ann. (1995a). *Meet the Marching Smithereens.* Illus. by Karmen Thompson. Orlando, FL: Harcourt Brace.

Hayes, Ann. (1995b). *Meet the Orchestra.* Illus. by Karmen Thompson. Orlando, FL: Harcourt Brace.

Hewitt, Sally. (1994). *Pluck and Scrape.* Illus. by Peter Millard. Chicago: Children's Press.

Storytelling and Fingerplays

Imai, Miko. (1995). *Sebastian's Trumpet*. Cambridge, MA: Candlewick Press.

Kalman, Bobbie. (1997). *Musical Instruments from A to Z*. New York: Crabtree Publishing.

Livo, Norma J. (1996). *Troubadour's Storybag: Musical Folktales of the World*. Golden, CO: Fulcrum Pub.

Millman, Isaac. (1998). *Moses Goes to a Concert*. New York: Farrar, Straus & Giroux.

Moss, Lloyd. (1996). *Zin! Zin! Zin! A Violin*. Illus. by Marjorie Priceman. New York: Simon & Schuster.

Pinkney, J. Brian. (1994). *Max Found Two Sticks*. New York: Simon & Schuster.

Raschka, Chris. (1992). *Charlie Parker Played Bebop*. New York: Orchard Books.

Raschka, Chris. (1997). *Mysterious Thelonious*. New York: Orchard Books.

Rachlin, Ann. Famous Children series. Illus. by Susan Hellard. Hauppauge, NY: Barron's Educational Series. (Paperback) *Bach* (1992); *Beethoven* (1994); *Brahms* (1993); *Chopin* (1993); *Handel* (1992); *Haydn* (1992); *Mozart* (1992); *Schubert* (1994); *Schumann* (1993); *Tchaikovsky* (1993).

Music, Multimedia

Child's Celebration of Showtunes [cassette]. (1992). Redway, CA: Music for Little People.

Jenkins, Ella. (1990). *Rhythm and Game Songs for the Little Ones* [cassette]. Washington, DC: Smithsonian/Folkways.

Jenkins, Ella. (1994). *This Is Rhythm* [compact disc]. Washington, DC: Smithsonian/Folkways.

Louchard, Ric. (1993). *Hey, Ludwig! Classical Piano Solos for Playful Times* [compact disc]. Redway, CA: Music for Little People.

Meter [video]. (1994). Princeton, NJ: Films for the Humanities & Sciences.

Pitch [video]. (1994). Princeton, NJ: Films for the Humanities & Sciences.

Stanley, Leotha. (1994). *Be a Friend: The Story of African American Music in Song, Words and Pictures* [book and cassette]. Illus. by Henry Hawkins. Middleton, WI: Zino Press.

Stewart, Georgiana. (1992). *Multicultural Rhythm Stick Fun* [compact disc]. Long Branch, NJ: Kimbo Educational.

Storytelling and Fingerplays

Numbers

Anno, Mitsumasa. (1995). *Anno's Magic Seeds*. New York: G. P. Putnam.

Big Fat Hen. (1994). Illus. by Keith Baker. Orlando, FL: Harcourt Brace.

Blackstone, Stella. (1996). *Grandma Went to Market: A Round-the-World Counting Rhyme*. Illus. by Bernard Lodge. Boston: Houghton Mifflin.

Brusca, Maria Christina. (1995). *Three Friends: A Counting Book/Tres Amigos: Un Cuento Para Contar*. New York: Holt.

Carlstrom, Nancy White. (1996). *Let's Count It Out, Jesse Bear*. Illus. by Bruce Degen. New York: Simon & Schuster.

Challoner, Jack. (1992). *Science Book of Numbers*. Orlando, FL: Harcourt Brace.

Cole, Norma. (1994). *Blast Off! A Space Counting Book*. Illus. by Marshall Peck III. Watertown, MA: Charlesbridge Publishers.

Dale, Penny. (1994). *Ten Out of Bed*. Cambridge, MA: Candlewick Press.

Five Little Ducks: An Old Rhyme. (1995). Illus. by Pamela Paparone. New York: North-South Books.

Fleming, Denise. (1992). *Count!* New York: Holt.

Geisert, Arthur. (1992). *Pigs from 1 to 10*. Boston: Houghton Mifflin.

Geisert, Arthur. (1996). *Roman Numerals I to MM*. Boston: Houghton Mifflin.

Giganti, Paul. (1992). *Each Orange Had 8 Slices: A Counting Book*. Illus. by Donald Crews. New York: Greenwillow.

Goennel, Heidi. (1994). *Odds and Evens: A Numbers Book*. New York: Tambourine Books.

Harley, Bill. (1996). *Sitting Down to Eat*. Illus. by Kitty Harvill. Little Rock, AR: August House Little Folk.

Jonas, Ann. (1995). *Splash!* New York: Greenwillow.

Mazzola, Frank. (1997). *Counting Is for the Birds*. Watertown, MA: Charlesbridge Publishers.

Noll, Sally. (1997). *Surprise!* New York: Greenwillow.

Ryan, Pam Munoz. (1996). *Crayon Counting Book*. Illus. by Frank Mazzola, Jr. Watertown, MA: Charlesbridge Publishers.

Schlein, Miriam. (1996). *More Than One*. Illus. by Donald Crews. New York: Greenwillow.

Sturges, Philemon. (1995). *Ten Flashing Fireflies*. Illus. by Anna Vojtech. New York: North-South Books.

Wells, Robert E. (1993). *Is a Blue Whale the Biggest Thing There Is?* Niles, IL: Albert Whitman & Co.

Yektai, Niki. (1996). *Bears at the Beach: Counting 10–20*. Brookfield, CT: Millbrook Press.

Storytelling and Fingerplays

Numbers, Multimedia

Counting and Sorting [CD-ROM]. (1997). New York: DK Multimedia.

Introduction to Letters and Numerals [video]. (1985). Hightstown, NJ: SRA/McGraw-Hill.

Jenkins, Ella. (1990). *Counting Games and Rhythms for the Little Ones* (Vol. 1). [cassette]. Washington, DC: Smithsonian/Folkways.

Millie's Math House [CD-ROM]. (1992). Redmond, WA: Edmark.

Palmer, Hap. (1986). *Learning Basic Skills* [video]. Freeport, NY: Educational Activities.

Palmer, Hap. *Math Readiness—Vocabulary and Concepts* [cassette]. Freeport, NY: Educational Activities.

Nursery Rhymes

Aylesworth, Jim. (1992). *"The Cat and the Fiddle" and More*. New York: Macmillan.

Aylesworth, Jim. (1994). *My Son John*. Illus. by David Frampton. New York: Holt.

Benjamin, Floella, ed. (1995). *Skip Across the Ocean: Nursery Rhymes from around the World*. Illus. by Sheila Moxley. New York: Orchard Books.

Big Fat Hen. (1994). Illus. by Keith Baker. Orlando, FL: Harcourt Brace.

Bornstein, Harry, et al. (1992). *Nursery Rhymes from Mother Goose: Told in Signed English*. Washington, DC: Kendall Green Publications.

Chorao, Kay. (1994). *Mother Goose Magic*. New York: Dutton.

Christelow, Eileen. (1998). *Five Little Monkeys Jumping on the Bed*. Boston: Houghton Mifflin.

Dyer, Jane. (1996). *Animal Crackers: A Delectable Collection of Pictures, Poems, and Lullabies for the Very Young*. Boston: Little, Brown.

Eagle, Kin. (1994). *It's Raining, It's Pouring*. Illus. by Robert Gilbert. Dallas, TX: Whispering Coyote Press.

Five Little Ducks: An Old Rhyme. (1995). Illus. by Pamela Paparone. New York: North-South Books.

Hale, Sara. (1995). *Mary Had a Little Lamb*. Illus. by Salley Mavor. New York: Orchard Books.

Heller, Nicholas. (1997). *This Little Piggy*. Illus. by Sonja Lamut. New York: Greenwillow.

Kroll, Virginia L. (1995). *Jaha and Jamil Go Down the Hill: An African Mother Goose*. Illus. by Katherine Roundtree. Watertown, MA: Charlesbridge Publishing.

Lansky, Bruce. (1993). *New Adventures of Mother Goose: Gentle Rhymes for Happy Times*. Illus. by Stephen Carpenter. New York: Simon & Schuster.

Little Robin Redbreast: A Mother Goose Rhyme. (1994). Illus. by Shari Halpern. New York: North-South Books.

Lobel, Arnold. (1997). *Arnold Lobel Book of Mother Goose*. New York: Random House.

Manson, Christopher. (1993). *Tree in the Wood: An Old Nursery Song*. New York: North-South Books.

Marks, Alan. (1991). *"Ring-a-Ring o'Roses" and "Ding, Dong, Bell": A Book of Nursery Rhymes*. New York: North-South Books.

Marks, Alan. (1993). *Over the Hills and Far Away: A Book of Nursery Rhymes*. New York: North-South Books.

Miranda, Anne. (1997). *To Market, to Market*. Illus. by Janet Stevens. Orlando, FL: Harcourt Brace.

My Very First Mother Goose. (1996). Edited by Iona Opie. Illus. by Rosemary Wells. Cambridge, MA: Candlewick Press.

Old Mother Hubbard and Her Wonderful Dog. (1991). Illus. by James Marshall. New York: Farrar, Straus & Giroux.

Opie, Iona Archibald. (1997). Cambridge, MA: Candlewick Press. *Humpty Dumpty and Other Rhymes; Pussycat Pussycat and Other Rhymes; Wee Willie Winkie and Other Rhymes*. (Board books)

Polacco, Patricia. (1995). *Babushka's Mother Goose*. New York: Philomel Books.

Scieszka, Jon. (1994). *The Book That Jack Wrote*. Illus. by Daniel Adel. New York: Viking.

Slier, Debby. (1993). *Real Mother Goose Book of American Rhymes*. Illus. by Patty McCloskey-Padgett et al. New York: Scholastic.

Sweet, Melissa. (1992). *Fiddle-i-ee: A Farmyard Song for the Very Young*. Boston: Little, Brown.

Van Rynbach, Iris. (1995). *Five Little Pumpkins*. Honesdale, PA: Boyds Mills Press.

Nursery Rhymes, Multimedia

Children's Treasury II: Rhymes, Poems, Stories [CD-ROM]. (1994). Fairfield, CT: Queue.

Mixed-Up Mother Goose [CD-ROM]. (1995). Bellevue, WA: Sierra On-Line.

Nursery Songs and Rhymes [video]. (1993). Sandy, UT: Waterford Institute.

Olde Mother Goose [cassette and paperback book]. (1993). Performed by the Hubbards. Illus. by Blanche Fisher Wright. August House Audio.

Palmer, Hap. (1991). *Hap Palmer Sings Classic Nursery Rhymes* [cassette]. Freeport, NY: Educational Activities.

Rusty and Rosy Nursery Songs and Rhymes [video]. (1993). Sandy, UT: Waterford Institute.

Occupations

Brandenberg, Alexa. (1996). *I Am Me*. Orlando, FL: Harcourt Brace.

Florian, Douglas. How We Work series. New York: Greenwillow. (Paperback.) *An Auto Mechanic* (1994); *A Chef* (1992); *A Fisher* (1994); *A Painter* (1993).

Gibbons, Gail. (1992). *Say Woof! The Day of a Country Veterinarian*. New York: Macmillan.

Grossman, Patricia. (1991). *The Night Ones*. Illus. by Lydia Dabcovich. Orlando, FL: Harcourt Brace.

Henkes, Kevin. (1995). *Good-Bye, Curtis*. Illus. by Marisabina Russo. New York: Greenwillow.

Isaacs, Gwynne. (1991). *While You Are Asleep*. Illus. by Cathi Hepworth. New York: Walker & Co.

Kalman, Maira. (1993). *Chicken Soup, Boots*. New York: Viking.

Kunhardt, Edith. I'm Going to Be series. New York: Scholastic. (Paperback.) *A Fire Fighter* (1995); *A Police Officer* (1995); *A Vet* (1996).

MacKinnon, Debbie. (1996). *What Am I?* Illus. by Anthea Sieveking. New York: Dial Books.

Maynard, Christopher. (1997). *Jobs People Do*. New York: DK Publishing.

Miller, Margaret. (1990). *Who Uses This?* New York: Greenwillow.

Miller, Margaret. (1994). *Guess Who?* New York: Greenwillow.

Miller, Margaret. (1997). *Whose Hat?* (Reprint). New York: Greenwillow. (Paperback)

Moses, Amy. (1997). *Doctors Help People*. Mankato, MN: Child's World.

Our Neighborhood series. San Francisco: Children's Book Press.

Duvall, Jill D. (1997). *Chef Ki Is Serving*.
    Duvall, Jill D. (1997). *Meet Rory Hohenstein, a Professional Dancer*.
    Duvall, Jill D. (1997). *Mr. Duvall Reports the News*.
    Duvall, Jill D. (1997). *Ms. Moja Makes Beautiful Clothes*.
    Duvall, Jill D. (1997). *Who Keeps the Water Clean?: Ms. Schindler!*
    Flanagan, Alice K. (1997). *Ask Nurse Pfaff, She'll Help You*.
    Flanagan, Alice K. (1996). *A Busy Day at Mr. Kang's Grocery Store*.
    Flanagan, Alice K. (1997). *A Day in Court with Mrs. Trinh*.
    Flanagan, Alice K. (1997). *Mrs. Murphy Fights Fires*.
    Flanagan, Alice K. (1996). *The Wilsons, a House-Painting Team*.

Paulsen, Gary. (1997). *Worksong*. Illus. by Ruth Wright Paulsen. Orlando, FL: Harcourt Brace.

Radford, Derek. (1995). *Harry at the Garage*. Cambridge, MA: Candlewick Press.

Ready, Dee. Community Helpers series. Chicago: Children's Book Press. *Astronauts* (1998); *Bakers* (1998); *Construction* (1998); *Doctors* (1997); *Farmers*

(1997); *Fire Fighters* (1997); *Garbage Collectors* (1998); *Nurses* (1998); *Police Officers* (1997); *Teacher* (1998); *Veterinarians* (1997); *Zoo Keeper* (1998).

Rylant, Cynthia. (1993). *Mr. Griggs' Work*. Illus. by Julie Downing. New York: Orchard Books.

Occupations, Multimedia

Big Job [CD-ROM]. (1995). Discovery Channel Multimedia.

Harriet's Magic Hats IV series [video]. (1986). Edmonton, Alberta: Access Network, Alberta and Educational Communication Corp. (15 min. Primary level.) *Dog Trainer; Hat Maker; Hotel Manager; Librarian; Museum Curator; Naturalist; Newspaper Reporter; Palaeontologist; Pasta Maker; Photographer; Potter; Puppeteer; Rodeo Cowboy; Sheep Farmer; Ski Instructor; Telephone Installer; Toy Tester; Vegetable Processor; Veterinarian; Water Treatment Engineer; Weather Forecaster; Welder; Zookeeper.*

Pets

Baker, Karen Lee. (1997). *Seneca*. New York: Greenwillow.

Caseley, Judith. (1995). *Mr. Green Peas*. New York: Greenwillow.

Evans, Mark. (1993). *Fish: A Practical Guide to Caring for your Fish*. New York: Dorling Kindersley.

Evans, Mark. (1993). *Hamster: A Practical Guide to Caring for Your Hamster*. New York: Dorling Kindersley.

Flanagan, Alice K. (1996). *Talking Birds*. San Francisco: Children's Book Press.

Gibbons, Gail. (1992). *Say Woof: The Day of a Country Veterinarian*. New York: Macmillan.

Johnson, Angela. (1993). *The Girl Who Wore Snakes*. Illus. by James Ransome. New York: Orchard Books.

Greenwood, Pamela D. (1993). *What about My Goldfish?* Illus. by Jennifer Plecas. New York: Clarion Books.

Griffith, Helen V. (1992). *"Mine Will," Said John* (Reprint). Newly illus. by Jos. A. Smith. New York: Greenwillow.

Johnson, Angela. (1993). *Julius*. Illus. by Dav Pilkey. New York: Orchard Books.

Joosse, Barbara M. (1997). *Nugget and Darling*. Illus. by Sue Truesdell. New York: Clarion Books.

King-Smith, Dick. (1995). *I Love Guinea Pigs*. Illus. by Anita Jeram. Cambridge, MA: Candlewick Press.

Nichols, Grace. (1997). *Asana and the Animals: A Book of Pet Poems.* Illus. by Sarah Adams. Cambridge, MA: Candlewick Press.

Petersen-Fleming, Judy, et al. (1996). *Kitten Training and Critters, Too!* New York: Tambourine Books.

Petersen-Fleming, Judy, et al. (1996). *Puppy Training and Critters, Too!* New York: Tambourine Books.

Pfeffer, Wendy. (1996). *What's It Like to Be a Fish?* Illus. by Holly Keller. New York: HarperCollins.

Reiser, Lynn W. (1992). *Any Kind of Dog.* New York: Greenwillow.

Ross, Michael Elsohn et al. (1998). *Ladybugology.* Illus. by Brian Grogan. Minneapolis: Lerner Publishing.

Rylant, Cynthia. (1997). *Mr. Putter and Tabby Row the Boat.* Illus. by Arthur Howard. Orlando: Harcourt Brace.

Smith, Lane. (1991). *The Big Pets.* New York: Viking.

Spangard, Kristine. (1997). *My Pet Rabbit.* Photos by Andy King. Minneapolis: Lerner Publishing.

Wolf, Jake. (1996). *Daddy, Could I Have an Elephant?* Illus. by Marylin Hafner. New York: Greenwillow.

Ziefert, Harriet. (1996). *Let's Get a Pet.* Illus. by Mavis Smith. New York: Puffin Books. (Paperback)

Zolotow, Charlotte. (1995). *The Old Dog* (Rev. ed.). Newly illus. by James Ransome. New York: HarperCollins.

Pets, Multimedia

Bourgeois, Paulette. (1995). *Franklin Wants a Pet* [book and cassette]. New York: Scholastic.

Cats [video]. (1985). Washington, DC: National Geographic.

Dogs [video]. (1985). Washington, DC: National Geographic.

Fish [video]. (1985). Washington, DC: National Geographic.

Keats, Ezra Jack. (1987). *Pet Show* [video]. Weston Woods.

Storytelling and Fingerplays

Plants

Ardley, Neil. (1991). *The Science Book of Things That Grow.* Orlando, FL: Harcourt Brace.

Berger, Melvin. (1994). *All about Seeds* (Reprint). New York: Scholastic.

Charman, Andrew. (1997). *I Wonder Why Trees Have Leaves and Other Questions about Plants.* Stanwood, WA: Kingfisher.

Christensen Bonnie. (1994). *An Edible Alphabet.* New York: Dial Books.

Dorros, Arthur. (1990). *Rain Forest Secrets.* New York: Scholastic.

Dunphy, Madeleine. (1994). *Here Is the Tropical Rain Forest.* Illus. by Michael Rothman. New York: Hyperion.

Fowler, Allan. (1998). *Good Mushrooms and Bad Toadstools.* Chicago: Children's Press.

Ganeri, Anita. (1995). *What's Inside Plants?* New York: Peter Bedrick Books.

Gibbons, Gail. (1991). *From Seed to Plant.* New York: Holiday House.

Guiberson, Brenda Z. (1991). *Cactus Hotel.* Illus. by Megan Lloyd. New York: Holt.

Jordan, Helene J. (1992). *How a Seed Grows* (Rev. ed.). Illus. by Loretta Krupinski. New York: HarperCollins.

Lucht, Irmgard. (1995). *Red Poppy.* Translated by Frank Jacoby-Nelson. New York: Hyperion.

Maestro, Betsy. (1992). *How Do Apples Grow?* Illus. by Giulio Maestro. New York: HarperCollins.

Maestro, Betsy. (1994). *Why Do Leaves Change Color?* Illus. by Loretta Krupinski. New York: HarperCollins.

Marzollo, Jean. (1996). *It's a Seed.* Illus. by Judith Moffatt. New York: Scholastic.

Morgan, Sally. (1996). *Flowers, Trees and Fruits.* Stanwood, WA: Kingfisher.

Nielsen, Nancy J. (1992). *Carnivorous Plants.* New York: Franklin Watts.

Robbins, Ken. (1990). *A Flower Grows.* New York: Dial Books.

Sekido, Isamu. (1993). *Fruits, Roots, and Fungi: Plants We Eat.* Minneapolis: Lerner Publications.

Visual Dictionary of Plants. (1992). New York: Dorling Kindersley.

What's Inside? Plants. (1992). New York: Dorling Kindersley.

Yolen, Jane. (1993). *Welcome to the Green House.* Illus. by Laura Regan. New York: G. P. Putnam.

Plants, Multimedia

Let's Explore the Jungle with Buzzy the Knowledge Bug [CD-ROM]. (1995). Woodinville, WA: Humongous Entertainment.

Tell Me Why: Vol. 3. Flowers, Plants and Trees [video]. (1987). Marina Del Rey, CA: Tell Me Why.

Wonders of Growing Plants (3rd ed.) [video]. (1992). Churchill Media/SVE.

Storytelling and Fingerplays

Puppets

Babbitt, Natalie. (1989). *Nellie: A Cat on Her Own.* New York: Farrar, Straus & Giroux.

Bulloch, Ivan. (1997). *I Want to Be a Puppeteer.* Illus. by Diane James. Chicago: World Book.

Collodi, Carlo. (1996). *Pinocchio.* Illus. by Ed Young. New York: Philomel Books.

Hoyt-Goldsmith, Diane. (1991). *Pueblo Storyteller.* Illus. by Lawrence Migdale. New York: Holiday House.

Jean Claverie's Fairy Tale Theater: Pop-Up Book with Puppets. (1996). Illus. by Jean Claverie. Hauppauge, NY: Barron's Educational Series.

Keats, Ezra Jack. (1983). *Louie.* New York: William Morrow.

Little Red Riding Hood. (1997). (Finger Puppet Theater.) Illus. by Peter Stevenson. St. Paul, MN: Cartwheel Books.

Wallis, Mary. (1994). *I Can Make Puppets.* Buffalo, NY: Firefly Books.

Weiss, George David, & Thiele, Bob. (1994). *What a Wonderful World.* Illus. by Ashley Bryan. New York: Simon & Schuster.

Puppets, Multimedia

Adventures of Pinocchio [video]. (1994). Charlotte, NC: United American Video.

Introduction to Puppet Making [video]. (1996). Jim Gamble Puppet Productions. Available from Library Video.

Johnson, Laura. (1987). "Puppet Pals." On *Homemade Games and Activities: Make Your Own Rhythm Band* [cassette]. Long Branch, NJ: Kimbo Educational.

Purple

Henkes, Kevin. (1996). *Lilly's Purple Plastic Purse.* New York: Greenwillow.

Hest, Amy. (1992). *The Purple Coat.* Illus. by Amy Schwartz. New York: Aladdin. (Paperback)

Johnson, Crockett. (1987). *Harold and the Purple Crayon.* New York: Harper-Colllins.

Mayer, Mercer. (1996). *Purple Pickle Juice.* New York: Random Library.

Munsch, Robert N. (1992). *Purple, Green and Yellow.* Illus. by Helene Desputeaux. Willowdale, Ontario: Annick Press.

Pearson, Tracey Campbell. (1997). *The Purple Hat.* New York: Farrar, Straus & Giroux.

Prelutsky, Jack. (1986). *Ride a Purple Pelican.* New York: William Morrow.

Rain

Baxter, Nicola. (1998). *Rain, Wind and Storm.* Austin, TX: Raintree/Steck-Vaughn.

Beecham, Caroline. (1996). *Rainbow.* New York: Random House.

Bogacki, Tomek. (1997). *Cat and Mouse in the Rain.* New York: Farrar, Straus & Giroux.

Branley, Franklyn M. (1997). *Down Comes the Rain.* New York: HarperCollins.

Buchanan, Ken, & Buchanan, Debby. (1994). *It Rained in the Desert Today.* Illus. by Libba Tracey. Flagstaff, AZ: Northland.

Calhoun, Mary. (1997). *Flood.* Illus. by Erick Ingraham. New York: William Morrow.

Canizares, Susan, & Chessen, Betsey. (1997). *Storms.* New York: Scholastic.

Carlstrom, Nancy White. (1993). *What Does the Rain Play?* New York: Macmillan.

Davies, Kay, & Oldfield, Wendy. (1995). *Rain.* Photos by Robert Pickett. Austin, TX: Raintree/Steck Vaughn.

Deming, Alhambra G. (1994). *Who Is Tapping at My Window?* Illus. by Monica Wellington. New York: Penguin Books.

Godfrey, Jan. (1994). *Why Is It Raining?* Illus. by D'Reen Neeves. Minneapolis: Augsburg Fortress Pub.

Hest, Amy. (1995). *In the Rain with Baby Duck.* Illus. by Jill Barton. Cambridge, MA: Candlewick Press.

Johnson, Angela. (1994). *Rain Feet.* Illus. by Rhonda Mitchell. New York: Orchard Books. (Board book)

Kuskin, Karla. (1995). *James and the Rain.* Illus. by Reg Cartwright. New York: Simon & Schuster.

Laser, Michael. (1997). *The Rain.* Illus. by Jeffrey Green. New York: Simon & Schuster.

Llewellyn, Claire, & Lewis, Anthony. (1995). *Wind and Rain.* Hauppauge, NY: Barron's Educational Series.

London, Jonathan. (1997). *Puddles.* Illus. by G. Brian Karas. New York: Viking.

Lynn, Sara and James, Diane. (1998). *Rain and Shine.* Illus. by Joe Wright. Chicago: World Book.

Storytelling and Fingerplays

Markle, Sandra. (1993). *A Rainy Day.* Illus. by Cathy Johnson. New York: Orchard Books.

May, Garelick. (1997). *Where Does the Butterfly Go When It Rains?* Illus. by Nicholas Wilton. Greenvale, NY: Mondo Publications.

McPhail, David M. (1998). *The Puddle.* New York: Farrar, Straus & Giroux.

Merk, Ann and Merk, Jim. (1994). *Rain, Snow and Ice.* Vero Beach, FL: Rourke Corp.

Nikola-Lisa, W. (1993). *Storm.* Illus. by Michael Hays. Colchester, CT: Atheneum.

Ray, Mary Lyn. (1996). *Mud.* Illus. by Lauren Stringer. Orlando, FL: Harcourt Brace.

Reay, Joanne. (1995). *Bumpa Rumpus and the Rainy Day.* Illus. by Adriano Gon. Boston: Houghton Mifflin.

Shannon, George. (1995). *April Showers.* Illus. by Jose Aruego and Ariane Dewey. New York: Greenwillow.

Simon, Norma. (1995). *Wet World.* Illus. by Alexi Natchev. Cambridge, MA: Candlewick Press.

Stallone, Linda. (1992). *The Flood That Came to Grandma's House.* Illus. by Joan Schooley. Dallas, PA: Upshur Press.

Stevenson, James. (1997). *Heat Wave at Mud Flat.* New York: Greenwillow.

Rain, Multimedia

"Clean Rain." (1990). On *Evergreen Everblue* [compact disc]. Shoreline Records.

Cleaver, Mary. (1993). "Rain Is Falling Down" and "The Incey Wincey Spider." On *Songs and Fingerplays for Little Ones* [video]. Cleaver Productions.

"On a Rainy Day." (1988). On *A Rainbow of Songs* [cassette]. Long Branch, NJ: Kimbo Educational.

"Why Does It Rain?" (1992). On *Our Earth* [CD-ROM]. Washington, DC: National Geographic.

Red

Barton, Byron. (1993). *The Little Red Hen.* New York: HarperCollins.

Bazilian, Barbara. (1997). *The Red Shoes.* Dallas, TX: Whispering Coyote Press.

Carle, Eric. (1998). *Hello, Red Fox.* New York: Simon & Schuster.

Carroll, Kathleen S. (1994). *One Red Rooster.* Illus. by Suzette Barbier. Boston: Sandpiper.

Casey, Mike. (1996). *Red Lace, Yellow Lace: Learn to Tie Your Shoe!* Hauppauge, NY: Barron's Educational Series.

Hoban, Tana. (1978). *Is It Red? Is It Yellow? Is It Blue?* New York: Greenwillow.

Lucht, Irmgard. (1995). *The Red Poppy.* New York: Hyperion.

Peek, Merle. (1998). *Mary Wore Her Red Dress, and Henry Wore His Green Sneakers.* Boston: Houghton Mifflin.

Serfozo, Mary. (1992). *Who Said Red?* New York: Aladdin Paperbacks.

Walsh, Ellen Stoll. (1989). *Mouse Paint.* Orlando, FL: Harcourt Brace.

Whitman, Candace. (1998). *Ready for Red.* New York: Abbeville Press.

Woolfitt, Gabrielle. (1992). *Red.* Minneapolis: Carolrhoda Books.

Red, Multimedia

Colors, Shapes and Size [CD-ROM]. (1995). StarPress Multimedia.

JumpStart Preschool [CD-ROM]. (1996). Glendale, CA: Knowledge Adventure.

"Little Red Caboose." (1998). On *Toddler Favorites* [cassette]. Redway, CA: Music for Little People.

Rock 'n Learn Colors, Shapes and Counting [video]. (1997). Conroe, TX: Rock 'N Learn.

Safety

Arnosky, Jim. (1990). *Crinkleroot's Guide to Walking in Wild Places.* New York: Simon & Schuster.

Boelts, Maribeth. (1997). *A Kid's Guide to Staying Safe around Water.* New York: Rosen Publishing.

Brown, Marc Tolon, & Krensky, Stephen. (1982). *Dinosaurs, Beware: A Safety Guide.* Boston: Little, Brown.

Butler, Daphne. (1996). *What Happens When Fire Burns?* Austin, TX: Raintree/Steck Vaughn.

Girard, L W. (1985). *Who Is a Stranger and What Should I Do?* Illus. by Helen Cogancherry. Niles, IL: Albert Whitman & Co.

Givon, Hannah Gelman. (1996). *We Shake in a Quake.* Illus. by David Uttal. Berkeley, CA: Tricycle Press.

Lakin, Patricia. (1995). *Aware and Alert.* Photos by Doub Cushman. Austin, TX: Raintree/Steck Vaughn.

Storytelling and Fingerplays

Loewen, Nancy. (1996). *Bicycle Safety.* Illus. by Penny Danny. Mankato, MN: Child's World.

Loewen, Nancy. (1996). *Traffic Safety.* Illus. by Penny Danny. Mankato, MN: Child's World.

Marzollo, Jean. (1996). *I Am Fire.* Illus. by Judith Moffatt. New York: Scholastic.

Rand, Gloria. (1996). *Willie Takes a Hike.* Illus. by Ted Rand. Orlando, FL: Harcourt Brace.

Rathmann, Peggy. (1995). *Officer Buckle and Gloria.* New York: G. P. Putnam.

Schulson, Rachel. (1997). *Guns—What You Should Know.* Illus. by Mary Jones. Niles, IL: Albert Whitman & Co.

Spelman, Cornelia. (1997). *Your Body Belongs to You.* Illus. by Teri Weidner. Niles, IL: Albert Whitman & Co.

Safety, Multimedia

Child Safety Outdoors [video]. (1994). Chino Hills, CA: KidSafety of America.

K.C.'s First Bus Ride [video]. (1994). Chino Hills, CA: KidSafety of America.

Play It Safe [kit; includes books, cassettes, video, etc.]. (1995). Bothell, WA: Wright Group.

Safety on Wheels [video]. (1994). Princeton, NJ: Films for the Humanities & Sciences.

Seat Belts Are for Kids Too [video]. (1987). AIMS Media.

Scissors

Birch, Barbara, & Lewis, Beverly. (1995). *Katie and the Haircut Mistake.* Illus. by Taia Morley. Minneapolis: Augsburg Fortress Publishers.

Klinting, Lars. (1996). *Bruno the Tailor.* New York: Holt.

Landstrom, Olof, et al. (1993). *Will Gets a Haircut.* Stockholm, NY: R&S Book Co.

Moore, Eva. (1997). *The Day of the Bad Haircut.* Illus. by Meredith Johnson. St. Paul, MN: Cartwheel Books. (Paperback)

Robins, Joan. (1993). *Addie's Bad Day.* Illus. by Sue Truesdell. New York: HarperCollins.

Ruediger, Beth. (1997). *The Barber of Bingo.* Illus. by John McPherson. Kansas City: Andrews & McMeel Pub.

Tusca, Tricia. (1994). *Camilla's New Hairdo* (Reprint). Pleasantville, NY: Sunburst Communications.

Storytelling and Fingerplays

Shapes

Dillon, Leo, et al. (1994). *What Am I? Looking through Shapes at Apples and Grapes.* New York: Scholastic.

Ehlert, Lois. (1990). *Color Farm.* New York: Lippincott.

Ehlert, Lois. (1989). *Color Zoo.* New York: Lippincott.

Grover, Max. (1996). *Circles and Squares Everywhere.* Orlando, FL: Harcourt Brace.

Hoban, Tana. (1986). *Shapes, Shapes, Shapes.* New York: William Morrow.

Hoban, Tana. (1992). *Spirals, Curves, Fanshapes and Lines.* New York: Greenwillow.

MacDonald, Suse. (1994). *Sea Shapes.* Orlando, FL: Harcourt Brace.

Morgan, Sally. World of Shapes series. Cincinnati, OH: Thomson Learning. *Circles and Spheres* (1994); *Spirals* (1995); *Squares and Cubes* (1994); *Triangles and Pyramids* (1995).

Serfozo, Mary. (1996). *There's a Square: A Book about Shapes.* Illus. by David A. Carter. New York: Scholastic.

Sharman, Lydia. (1994). *The Amazing Book of Shapes.* New York: Dorling Kindersley.

Shapes, Multimedia

Colors, Shapes and Size [CD-ROM]. (1995). San Francisco, CA: Star Press Multimedia.

Jumpstart Preschool [CD-ROM]. (1996). Glendale, CA: Knowledge Adventure.

Let's Start Learning [CD-ROM]. (1996). Freemont, CA: The Learning Co.

Millie's Math House [CD-ROM]. (1992). Redmond, WA: Edmark.

Rock 'N Learn Colors, Shapes and Counting [video]. (1997). Conroe, TX: Rock 'N Learn.

Shape Up! [CD-ROM]. (1995). Cupertino, CA: Sunburst Communications.

Traugh, Steven, et al. "Shapes." On *Music and Movement* [cassette]. Cypress, CA: Creative Teaching Press.

Storytelling and Fingerplays

Sports

Adler, David A. (1997). *Lou Gehrig: The Luckiest Man.* Illus. by Terry Widener. Orlando: Harcourt Brace.

Blackstone. Margaret. (1993). *This Is Baseball.* Illus. by John O'Brien. New York: Holt.

Borden, Louise. (1993). *Albie the Lifeguard.* Illus. by Elizabeth Sayles. New York: Scholastic.

Brown, Marc Tolon. (1993). *D.W. Rides Again!* Boston: Little, Brown.

Carrier, Roch. (1993). *The Longest Home Run.* Illus. by Sheldon Cohen. Plattsburgh, NY: Tundra Books.

Dragonwagon, Crescent. (1993). *Annie Flies the Birthday Bike.* Illus. by Emily Arnold McCully. Colchester, CT: Atheneum.

Florian, Douglas. (1994). *A Fisher.* New York: Greenwillow.

Gibbons, Gail. (1995). *Bicycle Book.* New York: Holiday House.

Hest, Amy. (1994). *Rosie's Fishing Trip.* Illus. by Paul Howard. Cambridge, MA: Candlewick Press.

Jakob, Donna. (1994). *My Bike.* Illus. by Nelle Davis. New York: Hyperion.

Johnston, Tony. (1996). *Fishing Sunday.* Illus. by Barry Root. New York: William Morrow.

Kessler, Leonard. (1988). *Old Turtle's Soccer Team.* New York: Greenwillow.

Kessler, Leonard. (1996). *Kick, Pass, and Run.* New York: HarperCollins.

Loewen, Nancy. (1996). *Bicycle Safety.* Illus. by Penny Danny. Mankato, MN: Child's World.

London, Jonathan. (1994). *Let's Go, Froggy!* Illus. by Frank Remkiewicz. New York: Viking.

London, Jonathan. (1995). *Froggy Learns to Swim.* Illus. by Frank Remkiewicz. New York: Viking.

Martin, Bill, & Sampson, Michael. (1997). *Swish.* Illus. by Michael Chesworth. New York: Holt.

McKissack, Patricia C. (1996). *A Million Fish . . . More or Less.* Illus. by Dena Schutzer. New York: Random House.

Moran, George. (1994). *Imagine Me on a Sit-Ski!* Illus. by Nadine Bernard Westcott. Beaver Dam, WI: Concept Books.

Norworth, Jack. (1992). *Take Me Out to the Ballgame.* Illus. by Alec Gillman. New York: Simon & Schuster.

Parish, Peggy. (1996). *Play Ball, Amelia Bedelia.* Illus. by Wallace Tripp. New York: HarperCollins.

Pulver, Robin. (1997). *Alicia's Tutu.* Illus. by Mark Graham. New York: Dial Books.

Rice, Eve. (1996). *Swim!* Illus. by Marisabina Russo. New York: Greenwillow.

Sampson, Michael. (1996). *The Football That Won . . .* Illus. by Ted Rand. New York: Holt.

Teague, Mark. (1992). *The Field beyond the Outfield.* New York: Scholastic.

Tryon, Leslie. (1996). *Albert's Ball Game.* Colchester, CT: Atheneum.

Welch, Willy. (1995). *Playing Right Field.* Illus. by Marc Simont. New York: Scholastic.

Wells, Rosemary. (1995). *Edward in Deep Water.* New York: Dial Books.

Weston, Martha. (1995). *Tuck in the Pool.* New York: Clarion Books.

Wolff, Ashley. (1993). *Stella and Roy.* New York: Dutton.

Sports, Multimedia

Brown, Marc Tolon. (1998). *Arthur Makes the Team* [book and cassette]. Old Greenwich, CT: Listening Library.

"Take Me Out to the Ballgame." (1997). On *Six Little Ducks* [compact disc]. Long Branch, NJ: Kimbo Educational.

Spring

Agell, Charlotte. (1994). *Mud Makes Me Dance in the Spring.* Gardner, ME: Tilbury House Publishers.

Baxter, Nicola. (1997). *Spring.* Illus. by Kim Woolley. Chicago: Children's Press.

Brown, Craig. (1994). *In the Spring.* New York: Greenwillow.

De Coteau Orie, Sandra. (1995). *Did You Hear Wind Sing Your Name? An Oneida Song of Spring.* Illus. by Christopher Canyon. New York: Walker & Co.

Emberley, Michael. (1993). *Welcome Back, Sun.* Boston: Little, Brown.

Janovitz, Marilyn. (1996). *Can I Help?* New York: North-South Books.

Kinsey-Warnock, Natalia. (1993). *When Spring Comes.* Illus. by Stacey Schuett. New York: Dutton.

Kroll, Virginia L. (1993). *Naomi Knows It's Springtime.* Illus. by Jill Kastner. Honesdale, PA: Boyds Mills Press.

Maass, Robert. (1996). *When Spring Comes.* Madison, WI: Demco Media.

Rau, Dana Meachen. (1995). *Robin at Hickory Street.* Illus. by Joel Snyder. Norwalk, CT: Soundprints Corp.

Ray, Mary Lyn. (1996). *Mud.* Illus. by Lauren Stringer. Orlando, FL: Harcourt Brace.

Storytelling and Fingerplays

321

Richardson, Judith Benet. (1996). *Old Winter*. Illus. by R. W. Alley. New York: Orchard Books.

Rockwell, Anne F. (1996). *My Spring Robin*. Madison, WI: Demco Media.

Shannon, George. (1996). *Spring: A Haiku Story*. Illus. By Malcah Zeldis. New York: Greenwillow.

Walters, Catherine. (1998). *When Will It Be Spring?* New York: Dutton.

Spring, Multimedia

Let's Find Out about Spring [video]. (1991). Hightstown, NJ: American School Publishers.

Through the Seasons with Birds: Spring [video]. (1994). Evanston, IL: Altschul Group Corp.

Summer

Agell, Charlotte. (1994). *I Wear Long Green Hair in Summer*. Gardner, ME: Tilbury House Publishers.

Aliki. (1996). *Those Summers*. New York: HarperCollins.

Appel, Karel. (1996). *Watermelon Day*. Illus. by Dale Gottlieb. New York: Holt.

Baxter, Nicola. (1997). *Summer*. Illus. by Kim Woolley. Chicago: Children's Press.

Crews, Nina. (1995). *One Hot Summer Day*. New York: Greenwillow.

George, Lindsay Barrett. (1996). *Around the Pond: Who's Been Here?* New York: Greenwillow.

Giovanni, Nikki. (1994). *Knoxville, Tennessee*. Illus. by Larry Johnson. New York: Scholastic.

Maass, Robert. (1995). *When Summer Comes*. New York: Holt.

Rylant, Cynthia. (1997). *Mr. Putter and Tabby Row the Boat*. Illus. by Arthur Howard. Orlando, FL: Harcourt Brace.

Van Leeuwen, Jean. (1997). *Touch the Sky Summer*. Illus. by Dan Andreasen. New York: Dial Books.

Yolen, Jane. (1993). *Jane Yolen's Songs of Summer*. Illus. by Cyd Moore. Honesdale, PA: Boyds Mills Press.

Yolen, Jane. (1995). *Before the Storm*. Illus. by Georgia Pugh. Honesdale, PA: Boyds Mills Press.

Storytelling and Fingerplays

Thanksgiving

Accorsi, William. (1992). *Friendship's First Thanksgiving*. New York: Holiday House.

Alden, Laura. (1993). *Thanksgiving*. Illus. by Susan Lexa-Senning. Chicago: Children's Press.

Bauer, Caroline Feller. (1994). *Thanksgiving: Stories and Poems*. Illus. by Nadine B. Westcott. New York: HarperCollins.

Behrens, June. (1996). *Thanksgiving Feast: The First American Holiday*. Illus. by Joann Rounds. Delmar, CA: York House Publishers.

Boynton, Alice B. (1996). *Priscilla Alden and the First Thanksgiving*. Morristown, NJ: Silver Burdett. (Paperback)

Capote, Truman. (1996). *Thanksgiving Visitor*. Illus. by Beth Peck. New York: Knopf.

Cowley, Joy. (1996). *Gracias, the Thanksgiving Turkey*. Illus. by Joe Cepeda. New York: Scholastic.

DeRubertis, Barbara. (1996). *Thanksgiving Day: Let's Meet the Wampanoags and the Pilgrims*. Illus. by Thomas Sperling. New York: Kane Press. (Paperback)

Dubowski, Cathy E. (1997). *Squanto: First Friend to the Pilgrims*. Illus. by Steven Peruccio. Milwaukee, WI: Gareth Stevens.

Hallinan, P. K. (1993). *Today Is Thanksgiving*. Lake Forest, IL: Forest House Publishing.

Hintz, Martin, & Hintz, Kate. (1998). *Thanksgiving*. Chicago: Children's Press.

Jackson, Alison et al. (1997). *I Know an Old Lady Who Swallowed a Pie*. Illus. by Byron Schachner. New York: Dutton.

MacMillan, Dianne M. (1997). *Thanksgiving Day*. Springfield, NJ: Enslow Publishers.

Ross, Katharine. (1995). *The Story of the Pilgrims*. Illus. by Carolyn Cross. New York: Random House.

Tryon, Leslie. (1994). *Albert's Thanksgiving*. New York: Simon & Schuster.

Woods, Andrew. (1996). *Young Squanto: The First Thanksgiving*. Illus. by Chris Powers. Mahwah, NJ: Troll.

Thanksgiving, Multimedia

Gallina, Jill. (1978). *Holiday Songs for All Occasions* [cassette]. Kimbo Records.

Holiday Action Songs [cassette]. Kimbo Records.

Squanto and the First Thanksgiving [video]. (1993). Rabbit Ears Productions.

Thanksgiving [video]. (1994). Schlessinger Video Productions.

Storytelling and Fingerplays

Trees

Aldridge, Josephine Haskell. (1993). *A Possible Tree.* Illus. by Daniel San Souci. New York: Simon & Schuster.

Arnosky, Jim. (1992). *Crinkleroot's Guide to Knowing the Trees.* New York: Simon & Schuster.

Bunting, Eve. (1993). *Someday a Tree.* Illus. by Ronald Himler. Boston: Houghton Mifflin.

Burns, Diane L. (1990). *Sugaring Season: Making Maple Syrup.* Illus. by Cheryl Walsh Bellville. Minneapolis: Carolrhoda Books.

Carrier, Lark. (1996). *A Tree's Tale.* New York: Dial Books.

Dorros, Arthur. (1997). *A Tree Is Growing.* Illus. by S. D. Schindler. New York: Scholastic.

Drawson, Blair. (1996). *Mary Margaret's Tree.* New York: Orchard Books.

Edwards, Richard. (1993). *Ten Tall Oaktrees.* Illus. by Caroline Crossland. New York: William Morrow.

Ehlert, Lois. (1991). *Red Leaf, Yellow Leaf.* Orlando, FL: Harcourt Brace.

Gackenbach, Dick. (1992). *Mighty Tree.* Orlando, FL: Harcourt Brace.

Hall, Zoe. (1996). *The Apple Tree.* Illus. by Shari Halpern. New York: Scholastic.

Jaspersohn, William. (1996). *Timber.* Boston: Little, Brown.

Levine, Ellen. (1995). *The Tree That Would Not Die.* Illus. by Ted Rand. New York: Scholastic.

Manson, Christopher. (1993). *The Tree in the Wood: An Old Nursery Song.* New York: North-South Books.

Maestro, Betsy. (1994). *Why Do Leaves Change Color?* Illus. by Loretta Krupinski. New York: HarperCollins.

Oppenheim, Joanne. (1995). *Have You Seen Trees?* Illus. by Jean and Mou-Sien Tseng. New York: Scholastic.

Pluckrose, Henry Arthur. (1990). *Trees.* Illus. by Joy Friedman. Chicago: Children's Press.

Reed-Jones, Carol. (1995). *The Tree in the Ancient Forest.* Illus. by Christopher Canyon. Nevada City, CA: Dawn Publications.

Sanders, Scott R. (1996). *Meeting Trees.* Illus. by Robert Hynes. Washington, DC: National Geographic Society.

Tresselt, Alvin. (1992). *The Gift of the Tree.* Illus. by Henri Sorenson. New York: Lothrop, Lee & Shepard.

Zalben, Jane Breskin. (1995). *Pearl Plants a Tree.* New York: Simon & Schuster.

Trees, Multimedia

Bean, Norman and Sandy. (1992). *A First Look at Trees* [video]. Van Nuys, CA: AIMS Media.

Cole, Joanna. (1995). *Goes the Seed* [video]. New York: KidVision. (Magic School Bus series)

Cutting, Michael. (1990). *The Little Crooked Christmas Tree* [video]. Stamford, CT: ABC Video.

Tell Me Why: Flowers, Plants and Trees [video]. (1987). Marina del Rey, CA: Tell Me Why.

What Is a Leaf? [video]. (1991). Washington, DC: National Geographic.

Valentine's Day

Bauer, Caroline Feller. (1993). *Valentine's Day: Stories and Poems.* Illus. by Blanche Sims. New York: HarperCollins.

Carrick, Carol. (1995). *Valentine.* Illus. by Paddy Bouma. Boston: Houghton Mifflin.

Devlin, Wende, & Devlin, Harry. (1991). *Cranberry Valentine.* New York: Simon & Schuster.

Hoban, Lillian. (1997). *Silly Tilly's Valentine.* New York: HarperCollins.

Hopkins, Lee Bennett. (1992). *Good Morning to You, Valentine.* Illus. by Tomie De Paola. Honesdale, PA: Boyds Mills Press.

Hurd, Thacher. (1990). *Little Mouse's Big Valentine.* New York: HarperCollins.

London, Jonathan. (1997). *Froggy's First Kiss.* Illus. by Frank Remkiewicz. New York: Viking.

Nerlove, Miriam. (1992). *Valentine's Day.* Niles, IL: Albert Whitman & Co.

Sabuda, Robert. (1992). *Saint Valentine.* New York: Simon & Schuster.

Shannon, George. (1995). *Heart to Heart.* Boston: Houghton Mifflin.

Sharmat, Marjorie Weinman. (1994). *Nate the Great and the Mushy Valentine.* Illus. by Marc Simont. New York: Dell Publishing.

Watson, Wendy. (1993). *A Valentine for You.* Boston: Houghton Mifflin. (Paperback)

Storytelling and Fingerplays

Valentine's Day, Multimedia

Coleman, Warren. (1993). *Valentine's Day* [video]. Niles, IL: United Learning.

Valentine's Day [video]. (1994). Schlessinger Video Productions.

Water

Arnold, Tedd. (1995). *No More Water in the Tub.* New York: Dial Books.

Asch, Frank. (1995). *Water.* San Diego: Gulliver Books.

Baker, Sanna A. (1996). *Mississippi Going North.* Illus. by Bill Farnsworth. Niles, IL: Albert Whitman & Co.

Bittinger, Gayle. (1993). *Exploring Water and the Ocean.* Illus. by Gary Mohrmann. Albertwood Manor, WA: Warren Publishing House.

Calhoun, Mary. (1997). *Flood.* Illus. by Erick Ingraham. New York: William Morrow.

Carlstrom, Nancy W. (1997). *Raven and River.* Illus. by Jon Van Zyle. Boston: Little, Brown.

Cast, C. Vance. (1992). *Where Does Water Come From?* Illus. by Sue Wilkinson. Hauppauge, NY: Barron's Educational Series. (Paperback)

Challoner, Jack. (1996). *Wet and Dry.* Austin, TX: Raintree/Steck Vaughn.

Dunphy, Madeline. (1998). *Here Is the Coral Reef.* Illus. by Tom Leonard. New York: Hyperion.

Fleming, Denise. (1993). *In the Small, Small Pond.* New York: Holt.

Fowler, Allan. (1995). *The Earth Is Mostly Ocean.* Chicago: Children's Press.

Fowler, Allan. (1997a). *It Could Still Be a Lake.* Chicago: Children's Press.

Fowler, Allan. (1997b). *Life in a Pond.* Chicago: Children's Press.

Gibbons, Gail. (1998). *Marshes and Swamps.* New York: Holiday House.

Gibson, Gary. (1995). *Making Things Float and Sink.* Illus. by Tony Kenyon. Brookfield, CT: Millbrook Press.

Gordon, Maria. (1995). *Float and Sink.* Illus. by Mike Gordon. Austin, TX: Raintree/Steck Vaughn.

Graham, Joan B. (1994). *Splish Splash.* Illus. By Steven M. Scott. New York: Ticknor and Fields.

Jackson, Shelley. (1998). *The Old Woman and the Wave.* New York: Dorling Kindersley.

Llewellyn, Claire. (1995). *Rivers and Seas (Why Do We Have . . .).* Illus. by Anthony Lewis. Hauppauge, NY: Barron's Educational Series.

Locker, Thomas. (1997). *Water Dance.* Orlando, FL: Harcourt Brace.

The Magic School Bus Wet All Over: A Book about the Water Cycle. (1996). New York: Scholastic. (Paperback)

Marzollo, Jean. (1996). *I Am Water.* Illus. by Judith Moffatt. New York: Scholastic. (Paperback)

Murata, Michinori. (1993). *Water and Light: Looking through Lenses.* Minneapolis: Lerner Publications.

Nielsen, Shelly, & Berg, Julie. (1993). *I Love Water*. Minneapolis: Abdo & Daughters.

O'Mara, Anna. (1996). *Oceans*. Chicago: Children's Press.

Rauzon, Mark J., & Bix, Cynthia O. (1994). *Water, Water Everywhere*. Santa Fe, NM: Sierra Club.

Speed, Toby. (1998). *Water Voices*. Illus. by Julie Downing. New York: G. P. Putnam.

Water, Multimedia

Circle of Water [video]. (1995). Washington, DC: National Geographic.

Oceans [video]. (1992). Science for You series. Agency for Instructional Technology.

Let's Explore Water [video] (1993). Science Is Elementary series. Agency for Instructional Technology.

What's in the Sea: Songs about Marine Life and Ocean Ecology [cassette]. Long Branch, NJ: Kimbo Educational.

Wheels

Butler, Daphne. (1995). *What Happens When Wheels Turn?* Austin, TX: Raintree/Steck Vaughn.

Cowen-Fletcher, Jane. (1993). *Mama Zooms*. New York: Scholastic.

Dahl, Michael. (1996). *Wheels and Axles*. Chicago: Children's Press.

Hayward, Linda et al. (1996). *Wheels*. New York: Random House.

Healey, Tim. (1993). *The Story of the Wheel*. Illus. by Nicholas Hewetson. Mahwah, NJ: Troll.

Hindley, Judy. (1994). *The Wheeling and Whirling-Around Book*. Illus. by Margaret Chamberlain. Cambridge, MA: Candlewick Press.

Kalman, Bobbie, & Gentile, Petrina. (1997). *Big Truck, Big Wheels*. New York: Crabtree Publishing.

Kovalski, Maryann. (1990). *The Wheels on the Bus*. Boston: Little, Brown. (Paperback)

Mellentin, Kath. (1998). *The Wheels on the Bus*. Illus. by Jenny Tulip. Reistertown, MD: Flying Frog Publishing.

Miller, Margaret. (1997). *Wheels Go Round*. New York: Simon & Schuster.

Nikola-Lisa, W. (1994). *Wheels Go Round*. Illus. by Jane Conteh-Morgan. New York: Doubleday.

Storytelling and Fingerplays

327

Raffi. (1998). *Wheels on the Bus*. New York: Crown Publishers.

Regan, Dana. (1996). *The Wheels on the Bus*. New York: Scholastic.

Rotner, Shelley. (1995). *Wheels Around*. Boston: Houghton Mifflin.

Rush, Caroline. (1997). *Wheels and Cogs*. Illus. by Mike Gordon. Austin, TX: Raintree/Steck-Vaughn.

Scarry, Richard. (1997). *Richard Scarry's Pop-Up Wheels*. New York: Simon & Schuster.

Zelinsky, Paul O. (1990). *The Wheels on the Bus: With Pictures That Move*. New York: Dutton.

Wheels, Multimedia

Fisher, Diana. (1996). *Wee Sing Wheels Sounds and Songs* [cassette]. New York: G. P. Putnam.

Winter

Agell, Charlotte. (1994). *I Slide Into the White of Winter*. Gardner, ME: Tilbury House.

Bancroft, Henrietta, & Van Gelder, Richard G. (1996). *Animals in Winter*. Newly illus. by Helen K. Davie. New York: HarperCollins.

Barasch, Lynne. (1993). *A Winter Walk*. New York: Ticknor & Fields.

Berger, Melvin and Berger, Gilda. (1995). *What Do Animals Do in Winter?* Illus. by Susan Harrison. Nashville, TN: Hambleton-Hill Publishing.

Capucilli, Alyssa Satin. (1995). *Peekaboo Bunny: Friend in the Snow*. Illus. by Mary Melcher. New York: Scholastic. (Peek a Book)

Carlstrom, Nancy White. (1993). *How Does the Wind Walk?* New York: Macmillan.

Chapman, Cheryl. (1994). *Snow on Snow on Snow*. Illus. by Synthia Saint James. New York: Dial Books.

Dunphy, Madeleine. (1993). *Here Is the Arctic Winter*. Illus. by Alan James Robinson. New York: Hyperion.

Ehlert, Lois. (1996). *Snowballs*. Orlando, FL: Harcourt Brace.

Evans, Lezlie. (1997). *Snow Dance*. Illus. by Cynthia Jabar. Boston: Houghton Mifflin.

Fain, Moria. (1996). *Snow Day*. New York: Walker & Co.

Fleming, Denise. (1996). *Time to Sleep*. New York: Holt.

Galbraith, Kathryn Osebold. (1992). *Look! Snow!* Illus. by Nina Montezinos. New York: Simon & Schuster.

Gammell, Stephen. (1997). *Is That You, Winter?* Orlando, FL: Harcourt Brace.

George, Jean Craighead. (1993). *Dear Rebecca, Winter Is Here.* Illus. by Loretta Krupinski. New York: HarperCollins.

George, Lindsay Barrett. (1995). *In the Snow: Who's Been Here?* New York: Greenwillow.

Hiscock, Bruce. (1995). *When Will It Snow?* New York: Simon & Schuster.

Howard, Kim. (1994). *In Wintertime.* New York: Lothrop, Lee & Shepard.

Joosse, Barbara M. (1995). *Snow Day!* Illus. by Jennifer Plecas. Boston: Houghton Mifflin.

Lee, Huy-Voun. (1995). *In the Snow.* New York: Holt.

Lerner, Carol. (1994). *Backyard Birds of Winter.* New York: William Morrow.

London, Jonathan. (1992). *Froggy Gets Dressed.* Illus. by Frank Remkiewicz. New York: Viking.

Maass, Robert. (1993). *When Winter Comes.* New York: Holt.

Richardson, Judith Benet. (1996). *Old Winter.* Illus. by R. W. Alley. New York: Orchard Books.

Ryder, Joanne. (1997). *Winter White.* Illus. by Carol Lacey. New York: William Morrow.

Simon, Seymour. (1994). *Winter across America.* New York: Hyperion Books.

Stoeke, Janet Morgan. (1994). *A Hat for Minerva Louise.* New York: Dutton.

Willard, Nancy. (1996). *A Starlit Somersault Downhill.* Illus. by Jerry Pinkney. Boston: Little, Brown. (Paperback)

Winter, Multimedia

Keats, Ezra Jack. *The Snowy Day* [book and cassette]. Kimbo Records.

Let's Find Out about Winter [video]. (1991). Hightstown, NJ: American School Publishers.

Piggyback Songs: Singable Poems Set to Favorite Tunes [compact disc]. (1995). Kimbo Records. (Includes 21 songs and poems for fall and winter)

Snowplows at Work [video]. (1994). Truckee, CA: Bill Aaron Productions.

Where Do Animals Go in Winter? [video]. (1995). Washington, DC: National Geographic.

Yellow

Bang, Molly. (1991). *Yellow Ball*. New York: William Morrow.

Cabrera, Jane. (1997). *Cat's Colors*. New York: Dial Books.

Carle, Eric. (1998). *Let's Paint a Rainbow*. New York: Scholastic.

Dodds, Dayle Ann. (1992). *The Color Box*. Illus. by Giles Laroche. Boston: Little, Brown.

Faulkner, Keith. (1995). *My Colors: Let's Learn about Colors*. New York: Simon & Schuster.

Heller, Ruth. (1995). *Color*. New York: G. P. Putnam.

Hoban, Tana. (1987). *Is It Red? Is It Yellow? Is It Blue?* New York: Greenwillow.

Hoban, Tana. (1995). *Colors Everywhere*. New York: Greenwillow.

Jackson, Ellen B. (1995). *Brown Cow, Green Grass, Yellow Mellow Sun* (Vol. 1). Illus. by Victoria Raymond. New York: Hyperion.

Lionni, Leo. (1994). *Little Blue and Little Yellow*. New York: William Morrow. (Paperback)

Munsch, Robert. (1992). *Purple, Green and Yellow*. Illus. by Helene Desputeaux. Willowdale, Ontario: Annick Press.

Rogers, Alan. (1997). *Yellow Hippo*. Chicago: World Book.

Rotner, Shelley. (1996). *Colors around Us*. New York: Simon & Schuster. (Lift the Flap Book)

Seuss, Dr. (1996). *My Many Colored Days*. Illus. by Steve Johnston. New York: Knopf.

Walsh, Ellen Stoll. (1989). *Mouse Paint*. Orlando, FL: Harcourt Brace.

Yellow, Multimedia

Big Yellow School Bus [cassette]. (1991). Alfred Publishing.

Bingham, Bing. (1988). "Primary Colors." On *A Rainbow of Songs* [cassette]. Kimbo Records.

Color, Shapes and Size [CD-ROM]. (1995). Harbor, WA: Star Press Multimedia.

My Silly CD of Colors [CD-ROM]. (1995). Toronto: Discis Knowledge Research.

Peter's Colors Adventure [CD-ROM]. (1994). Arborescence.

"A Yell for Yellow." (1976). On *There's Music in the Colors* [cassette]. Kimbo Records.

Zoo Animals

Aliki. (1997). *My Visit to the Zoo.* New York: HarperCollins.

Ancona, George, & Ancona, Mary Beth. (1991). *Handtalk Zoo.* New York: Simon & Schuster.

Arnold, Caroline. (1992). *Camel.* New York: William Morrow.

Arnold, Caroline. (1993a). *Elephant.* New York: William Morrow.

Arnold, Caroline. (1993b). *Lion.* New York: William Morrow.

Arnold, Caroline. (1993c). *Monkey.* New York: William Morrow.

Barton, Byron. (1996). *Zoo Animals.* New York: HarperCollins. (Board book)

Benjamin, Cynthia. (1995). *I Am a Zookeeper.* Illus. by Miriam Sagasti. Hauppauge, NY: Barron's Educational Series. (Board book)

Buehner, Caralyn, & Buehner, Mark. (1992). *The Escape of Marvin the Ape.* New York: Dial Books.

Denim, Sue, & Pilkey, Dave. (1996). *The Dumb Bunnies Go to the Zoo.* New York: Scholastic.

Finnegan, Evelyn, & Bruno, Margaret. (1998). *My Little Friend Goes to the Zoo.* Scituate, MA: Little Friend Press.

Ford, Miela. (1994). *Little Elephant.* Illus. by Tana Hoban. New York: Greenwillow.

Ford, Miela. (1995). *Bear Play.* New York: Greenwillow.

Ford, Miela. (1998). *Watch Us Play.* New York: Greenwillow.

Fowler, Allan. (1996). *The Biggest Animal on Land.* Chicago: Children's Press.

Gangelhoff, Jeanne M., & Belk, Bradford. (1993). *A Walk thru the Minnesota Zoo.* Illus. by Gene Gangelhoff. Cedar, MN: GJ & B Publishing.

Hazelaar, Cor. (1997). *Zoo Dreams.* New York: Farrar, Straus & Giroux.

Hendrick, Mary Jean. (1993). *If Anything Goes Wrong at the Zoo.* Illus. by Jane Dyer. Orlando, FL: Harcourt Brace.

Hewett, Joan. (1993). *Tiger, Tiger Growing Up.* Illus. by Richard Hewett. New York: Clarion Books.

Hosea Hilker, Cathryn. (1992). *A Cheetah Named Angel.* New York: Franklin Watts.

Kalman, Bobbie, & Sotzek, Hannelore. (1997). *A Koala Is Not a Bear.* New York: Crabtree Publishing.

Kenny, David et al. (1995). *Klondike and Snow: The Denver Zoo's Remarkable Story of Raising Two Polar Bear Cubs.* Niwot, CO: Roberts Rinehart Publishers. (Paperback)

Koebner, Linda. (1997). *Zoo Book.* New York: Tor Books.

Lee, Julie, & Northard, Jackie. (1995). *Animals A to Zoo.* Illus. by Kristine Kirkeby. Minnesota Zoo.

Storytelling and Fingerplays

Lemmon, Tess. (1993). *Apes*. Illus. by John Butler. New York: Ticknor & Fields.

Maestro, Betsy. (1992). *Take a Look at Snakes*. New York: Scholastic.

Martin, Ann M. (1998). *Baby Animal Zoo*. Illus. by Charles Tang. New York: Scholastic. (Paperback)

Martin, Bill. (1991). *Polar Bear, Polar Bear, What Do You Hear?* Illus. by Eric Carle. New York: Holt.

McMillan, Bruce. (1995). *The Baby Zoo*. New York: Scholastic. (Paperback)

Morozumi, Atsuko. (1998). *My Friend Gorilla*. New York: Farrar, Straus & Giroux.

Noble, Kate. (1994). *The Blue Elephant*. Illus. by Rachel Bass. Chicago: Silver Seahorse Press.

Ormerod, Jan. (1991). *When We Went to the Zoo*. New York: Lothrop, Lee & Shepard.

Oxenbury, Helen. (1991). *Monkey See, Monkey Do* (2nd ed.). New York: Dial Books. (Board book)

Paxton, Tom. (1996). *Going to the Zoo*. Illus. by Karen Schmidt. New York: William Morrow.

Rathmann, Peggy. (1994). *Good Night, Gorilla*. New York: G. P. Putnam.

Robinson, Martha. (1995). *The Zoo at Night*. Illus. by Antonio Frasconi. New York: Simon & Schuster.

Rowan, James P. (1990). *I Can Be a Zoo Keeper*. Chicago: Children's Press. (Paperback)

Simon, Seymour. (1992). *Snakes*. New York: HarperCollins.

Smith, Dale. (1997). *Nighttime at the Zoo*. Illus. by Gwen Clifford. Tacoma, WA: Golden Anchor Press.

Smith, Roland. (1992). *Cats in the Zoo*. Illus. by William Munoz. Brookfield, CT: Millbrook Press.

Tibbitts, Alison, & Roocraft, Alan. (1992). *Polar Bears*. New York: Capstone Press.

Waber, Bernard. (1996). *A Lion Named Shirley Williamson*. Boston: Houghton Mifflin.

Storytelling and Fingerplays

Zoo Animals, Multimedia

At Home with Zoo Animals [video]. (1992). Washington, DC: National Geographic Society.

National Zoo [videodisc]. (1989). Washington, DC: Smithsonian Institution.

Sharon, Lois, and Bram at the Zoo [video]. (1985). New York: Golden Book Video.

Zoo Keeper [computer file]. (1992). Davidson & Associates.

Helpful Hints!

The following are helpful hints for choosing books that are developmentally appropriate for the child:

▶ Share books with children and model reading behaviors.

▶ Reread favorite stories.

▶ Pronounce words clearly and read at a lively tempo.

▶ Use your voice as a tool to read with expression when sharing stories. You may whisper, sing, and raise your voice. To create interest, change your voice for particular characters.

▶ When reading, show the pictures to the child as you turn the pages to help him understand the story through the illustrations.

▶ Introduce unfamiliar words and use them throughout the day during interactions with the child.

▶ Allow comments to be added to the story while reading.

▶ Encourage participation and the child's attempts at reading and writing.

▶ Play games that involve specific directions, such as Simon Says, with three-, four-, and five-year-olds.

▶ Give books for presents.

▶ After reading, after the child has gained the necessary language skills, encourage her to retell the story to you.

▶ Take turns making up and sharing stories with your child as developmentally appropriate.

▶ Call attention to the written word by printing your child's name on materials.

▶ Point out labels and signs in the child's environment.

▶ Create a book with your child using photographs.

▶ Tape stories and let the child listen. Also, tape the child telling a story.

▶ Place books in the child's bedroom, as well as the play area.

▶ Visit a bookstore or library regularly.

▶ Provide colored pencils, felt-tip markers, and crayons for the child to write with.

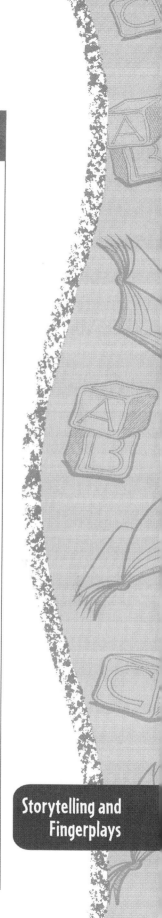

Storytelling and Fingerplays

Fingerplays

A fingerplay uses words and actions together, although some involve whole body actions. "This little piggy went to market, this little piggy stayed home, and this little piggy went wee wee all the way home" is an example. The younger the child, the simpler and shorter the rhyme needs to be. Visually, the young child will join you in the actions before learning the words. Typically, after repeated exposure, the child will gradually learn the words. Fingerplays help build listening skills and promote concept formation. The following are examples of fingerplay activities that children enjoy.

Fingerplay Activities

"Alligator"

The alligator likes to swim.
> (two hands flat on top of the other)
Sometimes his mouth opens wide.
> (hands open and shut)
But when he sees me on the shore,
Down under the water he'll hide.

"Ant Hill"

Once I saw an ant hill,
> (make a fist with one hand)
With no ants about.
So I said, "Dear little ants,
Won't you please come out?"
Then as if the little ants
Had heard my call,
One, two, three, four, five came out
> (extend fingers one at a time)
And that was all.

"An Apple"

An apple is what I'd like to be.
My shape would be round.
> (fingers in circular shape)
My color would be green.
> (point to something green)
Children could eat me each and
> *every day.*
I'm good in tarts and pies and cakes.
> (make these food shapes)
An apple is good to eat or to bake.
> (make stirring motion)

"The Apple"

Within its polished universe
The apple holds a star.
> (draw design of star with index
> finger)
A secret constellation
To scatter near and far.
> (point near and far)
Let a knife discover
Where the five points hide.
Split the shiny ruby
And find the star inside.
> (After introducing the fingerplay,
> you can cut an apple crosswise to
> find a star.)

"Apple Tree"

Way up high in the apple tree
> (stretch arm up high)
Two little apples smiled at me.
> (hold up two fingers)
I shook that tree as hard as I could
> (make shaking motion)
Down came the apples.
> (make downward motions)
Mmmm—They were good.
> (smile and rub stomach)

Storytelling and Fingerplays

335

"The Apple Tree"

This is the tree
With leaves so green.
   (make leaves with fingers outstretched)
Here are the apples
That hang in between
   (make fist)
When the wind blows
   (blow)
The apples will fall.
   (falling motion with hand)
Here is the basket to gather them all.
   (use arms to form basket)

"Autumn"

Autumn winds begin to blow
   (blow)
Colored leaves fall fast and slow.
   (make fast and slow motions with
   hands)
Twirling, whirling all around
   (turn around)
Til at last, they touch the ground.
   (fall to the ground)

"Bananas"

Bananas are my favorite fruit.
   (make fists as if holding banana)
I eat one every day.
   (hold up one finger)
I always take one with me
   (act as if putting one in pocket)
When I go out to play.
   (wave good-bye)
It gives me lots of energy
   (make a muscle)
To jump around and run.
   (move arms as if running)
Bananas are my favorite fruit.
   (rub tummy)
To me they're so much fun!
   (point to self and smile)

"The Big Turkey"

The big turkey on the farm is so very
   proud.
   (form fist)
He spreads his tail like a fan
   (spread fingers of other hand
   behind fist)
And struts through the animal
   crowd.
   (move two fingers of fist as if
   walking)
If you talk to him as he wobbles
   along
He'll answer back with a gobbling
   song.
"Gobble, gobble, gobble."
   (open and close hand)

🔲 "Bird Feeder"

Here is the bird feeder. Here are
*   seeds and crumbs.*
    (left hand out flat, right hand
    cupped)
Sprinkle them on and see what
*   comes.*
    (sprinkling motion with right hand
    over left hand)
One cardinal, one chickadee, one
*   junco, one jay,*
    (join fingers on right hand and
    peck at the bird feeder once for
    each bird)
Four of my bird friends are eating
*   today.*
    (hold up four fingers of left hand)

🔲 "Body Talk"

When I smile, I tell you that I'm
*   happy.*
    (point at the corner of mouth)
When I frown I tell you that I'm sad.
    (pull down corners of mouth)
When I raise my shoulders and tilt
*   my head I tell you, "I don't know."*
    (raise shoulders, tilt head, raise
    hands, shake head)

🔲 "Brushes in My Home"

These brushes in my home
Are simply everywhere.
I use them for my teeth each day,
    (brushing teeth motion)
And also for my hair.
    (hair-brushing motion)

We use them in the kitchen sink
    (scrubbing motion)
And in the toilet bowls
    (scrubbing motion)
For putting polish on my shoes
    (touch shoes and rub)
And to waterproof the soles.

Brushes are used to polish the floors
    (polishing motions)
And also paint the wall,
    (painting motion)
To clean the charcoal barbecue,
    (brushing motion)
It's hard to name them all.

🔲 "Brushing Teeth"

I jiggle the toothbrush again and
*   again.*
    (pretend to brush teeth)
I scrub all my teeth for awhile.
I swish the water to rinse them and
*   then*
    (puff out cheeks to swish)
I look at myself and I smile.
    (smile at one another)

**Storytelling and
Fingerplays**

🎲 "Build a Snowperson"

First you make a snowball,
   (rolling motion)
Big and fat and round.
   (extend arms in large circle)
Then you roll the snowball,
   (rolling motion)
All along the ground.
Then you build the snowperson
One-two-three!
   (place three pretend balls on top of
   each other)
Then you have a snowperson,
Don't you see?
   (point to eyes)
Then the sun shines all around and
Melts the snowperson to the ground.
   (drop to the ground in a melting
   motion)

🎲 "Bumblebee"

Brightly colored bumblebee
Looking for some honey.
Flap your wings and fly away
While it still is sunny.

🎲 "The Bunny"

Once there was a bunny
   (fist with two fingers tall)
And a green, green cabbage head.
   (fist of other hand)
"I think I'll have some breakfast," this
   little bunny said.
So he nibbled and he cocked his ears
   to say,
"I think it's time that I be on my
   way."

🎲 "Carpenter"

This is the way he saws the wood
   (make sawing motion)
Sawing, sawing, sawing.

This is the way she nails a nail
   (make hammering motion)
Nailing, nailing, nailing.

This is the way he paints a building
   (make brushing motion)
Painting, painting, painting.

🎲 "Carpenter's Tools"

The carpenter's hammer goes rap,
   rap, rap
   (make hammering motion with
   fist)
And his saw goes see, saw, see.
   (make sawing motion with arm
   and hand)
He planes and hammers and saws
   (make motions for each)
While he builds a building for me.
   (point to yourself)

🎲 "The Caterpillar"

A caterpillar crawled to the top of
   a tree.
   (index finger of left hand moves
   up right arm)
"I think I'll take a nap," said he.
So under a leaf, he began to creep
   (wrap right hand over left fist)
To spin his chrysalis and he fell
   asleep.
All winter long he slept in his
   chrysalis bed,
   (keep right hand over left fist)

Till spring came along one day, and
    said,
"Wake up, wake up little sleepy
    head."
    (shake left fist with right hand)
"Wake up, it's time to get out of
    bed!"
So, he opened his eyes that sunshiny
    day
    (shake fingers and look into hand)
Lo—he was a butterfly and flew
    away!
    (move hand into flying motion)

"Caught an Ant"

One, two, three, four, five
    (extend a finger for each number)
I caught an ant alive.
Six, seven, eight, nine, ten
    (extend fingers of other hand)
I let it go again.
Why did I let it go?
    (shrug shoulders)
It bit my finger so.
Which one did it bite?
    (shrug shoulders)
The little one on the right.
    (hold up right pinkie finger)

"Chickadees"

Five little chickadees sitting in a
    door
    (hold up hand)
One flew away and then there were
    four.
    (put down one finger at a time)
Four little chickadees sitting in a tree
One flew away and then there were
    three.
Three little chickadees looking at
    you
One flew away and then there were
    two.
Two little chickadees sitting in the
    sun
One flew away and then there was
    one.
One little chickadee sitting all alone
He flew away and then there were
    none.

"A Circle"

Around in a circle we will go.
Little tiny baby steps, make us go
    very slow.
And then we'll take some great giant
    steps,
As big as they can be.
Then in a circle we'll stand quietly.

🔲 "Circus Clown"

I'd like to be a circus clown
And make a funny face,
   (make a funny face)
And have all the people laugh at me
As I jump around the place.
   (act silly and jump around)

🔲 "Clay"

I stretch it.
   (pulling motion)
I pound it.
   (pounding motion)
I make it firm.
   (pushing motion)
I roll it.
   (rolling motion)
I pinch it.
   (pinching motion)
I make a worm.
   (wiggling motion)

🔲 "The Crossing Guard"

The crossing guard keeps us safe
As he works from day to day.
He holds the stop sign high in the air.
   (hold palm of hand up)
For the traffic to obey.
And when the cars have completely
   stopped
And it's as safe as can be,
He signals us to walk across
   (make a beckoning motion)
The street very carefully.

🔲 "Crossing Streets"

At the curb before I cross
I stop my running feet
   (point to feet)
And look both ways to left and right
   (look left and right)
Before I cross the street.
Lest autos running quietly
Might come as a surprise.
I don't just listen with my ears
   (point to ears)
But look with both my eyes.
   (point to eyes)

🔲 "Daisies"

One, two, three, four, five
   (pop up fingers, one at a time)
Yellow daisies all alive.
Here they are all in a row.
   (point to fingers standing)
The sun and the rain will help them
   grow.
   (make a circle with fingers, flutter
   fingers for rain)

🔲 "Dig a Little Hole"

Dig a little hole.
   (dig)
Plant a little seed.
   (drop a seed)
Pour a little water.
   (pour)
Pull a little weed.
   (pull and throw)

Chase a little bug.
   (chasing motion with hands)
Heigh-ho, there he goes.
   (shade eyes)
Give a little sunshine.
   (circle arms over head)
Grow a little bean!
   (hands grow upward)

"Draw a Bubble"

Draw a bubble, draw a bubble.
Make it very round.
   (make a shape in the air with
   index finger)
Draw a bubble, draw a bubble.
No corners can be found.
   (repeat actions)

"Draw a Circle"

Draw a circle, draw a circle
Made very round.
Draw a circle, draw a circle
No corners can be found.

"Draw a Square"

Draw a square, draw a square
Shaped like a tile floor.
Draw a square, draw a square
All with corners four.

"Draw a Triangle"

Draw a triangle, draw a triangle
With corners three.
Draw a triangle, draw a triangle
Draw it just for me.

"Eggs in a Nest"

Here's an egg in a nest up in a tree.
   (make a fist with right hand and
   place in palm of cupped left hand)
What's inside? What can it be?
   (shrug shoulders)
Peck, peck, peck,
Peep, peep, peep.
Out hatches a little bird
   (wiggle fingers of fisted hand)
Cute as can be!

"Eight Baby Pigs"

Two mother pigs lived in a pen.
   (thumbs)
Each had four babies and that
   made ten.
   (fingers of both hands)
These four babies were black and
   white.
   (fingers of one hand)
These four babies were black as
   night.
   (fingers of other hand)
All eight babies loved to play
   (wiggle fingers)
And they rolled in the mud all day!
   (roll hands)

Storytelling and Fingerplays

📖 "Elephants"

Elephants walk like this and like that.
  (sway body back and forth)
They're terribly big; they're terribly fat.
  (spread arms wide in a circular motion)
They have no hands, they have no toes,
And goodness gracious, what a NOSE!
  (put arms together and sway for elephant nose)

📖 "Farm Chores"

Five little farmers woke up with the sun.
  (hold up hand, palm forward)
It was early morning and the chores must be done.
The first little farmer went out to milk the cow.
  (hold up hand, point to thumb)
The second little farmer thought he'd better plow.
  (hold up hand, point to index finger)
The third little farmer cultivated weeds.
  (point to middle finger)
The fourth little farmer planted more seeds.
  (point to fourth finger)
The fifth little farmer drove his tractor round.
  (point to last finger)
Five little farmers, the best that can be found.
  (hold up hand)

📖 "Fish Story"

One, two, three, four, five
  (hold up fingers while counting)
Once I caught a fish alive.
Six, seven, eight, nine, ten
  (hold up additional fingers)
Then I let it go again.
Why did I let it go?
Because it bit my finger so.
Which finger did it bite?
The little finger on the right.
  (hold up pinky on the right hand)

📖 "Five Little Baby Mice"

Five little mice on the kitchen floor.
  (hold up five fingers)
This little mouse peeked behind the door.
  (point to thumb)
This little mouse nibbled at the cake.
  (point to index finger)
This little mouse not a sound did he make.
  (point to middle finger)
This little mouse took a bite of cheese.
  (point to ring finger)
This little mouse heard the kitten sneeze.
  (point to pinky)
"Ah-choo!" sneezed the kitten,
And "squeak" they cried.
As they found a hole and ran inside.
  (move hand behind back)

"Five Little Bear Cubs"

Five little bear cubs
Eating an apple core.
One had a sore tummy
And then there were four.

Four little bear cubs
Climbing in a tree.
One fell out
And then there were three.

Three little bear cubs
Playing peek-a-boo.
One was afraid
And then there were two.

Two little bear cubs
Sitting in the sun.
One ran away
And then there was one.

One little bear cub
Sitting all alone.
He saw his mommy
And then he ran home.

"Five Little Birds"

Five little birds without any home.
    (hold up five fingers)
Five little trees in a row.
    (raise hands high over head)
Come build your nests in our
        branches tall.
    (cup hands)
We'll rock them to and fro.

"Five Little Christmas Cookies"

(Hold up five fingers, take one
    away as directed by poem.)
Five little Christmas cookies on a
        plate by the door,
One was eaten and then there were
        four.

Four little Christmas cookies, gazing
        up at me,
One was eaten and then there were
        three.

Three little Christmas cookies,
        enough for me and you,
One was eaten and then there were
        two.

Two little Christmas cookies sitting
        in the sun,
One was eaten and then there was
        one.

One little Christmas cookie, better
        grab it fast,
As you can see, the others surely
        didn't last.

Storytelling and Fingerplays

📖 "Five Little Clowns"

Five little clowns running through
the door.
   (hold up one hand, put down one
   finger at each verse)
One fell down and then there were
four.

Four little clowns in an apple tree.
One fell out and then there were
three.

Three little clowns stirring up some
stew.
One fell in and then there were two.

Two little clowns having lots of fun.
One ran away and then there was
one.

One little clown left sitting in the sun.
He went home and then there were
none!

📖 "Five Little Donuts"

Down around the corner, at the
bakery shop
There were five little donuts with
sugar on top.
   (hold up five fingers)
Along came ——— (child's name), all
alone.
And she/he took the biggest one
home.
   (Continue the verses until all the
   donuts are gone.)

📖 "Five Little Ducks"

Five little ducks
   (hold up five fingers)
Swimming in the lake.
   (make swimming motions)
The first duck said,
   (hold up one finger)
"Watch the waves I make."
   (make wave motions)
The second duck said,
   (hold up two fingers)
"Swimming is such fun."
   (smile)
The third duck said,
   (hold up three fingers)
"I'd rather sit in the sun."
   (turn face to sun)
The fourth duck said,
   (hold up four fingers)
"Let's swim away."
   (swimming motions)
The fifth duck said,
   (hold up five fingers)
"Oh, let's stay."
Then along came a motorboat.
With a Pop! Pop! Pop!
   (clap three times)
And five little ducks
Swam away from the spot.
   (put five fingers behind back)

📖 "Five Little Fishes"

Five little fishes swimming in a pond
  (wiggle five fingers)
The first one said, "I'm tired," as he
  yawned.
  (yawn)
The second one said, "Well, let's
  take a nap."
  (put hands together on side of
  face)
The third one said, "Put on your
  sleeping cap."
  (pretend to pull on hat)
The fourth one said, "Wake up! Don't
  sleep."
  (shake finger)
The fifth one said, "Let's swim where
  it's deep."
  (point down and with a low voice
  say)
So, the five little fishes swam away.
  (wiggle fingers and put behind
  back)
But they came back the very next
  day.
  (wiggle fingers out front again)

📖 "Five Little Friends"

  (Hold up five fingers; subtract one
  with each action.)
Five little friends playing on the floor,
One got tired and then there were
  four.
Four little friends climbing in a tree,
One jumped down and then there
  were three.

Three little friends skipping to the
  zoo,
One went for lunch and then there
  were two.
Two little friends swimming in the
  sun,
One went home and then there was
  one.
One little friend going for a run,
Decided to take a nap and then
  there were none.

📖 "Five Little Monkeys Swinging from a Tree"

Five little monkeys swinging from
  the tree,
Teasing Mr. Alligator, "You can't
  catch me."
Along comes Mr. Alligator as sneaky
  as can be . . .
SNAP
Four little monkeys swinging from
  the tree.
Three little monkeys swinging from
  the tree.
Two little monkeys swinging from
  the tree.
One little monkey swinging from the
  tree.
No more monkeys swinging from the
  tree!

Storytelling and Fingerplays

"Five Little Pumpkins"

*Five little pumpkins sitting on a
   gate.
The first one said, "Oh my, it's
   getting late."
The second one said, "There are
   witches in the air."
The third one said, "But we don't
   care."
The fourth one said, "Let's run.
   Let's run."
The fifth one said, "It's Halloween
   fun."
"Wooooooooooo," went the wind,
And out went the lights.
And the five little pumpkins rolled
   out of sight.*

"Five Little Puppies I"

*Five little puppies were playing in
   the sun.*
   (hold up hands, fingers extended)
*This one saw a rabbit, and he began
   to run.*
   (bend down first finger)
*This one saw a butterfly, and he
   began to race.*
   (bend down second finger)
*This one saw a cat, and he began to
   chase.*
   (bend down third finger)
*This one tried to catch his tail, and
   he went round and round.*
   (bend down fourth finger)
*This one was so quiet, he never
   made a sound.*
   (bend down thumb)

**Storytelling and
Fingerplays**

"Five Little Puppies II"

*Five little puppies jumping on the
   bed,*
   (hold up five fingers)
One fell off and bumped his head,
   (hold up one finger—tap head)
*Mama called the doctor and the
   doctor said,*
*"No more puppies jumping on the
   bed."*
   (shake index finger)

"Five Little Snowpeople"

*Five little snowpeople standing in
   the door.
This one melted and then there were
   four.*
   (hold up all five fingers, put down
   thumb)
*Four little snowpeople underneath a
   tree.
This one melted and then there were
   three.*
   (put down pointer finger)
*Three little snowpeople with hats
   and mittens, too.
This one melted and then there were
   two.*
   (put down middle finger)
*Two little snowpeople outside in the
   sun.
This one melted and then there was
   one.*
   (put down ring finger)
*One little snowperson trying hard to
   run.
He melted, too, and then there were
   none.*
   (put down pinky)

🧊 "Five Little Valentines"

Five little valentines were having a
*   race.*
The first little valentine was frilly
*   with lace.*
    (hold up one finger)
The second little valentine had a
*   funny face.*
    (hold up two fingers)
The third little valentine said, "I love
*   you."*
    (hold up three fingers)
The fourth little valentine said, "I do,
*   too."*
    (hold up four fingers)
The fifth little valentine was sly as a
*   fox.*
He ran the fastest to the valentine
*   box.*
    (make five fingers run behind
    back)

🧊 "Five Little Witches"

Five little witches standing by the
*   door.*
    (hold up five fingers)
One flew out and then there were
*   four.*
    (flying motion with hand)
Four little witches standing by a
*   tree.*
    (four fingers)
One went to pick a pumpkin and
*   then there were three.*
    (picking motion, then three
    fingers)
Three little witches stirring their
*   brew.*
    (stir)

One fell in and then there were two.
    (two fingers)
Two little witches went for a run.
    (run with fingers)
One got lost and then there was one.
    (one finger)
One little witch, yes, only one.
    (one finger)
She cast a spell and now there are
*   none.*
    (make motions as if to cast spell
    and then put hands in lap)

🧊 "Five Police Officers"

Five strong police officers standing
*   by a store*
    (hold up the one hand)
One became a traffic cop, then there
*   were four.*
    (hold up four fingers)
Four strong police officers watching
*   over me*
One took a lost boy home, then there
*   were three.*
    (hold up three fingers)
Three strong police officers all
*   dressed in blue*
One stopped a speeding car and
*   then there were two.*
    (hold up two fingers)
Two strong police officers, how fast
*   they can run*
One caught a bad man and then
*   there was one.*
    (hold up one finger)
One strong police officer saw some
*   smoke one day*
He called a firefighter who put it out
*   right away.*

📖 "Five Red Apples"

Five red apples in a grocery store.
  (hold up five fingers)
Bobby bought one, and then there
  were four.
  (bend down one finger)
Four red apples on an apple tree.
Susie ate one, and then there were
  three.
  (bend down one finger)
Three red apples. What did Alice do?
Why, she ate one, and then there
  were two.
  (bend down one finger)
Two red apples ripening in the sun.
Timmy ate one, and then there was
  one.
  (bend down one finger)
One red apple and now we are done.
I ate the last one, and now there are
  none.
  (bend down last finger)

📖 "Flower Play"

If I were a little flower
Sleeping underneath the ground,
  (curl up)
I'd raise my head and grow and
  grow
  (raise head and begin to grow)
And stretch my arms and grow and
  grow
  (stretch arms)
And nod my head and say,
  (nod head)
"I'm glad to see you all today."

📖 "Football Players"

Five big football players standing
  in the locker room door.
One had a sore knee
And then there were four.

Four big football players down on
  their knees.
One made a touchdown
And then there were three.

Three big football players looking
  at you.
One made a tackle
And then there were two.

Two big football players running
  in the sun.
One was offsides
And then there was one.

One big football player standing
  all alone.
He decided to go home
And then there were none.

📖 "The Friendly Ghost"

I'm a friendly ghost—almost!
  (point to self)
And I chase you, too!
  (point to child)
I'll just cover me with a sheet
  (pretend to cover self ending with
  hands covering face)
And then call "scat" to you.
  (uncover face quickly and call out
  "scat")

Storytelling and Fingerplays

📖 "Friends"

I like my friends.
So when we are at play.
I try to be very kind
And nice in every way.

📖 "Frisky's Doghouse"

This is Frisky's doghouse,
    (pointer fingers touch to make a
    roof)
This is Frisky's bed.
    (motion of smoothing)
Here is Frisky's pan of milk,
    (cup hands)
So that he can be fed.

Frisky has a collar,
    (point to neck with fingers)
With his name upon it, too.
Take a stick and throw it,
    (motion of throwing)
He'll bring it back to you.
    (clap once)

📖 "Going to the Circus"

Going to the circus to have a lot of
    fun.
    (hold closed fist and raise fingers
    to indicate number)
The animals parading one by one.
Now they are walking two by two,
A great big lion and a caribou.
Now they are walking three by three,
The elephants and the chimpanzee.
Now they are walking four by four,
A striped tiger and a big old bear.
Now they are walking five by five,
It makes us laugh when they arrive.

📖 "Green Leaf"

Here's a green leaf
    (show hand)
And here's a green leaf.
    (show other hand)
That you see, makes two.

Here's a bud
    (cup hands together)
That makes a flower.
Watch it bloom for you!
    (open cupped hands gradually)

📖 "Halloween Fun"

Goblins and witches in high pointed
    hats,
    (hands above head to form hat)
Riding on broomsticks and chasing
    black cats.
    (ride broomstick)
Children in costumes might well
    give a fright.
    (look frightened)
Get things in order for Halloween
    night.
We like our treats
    (nod head)
And we'll play no mean pranks.
    (shake heads)
We'll do you no harm and we'll only
    say, "Thanks."

📖 "Halloween Witches"

One little, two little, three little
    witches,
    (hold up one hand, nod fingers at
    each count)
Fly over the haystacks
    (fly hand in up-and-down motion)
Fly over ditches

**Storytelling and
Fingerplays**

Slide down moonbeams without any hitches
   (glide hand downward)
Heigh-ho! Halloween's here!

"Hanukkah Lights"

One light, two lights, three lights, and four
   (hold up four fingers, one at a time)
Five lights, six lights, and three more.
   (hold up five fingers on other hand)
Twinkle, twinkle nine pretty lights,
   (move fingers)
In a golden menorah bright!
   (make cup with palm of hand)

"Hatching Chickens"

Five eggs and five eggs
   (hold up one hand and then the other)
Are underneath a hen.
Five eggs and five eggs
   (hold up all fingers)
And that makes ten.
The hen keeps the eggs warm for three long weeks
   (hold up three fingers)
Snap go the shells with tiny little beaks.
   (snap fingers)
Crack, crack, the shells go
   (clap four times)
The chickens every one
Fluff out their feathers
In the warm spring sun.
   (make circle of arms)

"Here Is a Bubble"

Here is a bubble
   (make a circle with thumb and index finger)
And here's a bubble
   (make a bigger circle with two thumbs and index finger)
And here is a great big bubble I see.
   (make a large circle with arms)
Let's count the bubbles we've made.
One, two, three.
   (repeat prior actions)

"Here Is a Car"

Here is a car, shiny and bright.
   (cup one hand and place on other palm)
This is the windshield that lets in the light.
   (hands open, fingertips touching)
Here are wheels that go round and round.
   (two fists)
I sit in the back seat and make not a sound.
   (sit quietly with hands in lap)

"Here Is the Beehive"

Here is the beehive. Where are the bees?
   (make a fist)
They're hiding away so nobody sees.
Soon they're coming creeping out of their hive,
One, two, three, four, five. Buzz-z-z-z.
   (draw fingers out of fist on each count)

"Here Is the Chimney"

Here is the chimney.
   (make fist and tuck in thumb)
Here is the top.
   (cover with hand)
Open it up quick
   (lift hand up)
And out Santa will pop.
   (pop out thumb)

"Hickory, Dickory, Dock"

Hickory, dickory, dock.
   (bend arm at elbow; hold up and
open palm)
The mouse ran up the clock.
   (run fingers up the arm)
The clock struck one,
   (hold up index finger)
The mouse ran down,
   (run fingers down arm)
Hickory, dickory, dock.

"Houses"

Here is a nest for a robin.
   (cup both hands)
Here is a hive for a bee.
   (fists together)
Here is a hole for the bunny;
   (finger and thumb make circle)
And here is a house for me!
   (fingertips together to make roof)

"How It Happens"

A muddy hump,
   (make a fist using both hands)
A small green lump,
   (poke up thumbs together as one)
Two leaves and then
Two leaves again
   (raise forefinger of each hand from
   fist, then middle fingers)
And shooting up, a stem and cup.
   (put elbows, forearms, and hands
   together, fingers slightly curved)
One last shower,
   (rain movements with spread arms
   and fingers)
Then a flower.
   (elbows, forearms together with
   hands wide apart, palms up)

"I Can Even Count Some More"

One, two, three, four
I can even count some more.
Five, six, seven, eight
All my fingers stand up straight
Nine, ten are my thumb men.

"I Looked inside My Looking Glass"

I looked inside my looking glass
To see what I could see.
It looks like I'm happy today,
Because that smiling face is me.

🎵 "I Want to Lead a Band"

I want to lead a band
With a baton in my hand.
   (wave baton in air)
I want to make sweet music high
   and low.
Now first I'll beat the drum
   (drum-beating motion)
With a rhythmic tum-tum-tum,
And then I'll play the bells
A-ting-a-ling-a-ling,
   (bell-playing motion)
And next I'll blow the flute
With a cheery toot-a-toot.
   (flute-playing motion)
Then I'll make the violin sweetly
   sing.
   (violin-playing motion)
Now I'm leading a band
With a baton in my hand.
   (wave baton in air again)

🎵 "Ice Cream"

I'm licking my ice cream
I'm licking it fast.
It's dripping down my arm.
It's disappearing fast.

🎵 "If I Could Play"

If I could play the piano
This is the way I would play.
   (move fingers like playing a piano)

If I had a guitar
I would strum the strings this way.
   (hold guitar and strum)

If I had a trumpet
I'd toot to make a tune.
   (play trumpet)

But if I had a drum
I'd go boom, boom, boom.
   (pretend to play a drum)

🎵 "If I Were"

If I were a dog
I'd have four legs to run and play.
   (down on all four hands and feet)
If I were a fish
I'd have fins to swim all day.
   (hands at side fluttering like fins)
If I were a bird
I could spread my wings out wide.
And fly all over the countryside.
   (arms out from sides fluttering like
   wings)
But I'm just me.
I have two legs, don't you see?
And I'm just as happy as can be.

Storytelling and Fingerplays

🎲 "If I Were a Bird"

If I were a bird, I'd sing a song
And fly about the whole day long.
   (twine thumbs together and move
   hands like wings)
And when the night comes, go to
   rest
   (tilt head and close eyes)
Up in my cozy little nest.
   (cup hands together to form a
   nest)

🎲 "If I Were a Horse"

If I were a horse, I'd gallop all
   around.
   (slap thighs and gallop in a circle)
I'd shake my head and say, "Neigh,
   neigh."
   (shake head)
I'd prance and gallop all over town.

🎲 "I've a Jack-o'-Lantern"

I've a jack-o'-lantern
   (make a ball with open fist, thumb
   at top)
With a great big grin.
   (grin)
I've got a jack-o'-lantern
With a candle in.
   (insert other index finger up
   through bottom of first)

🎲 "Jack-in-the-Box"

Jack-in-the-box all shut up tight
   (fingers wrapped around thumb)
Not a breath of air, not a ray of light.
   (other hand covers fist)
How tired he must be all down in a
   heap.
   (lift off)
I'll open the lid and up he will leap!
   (thumbs pop out)

🎲 "Jack-o'-Lantern"

I am a pumpkin, big and round.
   (show size with arms)
Once upon a time, I grew on the
   ground.
   (point to ground)
Now I have a mouth, two eyes, and a
   nose.
   (point to each)
What are they for, do you suppose?
   (point to forehead and "think")
Why—I'll be a jack-o'-lantern on
   Halloween night.

**Storytelling and
Fingerplays**

"The Jack-o'-Lantern"

Three little pumpkins growing on a vine.
  (three fingers)
Sitting in the sunlight, looking just fine.
  (arms up like sun)
Along came a ghost who picked just one
  (one finger)
To take on home for some Halloween fun.
  (smile)
He gave him two eyes to see where he goes.
  (paint two eyes)
He gave him a mouth and a big handsome nose.
  (point to mouth and nose)
Then he put a candle in.
  (pretend to put in candle)
Now see how he glows.
  (wiggle fingers from center of body out until arms are extended)

"Johnny's Hammer"

Johnny works with one hammer, one hammer, one hammer.
Johnny works with one hammer, then he works with two.
  (You can also change the name used in the fingerplay to include your child's name.)

"A Kitten Is Hiding"

A kitten is hiding under a chair.
  (hide one thumb in other hand)
I looked and looked for her everywhere.
  (peer about with hand on forehead)
Under the table and under the bed,
  (pretend to look)
I looked in the corner and then I said,
"Come Kitty, come Kitty, I have milk for you."
  (cup hands to make dish and extend)
Kitty came running and calling, "mew, mew."
  (run fingers up arm)

"Knocking"

Look at —— knocking on our door.
  (knock)
Look at —— knocking on our door.
  (knock)
Come on in out of the cold
  (shiver)
Into our nice, warm home.
  (rub hands together to be warm)

Storytelling and Fingerplays

📦 "Leaves"

Little leaves fall gently down
Red and yellow, orange and brown.
　(flutter hands as leaves falling)
Whirling, whirling around and
　around.
　(turn around)
Quietly without a sound.
　(put fingers to lips)
Falling softly to the ground
　(begin to fall slowly)
Down and down and down and
　down.
　(lie on floor)

📦 "Letter to Grandma"

Lick them, stamp them
　(make licking and stamping
　motions)
Put them in a box.
　(extend arms outward)
Hope that Grandma
Loves them a lot!
　(hug self)

📦 "Lickety Lick"

Lickety lick! Lickety lick!
　(form large circle with arm as
bowl; use other arm as spoon to stir)
The batter is getting all
Thickety-thick.
What shall we make?
　(arms spread out)
What shall we bake?
　(arms spread out more)
A great big delicious angel food
　cake.

📦 "Lines"

One straight finger makes a line.
　(hold up one index finger)
Two straight lines make one "t" sign.
　(cross index fingers)
Three lines made a triangle there
　(form triangle with index fingers
　touching and thumbs touching)
And one more line will make a
　square.
　(form square with hands)

📦 "Lion"

I knew a little lion who went roar,
　roar, roar.
　(make sounds)
Who walked around on all fours.
　(walk around on all fours)
He had a tail we could see behind
　the bars.
And when we visit we should stand
　back far.
　(move backwards)

📦 "Little Flowers"

The sun comes out and shines so
　bright
　(join hands over head in circle)
Then we have a shower.
　(wiggle fingers coming down)
The little bud pushes with all its
　might
　(one hand in a fist and the other
　clasped over it; move hands up
　slowly)
And soon we have a flower.
　(join thumbs and spread fingers
　for flower)

🔲 "Little Jack Horner"

Little Jack Horner
Sat in a corner
Eating a Christmas pie.
   (pretend you're eating)
He put in his thumb,
   (thumb down)
And pulled out a plum
   (thumb up)
And said, "What a good boy am I!"
   (say out loud)

🔲 "Little Mail Carrier"

I am a little mail carrier
   (point to self)
Who can do nothing better.
I walk.
   (walk in place)
I run.
   (run in place)
I hop to your house.
   (hop in place)
To deliver your letter.

🔲 "Little Miss Muffet"

Little Miss Muffet
Sat on a tuffet
Eating her curds and whey.
Along came a spider
And sat down beside her
And frightened Miss Muffet away!

🔲 "Little Mouse"

See the little mousie,
   (place index and middle finger on
   thumb to represent a mouse)
Creeping up the stair,
   (creep mouse slowly up the
   forearm)
Looking for a warm rest.
There—Oh! There!
   (spring mouse into an elbow
   corner)

🔲 "The Mail Carrier"

I come from the post office
   (walk from post office)
My mail sack on my back.
   (pretend to carry sack on back)
I go to all the houses
   (pretend to go up to a house)
Leaving letters from my pack.
   (pretend to drop letters into
   mailbox)
One, two, three, four
   (hold up fingers as you count)
What are these letters for?
   (pretend to hold letters as you
   count)
One for John. One for Lou.
   (pretend to hand out letters)
One for Tom and one for you!
   (pretend to hand out letters to
   others)

Storytelling and Fingerplays

"Making a Snowperson"

Roll it, roll it, get a pile of snow.
  (make rolling motions with hands)
Rolling, rolling, rolling, rolling, rolling,
  here we go.
Pat it, pat it, face it to the south.
  (patting motion)
Now my little snowperson's done,
  eyes and nose and mouth.
  (point to eyes, nose, and mouth)

"The Menorah Candle"

I'm a menorah candle
  (stand, point at self)
Growing shorter you can see.
  (bend down slowly)
Melting all my wax
  (go down more)
Until there's nothing left to see.
  (sit down)

"Miss Polly's Dolly"

Miss Polly had a dolly that was sick,
  sick, sick.
  (cradle arms and look sad)
She called for the doctor to come
  quick, quick, quick.
  (clap hands three times)
The doctor came with his coat and
  his hat.
  (point to your shirt and head)
And rapped on the door with a rap,
  rap, rap.
  (pretend to knock three times)
He looked at the dolly and he shook
  his head
  (shake head)

And he said, "Miss Polly, put her
  straight to bed."
  (shake finger)
Then he wrote on a paper for some
  pills, pills, pills.
  (hold left hand out flat, pretend to
  write with right hand)
I'll be back in the morning with my
  bill, bill, bill.
  (hold left hand out flat, wave it
  up and down as if waiting to be
  handed cash)
  (*Note:* The doctor may be male or
  female—substitute pronouns.)

"The Monkey"

The monkey claps, claps, claps his
  hands.
  (clap hands)
The monkey claps, claps, claps his
  hands.
  (clap hands)
Monkey see, monkey do.
The monkey does the same as you.
  (use pointer finger)
  (Then change actions.)

"Mouse"

Here is a mouse with ears so funny,
  (place index and middle finger on
  thumb to represent a mouse)
And here is a hole in the ground.
  (make a hole with the other fist)
When a noise he hears, he pricks up
  his ears.
And runs to his hole in the ground.
  (jump mouse into hole in other
  fist)

Storytelling and
Fingerplays

357

📖 "Mr. Carrot"

Nice Mr. Carrot
Makes curly hair.
   (hand on head)
His head grows underneath the
   ground,
   (bob head)
His feet up in the air.
   (raise feet)
And early in the morning
I find him in his bed
   (close eyes, lay head on hands)
And give his feet a great big pull
   (stretch legs out)
And out comes his head.

📖 "Mrs. Kitty's Dinner"

Mrs. Kitty, sleek and fat,
   (put thumb up with fingers folded
   on right hand)
With her kittens four.
   (hold up four fingers on right
   hand)
Went to sleep upon the mat
   (make a fist)
By the kitchen door.

Mrs. Kitty heard a noise.
Up she jumped in glee.
   (thumb up on right hand)
"Kittens, maybe that's a mouse?
   (all five fingers on right hand up)
Let's go and see!"

Creeping, creeping, creeping on.
   (slowly sneaking with five fingers
   on floor)
Silently they stole.
But the little mouse had gone
   (mouse is thumb on left hand)
Back into his hole.

📖 "Musical Instruments"

This is how a horn sounds
Toot! Toot! Toot!
   (play imaginary horn)

This is how guitars sound
Vrrroom, vrrroom, vrroom.
   (strum imaginary guitar)

This is how the piano sounds
Tinkle, grumble, brring.
   (run fingers over imaginary
   keyboard)

This is how the drum sounds
Rat-a-tat, grumble, brring.
   (strike drum, include cymbal)

📖 "My Apple"

Look at my apple, it's red and round.
   (make a ball shape with hands)
It fell from a tree down to the ground.
   (make downward motion)
Come let me share my apple, please
   do!
   (beckoning motion)
My mother can cut it right in two—
   (make slicing motion)
One half for me and one half for you.
   (holding out two hands, sharing
   halves)

Storytelling and Fingerplays

358

"My Bicycle"

*One wheel, two wheels on the
    ground.*
    (revolve hand in forward circle to
    form each wheel)
*My feet make the pedals go round
    and round.*
    (move feet in pedaling motion)
Handlebars help me steer so straight
    (pretend to steer bicycle)
Down the sidewalk, through the gate.

"My Dreidel"

I have a little dreidel.
    (cup hands to form a square)
I made it out of clay.
    (move fingers in a molding
motion)
And when it's dry and ready
    (flatten hands as if to hold in
    hand—palm up, pinkies together)
Then with it I will play.
    (pretend to spin dreidel on the floor)

"My Friend the Toothbrush"

*My toothbrush is a tool.
I use it every day.
I brush and brush and brush and
    brush
To keep the cavities away.*
    (pretend to brush teeth)

"My Garden"

This is my garden
    (extend one hand forward, palm up)
I'll rake it with care
    (raking motion with fingers)
And then some flower seeds
    (planting motion)
*I'll plant in right there.
The sun will shine*
    (make circle with hands)
And the rain will fall
    (let fingers flutter down to lap)
And my garden will blossom
    (cup hands together, extend
    upward slowly)
And grow straight and tall.

"My Hands"

*My hands can talk
In a special way.
These are some things
They help me to say:
"Hello"*
    (wave)
"Come here"
    (beckon toward self)
"It's A-OK"
    (form circle with thumb and
    pointer)
"Now stop"
    (hand out, palm up)
"Look"
    (hands shading eyes)
"Listen"
    (cup hand behind ear)
(or) "It's far, far away"
    (point out into the distance)
*And, "Glad to meet you, how are you
    today."*
    (shake someone's hand)

**Storytelling and
Fingerplays**

"My House"

I'm going to build a little house.
   (draw house with fingers by out-
   lining the air)
With windows big and bright,
   (spread out arms)
With chimney tall and curling smoke
   (show tall chimney with hands)
Drifting out of sight.
   (shade eyes with hands to look)
In winter when the snowflakes fall
   (use fingers to make the motion of
   snow falling downward)
Or when I hear a storm,
   (place hand to ear)
I'll go sit in my little house
   (draw house again)
Where I'll be snug and warm.
   (hug self)

"My Pumpkin"

See my pumpkin round and fat.
   (make circle with hands, fingers
   spread wide, touching)
See my pumpkin yellow.
   (make a smaller circle)
Watch him grin on Halloween.
   (point to mouth, which is grinning
   wide)
He is a very funny fellow.

"My Puppy"

I like to pet my puppy.
   (pet puppy)
He has such nice soft fur.
   (pet puppy)
And if I don't pull his tail
   (pull tail)
He won't say "Grr!"
   (make face)

"My Rabbit"

My rabbit has two big ears
   (hold up index and middle fingers
   for ears)
And a funny little nose.
   (join other three fingers for nose)
He likes to nibble carrots
   (move thumb away from other two
   fingers)
And he hops wherever he goes.
   (move whole hand jerkily)

"My Toothbrush"

I have a little toothbrush.
   (use pointer for a toothbrush)
I hold it very tightly.
   (make tight fist)
I brush my teeth each morning
   (pretend to brush teeth)
And then again at night.

"My Turtle"

This is my turtle
   (make fist and extend thumb)
He lives in a shell.
   (hide thumb in fist)
He likes his home very well.
He pokes his head out when he
   wants to eat
   (extend thumb)
And pulls it back in when he wants
   to sleep.
   (hide thumb in fist)

"Not Say a Single Word"

We'll hop, hop, hop like a bunny
    (make hopping motion with hands)
And run, run, run like a dog.
    (make running motion with
    fingers)
*We'll walk, walk, walk like an
    elephant*
    (make walking motion with arms)
And jump, jump, jump like a frog.
    (make jumping motions with arms)
*We'll swim, swim, swim like a gold-
    fish*
    (make swimming motion with
    hands)
And fly, fly, fly like a bird.
    (make flying motion with arms)
*We'll sit right down and fold our
    hands*
    (fold hands in lap)
And not say a single word!

"Old King Cole"

Old King Cole was a merry old soul
    (lift elbows up and down)
And a merry old soul was he.
    (nod head)
He called for his pipe.
    (clap two times)
He called for his bowl.
    (clap two times)
And he called for his fiddlers three.
    (clap two times, then pretend to
    play the violin)

"One Grape and One Grape"

*One grape and one grape, that
    makes two.*
    (hold up two fingers)
*But you have three friends, now
    what do you do?*
    (shrug shoulders and hold hands
    up)
Go to the store and buy a few more.
Then you'll have a whole bunch.
    (hold out arms to create circle
    shapes)
They're great with your lunch!

"One to Ten Circle"

Let's make a circle and around we go,
Not too fast and not too slow.
*One, two, three, four, five, six, seven,
    eight, nine, ten,*
*Let's face the other way and go
    around again.*
*One, two, three, four, five, six, seven,
    eight, nine, ten.*

"Open, Shut Them"

Open, shut them, open, shut them.
    (use index and middle finger to
make scissors motion)
Give a little snip, snip, snip.
    (three quick snips with fingers)
Open, shut them, open, shut them.
    (repeat scissors motion)
Make another clip.
    (make another scissors motion)

**Storytelling and
Fingerplays**

361

*This is the orange tree with leaves
    so green*
    (raise arms over head, making a
    circle)
*Here are the oranges that hang in
    between.*
    (make fists)
*When the wind blows the oranges
    will fall.*
Here is the basket to gather them all.
    (make circle with arms in front of
    body)

"Pat-a-Cake"

*Pat-a-cake, pat-a-cake, baker's man.
Bake me a cake as fast as you can!*
    (clap hands together lightly)
Roll it
    (roll hands)
And pat it
    (touch hands together lightly)
And mark it with a "B"
    (write "B" in the air)
*And put it in the oven for baby and
    me.*
    (point to baby and to yourself)

"Painting"

Hands are blue.
    (look at outstretched hands)
*Hands are green.
Fingers are red,
In between.*
    (wiggle fingers)
Paint on my face.
    (touch face)
Paint on my smock.
    (touch smock)
Paint on my shoes.
    (touch shoes)
Paint on my socks.
    (touch socks)

"Picking Apples"

Here's a little apple tree.
    (left arm up, fingers spread)
I look up and I can see
    (look at fingers)
Big red apples, good to eat!
    (raise hands to mouth)
Shake the little apple tree.
    (shake tree with hands)
See the apples fall on me.
    (raise cupped hands and let fall)
Here's a basket, big and round.
    (make circle with arms)
Pick the apples from the ground.
    (pick and put in basket)
Here's an apple I can see.
    (look up to the tree)
I'll reach up. It's ripe and sweet.
    (reach up to upper hand)
That's the apple I will eat!
    (hands to mouth)

**Storytelling and
Fingerplays**

📖 "Plants"

Plants need care to help them grow
    (make fist with hand)
Just like boys and girls you know.
Good soil, water, sunshine bright.
Then watch them pop overnight.
    (extend fingers from fist)

📖 "Presents"

See all the presents by the
    Christmas tree?
    (hand shades eyes)
Some for you,
    (point)
And some for me.
    (point)

Long ones,
    (extend arms)
Tall ones,
    (measure hand up from floor)
Short ones, too.
    (hand to floor, low)
And here is a round one
    (circle with arms)
Wrapped in blue.

Isn't it fun to look and see
    (hand shade eyes)
All of the presents by the Christmas
    tree?
    (arms open wide)

📖 "Purple Lollipop"

Here is a purple, sweet lollipop.
    (make a fist pretending to hold a
    stick of lollipop)
I bought it today at a candy shop.
One lick, mmm, it tastes so good.
    (pretend to lick)
Two licks, oh, I knew it would.
Three licks, yes, I like the taste.
Four licks, now I will not waste.
Five licks, keep on and on.
Six licks, oh! It's nearly gone!
Seven licks, it's getting small.
Eight licks and still not all.
Nine licks, my tongues goes fast.
Ten licks and that's the last!

📖 "Raindrops"

Rain is falling down.
Rain is falling down.
    (raise arm, flutter fingers to the
    ground, tapping the floor)
Pitter-patter
Pitter-patter
Rain is falling down.

**Storytelling and
Fingerplays**

🔲 "Red Light"

Red light, red light, what do you say?
I say, "Stop and stop right away!"
   (hold palms of both hands up)
Yellow light, yellow light, what do
   you say?
I say, "Wait till the light turns green."
   (hold one palm of hand up)
Green light, green light, what do you
   say?
I say, "Go, but look each way."
   (circle arm in forward motion and
   turn head to the right and left)
Thank you, thank you, red, yellow,
   green
Now I know what the traffic light
   means.

🔲 "Relaxing Flowers"

Five little flowers standing in the sun
   (hold up five fingers)
See their heads nodding, bowing
   one by one?
   (bend fingers several times)
Down, down, down comes the gentle
   rain
   (raise hands, wiggle fingers, and
   lower arms to simulate falling rain)
And the five little flowers lift their
   heads up again!
   (hold up five fingers)

🔲 "Right Circle, Left Square"

Close my eyes, shut them tight.
   (close eyes)
Make a circle with my one hand.
   (make circle with one hand)
Keep them shut; make it fair.
   (keep eyes shut)
With my other hand, make a square.
   (make square with other hand)

🔲 "Roly-Poly Caterpillar"

Roly-poly caterpillar
Into a corner crept.
Spun around himself a blanket
   (spin around)
Then for a long time slept.
   (place head on folded hands)

Roly-poly caterpillar
Wakened by and by.
   (stretch)
Found himself with beautiful wings
Changed into a butterfly.
   (flutter arms like wings)

🔲 "Sammy"

Sammy is a super snake.
   (wave finger on opposite palm)
He sleeps on the shore of a silver
   lake.
   (curl finger to indicate sleep)
He squirms and squiggles to snatch
   a snack
   (wave finger and pounce)
And snoozes and snores till his
   hunger is back.
   (curl finger on palm)

Storytelling and Fingerplays

 "Santa's Workshop"

Here is Santa's workshop.
  (form peak with both hands)
Here is Santa Claus.
  (hold up thumb)
Here are Santa's little elves
  (wiggle fingers)
Putting toys upon the shelves.

"School Bus"

I go to the bus stop each day
  (walk one hand across table)
Where the bus comes to take us
  away.
  (stop, have other hand wait also)
We stand single file
  (one behind the other)
And walk down the aisle
  (step up imaginary steps onto bus)
When the bus driver talks, we obey.

"Seeds"

Some little seeds have parachutes
To carry them around
  (cup hand downward)
The wind blows them swish, swish,
  swish.
  (flip fingers outward to form a
  parachute)
Then gently lays them on the
  ground.
  (let hand gently float down and
  rest on lap)

"See, See, See"

See, see, see
  (shade eyes with hands)
Three birds are in a tree.
  (hold up three fingers)

One can chirp
  (point to thumb)
And one can sing.
  (point to index finger)
One is just a tiny thing.
  (point to middle finger, then rock
  baby bird in arms)
See, see, see
Three birds are in a tree.
  (hold up three fingers)

Look, look, look
  (shade eyes)
Three ducks are in a brook.
  (hold up three fingers)
One is white, and one is brown.
One is swimming upside down.
  (point to a finger each time)
Look, look, look
Three ducks are in a brook.
  (hold up three fingers)

"Silly Teddy Bear"

Silly little teddy bear
Stood up in a rocking chair.
  (make rocking movements)
Now he has to stay in bed
  (lay head on hands)
With a bandage round his head.
  (circular movement of hand
  around head)

**Storytelling and
Fingerplays**

🔲 "The Snowperson and the Bunny"

A chubby little snowperson
   (make a fist)
Had a carrot nose.
   (poke thumb out)
Along came a bunny
And what do you suppose?
   (other hand, make rabbit ears)
That hungry little bunny
Looking for his lunch
   (bunny hops around)
Ate that snowperson's carrot nose.
   (bunny nibbles at thumb)
Crunch, crunch, crunch

🔲 "Speckled Frogs"

Five green-speckled frogs
Sitting on a speckled log
Eating the most delicious bugs,
Yum, yum!
   (rub tummy)

One jumped into the pool
Where it was nice and cool
Now there are four green-speckled
   frogs.
   (Repeat until there are no green-
   speckled frogs.)

🔲 "Stand Up Tall"

Stand up tall
Hands in the air.
Now sit down
In your chair.
Clap your hands
And make a frown.
Smile and smile.
Hop like a clown.

🔲 "Stretch, Stretch"

Stretch, stretch away up high:
On your tiptoes, reach the sky.
See the bluebirds flying high.
   (wave hands)
Now bend down and touch your
   toes.
Now sway as the North Wind blows.
Waddle as the gander goes!

🔲 "Swimming"

I can dive.
   (make diving motion with hands)
I can swim.
   (swimming motion)
I can float.
   (hands outstretched with head
   back)
I can fetch.
But dog paddle
   (paddle like dog)
Is the stroke I do best.

🔲 "Tap, Tap, Tap"

Tap, tap, tap goes the woodpecker
   (tap with right pointer finger on
   inside of left wrist)
As he pecks a hole in a tree.
   (make hole with pointer finger and
   thumb)
He is making a house with a window
To peep at you and me.
   (hold circle made with finger and
   thumb in front of eye)

"Ten Fluffy Chickens"

Five eggs and five eggs
    (hold up two hands)
That makes ten.
Sitting on top is the mother hen.
    (fold one hand over the other)
Crackle, crackle, crackle
    (clap hands three times)
What do I see?
Ten fluffy chickens
    (hold up ten fingers)
As yellow as can be!

"Ten Little Fingers"

I have ten little fingers and ten little
    toes.
    (point to portions of body as the
    child repeats words)
Two little arms and one little nose.
One little mouth and two little ears.
Two little eyes for smiles and tears.
One little head and two little feet.
One little chin, that makes me
    complete.

"Thanksgiving Dinner"

Every day we eat our dinner.
Our table is very small.
    (palms of hands close together)
There's room for father, mother,
    sister, brother, and me—that's all.
    (point to each finger)
But when it's Thanksgiving Day and
    the company comes,
You'd scarcely believe your eyes.
    (rub eyes)
For that very same reason
The table stretches until it is just
    this size!
    (stretch arms wide)

"There Was a Little Turtle"
    (by Vachel Lindsay)

There was a little turtle,
    (make small circle with hands)
He lived in a box.
    (make box with hands)
He swam in a puddle,
    (wiggle hands)
He climbed on the rocks.
    (climb fingers of one hand up over
    the other)

He snapped at a mosquito,
    (clap hands)
He snapped at a flea,
    (repeat)
He snapped at a minnow,
    (repeat)
He snapped at me!
    (point to self)

He caught the mosquito,
    (catching motion with hands and
    arms)
He caught the flea,
    (repeat)
He caught the minnow,
    (repeat)
But he didn't catch me!
    (shake head from side to side)

"This Little Cow"

This little cow eats grass.
    (hold up fingers of one hand, bend
    down one finger)
This little cow eats hay.
    (bend down another finger)
This little cow drinks water.
    (bend down another finger)
And this little cow does nothing.
    (bend down another finger)
But lie and sleep all day.

Storytelling and Fingerplays

🔲 "This Little Pig"

This little pig went to market.
   (point to one finger at a time)
This little pig stayed home.
This little pig had roast beef.
This little pig had none.
This little pig cried, "Wee, wee, wee,"
And ran all the way home.

🔲 "Three Cats"

One little cat and two little cats
Went out for a romp one day.
   (hold up one finger and then two
   fingers with the other hand)
One little cat and two little cats
Make how many cats at play?
   (ask how many that makes)
Three little cats had lots of fun
Till growing tired, away ran ——?
   (take one finger away and ask how
   many ran away)
I really think that he was most un-
   kind to the —— little cats that
   were left behind.
   (ask how many are left)

🔲 "Traffic Policeman"

The traffic policeman holds up his
   hand.
   (hold up hand, palm forward)
He blows the whistle,
   (pretend to blow whistle)
He gives the command.
   (hold up hand again)

When the cars are stopped
   (hold up hand again)
He waves at me.
Then I may cross the street, you see.
   (wave hand as if indicating for
   someone to go)

🔲 "Tulips"

Five little tulips—red and bright
   (hold up hand)
Let us water them every day.
   (make sprinkle motion with other
   hand)
Watch them open in the bright
   sunlight.
   (cup hand, then open)
Watch them close when it is night.
   (close hand again)

🔲 "Twirling Leaves"

The autumn wind blows—Oooo,
   Oooo, Oooo,
   (make wind sounds)
The leaves shake and shake then fly
   into the sky so blue.
   (children shake)
They whirl and whirl around them,
   twirl and twirl around.
   (turn around in circles)
But when the wind stops, the leaves
   sink slowly to the ground.
Lower, lower, lower, and land quietly
   without a sound.
   (sink very slowly and quietly)

"Two Little Apples"

Way up high in an apple tree
  (extend arms above head)
Two little apples smiled at me.
  (look at two clutched fists)
I shook that tree as hard as I could.
  (shake arms while continually
  looking up)
Down came the apples.
  (bring arms down to body trunk)
Mmmmm, were they good!
  (make circular motions over
  stomach and smile)
  (This traditional fingerplay can
  be adapted for lemons, oranges,
  grapefruit, limes, or mangoes.)

"Two Little Blackbirds"

Two little blackbirds sitting on a hill,
  (close fists, extend index fingers)
One named Jack. One named Jill.
  (talk to one finger; talk to other
  finger)
Fly away jack. Fly away Jill.
  (toss index fingers over shoulder
  separately)
Come back, Jack. Come back, Jill.
  (bring back hands separately with
  index fingers extended)

"Two Little Kittens"

Two little kittens found a ball of yarn
  (hold up two fingers and cup
hands together to form a ball)
As they were playing near a barn.

  (bring hands together pointed
  upward for barn)
One little kitten jumped in the hay,
  (hold up one finger and make
  jumping, then wiggling motion)
The other little kitten ran away.
  (make running motion with other
  hand)

"Vegetables and Fruits"

The food we like to eat that grows
On vines and bushes and trees
Are vegetables and fruits, my friend,
Like cherries, grapes, and peas.
Apples and oranges and peaches are
  fruits
And so are tangerines,
Lettuce and carrots are vegetables,
Like squash and beans.

"Wee Willie Winkle"

Wee Willie Winkle runs through the
  town
  (pretend to run)
Upstairs, downstairs in his
  nightgown,
  (point up, point down, then point
  to clothes)
Rapping at the window, crying
  through the lock
  (knock in the air, peek through a
  hole)
"Are the children all in bed? For now
  it's eight o'clock!"
  (shake finger)

Storytelling and Fingerplays

📖 "What Am I Making?"

This is a circle.
(draw circle in the air)
This is a square.
(draw square in the air)
Can you tell me?
What I'm making there?
(draw another shape in the air)

📖 "Wheels"

Wheels big (form big circles with
fingers)
Wheels small. (form little circles with
fingers)
Count them one by one.
Turning as they're pedaled (make
pedaling motion with hands)
In the springtime sun!
One-two-three-four-five.
(count fingers)

📖 "Where Are the Baby Mice?

Where are the baby mice?
(hide fists behind back)
Squeak, squeak, squeak!
I cannot see them.
Peek, peek, peek.
(show fist)
*Here they come out of their hole in
the wall.*
*One, two, three, four, five, and that
is all!*
(show fingers one at a time)

📖 "Where Should I Live?"

Where should I live?
In a castle with towers and a moat?
(make a point with arms over
head)
Or on a river in a houseboat?
(make wavelike motions)
*A winter igloo made of ice may be
just the thing*
(pretend to pack snow)
*But what would happen when it
turned to spring?*
(pretend to think)
*I like tall apartments and houses
made of stone,*
(stretch up tall)
*But I'd also like to live in a blue
mobile home.*
(shorten up)
*A cave or cabin in the woods would
give me lots of space*
(stretch out wide)
*But I guess my home is the best
place!*
(point to self)

📖 "Windshield Wiper"

I'm a windshield wiper
(bend arm at elbow with fingers
pointing up)
This is how I go
(move arm to left and right,
pivoting at elbow)
Back and forth, back and forth
(continue back and forth motion)
In the rain and snow.
(continue back and forth motion)

"Witch's Cat"

I am the witch's cat.
    (make a fist with two fingers
    extended for cat)
Meow, meow.
    (stroke fist with other hand)
My fur is black as darkest night.
My eyes are glaring green and
    bright.
    (circle eyes with thumb and fore-
    fingers)
I am the witch's cat.
    (make a fist again with two fingers
    extended and stroke it with the
    other hand)

"Zippers"

Three little zippers on my snowsuit,
    (hold up three fingers)
Fasten up as snug as snug can be.
It's a very easy thing as you can see
Just zip, zip, zip!
    (make three zipping motions)
I work the zippers on my snowsuit.
Zippers really do save time for me.
I can fasten them myself with one,
    two, three.
Just zip, zip, zip!
    (make three zipping motions)

"The Zoo"

The zoo holds many animals inside
    (make a circle with your hands
    and peer inside)
So unlatch the doors and open them
    wide.
    (open your hands wide)
Elephants, tigers, zebras, and bears,
    (hold up one finger for each kind
    of animal)
Are some of the animals you'll find
    there.

"Zoo Animals"

This is the way the elephant goes,
    (clasp hands together, extend
    arms, move back and forth)
With a curly trunk instead of a nose.
The buffalo, all shaggy and fat,
Has two sharp horns in place of a
    hat.
    (point to forehead)
The hippo with his mouth so wide—
Let's see what's inside.
    (hands together and open wide
    and close them)
The wiggly snake upon the ground,
Crawls along without a sound.
    (weave hands back and forth)
But monkey see and monkey do, is
    the
Funniest animal in the zoo.
    (place thumbs in ears and wiggle
    fingers)

**Storytelling and
Fingerplays**

Social Studies
and Excursions

Young children are notoriously curious. They are interested in the world around them—people, places, objects, foods, and customs. Listening to their conversations and questions you will note that many relate to other people such as community helpers, social skills, holidays, and current events.

For instance, they may ask:

- ▶ What is Hanukkah?
- ▶ Why does Sung Jee have a stepdad?
- ▶ What do postal workers do?
- ▶ Why does Luis's grandpa speak so loudly?

Value

Positive social experiences help children by:

- ▶ learning about people's roles, including family members and community helpers.
- ▶ learning how to share.
- ▶ developing good manners.
- ▶ learning to help others.
- ▶ developing an understanding of the necessary knowledge, skills, and activities for living in a democracy.
- ▶ learning to develop healthy relationships with others.
- ▶ developing respect and a healthy self-concept.
- ▶ developing respect and responsibility for caring for public property.
- ▶ respecting themselves and others, as well as seeing others' point of view.
- ▶ appreciating diversity.
- ▶ learning about celebrations.

Interacting Positively

Children need to learn how to interact positively with other people. They need to learn about social living. They also need to understand there are many ways to do things. All of these are concepts you can teach, directly or indirectly, every day. Many social studies concepts can be taught during the "teachable moment." As situations arise during daily activities and interactions, you can teach the related concepts. To illustrate, if you see a child hitting another child, this is a teachable moment. Point out to the hitter that hitting is not friendly behavior. Moreover, say of the child who was hit, "(Tunde) does not like being hit." Remember, it takes time to learn social skills. The child may be quite comfortable with siblings, relatives, and neighbors, yet in strange social situations, may become fearful, anxious, and clinging. When this occurs, avoid pushing the child forward and expecting skills that you would not expect of adults. Rather, provide the child support and reassurance, attempting to decrease the child's anxiety.

The type of verbal or nonverbal suggestions you use will have a significant influence on a young child's compliance. Studies show that suggestions tend to facilitate compliance more than commanding statements. Moreover, when positive actions are accompanied by a verbal suggestion, compliance is further facilitated. Then, too, after providing your suggestions, give the child time to comply. Patience and timing are important elements in working effectively with young children.

Celebrate Family Activities and Holidays

Children need to learn what it is like belonging to a family. They need to learn how family members work together to support one another. They also need to learn that there is a diversity of family types. For example, Sam might not have a father, Sally may have three grandmothers, and Luis may live with his grandmother.

By celebrating holidays in your home, the child will feel a connection with the human experience. Involve the child in planning special events and holidays. By introducing appropriate experiences, the child will learn the social importance of each holiday. The child will also be learning about the continuity of life.

Building Trust

Be honest and encourage trust in the child. Keeping your promises is the first step. Only make promises that you can keep. For instance, if you have promised to take the child to the library on Saturday, but when the day arrives, a close friend has become ill, explain your predicament to the child by explaining why you have to help your friend instead. Then set another date on which you can take the child to the library.

If you are shopping and the child asks for something you do not want him to have, be honest and discuss why you do not want him to have it. Pick words that suit the child's level of understanding. You may, if you are willing, suggest other choices of items that you would be willing to purchase. Explain why these choices would be more beneficial.

If your child asks a question and you do not know the answer, admit your shortcomings. This is another "teachable moment." In reality, no one has all the right answers. Use these times as an opportunity to teach your child where you might find the right answers. You may contact another person, use an encyclopedia or reference book, etc.

Building Confidence

Parents, grandparents, nannies, and other people special in the child's life need to encourage the child to demonstrate confidence in herself. Help the child learn to reflect positively on her own accomplishments. Self-pride is essential to self-confidence, so make a point of letting the child know that she should feel proud. Be specific in your feedback. You might say the following:

- "You should feel proud for completing the puzzle all by yourself."

- "You should feel proud for helping pick up the puzzle pieces."

- "You should feel proud for picking up the toys."

- "You should feel proud for making such a beautiful piece of art for your grandmother."

Encourage Sharing and Caring

Whenever possible, provide your child opportunities for caring and sharing. An act of compassion is a valuable reinforcer for developing compassion and generosity. There are numerous opportunities in a child's life to show sharing and caring. Encourage your child to:

▶ help you bake or purchase a birthday cake for someone special.

▶ bring a birthday card or present to a friend.

▶ help bake or make cookies for an elderly neighbor next door.

▶ give toys that he is no longer interested in to needy children or another charitable organization.

Promoting Positive Attitudes

Children reflect and become what they hear and see. Consequently, if they are surrounded by unfriendly talk, criticism, and pessimistic thought, they will act and speak accordingly. Likewise, if they are surrounded by positive thinking, praise, and encouragement, they will learn to project these qualities. To be effective in promoting positive attitudes, listen carefully to what you say and the tone of your voice when speaking it. If needed, work carefully to change your style. You also need to be sensitive to your nonverbal communications. Remember that making mistakes is all right. Rather than feeling like a failure when mistakes are made, children need help in determining how to learn from them.

Providing Intergenerational Contacts

Intergenerational contacts are another way for children to see that there is continuity to the human experience. These contacts are another way for children to learn about the past. The contact should also be an opportunity for them to avoid forming stereotypes of the elderly as being tired and sick. Children need to be exposed to a diverse population through personal contacts, as well as the media. Therefore, when choosing books for the child, be careful that the elderly people are not projected as being incapable, sick, or tired.

Excursions and Resource People

Young children learn social skills by learning about their home, culture, neighborhood, and community. They have had limited exposure to their world through the media. Their understanding comes from storybooks, pictures, and television. However, these experiences cannot replace the first-hand experiences gained during excursions in the neighborhood and community.

The best excursions help children develop and clarify concepts. They get to gather information firsthand. During the process, they also will be building their vocabularies. The following chart lists types of excursions that children enjoy.

Types of Excursions

Special excursions and events give opportunities for widening the young child's horizons. The following places or people are listed as suggestions:

Train station	Tree farm	Riding stable
Dentist office	Car wash	Barber shop
Post office	Children's houses	College dormitory
Grocery store	Garage mechanic	Shoe repair shop
Zoo	Television studio	Print shop
Dairy	Drug store	Artist's studio
Family garden	Bakery	Bowling alley
Poultry house	Hospital	Department store windows
Construction site	Meat market	
Beauty shop	Library	Potter's studio
Offices	Apple orchard	Teacher's house
Animal hospital	Farm	Street repair site
Fire station	Airport	

Plan activities after your excursion to help the child clarify the concepts. To illustrate, after a trip to the hair stylist, provide your child with tools a stylist uses. You could also read a storybook about hair stylists. Likewise, after a trip to a bakery, you could bake cookies, bread, or muffins. Moreover, you could read a story about a baker.

Social Studies and Excursions

Excursion Activities

Here is a list of excursions. Depending upon your geographical location and community, you may have others to add to the list.

Apple Orchard

Observe the workers picking, sorting, and/or selling the apples. Call attention to the colors and types of apples.

Bird Sanctuary

Take a field trip to a bird sanctuary, nature area, pond, or park. Observe where birds live.

Building Site

Visit a local building site if available. Observe and discuss the people who are working, how buildings look, and safety. Discuss the role of the construction worker. Take pictures. When the pictures are developed, share them.

Circus

If possible, go to a circus or circus parade in your area.

City Bus

Take the child for a ride around town on a city bus, if available. When boarding, allow the child to place his own money in the meter. Observe the length of the bus. While inside, watch how the bus driver operates the bus. Also have a school bus driver visit and tell about the job and the importance of safety on a bus.

Clothing Store

Visit a children's clothing store. Look at the different colors, sizes, and types of clothing.

Cycle Shop

Visit a cycle shop. Observe different sizes of wheels that are in the shop. Talk about the different materials that wheels can be made of.

Dentist's Office

Visit a dentist's office. Ask the dentist to demonstrate and explain the use of various brushes. Observe the furnishings and equipment.

Doctor's Office

Visit a doctor's office.

Farm

Take a trip to a farm to see the baby animals. Observe the animals and machinery. Ask the farmer to show the fruits and vegetables grown on the farm. While there, observe the various forms of plant life. It is an interesting place to visit during the spring. Also ask the farmer to show you the farm equipment, buildings, and animals.

Farmers' Market

Visit a farmers' market. Purchase fruits and vegetables that can be eaten as snacks.

Field Trips

Take field trips to the following:
- Bank
- Library
- Grocery store
- Police station
- Doctor/dentist office
- Beauty salon/barber
- Courthouse
- Television/radio station
- Airport
- Farm
- Restaurant

Fire Station

Take a trip to a fire station. Observe the clothing worn by firefighters, the building, the vehicles and the tools. Note the color of the engine, hats, sirens, etc. If permissible, let the child climb in the truck and observe the parts.

Greenhouse

Visit a florist or greenhouse to observe flowers and plants. Observe different plants and trees and inquire about their care. Observe the different kinds of yellow flowers.

Grocery Store

- Observe all the forms of apples sold in a grocery store, including the different colors and sizes of apples. To show differences in weight, take a large apple and place on a scale. Note the weight. Then take a small apple and repeat the process.
- Take a field trip to the grocery store and purchase the ingredients needed to make dog biscuits.
- Visit the dairy section of a grocery store. Look for dairy products.
- Ask the clerk to show the child how the food is delivered.
- View the freezer area and, if available, observe a refrigerated delivery truck.

Social Studies and Excursions

Hatchery

Visit a hatchery on a day when it is selling baby chicks.

Hat Store

Visit a hat store or hat department of a store. Examine the different kinds, sizes, and colors of hats.

Hospital

Visit a local hospital.

Ice Skating Rink

Visit an ice skating rink. Observe the ice and watch how it is cleaned.

Insect Walk

Go on a walk to a nearby park to find bugs. Look under rocks, in cracks, in sidewalks, in bushes, etc.

Kennel

Visit a kennel and observe the different sizes of cages and animals.

Laundromat

Take a walk to a local laundromat. Observe the facility. Point out sizes of the different kinds of washing machines and dryers. Explain the use of the laundry carts and folding tables.

Library

Visit a library. Observe how books are stored. Read a story while there. If possible, allow the child to check out books.

Machine Shop

Visit a machine parts shop. Look at the different gears, pulleys, and wheels. Discuss their sizes, shapes, and possible uses.

Mall

Visit the shopping mall. Talk about the mall being a large building that houses a variety of stores. Visit a few of the stores that may be of special interest to the child. Included may be a toy store, pet store, and sporting goods store.

Museum

- Take a field trip to a museum, if one is available. Observe art objects. Point out and discuss color and form.
- Arrange a visit to a nature museum or taxidermy studio to look at stuffed birds. Extend the activity by providing magnifying glasses.

Neighborhood Walk

- Walk around your neighborhood and observe blue items. Things to look for include cars, bikes, birds, houses, flowers, etc. When you return, have the child dictate a list. Record responses.
- Observe the various kinds of buildings. Talk about different sizes and colors of the buildings.
- Look for signs of new life. Observe different types and colors of flowers.
- Take a walk around the neighborhood when the leaves are at their peak of changing colors. Discuss differences in color and size.
- Walk around the neighborhood. Observe the construction workers' actions and tools.
- Take a walk around the neighborhood and look for red objects.
- Take a walk and look for yellow objects. When you return, prepare a language experience chart.

Nursing Home

Visit a nursing home allowing the child to interact with elderly friends.

Paint Store

- Visit a local paint store. Observe all the different shades of blue paint. Look carefully to see if they look similar. Ask the store manager for discarded sample cards. These cards can be added to the materials to use in the art area.
- Visit a paint store and observe the different shades of yellow. Collect samples of paint for use in the art area. If possible, also observe the manager mix yellow paint.

Patrol Car

Visit a police station and observe a squad car. The radio, siren, and flashing lights can be demonstrated. If possible, let the child sit in the car.

Pet Store

- Take a field trip to a pet store. Arrange to have the manager show the child birds and bird cages. Ask the manager how to care for birds.
- Ask the manager how to care for cats and/or dogs. Observe the different types of cats and dogs, cages, collars, leashes, toys, and food.
- Visit a pet store. Ask what kinds of insects are fed to the animals in the store. Do they sell any insects?

Phone Company

Visit a local phone company.

Picnic

Pack a picnic lunch or snack and take it to an area campground.

Post Office

- Visit a local post office. Observe how the mail is sorted. Observe the mailboxes, stamp machines, address books, scales, and rubber stamps. Mail a postcard back to yourself and count the number of days it takes to arrive.
- Visit the local post office. Valentine's Day cards made in the classroom can be mailed.

Pumpkin Patch

Visit a pumpkin patch. Discuss and observe how pumpkins grow, their size, shape, and color. Let the child pick a pumpkin to bring back.

Radio Station

Visit with a local disc jockey at the radio station.

Reflection Walk

Take a walk after it rains. Enjoy the puddles, overflowing gutters, and swirls of water caught by sewers. Look in the puddles. Does anyone see a reflection? Look up in the sky. Do you see any clouds, the sun, or a rainbow? What colors are in a rainbow?

Reserve Park

If your community has a reserve park, or an area where wild animals are caged in a natural environment, take the child to visit. Plan a picnic snack to take along.

Shape Walk

Walk around the neighborhood. During the walk, observe the shapes of the traffic signs and houses. After returning, record the shapes observed on a chart.

Shoe Repair Store

Visit a shoe repair store. Observe a shoe being repaired.

Sledding Hill

Visit a sledding hill. Bring sleds along and go sledding.

Snow Plow

Invite a snowplow operator to come and explain their duties. After a snowfall, the child can observe the plowing.

Sports Store

Visit a sporting goods store. Locate the hat section. Observe the types of hats used for different sports.

Television Station

If available, visit a local television station. Observe the cameras, microphones, and other communication devices.

Turkey Farm

Visit a turkey farm. The child can observe the behavior of the turkeys, as well as the food they eat.

Veterinarian's Office

- Take a field trip to a veterinarian's office or animal hospital. Compare its similarities and differences to a doctor's office.
- Invite a veterinarian to talk about how he or she helps pets and animals. Pet care can also be addressed.

Zoo

Visit the birdhouse at your local zoo. Observe the colors and sizes of birds.

Resource People

Animal/Pet Groomer

Visit with an animal groomer. Ask the groomer to show the equipment, emphasizing the importance of brushes. Observe how a pet is bathed and groomed.

Band Director

Visit a school band director. Observe the different instruments. Listen to their sounds.

Beekeeper

Invite an individual who raises bees to talk about the bees and how they make honey. Ask him to bring in a honeycomb to taste.

Camper Salesperson

Visit a recreational vehicle dealer and tour a large mobile home.

Candle Maker

Invite a resource person to demonstrate candle making, or take a field trip to a craft center so that the child can view candles being made.

Dog Trainer

Visit an obedience class.

Firefighter

Visit a fire station. Ask the firefighter to point out the special features such as the hose, siren, ladders, light, and special clothing kept on the truck. If permissible and safe, let the child climb onto the truck.

Florist/Floral Shop

- Invite a florist to show how flowers are arranged. Talk about why people send flowers. If convenient, the child can tour the greenhouse.
- Observe the different colors, types, and sizes of flowering plants. Then watch the florist design a bouquet or corsage.
- Visit a floral shop and specifically observe red flowers.
- Visit a flower store. Observe the different Valentine arrangements. Call attention to the beautiful color of the flowers, arrangements, and containers.

Hair Stylist

Visit a hair stylist. While there, observe a person's hair being cut. Notice the different scissors that are used and how they are used.

Musician

Invite a musician to play a variety of music for the child to express feelings.

Taxi Driver

Take the child on a taxi ride. Ask the taxi driver to show the features of the taxi.

Tailor/Seamstress

Visit a tailor or seamstress to show how they make, mend, and repair clothing. The seamstress or tailor can demonstrate tools and share some of the clothing articles that were constructed.

Weather Person

Take a field trip to a television station and see what equipment a weather person uses.

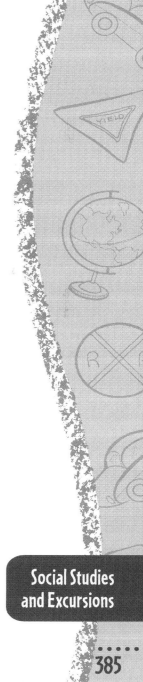

Some of the best resources for young children are grandparents, neighbors, and friends. Encourage these people to share their hobbies and interests. Whenever possible, children should be involved in "hands-on" experiences. This involvement will help make vague concepts more concrete. To illustrate, you may have a friend who plays the piano. After listening to your friend play, provide the child an opportunity to push the piano keys in an effort to produce sound. Encourage and demonstrate, if needed, how to lightly push a key. Listen. Then have the child push the key harder. Listen again. Then encourage the child to compare the two sounds. If needed, play the sounds again.

Helpful Hints!

▷ Reserve a time every day when you can have the child share something that happened to her during the day that she feels good about. Some families do this at dinner every evening.

▷ Serve as a model of respect. Use words such as "please," "thank you," and "excuse me" whenever possible. Young children take on the attitudes and values of people that are close to them.

▷ Project positive expectations. Begin by taking a few moments and make a list of the child's positive attributes. When the time is right, make a conscious effort to encourage these traits.

▷ Observe the child to determine his interests, behaviors, and attitudes. Take your cues from him. Then follow his lead for planning special activities and excursions.

▷ Remember that it is important for the young child to learn about herself. This is a prerequisite for learning about others. Therefore you need to give the child feedback.

▷ Choose books for the child that provide a balance of race and genders.

▷ Celebrate special occasions with family and friends.

▷ Take pictures of your child engaging in positive activities.

▷ Share stories and pictures of your own childhood with the child.

Social Studies Activities

The following are some social studies activities. If age appropriate, you can introduce them to the child.

Animal Babies

Collect pictures of animals and their young. Place adult animal pictures in one basket and pictures of baby animals in another basket. The child can match adult animals to their offspring.

Community Helper Hats

Many people in our community wear hats as part of their uniform. Collect several of these hats such as firefighter, police officer, mail carrier, baker, etc., and place in a bag. Allow the child to pull a hat out of the bag. Once the hat is removed, the child can identify the worker. An older child may be able to describe the activities of the identified worker.

Family Pictures

Display family pictures. Discuss ways in which families help and care for each other.

Fruit and Vegetable Book

The child can make a fruit and vegetable book. Possible titles include, "My favorite fruit is:" "My favorite vegetable is:" "I would like to grow:" and "I would most like to cook:". The child can paste pictures or adhere stickers to the individual pages.

Plant Walk

Walk around the neighborhood and try to identify as many plants as you can.

Room Match Game

Collect several boxes. On one box, print "kitchen"; on another, print "bathroom"; on another, print "living room"; and on another, print "bedroom". Then cut objects related to each of these rooms from catalogs. The child may sort objects by placing them in the appropriate boxes. To illustrate, dishes, silverware, and a coffeepot would be placed in the box labeled "kitchen."

Social Studies and Excursions

Safety Signs

Take a walk and watch for safety signs. Discuss colors and letters on each sign.

Sharing Baskets

Decorate eggs or baskets to give to a home for the elderly. If possible, take a walk and let the child deliver them.

Sorting Feelings

Cut pictures of happy and sad people out of magazines. On the outside of two boxes, draw a smiling face on one and a sad face on the other. The child can sort the pictures into the corresponding boxes.

Sound Tapes

Make a special tape of sounds heard in a home. Homes are full of different sounds. Included may be:

- People knocking on doors
- Wind chimes
- Telephone ringing
- Tea kettle whistling
- Clock ticking
- Toilet flushing
- Popcorn popping
- Vacuum cleaner
- Doorbell
- Running water
- Car horn

Play the tape and have the child listen carefully to identify the sounds.

Spring Cleanup

The child should be provided with a paper bag to collect litter on a walk to a park or in your neighborhood. The litter should be discarded when you return from the walk. Also, the child should be instructed to wash his hands after the walk.

Table Setting

On a sheet of tagboard, trace the outline of a plate, cup, knife, fork, spoon, and napkin. Laminate the tagboard. The child can match the silverware and dishes to the outline on the placemat in preparation for snack or meals. This activity can be extended by having the child turn the placemat over and arrange the place setting without the aid of an outline.

Travel

Discuss ways in which people travel in winter, such as sled, toboggan, snowmobile, snowshoes, skis, etc.

Weather Clothing

Provide examples of clothing worn in each of the four seasons. Provide four laundry baskets. Label each basket with a different picture representing either a sunny, hot day; a rainy day; a cold day; or a fall or spring day. Then encourage the child to sort the clothing according to the weather label on the basket.

Who Wears It?

Hold up different clothing items that family members would wear and ask the child who would wear it. Include baby clothes, sports uniforms, and occupational clothing, ladies clothes, men's clothes, etc.

Winter Book

Encourage the child to make a book about winter. Do one page a day. The following titles could be used:

- What I Wear in Winter
- What I Like to Do Outside in Winter
- What I Like to Do Inside in Winter
- My Favorite Food during Winter
- My Favorite Thing about Winter

This activity may be more appropriate for an older preschool child.

Bibliography

Books

Accorsi, William. (1992). *Friendship's First Thanksgiving.* New York: Holiday House.

Ackerman, Karen. (1992). *I Know a Place.* Illus. by Deborah Kogan Ray. Boston: Houghton Mifflin.

Ackerman, Karen. (1995). *The Sleeping Porch.* Illus. by Elizabeth Sayles. New York: William Morrow.

Adams, Adrienne. (1991). *Easter Egg Artists.* Madison, WI: Demco Media.

Adams, Georgie. (1993). *Fish, Fish, Fish.* New York: Dial Books.

Adler, David A. (1995). *One Yellow Daffodil: A Hanukkah Story.* Illus. by Lloyd Bloom. San Diego, CA: Gulliver Books.

Adler, David A. (1997a). *Chanukah in Chelm.* Illus. by Kevin O'Malley. New York: Lothrop, Lee & Shepard.

Adler, David A. (1997b). *Lou Gehrig: The Luckiest Man.* Illus. by Terry Widener. Orlando: Harcourt Brace.

Adler, David A. (1997c). *Young Cam Jansen and the Lost Tooth.* Illus. by Susanna Natti. New York: Viking.

Agell, Charlotte. (1994a). *I Slide into the White of Winter.* Gardner, ME: Tilbury House.

Agell, Charlotte. (1994b). *I Wear Long Green Hair in Summer.* Gardner, ME: Tilbury House.

Agell, Charlotte. (1994c). *Mud Makes Me Dance in the Spring.* Gardner, ME: Tilbury House.

Alden, Laura. (1993). *Thanksgiving.* Illus. by Susan Lexa-Senning. Chicago: Children's Press.

Aldridge, Josephine Haskell. (1993). *A Possible Tree.* Illus. by Daniel San Souci. New York: Simon & Schuster.

Aliki. (1991). *The Story of Johnny Appleseed.* New York: Simon & Schuster.

Aliki. (1992a). *I'm Growing.* New York: HarperCollins.

Aliki. (1992b). *Milk: From Cow to Carton.* New York: HarperCollins.

Aliki. (1993a). *Communication.* New York: Greenwillow.

Aliki. (1993b). *My Visit to the Aquarium.* New York: HarperCollins.

Aliki. (1995). *Best Friends Together Again.* New York: Greenwillow.

Aliki. (1996a). *Hello! Good-Bye.* New York: Greenwillow.

Aliki. (1996b). *Those Summers.* New York: HarperCollins.

Aliki. (1997). *My Visit to the Zoo.* New York: HarperCollins.

Allen, Sarah. (1996). *Cats.* Illus. by Charlotte Hard. Hauppauge, NY: Barron's Educational Series.

Ammon, Richard. (1996). *An Amish Christmas.* Illus. by Pamela Patrick. Colchester, CT: Atheneum.

Ancona, George, & Ancona, Mary Beth. (1991). *Handtalk Zoo.* New York: Simon & Schuster.

Andrews, Sylvia. (1995). *Rattlebone Rock.* Illus. by Jennifer Plecas. New York: HarperCollins.

Anholt, Laurence. (1994). *Camille and the Sunflowers: A Story about Vincent Van Gogh.* Hauppauge, NY: Barron's Educational Series.

Anno, Mitsumasa. (1995). *Anno's Magic Seeds.* New York: G. P. Putnam.

Appel, Karel. (1996). *Watermelon Day.* Illus. by Dale Gottlieb. New York: Holt.

Ardley, Neil. (1991). *The Science Book of Things That Grow*. Orlando: Harcourt Brace.

Arnold, Caroline. (1992). *Camel*. New York: William Morrow.

Arnold, Caroline. (1993a). *Elephant*. New York: William Morrow.

Arnold, Caroline. (1993b). *Lion*. New York: William Morrow.

Arnold, Caroline. (1993c). *Monkey*. New York: William Morrow.

Arnold, Ted. (1987). *No Jumping on the Bed*. New York: Dutton.

Arnold, Tedd. (1995). *No More Water in the Tub*. New York: Dial Books.

Arnosky, Jim. (1990). *Crinkleroot's Guide to Walking in Wild Places*. New York: Simon & Schuster.

Arnosky, Jim. (1992a). *Crinkleroot's Guide to Knowing the Birds*. New York: Simon & Schuster.

Arnosky, Jim. (1992b). *Crinkleroot's Guide to Knowing the Trees*. New York: Simon & Schuster.

Arnosky, Jim. (1993a). *Crinkleroot's 25 Birds Every Child Should Know*. Minneapolis: Bradbury Press.

Arnosky, Jim. (1993b). *Crinkleroot's 25 Fish Every Child Should Know*. New York: Simon & Schuster.

Arnosky, Jim. (1993c). *Every Autumn Comes the Bear*. New York: G. P. Putnam.

Arnosky, Jim. (1996). *Crinkleroot's Guide to Knowing Butterflies and Moths*. New York: Simon & Schuster.

Arnosky, Jim. (1997). *Watching Water Birds*. Washington, DC: National Geographic Society.

Asch, Frank. (1992). *Milk and Cookies*. Milwaukee, WI: Gareth Stevens.

Asch, Frank. (1995). *Water*. San Diego, CA: Gulliver Books.

Atwood, Margaret. (1995). *Princess Prunella and the Purple Peanut*. Illus. by Maryann Kowalski. New York: Workman Publishing.

Auch, Mary Jane. (1992). *The Easter Egg Farm*. New York: Holiday House.

Auch, Mary Jane. (1995). *Hen Lake*. New York: Holiday House.

Auch, Mary Jane. (1996). *Eggs Mark the Spot*. New York: Holiday House.

Aylesworth, Jim. (1992). *The Cat and the Fiddle and More*. New York: Macmillan.

Aylesworth, Jim. (1994). *My Son John*. Illus. by David Frampton. New York: Holt.

Babbitt, Natalie. (1989). *Nellie: A Cat on Her Own*. New York: Farrar, Straus & Giroux.

Bailey, Donna. (1990). *Fishing*. Austin, TX: Raintree/Steck Vaughn.

Baker, Karen Lee. (1997). *Seneca*. New York: Greenwillow.

Baker, Sanna A. (1996). *Mississippi Going North*. Illus. by Bill Farnsworth. Niles, IL: Albert Whitman & Co.

Ballard, Robin. (1994). *Good-Bye House*. New York: Greenwillow.

Bancroft, Catherine. (1993). *Felix's Hat*. Illus. by Hannah Coale Gruenberg. New York: Simon & Schuster.

Bancroft, Henrietta, & Van Gelder, Richard G. (1996). *Animals in Winter*. Newly illus. by Helen K. Davie. New York: Harper-Collins.

Bang, Molly. (1991). *Yellow Ball*. New York: William Morrow.

Bang, Molly Garrett. (1992). *Tye May and the Magic Brush*. New York: Mulberry Books. (Paperback)

Banks, Kate. (1997). *Spider, Spider*. Illus. by Georg Hallensleben. New York: Farrar, Straus & Giroux.

Barasch, Lynne. (1993). *A Winter Walk*. New York: Ticknor & Fields.

Bare, Colleen Stanley. (1995). *Toby the Tabby Kitten*. New York: Cobblehill Books.

Barker, Cicely Mary. (1996). *Flower Fairies: The Meaning of Flowers.* New York: Frederick Warne & Co.

Barker, Cicely Mary. (1998). *Flower Fairies of the Spring: A Celebration.* New York: Frederick Warne & Co.

Barner, Bob. (1996). *Dem Bones.* New York: Chronicle Books.

Barracca, Debra, et al. (1994). *A Taxi Dog Christmas.* Illus. by Alan Ayers. New York: Dial Books.

Barth, Edna. (1981). *Lilies, Rabbits, and Painted Eggs: The Story of the Easter Symbols.* Boston: Houghton Mifflin. (Paperback)

Bartlett, T. C. (1997). *Tuba Lessons.* Illus. by Monique Felix. Orlando: Harcourt Brace.

Barton, Byron. (1993). *The Little Red Hen.* New York: HarperCollins.

Barton, Byron. (1995a). *Tools.* New York: HarperCollins. (Board book)

Barton, Byron. (1995b). *Wee Little Woman.* New York: HarperCollins.

Barton, Byron. (1996). *Zoo Animals.* New York: HarperCollins. (Board book)

Barton, Byron. (1997). *Machines at Work.* New York: HarperCollins.

Bauer, Caroline Feller. (1993). *Valentine's Day: Stories and Poems.* Illus. by Blanche Sims. New York: HarperCollins.

Bauer, Caroline Feller. (1994). *Thanksgiving; Stories and Poems.* Illus. by Nadine B. Westcott. New York: HarperCollins.

Bauer, Marion Dane. (1995). *When I Go Camping with Grandma.* Illus. by Allen Garns. Morago, CA: Bridgewater Books.

Baxter, Nicola. (1997a). *Spring.* Illus. by Kim Woolley. Chicago: Children's Press.

Baxter, Nicola. (1997b). *Summer.* Illus. by Kim Woolley. Chicago: Children's Press.

Baxter, Nicola. (1998). *Rain, Wind and Storm.* Austin, TX: Raintree/Steck-Vaughn.

Bazilian, Barbara. (1997). *The Red Shoes.* Dallas, TX: Whispering Coyote Press.

Beecham, Caroline. (1996). *Rainbow.* New York: Random House.

Behrens, June. (1996). *Thanksgiving Feast; The First American Holiday.* Illus. by Joann Rounds. Del Mar, CA: York House Publishers.

Benjamin, Cynthia. (1995). *I Am a Zookeeper.* Illus. by Miriam Sagasti. Hauppauge, NY: Barron's Educational Series. (Board book)

Benjamin, Floella. (Ed.). (1995). *Skip across the Ocean: Nursery Rhymes from Around the World.* Illus. by Sheila Moxley. New York: Orchard Books.

Bennett, Penelope. (1995). *Town Parrot.* Illus. by Sue Heap. Cambridge, MA: Candlewick Press.

Berger, Bruce. (1995). *A Dazzle of Hummingbirds.* Illus. by John Chellman. Morristown, NJ: Silver Burdett.

Berger, Melvin. (1994). *All about Seeds.* Reprint ed. New York: Scholastic.

Berger, Melvin. (1995). *Germs Make Me Sick.* Rev. ed. Illus. by Marylin Hafner. New York: HarperCollins.

Berger, Melvin, & Berger, Gilda. (1995). *What Do Animals Do in Winter?* Illus. by Susan Harrison. Nashville, TN: Hambleton-Hill Publishing.

Bernhard, Emery. (1994). *Eagles: Lions of the Sky.* Illus. by Durga Bernhard. New York: Holiday House.

Berry, Joy. (1996). *Let's Talk About* series. Illus. by Maggie Smith. New York: Scholastic. *Feeling Afraid; Feeling Angry; Feeling Sad.* (Paperback)

Big Fat Hen. (1994). Illus. by Keith Baker. Orlando: Harcourt Brace.

Bingham, Caroline. *Mighty Machines* series. New York: Dorling Kindersley. *Big Rig.* Illus. by Mary Ling (1996); *Fire Truck: And Other Emergency Machines* (1995); *Monster Machines* (1998); *Race Car* (1996).

Birch, Barbara, & Lewis, Beverly. (1995). *Katie and the Haircut Mistake.* Illus. by

Taia Morley. Minneapolis: Augsburg Fortress Publishers.

Bittinger, Gayle. (1993). *Exploring Water and the Ocean.* Illus. by Gary Mohrmann. Alberwood Manor, WA: Warren Publishing House.

Blackstone, Margaret. (1993). *This Is Baseball.* Illus. by John O'Brien. New York: Holt.

Blackstone, Stella. (1996). *Grandma Went to Market: A Round-the-World Counting Rhyme.* Illus. by Bernard Lodge. Boston: Houghton Mifflin.

Blanchard, Arlene. (1995). *The Dump Truck.* Illus. by Tony Wells. Cambridge, MA: Candlewick Press.

Blizzard, Gladys. *Come Look with Me* series. West Palm Beach, FL: Lickle Publishing. *Animals in Art* (1992); *Enjoying Art with Children* (1991); *Exploring Landscape Art with Children* (1992); *World of Play* (1993).

Boelts, Maribeth. (1997). *A Kid's Guide to Staying Safe around Water.* New York: Rosen Publishing.

Bogacki, Tomek. (1997). *Cat and Mouse in the Rain.* New York: Farrar, Straus & Giroux.

Bogacki, Tomek, & Bogacki, Tomasz. (1998). *Story of a Blue Bird.* New York: Farrar, Straus & Giroux.

Boivin, Kelly. (1991). *What's in a Box?* Illus. by Janice Skivington. Chicago: Children's Press.

Boland, Janice D. (1996). *A Dog Named Sam.* Illus. by G. Brian Karas. New York: Dial Books.

Bond, Michael. (1992). *Paddington at the Circus.* Illus. by John Lobban. New York: HarperCollins.

Borden, Louise. (1993). *Albie the Lifeguard.* Illus. by Elizabeth Sayles. New York: Scholastic.

Bornstein, Harry. (1992). *Nursery Rhymes from Mother Goose: Told in Signed English.* Washington, DC: Kendall Green Publications.

Boyle, Doe. (1997). *Coral Reef Hideaway: The Story of a Clown Anemonefish.* Illus. by Steven James Petruccio. Norwalk, CT: Soundprints Corp.

Boynton, Alice B. (1996). *Priscilla Alden and the First Thanksgiving.* Morristown, NJ: Silver Burdett. (Paperback)

Brady, Peter. (1996a). *Bulldozers.* Mankato, MN: Bridgestone Books.

Brady, Peter. (1996b). *Cows.* Illus. by William Munoz. Mankato, MN: Bridgestone Books.

Brady, Peter, & Munoz, William. (1996). *Cows.* Mankato, MN: Bridgestone Books.

Brandenberg, Alexa. (1996). *I Am Me.* Orlando: Harcourt Brace.

Branley, Franklyn M. (1997). *Down Comes the Rain.* New York: HarperCollins.

Brazelton, T. Berry. (1996). *Going to the Doctor.* Photos by Alfred Womack. Portland, OR: Perseus Press.

Brenner, Barbara, & Takaya, Julia. (1996). *Chibi: A True Story from Japan.* Illus. by June Otani. New York: Clarion Books.

Brett, Jan. (1990). *Christmas Reindeer.* New York: G. P. Putnam.

Brett, Jan. (1991). *Berlioz the Bear.* New York: G. P. Putnam.

Brett, Jan. (1994). *Town Mouse, Country Mouse.* New York: G. P. Putnam.

Brett, Jan. (1997). *The Hat.* New York: G. P. Putnam.

Brillhart, Julie. (1997). *When Daddy Took Us Camping.* Niles, IL: Albert Whitman & Co.

Brimmer, Larry Dane. (1995). *Merry Christmas Old Armadillo.* Illus. by Dominic Catalano. Honesdale, PA: Boyds Mills Press.

Brown, Craig. (1994). *In the Spring.* New York: Greenwillow.

Brown, Laurene Krasny. (1995). *The Vegetable Show.* Boston: Little, Brown.

Brown, Laurene Krasny. (1996). *When Dinosaurs Die: A Guide to Understanding*

Death. Illus. by Marc Tolon Brown. Boston: Little, Brown.

Brown, Laurene Krasny, & Brown, Marc Tolon. (1990). *Dinosaurs Alive and Well! A Guide to Good Health.* Boston: Little, Brown.

Brown, M. K. (1995). *Let's Go Camping with Mr. Sillypants.* New York: Crown Publishers.

Brown, Margaret Wise. (1994). *A Pussycat's Christmas.* Newly illus. by Anne Mortimer. New York: HarperCollins.

Brown, Margaret Wise. (1996). *On Christmas Eve.* Newly illus. by Nancy Edwards Calder. New York: HarperCollins.

Brown, Marc Tolon. (1984). *Arthur Goes to Camp.* Madison, WI: Demco Media.

Brown, Marc Tolon. (1993). *D.W. Rides Again!* Boston: Little, Brown.

Brown, Marc Tolon. (1997). *Arthur's TV Trouble.* Boston: Little, Brown. (Paperback)

Brown, Marc Tolon, & Krensky, Stephen. (1982). *Dinosaurs, Beware: A Safety Guide.* Boston: Little, Brown.

Brown, Richard Eric. (1988). *100 Words about My House.* Orlando, FL: Harcourt Brace.

Brown, Ruth. (1991). *Alphabet Times Four: An International ABC.* New York: Dutton.

Brusca, Maria Christina. (1995). *Three Friends: A Counting Book / Tres Amigos: Un Cuento Para Contar.* New York: Holt.

Bryant-Mole, Karen. (1996). *Flowers.* Austin, TX: Raintree/Steck Vaughn.

Buchanan, Ken, & Buchanan, Debby. (1994). *It Rained in the Desert Today.* Illus. by Libba Tracey. Flagstaff, AZ: Northland.

Buck, Nola. (1996). *Sid and Sam.* Illus. by G. Brian Karas. New York: HarperCollins.

Buck, Nola. (1997). *Oh, Cats.* Illus. Nadine Bernard Westcott. New York: HarperCollins.

Buckley, Helen E. (1994a). *Grandfather and I.* Illus. by Jan Ormerod. New York: Lothrop, Lee & Shepard.

Buckley, Helen E. (1994b). *Grandmother and I.* Illus. by Jan Ormerod. New York: Lothrop, Lee & Shepard.

Buehner, Caralyn, & Buehner, Mark. (1992). *The Escape of Marvin the Ape.* New York: Dial Books.

Bulloch, Ivan. (1997). *I Want to Be a Puppeteer.* Illus. by Diane James. Chicago: World Book.

Bunting, Eve. (1991). *Fly Away Home.* Illus. by Ronald Himler. New York: Clarion Books.

Bunting, Eve. (1993). *Someday a Tree.* Illus. by Ronald Himler. Boston: Houghton Mifflin.

Bunting, Eve. (1994). *Flower Garden.* Illus. by Kathryn Hewitt. Orlando, FL: Harcourt Brace.

Bunting, Eve. (1997). *The Pumpkin Fair.* Illus. by Eileen Christelow. New York: Clarion Books.

Burnett, Frances H. (1993). *Land of the Blue Flower.* Illus. by Judith Ann Griffith. Tiburon, CA: H. J. Kramer.

Burnie, David. (1992). *Flowers.* New York: Dorling Kindersley.

Burns, Diane L. (1990). *Sugaring Season: Making Maple Syrup.* Illus. by Cheryl Walsh Bellville. Minneapolis: Carolrhoda Books.

Burningham, John. (1993). *Harvey Slumfenburger's Christmas Present.* Cambridge, MA: Candlewick Press.

Burningham, John. (1994). *Cannonball Simp.* Cambridge, MA: Candlewick Press.

Burton, Marilee Robin. (1994). *My Best Shoes.* Illus. by James E. Ransome. New York: William Morrow.

Burton, Robert. (1994). *Egg: A Photographic Story of Hatching.* Photos by Kim Taylor. New York: Dorling Kindersley.

Butler, Daphne. (1995). *What Happens When Wheels Turn?* Austin, TX: Raintree/Steck Vaughn.

Butler, Daphne. (1996). *What Happens When Fire Burns?* Austin, TX: Raintree/Steck Vaughn.

Butrum, Ray. (1998). *I'm Sorry You Can't Hatch an Egg.* Sisters, OR: Multnomah Press.

Cabrera, Jane. (1997). *Cat's Colors.* New York: Dial Books.

Caffey, Donna. (1998). *Yikes—Lice!* Illus. by Patrick Girouard. Niles, IL: Albert Whitman & Co.

Calhoun, Mary. (1997). *Flood.* Illus. by Erick Ingraham. New York: William Morrow.

Campilonga, Margaret S. (1996). *Blue Frogs.* Illus. by Carl Lindahl. Circleville, NY: Chicken Soup Press.

Canizares, Susan, & Chessen, Betsey. (1997). *Storms.* New York: Scholastic.

Cannon, Janell. (1993). *Stellaluna.* Orlando, FL: Harcourt Brace.

Capote, Truman. (1996). *Thanksgiving Visitor.* Illus. by Beth Peck. New York: Knopf.

Capucilli, Alyssa Satin. (1995). *Peekaboo Bunny: Friend in the Snow.* Illus. by Mary Melcher. New York: Scholastic. (Peek a Book)

Carle, Eric. (1995a). *The Very Lonely Firefly.* New York: Philomel Books.

Carle, Eric. (1995b). *Walter the Baker.* New York: Simon & Schuster.

Carle, Eric. (1998a). *Hello, Red Fox.* New York: Simon & Schuster.

Carle, Eric. (1998b). *Let's Paint a Rainbow.* New York: Scholastic.

Carlson, Laurie. (1998). *Boss of the Plains: The Hat That Won the West.* Illus. by Holly Meade. New York: Dorling Kindersley.

Carlson, Nancy L. (1994). *How to Lose All Your Friends.* New York: Viking.

Carlson, Nancy L. (1997). *ABC I Like Me.* New York: Viking.

Carlstrom, Nancy White. (1993a). *How Does the Wind Walk?* New York: Macmillan.

Carlstrom, Nancy White. (1993b). *What Does the Rain Play?* New York: Macmillan.

Carlstrom, Nancy White. (1995a). *I Am Christmas.* Illus. by Lori McElrath-Eslick. Grand Rapids, MI: Wm. B. Eerdmans Publishing Co.

Carlstrom, Nancy White. (1995b). *Who Said Boo?: Halloween Poems for the Very Young.* Illus. by R. W. Alley. New York: Simon & Schuster.

Carlstrom, Nancy White. (1996). *Let's Count It Out, Jesse Bear.* Illus. by Bruce Degen. New York: Simon & Schuster.

Carlstrom, Nancy White. (1997). *Raven and River.* Illus. by Jon Van Zyle. Boston: Little, Brown.

Carrick, Carol. (1995). *Valentine.* Illus. by Paddy Bouma. Boston: Houghton Mifflin.

Carrier, Lark. (1996). *A Tree's Tale.* New York: Dial Books.

Carrier, Roch. (1993). *The Longest Home Run.* Illus. by Sheldon Cohen. Plattsburgh, NY: Tundra Books.

Carroll, Kathleen S. (1994). *One Red Rooster.* Illus. by Suzette Barbier. Boston: Sandpiper.

Carter, David A. (1990). *More Bugs in Boxes Pop-Up Book: A Pop-Up Book about Color.* New York: Simon & Schuster.

Caseley, Judith. (1990). *Grandpa's Garden Lunch.* New York: Greenwillow.

Caseley, Judith. (1991). *Harry and Willy and Carrothead.* New York: Greenwillow.

Caseley, Judith. (1995). *Mr. Green Peas.* New York: Greenwillow.

Caseley, Judith. (1996). *Witch Mama.* New York: Greenwillow.

Casey, Mike. (1996). *Red Lace, Yellow Lace: Learn to Tie Your Shoe!* Hauppauge, NY: Barron's Educational Series.

Casey, Patricia. (1996). *My Cat Jack.* Cambridge, MA: Candlewick Press.

Cassie, Brian, & Pallotta, Jerry. (1995). *The Butterfly Alphabet Book.* Illus. by Mark Astrella. Watertown, MA: Charlesbridge Publishers.

Cast, C. Vance. (1992). *Where Does Water Come From?* Illus. by Sue Wilkinson. Hauppauge, NY: Barron's Educational Series. (Paperback)

Catalanotto, Peter. (1995). *The Painter.* New York: Orchard Books, 1995.

Challoner, Jack. (1992). *Science Book of Numbers.* Orlando, FL: Harcourt Brace.

Challoner, Jack. (1996). *Wet and Dry.* Austin, TX: Raintree/Steck Vaughn.

Champion, Joyce. (1993). *Emily and Alice.* Illus. by Sucie Stevenson. Orlando, FL: Harcourt Brace.

Chapman, Cheryl. (1994). *Snow on Snow on Snow.* Illus. by Synthia Saint James. New York: Dial Books.

Charles, N. N. (1994). *What Am I? Looking through Shapes at Apples and Grapes.* Illus. by Leo and Diane Dillon. New York: Scholastic.

Charman, Andrew. (1997). *I Wonder Why Trees Have Leaves and Other Questions about Plants.* Stanwood, WA: Kingfisher.

Cherry, Lynne. (1997). *Flute's Journey: The Life of a Wood Thrush.* San Diego, CA: Gulliver Books.

Childress, Mark. (1996). *Joshua and the Big Bad Blue Crabs.* Illus. by Mary B. Brown. Boston: Little, Brown.

Chinery, Michael. (1991). *Ant.* Mahwah, NJ: Troll. (Paperback)

Chorao, Kay. (1994). *Mother Goose Magic.* New York: Dutton.

Christelow, Eileen. (1998a). *Five Little Monkeys Jumping on the Bed.* Boston: Houghton Mifflin.

Christelow, Eileen. (1998b). *Jerome Camps Out.* New York: Clarion Books.

Christensen, Bonnie. (1994). *An Edible Alphabet.* New York: Dial Books.

Chwast, Seymour. (1993). *The Twelve Circus Rings.* Orlando, FL: Harcourt Brace.

Ciavonne, Jean. (1995). *Carlos, Light the Farolito.* Illus. by Donna Clair. New York: Clarion Books.

Clark, Elizabeth. (1990). *Fish.* Illus. by John Yates. Minneapolis: Carolrhoda Books.

Claverie, Jean. (1996). *Jean Claverie's Fairy Tale Theater: Pop-Up Book with Puppets.* Illus. by Jean Claverie. Hauppauge, NY: Barron's Educational Series.

Climo, Shirley. (1995). *The Little Red Ant and the Great Big Crumb: A Mexican Fable.* New York: Clarion Books.

Coffelt, Nancy. (1995). *The Dog Who Cried Woof.* Orlando, FL: Harcourt Brace.

Cole, Henry. (1995). *Jack's Garden.* New York: Greenwillow.

Cole, Joanna. (1991). *My Puppy Is Born.* Rev. ed. Newly illustrated with photos by Margaret Miller. New York: William Morrow.

Cole, Joanna. (1995a). *The Magic School Bus Plants Seeds: A Book about How Living Things Grow.* Illus. by Bruce Degen. New York: Scholastic. (Paperback)

Cole, Joanna. (1995b). *My New Kitten.* Photos by Margaret Miller. New York: William Morrow.

Cole, Joanna. (1995c). *Spider's Lunch: All about Garden Spiders.* Illus. by Ron Broda. New York: Grosset & Dunlap. (Paperback)

Cole, Joanna. (1996a). *The Magic School Bus Gets Ants in Its Pants: A Book about Ants.* New York: Scholastic.

Cole, Joanna. (1996b). *The Magic School Bus Inside a Beehive.* Illus. by Bruce Degen. New York: Scholastic.

Cole, Joanna. (1997a). *The Magic School Bus Goes Upstream: A Book about Salmon on Migration.* Illus. by Bruce Degen. New York: Scholastic. (Paperback)

Cole, Joanna. (1997b). *The Magic School Bus Spins a Web: A Book about Spiders.* Illus. by Bruce Degen. New York: Scholastic. (Paperback)

Cole, Norma. (1994). *Blast Off! A Space Counting Book*. Illus. by Marshall Peck III. Watertown, MA: Charlesbridge Publishers.

Collodi, Carlo. (1996). *Pinocchio*. Illus. by Ed Young. New York: Philomel Books.

Conlin, Susan, et al. (1991). *All My Feelings at Preschool: Nathan's Day*. Seattle, WA: Parenting Press.

Conway, Diana Cohen. (1994). *Northern Lights: A Hanukkah Story*. Rockville, MD: Kar-Ben Copies.

Cooney, Barbara. (1990). *Hattie and the Wild Waves*. New York: Viking.

Copeland, Eric. (1994). *Milton, My Father's Dog*. Plattsburgh, NY: Tundra Books.

Cote, Nancy. (1993). *Palm Trees*. New York: Four Winds Press.

Cowen-Fletcher, Jane. (1993). *Mama Zooms*. New York: Scholastic.

Cowley, Joy. (1995). *Mouse Bride*. Illus. by David Christiana. New York: Scholastic.

Cowley, Joy. (1996). *Gracias, the Thanksgiving Turkey*. Illus. by Joe Cepeda. New York: Scholastic.

Crary, Elizabeth. *Dealing with Feelings* series. Illus. by Jean Whitney. Seattle, WA: Parenting Press. *I'm Excited* (1996); *I'm Frustrated* (1992); *I'm Furious* (1996); *I'm Mad* (1992); *I'm Proud* (1992); *I'm Scared* (1996).

Crespi, Francesca. (1995). *A Walk in Monet's Garden: Full Color Pop-Up with Guided Tour*. Boston: Little, Brown.

Crewe, Sabrina. (1997). *The Bee*. Austin, TX: Raintree/Steck Vaughn.

Crews, Donald. (1984). *School Bus*. New York: William Morrow.

Crews, Nina. (1995). *One Hot Summer Day*. New York: Greenwillow.

Curtis, Munzee. (1997). *When the Big Dog Barks*. Illus. by Susan Ayishai. New York: Greenwillow.

Curtis, Neil & Greenland, Peter. (1992). *How Bread Is Made (I Wonder)*. Minneapolis: Lerner Publications.

Cutler, Jane. (1996). *Mr. Carey's Garden*. Illus. by G. Brian Karas. Boston: Houghton Mifflin.

Czernecky, Stefan, et al. (1992). *The Sleeping Bread*. New York: Hyperion.

Dahl, Michael. (1996). *Wheels and Axles*. Chicago: Children's Press.

Dale, Penny. (1994). *Ten Out of Bed*. Cambridge, MA: Candlewick Press.

Dallinger, Jane. (1990). *Grasshoppers*. Illus. by Yuko Sato. Minneapolis: First Avenue Editions.

Davies, Kay, & Oldfield, Wendy. (1995). *Rain*. Photos by Robert Pickett. Austin, TX: Raintree/Steck Vaughn.

Davies, Nicola. (1997). *Big Blue Whale*. Illus. by Nick Maland. Cambridge, MA: Candlewick Press.

Davis, Rebecca. (1995). *The 12 Days of Christmas*. Illus. by Linnea Asplind Riley. New York: Simon & Schuster.

Davis, Wendy. (1997). *From Metal to Music: A Photo Essay*. Chicago: Children's Press.

Day, Alexandra. (1994). *Carl's Christmas*. Orlando, FL: Harcourt Brace.

De Bourgoing, Pascale. (1992). *The Egg*. Illus. by René Mettle. New York: Scholastic.

De Coteau Orie, Sandra. (1995). *Did You Hear Wind Sing Your Name? An Oneida Song of Spring*. Illus. by Christopher Canyon. New York: Walker & Co.

Dee, Ready. *Community Helpers* series. San Francisco: Children's Book Press. *Astronauts* (1998); *Bakers* (1998); *Construction* (1998); *Doctors* (1997); *Farmers* (1997); *Fire Fighters* (1997); *Garbage Collectors* (1998); *Nurses* (1998); *Police Officers* (1997); *Teacher* (1998); *Veterinarians* (1997); *Zoo Keeper* (1998).

Delafosse, Claude. (Ed.). (1998). *Houses*. New York: Scholastic.

Delaney, A. (1997). *Pearl's First Prize Plant.* New York: HarperCollins.

Demarest, Chris L. (1995). *My Blue Boat.* Orlando, FL: Harcourt Brace.

Demi. (1988). *Liang and the Magic Paintbrush.* New York: Holt. (Paperback)

Deming, Alhambra G. (1994). *Who Is Tapping at My Window?* Illus. by Monica Wellington. New York: Penguin Books.

Demuth, Patricia. (1994). *Cradles in the Trees: The Story of Bird Nests.* Illus. by Suzanne Barnes. New York: Simon & Schuster.

Demuth, Patricia Brennan. (1994). *Those Amazing Ants.* Illus. by S. D. Schindler. New York: Simon & Schuster.

Denim, Sue, & Pilkey, Dave. (1996). *The Dumb Bunnies Go to the Zoo.* New York: Scholastic.

De Paola, Tomie. (1988). *The Legend of the Indian Paintbrush.* New York: G. P. Putnam.

De Paola, Tomie. (1989). *Art Lesson.* New York: G. P. Putnam.

De Paola, Tomie. (1992). *Jingle, the Christmas Clown.* New York: G. P. Putnam.

De Paola, Tomie. (1994). *Legend of the Poinsettia.* New York: G. P. Putnam.

DePaola, Tomie. (1996). *The Baby Sister.* New York: G. P. Putnam.

De Paola, Tomie. (1997). *Antonio the Bread Boy.* New York: G. P. Putnam.

DeRubertis, Barbara. (1996). *Thanksgiving Day; Let's Meet the Wampanoags and the Pilgrims.* Illus. by Thomas Sperling. New York: Kane Press. (Paperback)

Devlin, Wende, & Devlin, Harry. (1991). *Cranberry Valentine.* New York: Simon & Schuster.

Dillon, Jana. (1992). *Jeb Scarecrow's Pumpkin Patch.* Boston: Houghton Mifflin.

Dillon, Leo, et al. (1994). *What Am I? Looking through Shapes at Apples and Grapes.* New York: Scholastic.

Dixon, Annabelle. (1990). *Clay.* Photos by Ed Barber. Ada, OK: Garrett.

Dodds, Dayle Ann. (1992). *The Color Box.* Illus. by Giles Laroche. Boston: Little, Brown.

Dooley, Norah. (1995). *Everybody Bakes Bread.* Illus. by Peter J. Thornton. Minneapolis: Carolrhoda Books.

Dooley, Virginia. (1996). *Tubes in My Ears: My Trip to the Hospital.* Illus. by Miriam Katin. Greenvale, NY: Mondo Publications. (Paperback)

Dorros, Arthur. (1987). *Ant Cities.* Bellevue, WA: Ty Crowell Co.

Dorros, Arthur. (1990). *Rain Forest Secrets.* New York: Scholastic.

Dorros, Arthur. (1992). *This Is My House.* New York: Scholastic.

Dorros, Arthur. (1997). *A Tree Is Growing.* Illus. by S. D. Schindler. New York: Scholastic.

Dragonwagon, Crescent. (1991). *This Is the Bread I Baked for Ned.* Illus. by Isadore Seltzer. New York: Simon & Schuster.

Dragonwagon, Crescent. (1993). *Annie Flies the Birthday Bike.* Illus. by Emily Arnold McCully. Colchester, CT: Atheneum.

Drawson, Blair. (1996). *Mary Margaret's Tree.* New York: Orchard Books.

Drew, Helen. (1993). *My First Music Book.* New York: Dorling Kindersley.

Dubowski, Cathy E. (1997). *Squanto: First Friend to the Pilgrims.* Illus. by Steven Peruccio. Milwaukee, WI: Gareth Stevens.

Duffey, Betsy. (1996). *Camp Knock Knock.* Illus. by Fiona Dunbar. New York: Delacorte Press.

Dugan, Barbara. (1992). *Loop the Loop.* Illus. by James Stevenson. New York: Greenwillow.

Duke, Kate. (1992). *Isabelle Tells a Good One.* New York: Dutton.

Duncan, Lois. (1993). *The Circus Comes Home: When the Greatest Show on Earth Rode the Rails.* Illus. by Joseph Janney Steinmetz. New York: Doubleday.

Dunphy, Madeleine. (1993). *Here Is the Arctic Winter.* Illus. by Alan James Robinson. New York: Hyperion.

Dunphy, Madeleine. (1994). *Here Is the Tropical Rain Forest.* Illus. by Michael Rothman. New York: Hyperion.

Dunphy, Madeleine. (1998). *Here Is the Coral Reef.* Illus. by Tom Leonard. New York: Hyperion.

Dunrea, Olivier. (1995). *The Painter Who Loved Chickens.* New York: Farrar, Straus & Giroux.

Duvall, Jill D. (1997). *Meet Rory Hohenstein, a Professional Dancer.* Photos by Lili S. Duvall. Chicago: Children's Press.

Dyer, Jane. (1996). *Animal Crackers: A Delectable Collection of Pictures, Poems, and Lullabies for the Very Young.* Boston: Little, Brown.

Dyjak, Elisabeth. (1995). *Bertha's Garden.* Illus. by Janet Wilkins. Boston: Houghton Mifflin.

Eagle, Kin. (1994). *It's Raining, It's Pouring.* Illus. by Robert Gilbert. Dallas, TX: Whispering Coyote Press.

Early, Margaret. (1991). *William Tell.* New York: Harry N. Abrams.

Edwards, Pamela Duncan. (1996). *Livingstone Mouse.* Illus. by Henry Cole. New York: HarperCollins.

Edwards, Pamela Duncan. (1998). *The Grumpy Morning.* Illus. by Loretta Krupinski. New York: Hyperion.

Edwards, Richard. (1993). *Ten Tall Oaktrees.* Illus. by Caroline Crossland. New York: William Morrow.

Egan, Tim. (1996). *Metropolitan Cow.* Boston: Houghton Mifflin.

Ehlert, Lois. (1989). *Color Zoo.* New York: Lippincott.

Ehlert, Lois. (1990a). *Color Farm.* New York: Lippincott.

Ehlert, Lois. (1990b). *Fish Eyes: A Book You Can Count On.* Orlando, FL: Harcourt Brace.

Ehlert, Lois. (1991). *Red Leaf, Yellow Leaf.* Orlando, FL: Harcourt Brace.

Ehlert, Lois. (1992). *Circus.* New York: HarperCollins.

Ehlert, Lois. (1994). *Eating the Alphabet: Fruits and Vegetables from A to Z.* Orlando, FL: Harcourt Brace.

Ehlert, Lois. (1996). *Snowballs.* Orlando, FL: Harcourt Brace.

Ehlert, Lois. (1997). *Cuckoo: A Mexican Folktale.* Orlando, FL: Harcourt Brace.

Ehrlich, Amy. (1993). *Parents in the Pigpen, Pigs in the Tub.* Illus. by Steven Kellogg. New York: Dial Books.

Eick, Jean. (1997). *Giant Dump Trucks.* Illus. by Michael Sellner. Minneapolis: Abdo & Daughters.

Emberley, Ed. (1993). *Go Away, Big Green Monster!* Boston: Little, Brown.

Emberley, Ed. (1997). *Glad Monster, Sad Monster: A Book about Feelings.* Illus. by Anne Miranda. Boston: Little, Brown.

Emberley, Michael. (1993). *Welcome Back, Sun.* Boston: Little, Brown.

Enderle, Judith Ross. (1992). *Six Creepy Sheep.* Illus. by John O'Brien. Honesdale, PA: Boyds Mills Press.

Ericsson, Jennifer A. (1993). *No Milk.* Illus. by Ora Eitan. New York: Tambourine Books.

Ernst, Lisa Campbell. (1992a). *Walter's Tail.* New York: Simon & Schuster.

Ernst, Lisa Campbell. (1992b). *Zinnia and Dot.* New York: Viking.

Ernst, Lisa Campbell. (1996). *Ginger Jumps.* Madison, WI: Demco Media.

Esbensen, Barbara Juster. (1991). *Tiger with Wings: The Great Horned Owl.* Illus. by Mary Barrett Brown. New York: Orchard Books.

Esbensen, Barbara Juster. (1995). *Dance with Me.* Illus. by Megan Lloyd. New York: HarperCollins.

Evans, Lezlie. (1997). *Snow Dance.* Illus. by Cynthia Jabar. Boston: Houghton Mifflin.

Evans, Mark. (1993a). *Fish: Practical Guide to Caring for Your Fish.* New York: Dorling Kindersley.

Evans, Mark. (1993b). *Hamster: A Practical Guide to Caring for Your Hamster.* New York: Dorling Kindersley.

Eversole, Robyn. (1995). *Flute Player / La Flautista.* Illus. by G. Brian Karas. New York: Orchard Books.

Ezra, Mark. (1997). *The Frightened Little Owl.* Illus. by Gavin Rowe. New York: Crocodile Books.

Fain, Moria. (1996). *Snow Day.* New York: Walker & Co.

Falwell, Cathryn. (1996). *Dragon Tooth.* New York: Clarion Books.

Farjeon, Eleanor. (1996). *Cats Sleep Anywhere.* Illus. by Anne Mortimer. New York: HarperCollins.

Farris, Pamela J. (1996). *Young Mouse and Elephant: An East African Folktale.* Illus. by Valeri Gorbachev. Boston: Houghton Mifflin.

Faulkner, Keith. (1995). *My Colors: Let's Learn about Colors.* New York: Simon & Schuster.

Fearrington, Ann. (1996). *Christmas Lights.* Boston: Houghton Mifflin.

Fine, Anne. (1992). *Poor Monty.* Illus. by Clara Vulliamy. New York: Clarion Books.

Finnegan, Evelyn M. (1995). *My Little Friend Goes to the Dentist.* Illus. by Diane R. Houghton. Scituate, MA: Little Friend Press.

Finnegan, Evelyn, & Bruno, Margaret. (1998). *My Little Friend Goes to the Zoo.* Scituate, MA: Little Friend Press.

Fisher, Aileen Lucia. (1997). *The Story of Easter.* Illus. by Stefano Vitale. New York: HarperCollins.

Fisher, Leonard Everett. (1996). *William Tell.* New York: Farrar, Straus & Giroux.

Five Little Ducks: An Old Rhyme. (1995). Illus. by Pamela Paparone. New York: North South Books.

Flanagan, Alice K. (1996). *New True Book* series. Chicago: Children's Press. *Desert Birds; Night Birds; Seabirds; Songbirds; Talking Birds.*

Flanagan, Alice K. (1997a). *Ask Nurse Pfaff, She'll Help You.* Photos by Christine Osinski. Chicago: Children's Press.

Flanagan, Alice K. (1997b). *Ms. Murphy Fights Fires.* Photos by Christine Osinski. Chicago: Children's Press.

Flanagan, Romie, & Flanagan, Alice K. (1998). *Mr. Santizo's Tasty Treats.* Chicago: Children's Press.

Fleming, Candace. (1997). *Gabriella's Song.* Illus. by Giselle Potter. Colchester, CT: Atheneum.

Fleming, Denise. (1992a). *Count!* New York: Holt.

Fleming, Denise. (1992b). *Lunch.* New York: Holt.

Fleming, Denise. (1993). *In the Small, Small Pond.* New York: Holt.

Fleming, Denise. (1994). *Barnyard Banter.* New York: Holt.

Fleming, Denise. (1996). *Time to Sleep.* New York: Holt.

Florian, Douglas. *How We Work* series. New York: Greenwillow. *An Auto Mechanic* (1994); (Paperback); *A Chef* (1992); *A Fisher* (1994); *A Painter* (1993).

Florian, Douglas. (1991). *Vegetable Garden.* Orlando, FL: Harcourt Brace.

Florian, Douglas. (1993). *Painter.* New York: Greenwillow.

Florian, Douglas. (1994). *A Fisher.* New York: Greenwillow.

Flournoy, Valerie. (1995). *Tanya's Reunion.* Illus. by Jerry Pinkney. New York: Dial Books.

Folk Art Counting Book. (1992). Developed by Amy Watson & the staff of the Abby Aldrich Rockefeller Folk Art Center. New York: Abrams.

Fontanel, Beatrice. (1992). *The Penguin.* Illus. by Valerie Tracqui. Watertown, MA: Charlesbridge Publishers. (Paperback)

Ford, Miela. (1994). *Little Elephant.* Illus. by Tana Hoban. New York: Greenwillow.

Ford, Miela. (1995a). *Bear Play.* New York: Greenwillow.

Ford, Miela. (1995b). *Sunflower.* Illus. by Sally Noll. New York: Greenwillow.

Ford, Miela. (1998). *Watch Us Play.* New York: Greenwillow.

Foster, Joanna. (1995). *The Magpies' Nest.* Illus. by Julie Downing. New York: Clarion Books.

Fowler, Allan. (1992a). *How Do You Know It's Fall?* Chicago: Children's Press.

Fowler, Allan. (1992b). *Thanks to Cows.* Chicago: Children's Press.

Fowler, Allan. (1993a). *The Chicken or the Egg!* Chicago: Children's Press.

Fowler, Allan. (1993b). *It Could Still Be a Leaf.* Chicago: Children's Press.

Fowler, Allan. (1995a). *The Best Way to See a Shark.* Chicago: Children's Press.

Fowler, Allan. (1995b). *Corn—On and Off the Cob.* Chicago: Children's Press. (Paperback)

Fowler, Allan. (1995c). *The Earth Is Mostly Ocean.* Chicago: Children's Press.

Fowler, Allan. (1996a). *The Biggest Animal on Land.* Chicago: Children's Press.

Fowler, Allan. (1996b). *It's a Fruit, It's a Vegetable, It's a Pumpkin.* Illus. by Robert L. Hillerich. Chicago: Children's Press.

Fowler, Allan. (1996c). *Spiders Are Not Insects.* Chicago: Children's Press.

Fowler, Allan. (1997a). *It Could Still Be a Butterfly.* Chicago: Children's Press.

Fowler, Allan. (1997b). *It Could Still Be a Lake.* Chicago: Children's Press.

Fowler, Allan. (1997c). *Life in a Pond.* Chicago: Children's Press.

Fowler, Allan. (1998a). *Good Mushrooms and Bad Toadstools.* Chicago: Children's Press.

Fowler, Allan. (1998b). *Inside an Ant Colony.* Chicago: Children's Press.

Francisco, X. Mora. (1993). *La Gran Fiesta.* Fort Atkinson, WI: Highsmith Co.

French, Vivian. (1995). *Oliver's Vegetables.* Illus. by Alison Bartlett. New York: Orchard Books.

Fuchs, Diane Marcial. (1995). *A Bear for All Seasons.* Illus. by Kathryn Brown. New York: Holt.

Gackenbach, Dick. (1992). *Mighty Tree.* Orlando, FL: Harcourt Brace.

Galbraith, Kathryn Osebold. (1992). *Look! Snow!* Illus. by Nina Montezinos. New York: Simon & Schuster.

Galvin, Laura Gates, et al. (1998). *Deer Mouse at Old Farm Road.* Illus. Katy Bratun. Norwalk, CT: Soundprints Corp.

Gammell, Stephen. (1997). *Is That You, Winter?* Orlando, FL: Harcourt Brace.

Ganeri, Anita. (1995). *What's inside Plants?* New York: Peter Bedrick Books.

Gans, Roma, & Mirocha, Paul. (1996). *How Do Birds Find Their Way?* New York: HarperCollins.

Gardella, Tricia. (1997). *Casey's New Hat.* Illus. by Margot Apple. Boston: Houghton Mifflin.

Gauch, Patricia Lee. (1994). *Tanya and Emily in a Dance for Two.* Illus. by Satomi Ichikawa. New York: Philomel Books.

Geisert, Arthur. (1992). *Pigs from 1 to 10.* Boston: Houghton Mifflin.

Geisert, Arthur. (1996). *Roman Numerals I to MM.* Boston: Houghton Mifflin.

George, Jean Craighead. (1993). *Dear Rebecca, Winter Is Here*. Illus. by Loretta Krupinski. New York: HarperCollins.

George, Lindsay Barrett. (1995a). *In the Snow: Who's Been Here?* New York: Greenwillow.

George, Lindsay Barrett. (1995b). *In the Woods: Who's Been Here?* New York: Greenwillow.

George, Lindsay Barrett. (1996). *Around the Pond: Who's Been Here?* New York: Greenwillow.

George, William T. (1992). *Christmas at Long Pond*. Illus. by Lindsay Barrett George. New York: Greenwillow.

Gerholdt, James E. (1996a). *Black Widow Spiders*. Minneapolis: Abdo & Daughters.

Gerholdt, James E. (1996b). *Jumping Spider*. Austin, TX: Raintree/Steck Vaughn.

Gerholdt, James E. (1996c). *Trapdoor Spiders*. Minneapolis: Abdo & Daughters.

Gerholdt, James E. (1996d). *Wolf Spiders*. Minneapolis: Abdo & Daughters.

Geringer, Laura. (1987). *A Three Hat Day*. Illus. by Arnold Lobel. New York: HarperCollins.

Gershator, David, et al. (1995). *Bread Is for Eating*. New York: Holt.

Gershator, Phillis. (1996). *Sweet, Sweet Fig Banana*. Illus. by Fritz Millvoix. Niles, IL: Albert Whitman & Co.

Gibbons, Gail. (1982). *Tool Book*. New York: Holiday House.

Gibbons, Gail. (1985). *The Milk Makers*. New York: Simon & Schuster.

Gibbons, Gail. (1986). *Up Goes the Sky-scraper!* New York: Macmillan.

Gibbons, Gail. (1987a). *Fill It Up: All about Service Stations*. New York: HarperCollins.

Gibbons, Gail. (1987b). *The Post Office Book: Mail and How It Moves*. New York: HarperCollins.

Gibbons, Gail. (1988). *Farming*. New York: Holiday House.

Gibbons, Gail. (1989). *Easter*. New York: Holiday House.

Gibbons, Gail. (1990). *How a House Is Built*. New York: Holiday House.

Gibbons, Gail. (1991). *From Seed to Plant*. New York: Holiday House.

Gibbons, Gail. (1992a). *Say Woof! The Day of a Country Veterinarian*. New York: Macmillan.

Gibbons, Gail. (1992b). *Sharks*. New York: Holiday House.

Gibbons, Gail. (1993a). *Puff—Flash—Bang: A Book about Signals*. New York: William Morrow.

Gibbons, Gail. (1993b). *Spiders*. New York: Holiday House.

Gibbons, Gail. (1995). *Bicycle Book*. New York: Holiday House.

Gibbons, Gail. (1996a). *Cats*. New York: Holiday House.

Gibbons, Gail. (1996b). *Dogs*. New York: Holiday House.

Gibbons, Gail. (1997a). *Gulls—Gulls—Gulls*. New York: Holiday House.

Gibbons, Gail. (1997b). *The Honey Makers*. New York: William Morrow.

Gibbons, Gail. (1998a). *Marshes and Swamps*. New York: Holiday House.

Gibbons, Gail. (1998b). *Soaring with the Wind: The Bald Eagle*. New York: William Morrow.

Gibson, Gary. (1995). *Making Things Float and Sink*. Illus. by Tony Kenyon. Brook-field, CT: Millbrook Press.

Giganti, Paul. (1992). *Each Orange Had 8 Slices: A Counting Book*. Illus. by Donald Crews. New York: Greenwillow.

Giovanni, Nikki. (1994). *Knoxville, Tennessee*. Illus. by Larry Johnson. New York: Scholastic.

Girard, L W. (1985). *Who Is a Stranger and What Should I Do?* Illus. by Helen Cogancherry. Niles, IL: Albert Whitman & Co.

Givon, Hannah Gelman. (1996). *We Shake in a Quake*. Illus. by David Uttal. Berkeley, CA: Tricycle Press.

Glaser, Linda. (1996). *Compost! Growing Gardens from Your Garbage*. Illus. by Anca Hariton. Brookfield, CT: Millbrook Press.

Gliori, Debi. (1996). *The Snow Lambs*. New York: Scholastic.

Godfrey, Jan. (1994). *Why Is It Raining?* Illus. by D'Reen Neeves. Minneapolis: Augsburg Fortress Pub.

Godfrey, Neale S. (1995). *Here's the Scoop: Follow an Ice-Cream Cone around the World*. Illus. by Randy Verougstraete. Morristown, NJ: Silver Burdett Press.

Godkin, Celia. (1998). *What about Ladybugs?* Boston: Little, Brown. (Paperback)

Goennel, Heidi. (1994). *Odds and Evens: A Numbers Book*. New York: Tambourine Books.

Gomi, Taro. (1994). *The Crocodile and the Dentist*. Brookfield, CT: Millbrook Press.

Gordon, Maria. (1995). *Float and Sink*. Illus. by Mike Gordon. Austin, TX: Raintree/Steck Vaughn.

Gosselin, Kim. (1998). *Taking Diabetes to School* (2nd ed.). Illus. by Moss Freedman. Valley Park, MO: JayJo Books.

Graham, Joan B. (1994). *Splish Splash*. Illus. By Steven M. Scott. New York: Ticknor and Fields.

Granowsky, Alvin. (1996). *The Help Yourself, Little Red Hen! (Another side to the story.)*. Illus. by Wendy Edelson & Jane K. Manning. Austin, TX: Raintree/Steck Vaughn.

Gray, Libba Moore. (1994). *The Little Black Truck*. Illus. by Elizabeth Sayles. New York: Simon & Schuster.

Gray, Libba Moore. (1995). *My Mama Had a Dancing Heart*. Illus. by Raul Colon. New York: Orchard Books.

Gray, Libba Moore. (1997). *Is There Room on the Feather Bed?* Illus. by Nadine Bernard Westcott. New York: Orchard Books.

Greenberg, David T. (1997). *Bugs!* Illus. by Lynn Munsinger. Boston: Little, Brown.

Greenstein, Elaine. (1996). *Mrs. Rose's Garden*. New York: Simon & Schuster.

Greenwood, Pamela D. (1993). *What about My Goldfish?* Illus. by Jennifer Plecas. New York: Clarion Books.

Gregory, Nan. (1995). *How Smudge Came*. Illus. by Ron Lightburn. New York: Red Deer College Press.

Griffith, Helen V. (1992). *"Mine Will," Said John*. Newly illus. edition by Jos. A. Smith. New York: Greenwillow.

Grimm, Jakob. (1996). *The Twelve Dancing Princesses*. Retold by Jane Ray. New York: Dutton.

Grohmann, Almute, et al. (1998). *Dragon Teeth and Parrot Beaks: Even Creatures Brush Their Teeth*. Carol Stream, IL: Edition Q.

Grossman, Bill, & Chess, Victoria. (1991). *Tommy at the Grocery Store*. New York: HarperCollins.

Grossman, Patricia. (1991). *The Night Ones*. Illus. by Lydia Dabcovich. Orlando, FL: Harcourt Brace.

Grover, Max. (1996). *Circles and Squares Everywhere*. Orlando, FL: Harcourt Brace.

Guiberson, Brenda Z. (1991). *Cactus Hotel*. Illus. by Megan Lloyd. New York: Holt.

Hale, Sara. (1995). *Mary Had a Little Lamb*. Illus. by Salley Mavor. New York: Orchard Books.

Hall, Donald. (1994). *I Am the Dog, I Am the Cat*. Illus. by Barry Moser. New York: Dial Books.

Hall, Kirsten. (1994). *The Tooth Fairy*. Illus. by Nan Brooks. Chicago: Children's Press.

Hall, Zoe. (1994). *It's Pumpkin Time!* Illus. by Shari Halpern. New York: Scholastic.

Hall, Zoe. (1996a). *The Apple Pie Tree*. Illus. by Shari Halpern. New York: Scholastic.

Hall, Zoe. (1996b). *The Apple Tree*. Illus. by Shari Halpern. New York: Scholastic.

Hallinan, P. K. (1993a). *Today Is Easter!* Nashville, TN: Ideals Children's Books. (Paperback)

Hallinan, P. K. (1993b). *Today Is Thanksgiving.* Lake Forest, IL: Forest House Publishing.

Hamilton, Dewitt. (1995). *Sad Days, Glad Days: A Story about Depression.* Illus. by Gail Owens. Beaver Dam, WI: Concept Books.

Hanel, Wolfram. (1995). *The Extraordinary Adventures of an Ordinary Hat.* Illus. by Christa Unzner-Fischer. New York: North-South Books. (Paperback)

Hariton, Anca. (1995). *Butterfly Story.* New York: Dutton.

Harley, Bill. (1996). *Sitting Down to Eat.* Illus. by Kitty Harvill. Little Rock, AR: August House Little Folk.

Harper, Isabelle. (1994). *My Dog Rosie.* Illus. by Barry Moser. New York: Scholastic.

Harper, Isabelle. (1995). *My Cats Nick and Nora.* Illus. by Barry Moser. New York: Scholastic.

Harper, Isabelle. (1996). *Our New Puppy.* Illus. by Barry Moser. New York: Scholastic.

Hausherr, Rosmarie. (1997). *Celebrating Families.* New York: Scholastic.

Hausman, Gerald. (1998). *The Story of Blue Elk.* Illus. by Kristina Rodanas. Boston: Houghton Mifflin.

Hautzig, David. (1994). *At the Supermarket.* New York: Orchard Books.

Havill, Juanita. (1993). *Jamaica and Brianna.* Illus. by Anne Sibley O'Brien. Boston: Houghton Mifflin.

Hayes, Ann. (1995a). *Meet the Marching Smithereens.* Illus. by Karmen Thompson. Orlando, FL: Harcourt Brace.

Hayes, Ann. (1995b). *Meet the Orchestra.* Illus. by Karmen Thompson. Orlando, FL: Harcourt Brace.

Hayward, Linda, et al. (1996). *Wheels.* New York: Random House.

Hazelaar, Cor. (1997). *Zoo Dreams.* New York: Farrar, Straus & Giroux.

Healey, Tim. (1993). *The Story of the Wheel.* Illus. by Nicholas Hewetson. Mahwah, NJ: Troll.

Heath, Amy. (1992). *Sophie's Role.* Illus. by Sheila Hamanaka. New York: Simon & Schuster.

Heiligman, Deborah. (1996). *From Caterpillar to Butterfly.* Illus. by Bari Weissman. New York: HarperCollins.

Heinz, Brian J. (1996). *The Monsters' Test.* Illus. by Sal Murdocca. Brookfield, CT: Millbrook Press.

Heller, Nicholas. (1997). *This Little Piggy.* Illus. by Sonja Lamut. New York: Greenwillow.

Heller, Ruth. (1981). *Chickens Aren't the Only Ones.* New York: G. P. Putnam.

Heller, Ruth. (1995). *Color.* New York: G. P. Putnam.

Hendrick, Mary Jean. (1993). *If Anything Goes Wrong at the Zoo.* Illus. by Jane Dyer. Orlando, FL: Harcourt Brace.

Henkes, Kevin. (1995). *Good-Bye, Curtis.* Illus. by Marisabina Russo. New York: Greenwillow.

Henkes, Kevin. (1996). *Lilly's Purple Plastic Purse.* New York: Greenwillow.

Hepworth, Catherine. (1992). *Antics! An Alphabetical Anthology.* New York: G. P. Putnam.

Hesse, Karen. (1993). *Lester's Dog.* Illus. by Nancy Carpenter. New York: Crown Publishers.

Hest, Amy. (1992). *The Purple Coat.* Illus. by Amy Schwartz. New York: Aladdin Paperback. (Paperback)

Hest, Amy. (1994). *Rosie's Fishing Trip.* Illus. by Paul Howard. Cambridge, MA: Candlewick Press.

Hest, Amy. (1995). *In the Rain with Baby Duck.* Illus. by Jill Barton. Cambridge, MA: Candlewick Press.

Hest, Amy. (1996). *Jamaica Louise James*. Illus. by Sheila White Samton. Cambridge, MA: Candlewick Press.

Hewett, Joan. (1993). *Tiger, Tiger Growing Up*. Illus. by Richard Hewett. New York: Clarion Books.

Hewitt, Sally. (1994). *Pluck and Scrape*. Illus. by Peter Millard. Chicago: Children's Press.

Hill, Elizabeth Starr. (1991). *Evan's Corner* Rev. ed. Newly illus. by D. Brodie. New York: Viking.

Hillyard, P. D. (1993). *Insects and Spiders*. New York: Dorling Kindersley.

Hilton, Nette. (1991). *The Long Red Scarf*. Illus. by Margaret Power. Minneapolis: Carolrhoda Books.

Hindley, Judy. (1994). *The Wheeling and Whirling-Around Book*. Illus. by Margaret Chamberlain. Cambridge, MA: Candlewick Press.

Hines, Anna Grossnickle. (1997). *Miss Emma's Wild Garden*. New York: Greenwillow.

Hines, Gary. (1993). *Flying Firefighters*. Illus. by Anna Grossnickle Hines. New York: Clarion Books.

Hintz, Martin & Hintz, Kate. (1998). *Thanksgiving*. Chicago: Children's Press.

Hirschi, Ron. (1991). *What Is a Cat?* New York: Walker & Co.

Hiscock, Bruce. (1995). *When Will It Snow?* New York: Simon & Schuster.

Hoban, Julia. (1992). *Buzby*. Illus. by John Himmelman. New York: HarperCollins.

Hoban, Lillian. (1987). *Arthur's Loose Tooth: Story and Pictures*. New York: HarperCollins.

Hoban, Lillian. (1996). *Arthur's Back to School Day*. New York: HarperCollins.

Hoban, Lillian. (1997). *Silly Tilly's Valentine*. New York: HarperCollins.

Hoban, Russell. (1993). *Bread and Jam for Frances*. Illus. by Lillian Hoban. New York: HarperCollins.

Hoban, Russell. (1994). *Best Friends for Frances*. Illus. by Lillian Hoban. New York: HarperCollins.

Hoban, Tana. (1978). *Is It Red? Is It Yellow? Is It Blue?* New York: Greenwillow.

Hoban, Tana. (1986). *Shapes, Shapes, Shapes*. New York: William Morrow.

Hoban, Tana. (1992). *Spirals, Curves, Fanshapes and Lines*. New York: Greenwillow.

Hoban, Tana. (1995a). *Animal, Vegetable, or Mineral?* New York: Greenwillow.

Hoban, Tana. (1995b). *Colors Everywhere*. New York: Greenwillow.

Hoban, Tana. (1997). *Construction Zone*. New York: Greenwillow.

Hoberman, Mary Ann. (1978). *A House Is a House for Me*. Illus. by Betty Fraser. New York: Viking.

Hodges, Margaret. (1997). *The True Tale of Johnny Appleseed*. New York: Holiday House.

Hoff, Syd. (1996). *Danny and the Dinosaur Go to Camp*. New York: HarperCollins.

Hoffman, Mary. (1997). *An Angel Just Like Me*. Illus. by Cornelius Van Wright. New York: Dial Books.

Holabird, Katharine. (1993). *Angelina Ice Skates*. Illus. by Helen Craig. New York: C. N. Potter Publishers.

Holmes, Kevin J. (1998). *Sharks*. Chicago: Children's Press.

Hoopes, Lyn Littlefield. (1996). *The Unbeatable Bread*. Illus. by Brad Sneed. New York: Dial Books.

Hopkins, Lee Bennett. (1992). *Good Morning to You, Valentine*. Illus. by Tomie De Paola. Honesdale, PA: Boyds Mills Press.

Hopkins, Lee Bennett. (1993). *Easter Buds Are Springing; Poems for Easter*. Illus. by Tomie De Paola. Honesdale, PA: Boyds Mills Press.

Hosea Hilker, Cathryn. (1992). *A Cheetah Named Angel*. New York: Franklin Watts.

Howard, Elizabeth Fitzgerald. (1991). *Aunt Flossie's Hats and Crab Cakes Later.* Illus. by James Ransome. New York: Clarion Books.

Howard, Kim. (1994). *In Wintertime.* New York: Lothrop, Lee & Shepard.

Howe, James. (1994). *The Hospital Book.* Photos by Mal Warshaw. New York: William Morrow.

Howe, James. (1995). *Pinky and Rex and the Double-Dad Weekend.* Illus. by Melissa Sweet. Colchester, CT: Atheneum.

Howland, Naomi. (1994). *ABCDrive! A Car Trip Alphabet.* New York: Clarion Books.

Hoyt-Goldsmith, Diane. (1991). *Pueblo Storyteller.* Illus. by Lawrence Migdale. New York: Holiday House.

Humphrey, Paul. (1996). *Frog's Eggs.* Austin, TX: Raintree/Steck Vaughn. (Paperback)

Hunter, Anne. (1996). *Possum's Harvest Moon.* Boston: Houghton Mifflin.

Hurd, Thacher. (1990). *Little Mouse's Big Valentine.* New York: HarperCollins.

Hurd, Thacher. (1996). *Art Dog.* New York: HarperCollins.

Hurwitz, Johanna. (1993). *New Shoes for Silvia.* Illus. by Jerry Pinkney. New York: William Morrow.

Hutchings, Amy. (1994). *Picking Apples and Pumpkins.* Illus. by Richard Hutchings. St. Paul, MN: Cartwheel Books. (Paperback)

Hutchins, Pat. (1993). *My Best Friend.* New York: Greenwillow.

Hutchins, Pat. (1994). *Little Pink Pig.* New York: Greenwillow.

Hutchins, Pat. (1996). *Titch and Daisy.* New York: Greenwillow.

Imai, Miko. (1995). *Sebastian's Trumpet.* Cambridge, MA: Candlewick Press.

Inkpen, Mick. (1996). *The Blue Balloon* (Vol. 1). Boston: Little, Brown.

Isaacs, Gwynne. (1991). *While You Are Asleep.* Illus. by Cathi Hepworth. New York: Walker & Co.

Isadora, Rachel. (1993). *Lili at Ballet.* New York: G. P. Putnam.

Isadora, Rachel. (1997). *Lili Backstage.* New York: G. P. Putnam.

Jackson, Alison, et al. (1997). *I Know An Old Lady Who Swallowed a Pie.* Illus. by Byron Schachner. New York: Dutton.

Jackson, Ellen. (1995). *Brown Cow, Green Grass, Yellow Mellow Sun.* Illus. by Victoria Raymond. New York: Hyperion.

Jackson, Shelley. (1998). *The Old Woman and the Wave.* New York: Dorling Kindersley.

Jaffe, Nina. (1992). *In the Month of Kislev: A Story for Hanukkah.* Illus. by Louise August. New York: Viking.

Jakob, Donna. (1994). *My Bike.* Illus. by Nelle Davis. New York: Hyperion.

James, Alan. (1989). *Homes on Water.* Minneapolis: Lerner Publications.

Janovitz, Marilyn. (1994). *Is It Time?* New York: North-South Books.

Janovitz, Marilyn. (1996). *Can I Help?* New York: North-South Books.

Jaspersohn, William. (1996). *Timber.* Boston: Little, Brown.

Jaspersohn, William. (1994). *My Hometown Library.* Boston: Houghton Mifflin.

Jenkins, Priscilla Belz. (1995). *Nest Full of Eggs.* Illus. by Lizzy Rockwell. New York: HarperCollins.

Jensen, Patsy. (1993). *Paul Bunyan and His Blue Ox.* Illus. by Jean Pidgeon. Mahwah, NJ: Troll.

Jeunesse, Gallimard. (1991). *Colors.* Illus. by P. M. Valet. New York: Scholastic.

Jeunesse, Gallimard. (1997a). *Bees.* New York: Scholastic.

Jeunesse, Gallimard. (1997b). *Butterflies.* New York: Scholastic.

Johnson, Angela. (1990). *When I Am Old with You.* Illus. by David Soman. New York: Orchard Books.

Johnson, Angela. (1991). *One of Three*. Illus. by David Soman. New York: Orchard Books.

Johnson, Angela. (1993a). *The Girl Who Wore Snakes*. Illus. by James Ransome. New York: Orchard Books.

Johnson, Angela. (1993b). *Julius*. Illus. by Dave Pilkey. New York: Orchard Books.

Johnson, Angela. (1994). *Rain Feet*. Illus. by Rhonda Mitchell. New York: Orchard Books. (Board book)

Johnson, Crockett. (1987). *Harold and the Purple Crayon*. New York: HarperColllins.

Johnson, Neil. (1995). *Big-Top Circus*. New York: Dial Books.

Johnson, Sylvia A. (1992). *Inside an Egg*. Photos by Kiyoshi Shimizu. Minneapolis: Lerner Publishing. (Paperback)

Johnston, Tony. (1990). *The Soup Bone*. Illus. by Margot Tomes. Orlando, FL: Harcourt Brace.

Johnston, Tony. (1995). *Very Scary*. Illus. by Douglas Florian. Orlando, FL: Harcourt Brace.

Johnston, Tony. (1996). *Fishing Sunday*. Illus. by Barry Root. New York: William Morrow.

Jonas, Ann. (1995). *Splash!* New York: Greenwillow.

Jones, Rebecca C. (1995). *Great Aunt Martha*. Illus. by Shelley Jackson. New York: Dutton.

Joosse, Barbara M. (1991). *Mama, Do You Love Me?* Illus. by Barbara Lavalle. San Francisco: Chronicle Books.

Joosse, Barbara M. (1995). *Snow Day!* Illus. by Jennifer Plecas. Boston: Houghton Mifflin.

Joosse, Barbara M. (1997). *Nugget and Darling*. Illus. by Sue Truesdell. New York: Clarion Books.

Jordan, Helene J. (1992). *How a Seed Grows*. Rev. ed. Illus. by Loretta Krupinski. New York: HarperCollins.

Jordan, Sandra. (1993). *Christmas Tree Farm*. New York: Orchard Books.

Joyce, William. (1992). *Bently and Egg*. New York: HarperCollins.

Kalbacken, Joan. (1997). *Peacocks and Peahens*. Chicago: Children's Press.

Kallen, Stuart A. (1996). *Cats* series. Minneapolis: Abdo & Daughters. *Abyssinian Cats*; *Siamese Cats*; *Tabby Cats*.

Kallen, Stuart A. (1997). *The Fire Station*. Minneapolis: Abdo & Daughters.

Kalman, Bobbie. (1994). *Homes around the World*. New York: Crabtree Publishing.

Kalman, Bobbie D. (1995). *Summer Camp*. New York: Crabtree Publishing.

Kalman, Bobbie. (1997). *Musical Instruments from A to Z*. New York: Crabtree Publishing.

Kalman, Bobbie. (1998). *Bandanas, Chaps, and Ten-Gallon Hats*. New York: Crabtree Publishing.

Kalman, Bobbie, & Gentile, Petrina. (1997). *Big Truck, Big Wheels*. New York: Crabtree Publishing.

Kalman, Bobbie, & Sotzek, Hannelore. (1997). *A Koala Is Not a Bear*. New York: Crabtree Publishing.

Kalman, Maira. (1993). *Chicken Soup, Boots*. New York: Viking.

Katz, Bobbi. (1997). *Truck Talk: Rhymes on Wheels*. St. Paul, MN: Cartwheel Books.

Keats, Ezra Jack. (1983). *Louie*. New York: William Morrow.

Keats, Ezra Jack. (1998). *A Letter to Amy*. Reprint edition. San Francisco: Children's Books.

Keillor, Garrison. (1996). *The Old Man Who Loved Cheese*. Illus. by Anne Wilsdorf. Boston: Little, Brown.

Keller, Holly. (1995). *Rosata*. New York: Greenwillow.

Keller, Stella, & Holm, John. (1990). *Ice Cream*. Austin, TX: Raintree/Steck Vaughn.

Kennedy, Pamela. (1991). *An Easter Celebration: Traditions and Customs from around the World.* Nashville, TN: Ideals Children's Books.

Kenny, David, et al. (1995). *Klondike and Snow: The Denver Zoo's Remarkable Story of Raising Two Polar Bear Cubs.* Niwot, CO: Roberts Rinehart Publishers. (Paperback)

Kessler, Leonard. (1988). *Old Turtle's Soccer Team.* New York: Greenwillow.

Kessler, Leonard. (1996). *Kick, Pass, and Run.* New York: HarperCollins.

Kimmel, Eric A. (1996). *The Magic Dreidels: A Hanukkah Story.* Illus. by Katya Krenina. New York: Holiday House.

King, Elizabeth. (1993). *Backyard Sunflower.* New York: Dutton.

King, Mary Ellen. (1997). *A Good Day for Listening.* Harrisburg, PA: Morehouse Publishing.

King, Sandra. (1993). *Shannon: An Ojibway Dancer.* Minneapolis: Lerner Publications.

King, Stephen Michael. (1996). *A Special Kind of Love.* New York: Scholastic.

King-Smith, Dick. (1995). *I Love Guinea Pigs.* Illus. by Anita Jeram. Cambridge, MA: Candlewick Press.

Kinsey-Warnock, Natalia. (1993). *When Spring Comes.* Illus. by Stacey Schuett. New York: Dutton.

Kirk, Daniel. (1997). *Trash Trucks.* New York: G. P. Putnam.

Kleven, Elisa. (1992). *The Lion and the Little Red Bird.* New York: Dutton.

Klinting, Lars. (1996a). *Bruno the Carpenter.* New York: Holt.

Klinting, Lars. (1996b). *Bruno the Tailor.* New York: Holt.

Klove, Lars. (1996). *I See a Sign.* New York: Aladdin Paperbacks.

Knight, Margy Burns. (1994). *Welcoming Babies.* Illus. by Anne Sibley O'Brien. Gardner, ME: Tilbury House.

Koebner, Linda. (1997). *Zoo Book.* New York: Tor Books.

Kovalski, Maryann. (1990). *The Wheels on the Bus.* Boston: Little, Brown. (Paperback)

Krensky, Stephen. (1995). *Three Blind Mice Mystery.* Illus. by Lynn Munsinger. New York: Delacorte.

Kroll, Virginia L. (1993). *Naomi Knows It's Springtime.* Illus. by Jill Kastner. Honesdale, PA: Boyds Mills Press.

Kroll, Virginia L. (1994). *Beginnings: How Families Came to Be.* Illus. by Stacey Schuett. Niles, IL: Albert Whitman & Co.

Kroll, Virginia L. (1995). *Jaha and Jamil Go Down the Hill: An African Mother Goose.* Illus. by Katherine Roundtree. Watertown, MA: Charlesbridge Publishing.

Kroll, Virginia L. (1996). *Can You Dance, Dalila?* Illus. by Nancy Carpenter. New York: Simon & Schuster.

Krueger, David. (1996). *What Is a Feeling?* Seattle, WA: Parenting Press.

Krulik, Nancy E., & Cole, Joanna. (1996). *The Magic School Bus: Butterfly and the Bog Beast: A Book about Butterfly Camouflage.* Illus. by Dana and Del Thompson. New York: Scholastic. (Paperback)

Kuklin, Susan. (1988). *Taking My Cat to the Vet.* Minneapolis: Bradbury Press.

Kuklin, Susan. (1992). *How My Family Lives in America.* Minneapolis: Bradbury Press.

Kuklin, Susan. (1993). *Fighting Fires.* New York: Simon & Schuster.

Kunhardt, Edith. *I'm Going to Be* series. New York: Scholastic. *A Fire Fighter.* (1995); *A Police Officer.* (1995); *A Vet.* (1996). (Paperback)

Kunhardt, Edith. (1995). *I'm Going to Be a Fire Fighter.* St. Paul, MN: Cartwheel Books. (Paperback)

Kuskin, Karla. (1995a). *A Great Miracle Happened There: A Chanukah Story.* Madison, WI: Demco Media.

Kuskin, Karla. (1995b). *James and the Rain.* Illus. by Reg Cartwright. New York: Simon & Schuster.

Lachner, Dorothea. (1995). *Andrew's Angry Words*. Illus. by Tjong-Khing The. New York: North-South Books.

Lachner, Dorothea. (1997). *Meredith: The Witch Who Wasn't*. Illus. by Christa Unzner. New York: North-South Books.

Lakin, Patricia. (1994). *Dad and Me in the Morning*. Illus. by Robert G. Steele. Niles, IL: Albert Whitman & Co.

Lakin, Patricia. (1995a). *Aware and Alert*. Photos by Doub Cushman. Austin, TX: Raintree/Steck Vaughn.

Lakin, Pat. (1995b). *The Fire Fighter: Where There's Smoke*. Austin, TX: Raintree/Steck Vaughn.

Lakin, Pat. (1995c). *Red-Letter Day*. Illus. by Doug Cushman. Austin, TX: Raintree/Steck Vaughn.

Landstrom, Olof, & Landstrom, Lena. (1994). *Will Goes to the Post Office*. New York: Farrar, Straus & Giroux.

Landstrom, Olof, et al. (1993). *Will Gets a Haircut*. New York: R&S Book Co.

Langreuter, Jutta. (1997). *Little Bear Brushes His Teeth*. Illus. by Vera Sobat. Brookfield, CT: Millbrook Press.

Lansky, Bruce. (1993). *New Adventures of Mother Goose: Gentle Rhymes for Happy Times*. Illus. by Stephen Carpenter. New York: Simon & Schuster.

Laser, Michael. (1997). *The Rain*. Illus. by Jeffrey Green. New York: Simon & Schuster.

Laughlin, Robin Kittrell. (1996). *Backyard Bugs*. Illus. by Sue Hubbell. San Francisco: Chronicle Books.

Lee, Huy-Voun. (1995). *In the Snow*. New York: Holt.

Lee, Jeanne M. (1991). *Silent Lotus*. New York: Farrar, Straus & Giroux.

Lee, Julie, & Northard, Jackie. (1995). *Animals A to Zoo*. Illus. by Kristine Kirkeby. Minnesota Zoo.

Leedy, Loreen. (1990). *The Furry News: How to Make a Newspaper*. New York: Holiday House.

Leedy, Loreen. (1994). *The Edible Pyramid: Good Eating Every Day*. New York: Holiday House.

Leedy, Loreen. (1995). *Who's Who in My Family*. New York: Holiday House.

Leedy, Loreen. (1996). *How Humans Make Friends*. New York: Holiday House.

Lemmon, Tess. (1993). *Apes*. Illus. by John Butler. New York: Ticknor & Fields.

Lerner, Carol. (1994). *Backyard Birds of Winter*. New York: William Morrow.

Lesser, Carolyn. (1995). *What a Wonderful Day to Be a Cow*. Illus. by Melissa Bay Mathis. New York: Knopf.

Lester, Helen. (1995). *Listen, Buddy*. Illus. by Lynn Munsinger. Boston: Houghton Mifflin.

Le Tord, Bijou. (1995). *Blue Butterfly: A Story about Claude Monet*. New York: Bantam.

Levine, Abby. (1997). *This Is the Pumpkin*. Niles, IL: Albert Whitman & Co.

Levine, Ellen. (1995). *The Tree That Would Not Die*. Illus. by Ted Rand. New York: Scholastic.

Levinson, Nancy Smiler. (1992). *Snowshoe Thompson*. Illus. by Joan Sandin. New York: HarperCollins.

Lewin, Betsy. (1995). *Booby Hatch*. New York: Clarion Books.

Lillegard, Dee. (1992). *Sitting in My Box*. Illus. by Jon Agee. New York: Puffin. (Paperback)

Lillegard, Dee. (1997). *Tortoise Brings the Mail*. Illus. by Jillian Lund. New York: Dutton.

Lindbergh, Reeve. (1990). *Johnny Appleseed*. Illus. by Kathy Jakobsen. Boston: Little, Brown.

Ling, Mary. (1991). *Amazing Fish*. Photos by Jerry Young. New York: Knopf.

Ling, Mary. (1992). *Butterfly*. Photos by Kim Taylor. New York: Dorling Kindersley.

Lionni, Leo. (1994). *An Extraordinary Egg*. New York: Knopf.

Lionni, Leo. (1995). *Little Blue and Little Yellow*. New York: Mulberry Books. (Paperback)

Little Red Riding Hood. (1997). Illus. by Peter Stevenson. St. Paul, MN: Cartwheel Books. (Finger Puppet Theater)

Little Robin Redbreast: A Mother Goose Rhyme. (1994). Illus. by Shari Halpern. New York: North-South Books.

Livo, Norma J. (1996). *Troubadour's Storybag: Musical Folktales of the World*. Golden, CO: Fulcrum Pub.

Llewellyn, Claire. (1991). *First Look at Growing Food*. Milwaukee, WI: Gareth Stevens.

Llewellyn, Claire. (1995). *Rivers and Seas (Why Do We Have . . .)*. Illus. by Anthony Lewis. Hauppauge, NY: Barron's Educational Series.

Llewellyn, Claire, & Lewis, Anthony. (1995). *Wind and Rain*. Hauppauge, NY: Barron's Educational Series.

Lobel, Anita. (1990). *Alison's Zinnia*. New York: Greenwillow.

Lobel, Arnold. (1997). *Arnold Lobel Book of Mother Goose*. New York: Random House.

Locker, Thomas. (1984). *Where the River Begins*. New York: Dial Books.

Locker, Thomas. (1997). *Water Dance*. Orlando, FL: Harcourt Brace.

Loewen, Nancy. (1996a). *Bicycle Safety*. Illus. by Penny Danny. Mankato, MN: Child's World.

Loewen, Nancy. (1996b). *Traffic Safety*. Illus. by Penny Danny. Mankato, MN: Child's World.

London, Jonathan. (1992a). *Froggy Gets Dressed*. Illus. by Frank Remkiewicz. New York: Viking.

London, Jonathan. (1992b). *The Lion Who Had Asthma*. Illus. by Nadine B. Westcott. Beaver Dam, WI: Concept Books.

London, Jonathan. (1994). *Let's Go, Froggy!* Illus. by Frank Remkiewicz. New York: Viking.

London, Jonathan. (1995). *Froggy Learns to Swim*. Illus. by Frank Remkiewicz. New York: Viking.

London, Jonathan. (1997a). *Froggy's First Kiss*. Illus. by Frank Remkiewicz. New York: Viking.

London, Jonathan. (1997b). *Puddles*. Illus. by G. Brian Karas. New York: Viking.

Loredo, Elizabeth. (1997). *Boogie Bones*. Illus. by Kevin Hawkes. New York: G. P. Putnam.

Lotz, Karen E. (1993). *Snowsong Whistling*. Illus. by Elisa Kleven. New York: Dutton.

Lowery, Linda. (1995). *Twist with a Burger, Jitter with a Bug*. Boston: Houghton Mifflin.

Lucht, Irmgard. (1995). *The Red Poppy*. Illus. by Frank Jacoby-Nelson. New York: Hyperion.

Luttrell, Ida. (1997). *Milo's Toothache*. Illus. by Enzo Giannini. New York: Puffin. (Paperback)

Lynn, Sara. (1993). *Play with Paint*. Minneapolis: Carolrhoda Books.

Lynn, Sara, & James, Diane. (1998). *Rain and Shine*. Illus. by Joe Wright. Chicago: World Book.

Maass, Robert. (1993). *When Winter Comes*. New York: Holt.

Maass, Robert. (1995). *When Summer Comes*. New York: Holt.

Maass, Robert. (1996). *When Spring Comes*. Reprint ed. Madison, WI: Demco Media.

MacDonald, Amy. (1996a). *Cousin Ruth's Tooth*. Illus. by Marjorie Priceman. Boston: Houghton Mifflin.

MacDonald, Amy. (1996b). *The Spider Who Created the World*. Illus. by G. Brian Karas. New York: Orchard Books.

MacDonald, Suse. (1994). *Sea Shapes*. Orlando, FL: Harcourt Brace.

MacKinnon, Debbie. (1996). *What Am I?* Illus. by Anthea Sieveking. New York: Dial Books.

MacLachlan, Patricia. (1994). *All the Places to Love.* Illus. by Mike Wimmer. New York: HarperCollins.

MacMillan, Dianne M. (1997). *Thanksgiving Day.* Springfield, NJ: Enslow Publishers.

MacQuitty, Miranda. (1996). *Amazing Bugs.* New York: Dorling Kindersley.

Maestro, Betsy. (1992a). *How Do Apples Grow?* New York: HarperCollins.

Maestro, Betsy. (1992b). *Take a Look at Snakes.* New York: Scholastic.

Maestro, Betsy. (1994). *Why Do Leaves Change Color?* Illus. by Loretta Krupinski. New York: HarperCollins.

The Magic School Bus Wet All Over: A Book about the Water Cycle. (1996). New York: Scholastic.

Mahy, Margaret. (1994). *The Rattlebang Picnic.* Illus. by Steven Kellogg. New York: Dial Books.

Malka, Lucy. (1995). *Fun with Hats.* Illus. by Melinda Levine. Greenvale, NY: Mondo Pub. (Paperback)

Manson, Christopher. (1993). *Tree in the Wood: An Old Nursery Song.* New York: North-South Books.

Markle, Sandra. (1993). *A Rainy Day.* Illus. by Cathy Johnson. New York: Orchard Books.

Marks, Alan. (1991). *Ring-a-Ring o'Roses and A Ding, Dong, Bell: A Book of Nursery Rhymes.* New York: North-South Books.

Marks, Alan. (1993). *Over the Hills and Far Away: A Book of Nursery Rhymes.* New York: North-South Books.

Marston, Hope Irvin. (1993). *Big Rigs.* New York: Cobblehill Books.

Martin, Ann M. (1998). *Baby Animal Zoo.* Illus. by Charles Tang. New York: Scholastic. (Paperback)

Martin, Bill. (1991). *Polar Bear, Polar Bear, What Do You Hear?* Illus. by Eric Carle. New York: Holt.

Martin, Bill. (1993). *Old Devil Wind.* Illus. by Barry Root. Orlando, FL: Harcourt Brace.

Martin, Bill, & Sampson, Michael. (1997). *Swish.* Illus. by Michael Chesworth. New York: Holt.

Marzollo, Jean. (1996a). *I Am Fire.* Illus. by Judith Moffatt. New York: Scholastic.

Marzollo, Jean. (1996b). *I Am Water.* Illus. by Judith Moffatt. New York: Scholastic. (Paperback)

Marzollo, Jean. (1996c). *I'm a Seed.* Madison, WI: Demco Media.

Marzollo, Jean. (1996d). *It's a Seed.* Illus. by Judith Moffatt. New York: Scholastic.

Marzollo, Jean. (1997). *I Am an Apple.* Illus. by Judith Moffatt. St. Paul, MN: Cartwheel Books. (Paperback)

Masurel, Claire. (1997). *No, No, Titus!* Illus. by Shari Halpern. New York: North-South Books.

Mavor, Salley. (1997). *You and Me: Poems of Friendship.* New York: Orchard Books.

May, Garelick. (1997). *Where Does the Butterfly Go When It Rains?* Illus. by Nicholas Wilton. Greenvale, NY: Mondo Publications.

Mayer, Mercer. (1996). *Purple Pickle Juice.* New York: Random Library.

Maynard, Christopher. (1997a). *Jobs People Do.* New York: DK Publishing.

Maynard, Christopher. (1997b). *Why Are All Families Different? Questions Children Ask about Families.* New York: Dorling Kindersley.

Maynard, Thane. (1997). *Ostriches.* Mankato, MN: Child's World.

Mazen, Barbara S. (1994). *Pass the Cheese Please.* Illus. by Paul Harvey. Delran, NJ: Newbridge.

Mazzola, Frank. (1997). *Counting Is for the Birds.* Watertown, MA: Charlesbridge Publishers.

McBratney, Sam. (1996). *The Dark at the Top of the Stairs.* Illus. by Ivan Bates. Cambridge, MA: Candlewick Press.

McCully, Emily Arnold. (1992). *Mirette on the Highwire.* New York: G. P. Putnam.

McDonald, Megan. (1995). *Insects Are My Life*. Illus. by Paul Brett Johnson. New York: Orchard Books.

McDonald, Megan. (1996). *My House Has Stars*. Illus. by Peter Catalanotto. New York: Orchard Books.

McDonnell, Flora. (1994). *I Love Animals*. Cambridge, MA: Candlewick Press.

McDonnell, Janet. (1993). *The Easter Surprise*. Illus. by Linda Hohag. Chicago: Children's Press.

McGeorge, Constance W. (1994). *Boomer's Big Day*. Illus. by Mary Whyte. New York: Chronicle.

McGovern, Ann. (1997). *The Lady in the Box*. Illus. by Marni Backer. New York: Turtle Books.

McKissack, Patricia C. (1996). *A Million Fish . . . More or Less*. Illus. by Dena Schutzer. New York: Random House.

McMillan, Bruce. (1993). *Mouse Views: What the Class Pet Saw*. New York: Holiday House.

McMillan, Bruce. (1995a). *The Baby Zoo*. New York: Scholastic. (Paperback)

McMillan, Bruce. (1995b). *Nights of the Pufflings*. Boston: Houghton Mifflin.

McPhail, David M. (1998). *The Puddle*. New York: Farrar, Straus & Giroux.

Meddaugh, Susan. (1994). *Witches Supermarket*. Madison, WI: Demco Media.

Mellentin, Kath. (1998). *The Wheels on the Bus*. Illus. by Jenny Tulip. Reistertown, MD: Flying Frog Publishing.

Mendel, Lydia J. (1993). *All Dressed Up and Nowhere to Go*. Illus. by Normand Chartier. Boston: Houghton Mifflin.

Merk, Ann, & Merk, Jim. (1994). *Rain, Snow and Ice*. Vero Beach, FL: Rourke Corp.

Micucci, Charles. (1992). *The Life and Times of the Apple*. New York: Orchard Books.

Milich, Melissa. (1997). *Miz Fannie Mae's Fine New Easter Hat*. Illus. by Yong Chen. Boston: Little, Brown.

Miller, Margaret. (1988). *Whose Hat?* New York: William Morrow.

Miller, Margaret. (1990). *Who Uses This?* New York: Greenwillow.

Miller, Margaret. (1997). *Wheels Go Round*. New York: Simon & Schuster.

Miller, Marilyn. (1996a). *Behind the Scenes at the Hospital*. Illus. by Ingo Fast. Austin, TX: Raintree/Steck Vaughn.

Miller, Marilyn. (1996b). *Behind the Scenes at the Shopping Mall*. Illus. by Ingo Fast. Austin, TX: Raintree/Steck Vaughn.

Miller, Robert H. (1994). *The Story of "Stagecoach" Mary Fields*. Illus. by Cheryl Hanna. Morristown, NJ: Silver Press.

Millman, Isaac. (1998). *Moses Goes to a Concert*. New York: Farrar, Straus & Giroux.

Miranda, Anne. (1997). *To Market, to Market*. Illus. by Janet Stevens. Orlando, FL: Harcourt Brace.

Monson, A. M. (1997). *Wanted: Best Friend*. Illus. by Lynn Munsinger. New York: Dial Books.

Moon, Nicola. (1997). *Lucy's Picture*. Illus. by Lynn Munsinger. New York: Dial Books.

Moore, Clement C. (1994). *The Night before Christmas: Told in Signed English*. Washington, DC: Gallaudet University Press.

Moore, Clement C. (1995). *Twas the Night before Christmas*. Illus. by Ted Rand. New York: North-South Books.

Moore, Clement C. (1996). *Twas the Night b'fore Christmas: An African-American Version*. Melodye Rosales. New York: Scholastic.

Moore, Elaine. (1994). *Grandma's Garden*. Illus. by Dan Andreasen. New York: Lothrop, Lee & Shepard.

Moore, Elaine. (1995). *Grandma's Smile*. Illus. by Dan Andreasen. New York: Lothrop, Lee & Shepard.

Moore, Eva. (1996). Buddy: *The First Seeing Eye Dog*. Illus. by Don Bolognese. New York: Scholastic.

Moore, Eva. (1997). *The Day of the Bad Haircut.* Illus. by Meredith Johnson. St. Paul, MN: Cartwheel Books. (Paperback)

Moran, George. (1994). *Imagine Me on a Sit-Ski!* Illus. by Nadine Bernard Westcott. Beaver Dam, WI: Concept Books.

Morgan, Sally. *World of Shapes* series. Cincinatti, OH: Thomson Learning. *Circles and Spheres* (1994a); *Squares and Cubes* (1994b); *Spirals* (1995a); *Triangles and Pyramids* (1995b).

Morgan, Sally. (1996). *Flowers, Trees and Fruits.* Stanwood, WA: Kingfisher.

Morley, Christine, et al. (1997). *Me and My Pet Fish.* Chicago: World Book.

Morozumi, Atsuko. (1998). *My Friend Gorilla.* New York: Farrar, Straus & Giroux.

Morris, Ann. (1989). *Hats, Hats, Hats.* Photos by Ken Heyman. New York: Lothrop, Lee & Shepard.

Morris, Ann. (1990). *Loving.* Photos by Ken Heyman. New York: Lothrop, Lee & Shepard.

Morris, Ann. (1992a). *Houses and Homes.* Photos by Ken Heyman. New York: Lothrop, Lee & Shepard.

Morris, Ann. (1992b). *Tools.* Photos by Ken Heyman. New York: Lothrop, Lee & Shepard.

Morris, Ann. (1995a). *The Daddy Book.* Photos by Ken Heyman. Englewood Cliffs, NJ: Silver Press.

Morris, Ann. (1995b). *The Mommy Book.* Photos by Ken Heyman. Englewood Cliffs, NJ: Silver Press.

Morris, Ann. (1995c). *Shoes, Shoes, Shoes.* New York: Lothrop, Lee & Shepard.

Morrison, Gordon. (1998). *Bald Eagle.* Boston: Houghton Mifflin.

Moses, Amy. (1997). *Doctors Help People.* Mankato, MN: Child's World.

Moss, Lloyd. (1996). *Zin! Zin! Zin! A Violin.* Illus. by Marjorie Priceman. New York: Simon & Schuster.

Munsch, Robert. (1992). *Purple, Green and Yellow.* Illus. by Helene Desputeaux. Willowdale, Ontario: Annick Press.

Murata, Michinori. (1993). *Water and Light: Looking through Lenses.* Minneapolis: Lerner Publications.

Murphy, Stuart. (1996). *A Pair of Socks.* Illus. by Lois Ehlert. New York: HarperCollins.

Naylor, Phyllis Reynolds. (1991). *King of the Playground.* Illus. by Nola Langner Malone. Colchester, CT: Atheneum.

Neitzel, Shirley. (1989). *The Jacket I Wear in the Snow.* Illus. by Nancy Winslow Parker. New York: Greenwillow.

Neitzel, Shirley. (1992). *The Dress I'll Wear to the Party.* Illus. by Nancy Winslow Parker. New York: Greenwillow.

Neitzel, Shirley. (1997). *The House I'll Build for the Wrens.* New York: Greenwillow.

Nelson, Nigel. (1994a). *Codes.* Illus. by Tony De Saulles. Cincinnati, OH: Thomson Learning.

Nelson, Nigel. (1994b). *Writing and Numbers.* Illus. by Tony De Saulles. Cincinnati, OH: Thomson Learning.

Nerlove, Miriam. (1992). *Valentine's Day.* Niles, IL: Albert Whitman & Co.

Newberry, Clare Turlay. (1993). *April's Kittens.* New York: HarperCollins.

Newcome, Zita. (1997). *Toddlerobics.* Cambridge, MA: Candlewick Press.

Nichols, Grace. (1997). *Asana and the Animals: A Book of Pet Poems.* Illus. by Sarah Adams. Cambridge, MA: Candlewick Press.

Nielsen, Nancy J. (1992). *Carnivorous Plants.* New York: Franklin Watts.

Nielsen, Shelly. (1992). *Celebrating Easter.* Minneapolis: Abdo & Daughters.

Nielsen, Shelly, & Berg, Julie. (1993). *I Love Water.* Minneapolis: Abdo & Daughters.

Nikola-Lisa, W. (1993). *Storm.* Illus. by Michael Hays. Colchester, CT: Atheneum.

Nikola-Lisa, W. (1994). *Wheels Go Round.* Illus. by Jane Conteh-Morgan. New York: Doubleday.

Nikola-Lisa, W. (1997). *Shake Dem Halloween Bones.* Boston: Houghton Mifflin.

Noble, Kate. (1994). *The Blue Elephant.* Illus. by Rachel Bass. Chicago: Silver Seahorse Press.

Noll, Sally. (1997). *Surprise!* New York: Greenwillow.

Norworth, Jack. (1992). *Take Me Out to the Ballgame.* Illus. by Alec Gillman. New York: Simon & Schuster.

Novak, Matt. (1996). *Elmer Blunt's Open House.* New York: Orchard Books. (Paperback)

Oberman, Sheldon. (1997). *By the Hanukkah Light.* Illus. by Neil Waldman. Honesdale, PA: Boyds Mills Press.

Oborne, Martine. (1997). *Juice the Pig.* Illus. by Axel Scheffler. New York: Holt.

O'Brien, Claire. (1997). *Sam's Sneaker Search.* Illus. by Charles Fuge. New York: Simon & Schuster.

O'Connor, Jane. (1993). *Nina, Nina Ballerina.* Illus. by DyAnne DiSalvo-Ryan. New York: Grosset & Dunlap.

Old Mother Hubbard and Her Wonderful Dog. (1991). Illus. by James Marshall. New York: Farrar, Straus & Giroux.

Older, Jules. (1997). *Cow.* Illus. by Lyn Severance. Watertown, MA: Charlesbridge Publishers.

O'Mara, Anna. (1996). *Oceans.* Chicago: Children's Press.

Onyefulu, Ifeoma. (1997). *Chidi Only Likes Blue: An African Book of Colors.* New York: Cobblehill.

Opie, Iona. (Ed.). (1996). *My Very First Mother Goose.* Illus. by Rosemary Wells. Cambridge, MA: Candlewick Press.

Opie, Iona Archibald. (1997). Cambridge, MA: Candlewick Press. (Board books) *Humpty Dumpty and Other Rhymes; Pussycat Pussycat and Other Rhymes; Wee Willie Winkie and Other Rhymes.*

Oppenheim, Joanne. (1995). *Have You Seen Trees?* Illus. by Jean Tseng & Mou-Sien Tseng. New York: Scholastic.

Oppenheim, Joanne. (1998). *Have You Seen Bugs?* Illus. by Ron Broda. New York: Scholastic.

Oram, Hiawyn. (1993). *Out of the Blue: Poems about Color.* Illus. by David McKee. New York: Hyperion.

Ormerod, Jan. (1991). *When We Went to the Zoo.* New York: Lothrop, Lee & Shepard.

Osofsky, Audrey. (1992). *My Buddy.* Illus. by Ted Rand. New York: Holt.

Ostheeren, Ingrid et al. (1996). *The Blue Monster.* New York: North-South Books.

Our Neighborhood series. San Francisco: Children's Book Press.

Duvall, Jill D. (1997a). *Chef Ki Is Serving Our Dinner.*

Duvall, Jill D. (1997b). *Meet Rory Hohenstein, a Professional Dancer.*

Duvall, Jill D. (1997c). *Mr. Duvall Reports the News.*

Duvall, Jill D. (1997d). *Ms. Moja Makes Beautiful Clothes.*

Duvall, Jill D. (1997e). *Who Keeps the Water Clean? Ms. Schindler!*

Flanagan, Alice K. (1996a). *A Busy Day at Mr. Kang's Grocery Store.*

Flanagan, Alice K. (1996b). *The Wilsons, a House-Painting Team.*

Flanagan, Alice K. (1997a). *A Day in Court with Mrs. Trinh.*

Flanagan, Alice K. (1997b). *Ask Nurse Pfaff, She'll Help You.*

Flanagan, Alice K. (1997c). Mrs. Murphy Fights Fires.

Owens, Mary Beth. (1993). *Counting Cranes.* Boston: Little, Brown.

Oxenbury, Helen. (1991). *Monkey See, Monkey Do* (2nd ed.). New York: Dial Books. (Board book)

Oxlade, Chris. (1997a). *Car (Take It Apart).* Morristown, NJ: Silver Burdett.

Oxlade, Chris. (1997b). *Electronic Communication*. Illus. by Colin Mier. New York: Franklin Watts.

Packard, Mary. (1995). *I'm a Fire Fighter*. Illus. by Julie Durrell. Madison, WI: Demco Media.

Packard, Mary. (1997). *Christmas Kitten*. Illus. by Jenny Williams. San Francisco: Children's Book Press.

Palazzo-Craig, Janet. (1995). *Max and Maggie in Spring*. Illus. by Paul Meisel. Mahwah, NJ: Troll.

Pallotta, Jerry. (1990). *Flower Alphabet Book*. Illus. by Leslie Evans. Watertown, MA: Charlesbridge Publishers.

Pallotta, Jerry. (1993). *The Icky Bug Alphabet Book*. Illus. by Ralph Masiello. Watertown, MA: Charlesbridge Books.

Parish, Peggy. (1996). *Play Ball, Amelia Bedelia*. Illus. by Wallace Tripp. New York: HarperCollins.

Parry-Jones, Jemima. (1992). *Amazing Birds of Prey*. Illus. by Mike Dunning. New York: Knopf.

Patent, Dorothy Hinshaw. (1998). *Apple Trees*. Photos by William Munoz. Minneapolis: Lerner Publications.

Patent, Dorothy Hinshaw. (1991). *Where Food Comes From*. Illus. by William Munoz. New York: Holiday House.

Patrick, Denise Lewis. (1993a). *The Car Washing Street*. Illus. by John Ward. New York: William Morrow.

Patrick, Denise Lewis. (1993b). *Red Dancing Shoes*. Illus. by James Ransome. New York: William Morrow.

Paulsen, Gary. (1997). *Worksong*. Illus. by Ruth Wright Paulsen. Orlando, FL: Harcourt Brace.

Paxton, Tom. (1996a). *Going to the Zoo*. Illus. by Karen Schmidt. New York: William Morrow.

Paxton, Tom. (1996b). *The Story of the Tooth Fairy*. Illus. by Rob Sauber. New York: William Morrow.

Paxton, Tom. (1997). *Engelbert Joins the Circus*. Illus. by Roberta Wilson. New York: William Morrow.

Pearson, Tracey Campbell. (1997). *The Purple Hat*. New York: Farrar, Straus & Giroux.

Peek, Merle. (1998). *Mary Wore Her Red Dress, and Henry Wore His Green Sneakers*. Boston: Houghton Mifflin.

Pellam, David. (1991). *Sam's Sandwich*. New York: Dutton. (Flap book)

Pellegrini, Nina. (1991). *Families are Different*. New York: Holiday House.

Penn, Malka. (1994). *The Miracle of the Potato Latkes: A Hanukkah Story*. Illus. by Giora Carmi. New York: Holiday House.

Perkins, Lynne Rae. (1995). *Home Lovely*. New York: Greenwillow.

Petersen-Fleming, Judy, et al. (1996a). *Kitten Care and Critters, Too!* New York: William Morrow.

Petersen-Fleming, Judy, et al. (1996b). *Kitten Training and Critters, Too!* New York: Tambourine Books.

Petersen-Fleming, Judy, et al. (1996c). *Puppy Training and Critters, Too!* New York: Tambourine Books.

Peterson, Cris. (1994). *Extra Cheese, Please! Mozzarella's Journey from Cow to Pizza*. Illus. by Alvis Upitis. Honesdale, PA: Boyds Mills Press.

Peterson, Jeanne Whitehouse. (1994). *My Mama Sings*. Illus. by Sandra Speidel. New York: HarperCollins.

Pfeffer, Wendy. (1996a). *Mute Swans*. Morristown, NJ: Silver Burdett Press.

Pfeffer, Wendy. (1996b). *What's It Like to Be a Fish?* Illus. by Holly Keller. New York: HarperCollins.

Pfister, Marcus. (1992). *The Rainbow Fish*. Trans. by J. Alison James. New York: North-South Books.

Pfister, Marcus. (1995). *Rainbow Fish to the Rescue*. Illus. by J. Alison James. New York: North-South Books.

Pilkey, Dav. (1995). *Hallo-Wiener*. New York: Scholastic.

Pinczes, Elinor. (1993). *One Hundred Hungry Ants*. Illus. by Bonnie MacKain. Boston: Houghton Mifflin.

Pinczes, Elinor. (1995). *A Remainder of One*. Illus. by Bonnie MacKain. Boston: Houghton Mifflin.

Plourde, Lynn. (1997). *Pigs in the Mud in the Middle of the Rud*. Illus. by John Schoenherr. New York: Scholastic.

Pluckrose, Henry Arthur. (1990). *Trees*. Illus. by Joy Friedman. Chicago: Children's Press.

Pinkney, J. Brian. (1994). *Max Found Two Sticks*. New York: Simon & Schuster.

Polacco, Patricia. (1988). *Rechenka's Eggs*. New York: G. P. Putnam.

Polacco, Patricia. (1992a). *Chicken Sunday*. New York: Philomel Books.

Polacco, Patricia. (1992b). *Mrs. Katz and Tush*. New York: Bantam.

Polacco, Patricia. (1993). *The Bee Tree*. New York: Philomel Books.

Polacco, Patricia. (1995). *Babushka's Mother Goose*. New York: Philomel Books.

Polacco, Patricia. (1996). *Trees of the Dancing Goats*. New York: Simon & Schuster.

Pomeroy, Diana. (1997). *Wildflower ABC: An Alphabet of Potato Prints*. Orlando, FL: Harcourt Brace.

Porte, Barbara Ann. (1993). *"Leave That Cricket Be, Alan Lee."* Illus. by Donna Ruff. New York: Greenwillow.

Porte, Barbara Ann. (1995). *Chickens! Chickens!* Illus. by Greg Henry. New York: Orchard Books.

Powell, Jillian. (1997a). *Fruit*. Austin, TX: Raintree/Steck Vaughn.

Powell, Jillian. (1997b). *Health Matters* series. Austin, TX: Raintree/Steck Vaughn. *Exercise and Your Health; Food and Your Health; Hygiene and Your Health*.

Pratt, Pierre. (1992). *Follow That Hat!* Willowdale, Ontario: Annick Press.

Prelutsky, Jack. (1986). *Ride a Purple Pelican*. New York: William Morrow.

Priceman, Marjorie. (1994). *How to Make an Apple Pie and See the World*. New York: Knopf.

Pulver, Robin. (1994). *Mrs. Toggle's Beautiful Blue Shoe*. Illus. by R. W. Alley. New York: Simon & Schuster.

Pulver, Robin. (1997). *Alicia's Tutu*. Illus. by Mark Graham. New York: Dial Books.

Rachlin, Ann. *Famous Children* series. Illus. by Susan Hellard. Hauppauge, NY: Barron's Educational Series. *Bach* (1992); *Beethoven* (1994); *Brahms* (1993); *Chopin* (1993); *Handel* (1992); *Haydn* (1992); *Mozart* (1992); *Schubert* (1994); *Schumann* (1993); *Tchaikovsky* (1993). (Paperback)

Radford, Derek. (1994). *Building Machines and What They Do*. Reprint ed. Cambridge, MA: Candlewick Press.

Radford, Derek. (1997). *Harry at the Garage*. Cambridge, MA: Candlewick Press.

Raffi. (1998). *Wheels on the Bus*. New York: Crown Books.

Rahaman, Vashanti. (1996). *O Christmas Tree*. Illus. by Frane Lessac. Honesdale, PA: Boyds Mills Press.

Rand, Gloria. (1996). *Willie Takes a Hike*. Illus. by Ted Rand. Orlando, FL: Harcourt Brace.

Rankin, Laura. (1991). *The Handmade Alphabet*. New York: Dial Books.

Raschka, Christopher. (1992). *Charlie Parker Played Be Bop*. New York: Orchard Books.

Raschka, Christopher. (1993). *Yo! Yes?* New York: Orchard Books.

Raschka, Christopher. (1997). *Mysterious Thelonious*. New York: Orchard Books.

Rathmann, Peggy. (1994). *Good Night, Gorilla*. New York: G. P. Putnam.

Rathmann, Peggy. (1995). *Officer Buckle and Gloria*. New York: G. P. Putnam.

Rau, Dana Meachen. (1995). *Robin at Hickory Street*. Illus. by Joel Snyder. Norwalk, CT: Soundprints/Smithsonian Institution.

Rau, Dana Meachen. (1997). *A Box Can Be Many Things*. Illus. by Paige Bellin-Frye. Chicago: Children's Press.

Rauzon, Mark J., & Bix, Cynthia O. (1994). *Water, Water Everywhere*. Santa Fe, NM: Sierra Club.

Ray, Mary Lyn. (1996). *Mud*. Illus. by Lauren Stringer. Orlando, FL: Harcourt Brace.

Ready, Dee. (1997a). *Dentists*. Chicago: Children's Press.

Ready, Dee. (1997b). *Doctors*. Chicago: Children's Press.

Ready, Dee. (1997c). *Fire Fighters*. Danbury, CT: Grolier Pub.

Ready, Dee. (1997d). *Nurses*. Chicago: Children's Press.

Ready, Dee. (1998). *School Bus Driver*. New York: Capstone.

Reasoner, Charles. (1994). *Who's Hatching?* (A Sliding Surprise Book). New York: Price Stern Sloan.

Reay, Joanne. (1995). *Bumpa Rumpus and the Rainy Day*. Illus. by Adriano Gon. Boston: Houghton Mifflin.

Redberg, Rita F., et al. (1996). *You Can Be a Woman Cardiologist*. Culver City, CA: Cascade Pass. (Paperback)

Reed, Lynn Rowe. (1995). *Pedro, His Perro, and the Alphabet Sombrero*. New York: Hyperion.

Reed-Jones, Carol. (1995). *The Tree in the Ancient Forest*. Illus. by Christopher Canyon. Nevada City, CA: Dawn Publications.

Regan, Dana. (1996). *The Wheels on the Bus*. New York: Scholastic.

Reid, Mary Ebeltoft. (1997). *Let's Find Out about Ice Cream*. New York: Scholastic.

Reiser, Lynn. (1992). *Any Kind of Dog*. New York: Greenwillow.

Reiser, Lynn. (1993). *Margaret and Margarita / Margarita y Margaret*. New York: Greenwillow.

Reiser, Lynn. (1995). *Two Mice in Three Fables*. New York: Greenwillow.

Reiser, Lynn. (1997). *Best Friends Think Alike*. New York: Greenwillow.

Rice, Eve. (1996). *Swim!* Illus. by Marisabina Russo. New York: Greenwillow.

Richardson, Joy. (1993). *Inside the Museum: A Children's Guide to the Metropolitan Museum of Art*. New York: Abrams.

Richardson, Joy. (1994a). *Cars*. New York: Franklin Watts.

Richardson, Joy. (1994b). *Skyscrapers*. New York: Franklin Watts.

Richardson, Judith Benet. (1996). *Old Winter*. Illus. by R. W. Alley. New York: Orchard Books.

Riley, Linnea Asplind. (1997). *Mouse Mess*. New York: Blue Sky Press.

Ring, Elizabeth. (1994). *Night Flier*. Photos by Dwight Kuhn. Brookfield, CT: Millbrook Press.

Ring, Elizabeth. (1995). *Lucky Mouse*. Illus. by Dwight Kuhn. Brookfield, CT: Millbrook Press.

Robbins, Ken. (1990). *A Flower Grows*. New York: Dial Books.

Robbins, Ken. (1993). *Power Machines*. New York: Holt.

Robbins, Ken. (1998). *Fall Leaves*. New York: Scholastic.

Roberts, Bethany. (1995). *Halloween Mice!* Illus. by Doug Cushman. New York: Clarion Books.

Robertus, Polly M. (1991). *The Dog Who Had Kittens*. Illus. by Janet Stevens. New York: Holiday House.

Robins, Joan. (1993). *Addie's Bad Day*. Illus. by Sue Truesdell. New York: HarperCollins.

Robinson, Fay. (1994). *Vegetables, Vegetables*. Chicago: Children's Press.

Robinson, Martha. (1995). *The Zoo at Night*. Illus. by Antonio Frasconi. New York: Simon & Schuster.

Robson, Pam. (1998a). *Banana*. Chicago: Children's Press.

Robson, Pam. (1998b). *Corn*. Chicago: Children's Press.

Rockwell, Anne F. (1990). *Toolbox*. New York: Aladdin.

Rockwell, Anne. (1991). *Apples and Pumpkins*. Illus. by Lizzy Rockwell. New York: Simon & Schuster.

Rockwell, Anne F. (1992a). *Cars*. New York: Dutton.

Rockwell, Anne. (1992b). *Our Yard Is Full of Birds*. New York: Macmillan.

Rockwell, Anne F. (1993). *Mr. Panda's Painting*. New York: Simon & Schuster.

Rockwell, Anne F. (1996). *My Spring Robin*. Madison, WI: Demco Media.

Rockwell, Harlow. (1987). *My Dentist*. New York: William Morrow. (Paperback)

Rockwell, Harlow. (1992). *My Doctor*. New York: Macmillan.

Rogers, Alan. (1997). *Yellow Hippo*. Chicago: World Book.

Rogers, Fred. (1997). *Going to the Hospital*. Illus. by Jim Judkis. New York: G. P. Putnam.

Rosen, Michael J. (1992a). *Elijah's Angel: A Story for Chanukah and Christmas*. Illus. by Aminah B. L. Robinson. Orlando, FL: Harcourt Brace.

Rosen, Michael (Ed.) (1992b). *Home*. New York: HarperCollins.

Rosen, Michael. (1996). *This Is Our House*. Illus. by Bob Graham. Cambridge, MA: Candlewick Press.

Rosenberg, Maxine B. (1991). *Brothers and Sisters*. Photos by George Ancona. New York: Clarion Books.

Rosenberg, Maxine B. (1997). *Mommy's in the Hospital Having a Baby*. Photos by Robert Maass. New York: Clarion Books.

Ross, Katharine. (1995). *The Story of the Pilgrims*. Illus. by Carolyn Cross. New York: Random House.

Ross, Michael Elsohn, et al. (1998). *Ladybugology*. Illus. by Brian Grogan. Minneapolis: Lerner Publishing.

Roth, Susan L. (1997). *My Love for You*. New York: Dial Books.

Rotner, Shelley. (1995). *Wheels Around*. Boston: Houghton Mifflin.

Rotner, Shelley. (1996). *Colors around Us*. New York: Simon & Schuster. (Lift the Flap Book)

Rotner, Shelley, & Kelly, Sheila. (1996). *Lots of Moms*. New York: Dial Books.

Rotner, Shelley, & Kelly, Sheila. (1997). *Lots of Dads*. New York: Dial Books.

Rounds, Glen. (1995). *Sod Houses on the Great Plains*. New York: Holiday House.

Rowan, James P. (1990). *I Can Be a Zoo Keeper*. Chicago: Children's Press. (Paperback)

Royston, Angela. (1991). *Cars*. Photos by Tim Ridley. New York: Macmillan.

Royston, Angela. (1992). *Birds*. New York: Aladdin Books.

Ruediger, Beth. (1997). *The Barber of Bingo*. Illus. by John McPherson. Kansas City: Andrews & McMeel Pub.

Rush, Caroline. (1997). *Wheels and Cogs*. Illus. by Mike Gordon. Austin, TX: Raintree/Steck Vaughn.

Russo, Marisabina. (1994). *I Don't Want to Go Back to School*. New York: Greenwillow.

Russo, Marisabina. (1998). *When Mama Gets Home*. New York: Greenwillow.

Ruurs, Margriet. (1997). *Emma's Eggs*. Illus. by Barbara Spurll. New York: Stoddart Kids.

Ryan, Pam Munoz. (1996). *Crayon Counting Book*. Illus. by Frank Mazzola Jr. Watertown, MA: Charlesbridge Publishers.

Ryden, Hope. (1996). *ABC of Crawlers and Flyers*. New York: Clarion Books.

Ryder, Joanne. (1994). *My Father's Hands*. Illus. by Mark Graham. New York: William Morrow.

Ryder, Joanne. (1997a). *Shark in the Sea*. Illus. by Michael Rothman. New York: William Morrow.

Ryder, Joanne. (1997b). *Winter White.* Illus. by Carol Lacey. New York: William Morrow.

Rylant, Cynthia. (1991). *Bookshop Dog.* New York: Scholastic.

Rylant, Cynthia. (1993a). *Everyday Garden.* New York: Simon & Schuster. (Board book)

Rylant, Cynthia. (1993b). *Everyday House.* New York: Simon & Schuster. (Board book)

Rylant, Cynthia. (1993c). *Mr. Griggs' Work.* Illus. by Julie Downing. New York: Orchard Books.

Rylant, Cynthia. (1994). *Mr. Putter and Tabby Walk the Dog.* Illus. by Arthur Howard. Orlando: Harcourt Brace.

Rylant, Cynthia. (1995). *Mr. Putter and Tabby Pick the Pears.* Orlando, FL: Harcourt Brace.

Rylant, Cynthia. (1997a). *Mr. Putter and Tabby Row the Boat.* Illus. by Arthur Howard. Orlando, FL: Harcourt Brace.

Rylant, Cynthia. (1997b). *Silver Packages: An Appalachian Christmas Story.* Illus. by Chris K. Soentpiet. New York: Orchard Books.

Sabuda, Robert. (1992). *Saint Valentine.* New York: Simon & Schuster.

Sampson, Michael. (1996). *The Football That Won . . .* Illus. by Ted Rand. New York: Holt.

Samson, Suzanne. (1994). *Fairy Dusters and Blazing Stars: Exploring Wildflowers with Children.* Illus. by Neel Preston. Niwot, CO: Roberts Rinehart Publishers.

Samson, Suzanne. (1995). *Sea Dragons and Rainbow Runners: Exploring Fish with Children.* Illus. by Preston Neel. Niwot, CO: Roberts Rinehart Publishers.

Sanders, Scott R. (1996). *Meeting Trees.* Illus. by Robert Hynes. Washington, DC: National Geographic Society.

Sathre, Vivian. (1995). *Mouse Chase.* Illus. by Ward Schumaker. Orlando, FL: Harcourt Brace.

Saul, Carol P. (1995). *Someplace Else.* Illus. by Barry Root. New York: Simon & Schuster.

Saunders-Smith, Gail. (1997). *Autumn Leaves.* Mankato, MN: Pebble Books.

Savage, Stephen. (1995a). *Ant.* Illus. by Clive Pritchard. Cincinnati, OH: Thomson Learning.

Savage, Stephen. (1995b). *Butterfly.* Cincinnati, OH: Thomson Learning.

Savage, Stephen. (1995c). *Duck.* Illus. by Steve Lings. Cincinnati, OH: Thomson Learning.

Savage, Stephen. (1995d). *Seagull.* Illus. by Andre Boos. Cincinnati, OH: Thomson Learning.

Savage, Stephen. (1995e). *Spider.* Illus. by Phil Weare. Cincinnati, OH: Thomson Learning.

Say, Allen. (1989). *The Lost Lake.* Boston: Houghton Mifflin.

Say, Allen. (1991). *Tree of Cranes.* Boston: Houghton Mifflin.

Say, Allen. (1997). *Allison.* Illus. by Susan Guevara. Boston: Houghton Mifflin.

Scarry, Richard. (1997). *Richard Scarry's Pop-Up Wheels.* New York: Simon & Schuster.

Schertle, Alice. (1994). *How Now Brown Cow?* Illus. by Amanda Schaffer. San Diego, CA: Browndeer Press.

Schindel, John. (1994). *What's for Lunch?* Illus. by Kevin O'Malley. New York: Lothrop, Lee & Shepard.

Schindel, John. (1995). *Dear Daddy.* Illus. by Dorothy Donohue. Niles, IL: Albert Whitman & Co.

Schlein, Miriam. (1996). *More Than One.* Illus. by Donald Crews. New York: Greenwillow.

Schnur, Steven. (1995). *The Tie Man's Miracle: A Chanukah Story.* Illus. by Stephen Johnson. New York: William Morrow.

Schomp, Virginia. (1997). *If You Were a . . . Ballet Dancer.* Tarrytown, NY: Marshall Cavendish.

Schomp, Virginia. (1998). *If You Were a Veterinarian.* Tarrytown, NY: Marshall Cavendish.

Schotter, Roni. (1993). *Hanukkah!* Illus. by Marylin Hafner. Madison, WI: Demco Media.

Schulson, Rachel. (1997). *Guns—What You Should Know.* Illus. by Mary Jones. Niles, IL: Albert Whitman & Co.

Schumaker, Ward. (1997). *Sing a Song of Circus.* Orlando, FL: Harcourt Brace.

Schwartz, Amy. (1994). *A Teeny Tiny Baby.* New York: Orchard Books.

Schweninger, Ann. (1993). *Autumn Days.* New York: Puffin. (Paperback)

Scieszka, Jon. (1994). *The Book That Jack Wrote.* Illus. by Daniel Adel. New York: Viking.

Scott, Ann Herbert. (1994). *Hi.* Illus. by Glo Coalson. New York: Philomel Books.

Scott, Carey. (1997). *Kittens.* New York: Dorling Kindersley.

Seabrook, Elizabeth. (1997). *Cabbages and Kings.* Illus. by Jamie Wyeth. New York: Viking.

Sekido, Isamu. (1993). *Fruits, Roots, and Fungi: Plants We Eat.* Minneapolis: Lerner Publications.

Seltzer, Isadore. (1992). *The House I Live In: At Home in America.* Colchester, CT: Atheneum.

Serfozo, Mary. (1992). *Who Said Red?* New York: Aladdin Paperbacks.

Serfozo, Mary. (1993). *Benjamin Bigfoot.* Illus. by Joseph A. Smith. New York: Margaret McElderry.

Serfozo, Mary. (1996). *There's a Square: A Book about Shapes.* Illus. by David A. Carter. New York: Scholastic.

Seuss, Dr. (1992). *Scrambled Eggs Super!* New York: Random House.

Seuss, Dr. (1996). *My Many Colored Days.* Lou Fancher (Ed). Illus. by Steve Johnson. New York: Knopf.

Seymour, Tres. (1993). *Hunting the White Cow.* Illus. by Wendy Anderson Halperin. New York: Orchard Books.

Shannon, George. (1994). *Seeds.* Illus. by Steve Bjorkman. Boston: Houghton Mifflin.

Shannon, George. (1995a). *April Showers.* Illus. by Jose Aruego & Ariane Dewey. New York: Greenwillow.

Shannon, George. (1995b). *Heart to Heart.* Boston: Houghton Mifflin.

Shannon, George. (1996). *Spring: A Haiku Story.* Illus. By Malcah Zeldis. New York: Greenwillow.

Shapiro, Arnold. (1997). *Mice Squeak, We Speak.* Illus. by Tomie De Paola. New York: G. P. Putnam.

Sharman, Lydia. (1994). *The Amazing Book of Shapes.* New York: Dorling Kindersley.

Sharmat, Marjorie Weinman. (1994). *Nate the Great and the Mushy Valentine.* Illus. by Marc Simont. New York: Dell Publishing.

Sharp, N. L. (1993). *Today I'm Going Fishing with My Dad.* Illus. by Chris L. Demarest. Honesdale, PA: Boyds Mills Press.

Shaw, Nancy E. (1994). *Sheep Take a Hike.* Illus. by Margot Apple. Boston: Houghton Mifflin.

Shaw, Nancy. (1997). *Sheep Trick or Treat.* Boston: Houghton Mifflin.

Shelby, Anne. (1996). *The Someday House.* Illus. by Rosanne Litzinger. New York: Orchard Books.

Shemie, Bonnie. (1990). *Houses of Bark.* San Francisco: Children's Book Press.

Shories, Pat. (1996). *Over under in the Garden: An Alphabet Book.* New York: Farrar, Straus & Giroux.

Showers, Paul. (1991a). *How Many Teeth?* New York: HarperCollins. (Paperback)

Showers, Paul. (1991b). *Listening Walk.* Revised ed. New York: HarperCollins.

Showers, Paul. (1997). *Sleep Is for Everyone.* Illus. by Wendy Watson. New York: HarperCollins.

Sierra, Judy. (1995). *The House That Drac Built*. Illus. by Will Hillenbrand. Orlando, FL: Harcourt Brace.

Sill, Cathryn P. (1991). *About Birds: A Guide for Children*. Illus. by John Sill. Atlanta: Peachtree Publishers.

Silverman, Erica. (1992). *Big Pumpkin*. Illus. by S. D. Schindler. New York: Macmillan.

Simon, Norma. (1995a). *Fire Fighters*. Illus. by Pam Paparone. New York: Simon & Schuster.

Simon, Norma. (1995b). *Wet World*. Illus. by Alexi Natchev. Cambridge, MA: Candlewick Press.

Simon, Seymour. (1991). *Big Cats*. New York: HarperCollins.

Simon, Seymour. (1992). *Snakes*. New York: HarperCollins.

Simon, Seymour. (1993). *Autumn across America*. New York: Hyperion.

Simon, Seymour. (1994). *Winter across America*. New York: Hyperion Books.

Siracusa, Catherine. (1991). *Bingo, the Best Dog in the World*. Illus. by Sidney Levitt. New York: HarperCollins.

Skurzynksi, Gloria. (1992). *Here Comes the Mail*. New York: Macmillan.

Slawson, Michele Benoit. (1994). *Apple Picking Time*. Illus. by Deborah Kogan Ray. New York: Crown Publishers.

Slier, Debby. (1993). *Real Mother Goose Book of American Rhymes*. Illus. by Patty McCloskey-Padgett et al. New York: Scholastic.

Small, David. (1996). *Fenwick's Suit*. New York: Farrar, Straus & Giroux.

Smath, Jerry. (1995). *A Hat So Simple*. Mahwah, NJ: Troll. (Paperback)

Smith, Dale. (1997). *Nighttime at the Zoo*. Illus. by Gwen Clifford. Tacoma, WA: Golden Anchor Press.

Smith, Lane. (1991). *The Big Pets*. New York: Viking.

Smith, Roland. (1992). *Cats in the Zoo*. Illus. by William Munoz. Brookfield, CT: Millbrook Press.

Soto, Gary. (1995). *Chato's Kitchen*. Illus. by Susan Guevara. New York: G. P. Putnam.

Spanguard, Kristine. (1997). *My Pet Rabbit*. Photos by Andy King. Minneapolis: Lerner Publishing.

Speed, Toby. (1998). *Water Voices*. Illus. by Julie Downing. New York: G. P. Putnam.

Spelman, Cornelia. (1997). *Your Body Belongs to You*. Illus. by Teri Weidner. Niles, IL: Albert Whitman & Co.

Spier, Peter. (1992). *Peter Spier's Circus*. New York: Delacorte Press.

Spohn, Kate. (1996). *Dog and Cat Shake a Leg*. New York: Viking.

Stallone, Linda. (1992). *The Flood That Came to Grandma's House*. Illus. by Joan Schooley. Dallas, PA: Upshur Press.

Stanley, Diane. (1994). *The Gentleman and the Kitchen Maid*. Illus. by Dennis Nolan. New York: Dial Books.

Stevenson, Harvey. (1994). *Grandpa's House*. New York: Hyperion.

Stevenson, James. (1996). *The Oldest Elf*. New York: William Morrow.

Stevenson, James. (1997a). *Heat Wave at Mud Flat*. New York: Greenwillow.

Stevenson, James. (1997b). *The Mud Flat Mystery*. New York: Greenwillow.

Stewart, Sarah. (1997). *The Gardener*. Illus. by David Small. New York: Farrar, Straus & Giroux.

Stock, Catherine. (1990). *Halloween Monster*. New York: Simon & Schuster.

Stock, Catherine. (1994). *Sophie's Bucket*. Orlando, FL: Harcourt Brace. (Paperback)

Stoeke, Janet Morgan. (1994). *A Hat for Minerva Louise*. New York: Dutton.

Sturges, Philemon. (1995). *Ten Flashing Fireflies*. Illus. by Anna Vojtech. New York: North-South Books.

Stutson, Caroline. (1993). *By the Light of the Halloween Moon.* Illus. by Kevin Hawkes. New York: Lothrop, Lee & Shepard.

Summers, Kate. (1997). *Milly and Tilly: The Story of a Town Mouse and a Country Mouse.* Illus. by Maggie Kneen. New York: Dutton.

Sun, Chyng-Feng. (1996). *Cat and Cat-Face.* Illus. by Lesley Liu. Boston: Houghton Mifflin.

Sweet, Melissa. (1992). *Fiddle-i-ee: A Farmyard Song for the Very Young.* Boston: Little, Brown.

Swinburne, Stephen R. (1996). *Swallows in the Birdhouse.* Illus. by Robin Brickman. Brookfield, CT: Millbrook Press.

Sykes, Julie. (1996). *This and That.* Illus. by Tanya Linch. New York: Farrar, Straus & Giroux.

Tafuri, Nancy. (1987). *Do Not Disturb.* New York: William Morrow.

Tafuri, Nancy. (1994). *This Is the Farmer.* New York: Greenwillow.

Tamar, Erika. (1996). *The Garden of Happiness.* Illus. by Barbara Lambase. Orlando, FL: Harcourt Brace.

Teague, Mark. (1992). *The Field beyond the Outfield.* New York: Scholastic.

Teague, Mark. (1994). *Pigsty.* New York: Scholastic.

Thomassie, Tynia. (1996). *Mimi's Tutu.* Illus. by Jan Spivey Gilchrist. New York: Scholastic.

Thompson, Carol. (1997). *Piggy Washes Up.* Cambridge, MA: Candlewick Press.

Thompson, Mary. (1996). *Gran's Bees.* Illus. by Donna Peterson. Brookfield, CT: Millbrook Press.

Tibbitts, Alison, & Roocraft, Alan. (1992). *Polar Bears.* New York: Capstone Press.

Tibo, Gilles. (1995). *Simon and His Boxes.* Plattsburgh, NY: Tundra Books.

Tompert, Ann. (1994). *A Carol for Christmas.* Illus. by Laura Kelly. New York: Simon & Schuster.

Torres, Leyla. (1993). *Subway Sparrow.* New York: Farrar, Straus & Giroux.

Trapani, Iza. (1993). *The Itsy Bitsy Spider.* Dallas, TX: Whispering Coyote Press.

Tresselt, Alvin. (1991). *Wake Up, Farm.* Newly illus. by Carolyn Ewing. New York: Lothrop, Lee & Shepard.

Tresselt, Alvin. (1992). *The Gift of the Tree.* Illus. by Henri Sorenson. New York: Lothrop, Lee & Shepard.

Tryon, Leslie. (1993). *Albert's Field Trip.* New York: Simon & Schuster.

Tryon, Leslie. (1994). *Albert's Thanksgiving.* New York: Simon & Schuster.

Tryon, Leslie. (1996). *Albert's Ball Game.* Colchester, CT: Atheneum.

Van Cleave, Janice. (1998). *Janice Van Cleave's Play and Find Out about the Human Body.* Somerset, NY: Wiley.

Van Laan, Nancy. (1993). *Tiny Tiny Boy and the Big Big Cow: A Scottish Folk Tale.* Illus. by Marjorie Priceman. New York: Knopf.

Van Laan, Nancy. (1998). *Little Fish, Lost.* Illus. by Jane Conteh-Morgan. New York: Simon & Schuster.

Van Leeuwen, Jean. (1997). *Touch the Sky Summer.* Illus. by Dan Andreasen. New York: Dial Books.

Van Rynbach, Iris. (1995). *Five Little Pumpkins.* Honesdale, PA: Boyds Mills Press.

Venezia, Mike. (1988–1997). *Getting to Know the World's Greatest Artists series.* Chicago: Children's Press. (23+ titles).

Vigna, Judith. (1997). *I Live with Daddy.* Niles, IL: Albert Whitman & Co.

Vincent, Gabrielle. (1989). *Ernest and Celestine at the Circus.* New York: Greenwillow.

Visual Dictionary of Plants. (1992). New York: Dorling Kindersley.

Waber, Bernard. (1995a). *Do You See a Mouse?* Boston: Houghton Mifflin.

Waber, Bernard. (1995b). *Gina.* Boston: Houghton Mifflin.

Waber, Bernard. (1996). *A Lion Named Shirley Williamson*. Boston: Houghton Mifflin.

Waddell, Martin. (1992). *Farmer Duck*. Illus. by Helen Oxenbury. Cambridge, MA: Candlewick Press.

Waddell, Martin. (1993). *Let's Go Home, Little Bear*. Illus. by Barbara Firth. Cambridge, MA: Candlewick Press.

Waldron, Jan L. (1997). *Angel Pig and the Hidden Christmas*. Illus. by David M. McPhail. New York: Dutton.

Wallace, Ian. (1997). *A Winter's Tale*. Washington, DC: Groundwood Books.

Wallace, John. (1997). *Building a House with Mr. Bumble*. Cambridge, MA: Candlewick Press.

Wallace, Karen. (1993). *Think of an Eel*. Illus. by Mike Bostock. Cambridge, MA: Candlewick Press.

Wallace, Karen. (1994). *My Hen Is Dancing*. Illus. by Anita Jeram. Cambridge, MA: Candlewick Press.

Wallis, Mary. (1994). *I Can Make Puppets*. Buffalo, NY: Firefly Books.

Walsh, Ellen Stoll. (1989). *Mouse Paint*. Orlando, FL: Harcourt Brace.

Walsh, Ellen Stoll. (1993). *Hop Jump*. Orlando, FL: Harcourt Brace.

Walsh, Ellen Stoll. (1996). *Samantha*. Orlando, FL: Harcourt Brace.

Walters, Catherine. (1998). *When Will It Be Spring?* New York: Dutton.

Ward, Heather P. (1994). *I Promise I'll Find You*. Illus. by Sheila McGraw. Buffalo, NY: Firefly Books.

Waters, Kate. (1990). *Lion Dancer: Ernie Wan's Chinese New Year*. New York: Scholastic.

Watson, Wendy. (1993). *A Valentine for You*. Boston: Houghton Mifflin. (Paperback)

Wax, Wendy, ed. (1993). *Hanukkah, Oh Hanukkah! A Treasury of Stories, Songs, and Games to Share*. Illus. by John Speirs. New York: Bantam Doubleday.

Wechsler, Doug. (1995). *Bizarre Bugs*. New York: Cobblehill.

Weiss, George David and Bob Thiele. (1994). *What a Wonderful World*. Illus. by Ashley Bryan. New York: Simon & Schuster.

Welch, Willy. (1995). *Playing Right Field*. Illus. by Marc Simont. New York: Scholastic.

Weller, Janet. (1997). *The Written Word*. Illus. by Colin Mier. New York: Franklin Watts.

Wells, Robert E. (1993). *Is a Blue Whale the Biggest Thing There Is?* Niles, IL: Albert Whitman & Co.

Wells, Rosemary. (1995). *Edward in Deep Water*. New York: Dial Books.

Wells, Rosemary. (1997). *McDuff Moves In*. Illus. by Susan Jeffers. New York: Hyperion.

Westcott, Nadine. (1990). *There's a Hole in the Bucket*. New York: Harper & Row.

Weston, Martha. (1995). *Tuck in the Pool*. New York: Clarion Books.

What's Inside? Plants. (1992). New York: Dorling Kindersley.

Wheeler, Cindy. (1994). *Bookstore Cat*. New York: Random House.

Wheeler, Cindy. (1998). *More Simple Signs*. New York: Viking.

White, Linda. (1996). *Too Many Pumpkins*. Illus. by Megan Lloyd. New York: Holiday House.

Whitman, Candace. (1998a). *Bring on the Blue*. New York: Abbeville Press.

Whitman, Candace. (1998b). *Ready for Red*. New York: Abbeville Publishing.

Wiesner, David. (1992). *June 29, 1999*. New York: Clarion Books.

Wild, Margaret. (1994a). *Our Granny*. Illus. by Julie Vivas. New York: Ticknor & Fields.

Wild, Margaret. (1994b). *Toby*. Illus. by Noela Young. New York: Ticknor & Fields.

Wilder, Laura Ingalls. (1994). *Dance at Grandpa's: Adapted from the Little House Books*. New York: HarperCollins.

Wilkins, Verna Allette, et al. *Mum Can Fix It*. Lawrenceville, NJ: Red Sea Press.

Willard, Nancy. (1996). *A Starlit Somersault Downhill.* Illus. by Jerry Pinkney. Boston: Little, Brown. (Paperback)

Williams, John. (1997). *Houses and Homes.* Austin, TX: Raintree/Steck Vaughn.

Williams, Vera B. (1983). *Three Days on a River in a Red Canoe.* New York: Greenwillow.

Williams, Vera B. (1990). *"More More More" Said the Baby.* New York: Greenwillow.

Willis, Nancy Carol. (1996). *The Robins in Your Backyard.* Montchanin, DE: Cucumber Island Storytellers.

Wilson, Gina. (1995). *Prowlpuss.* Illus. by David Parkins. Cambridge, MA: Candlewick Press.

Winkleman, Katherine. (1994). *Firehouse.* Illus. by John S. Winkleman. New York: Walker & Co.

Winter, Jeanette. (1996). *Josefina.* Orlando, FL: Harcourt Brace.

Wolf, Jake. (1996). *Daddy, Could I Have an Elephant?* Illus. by Marylin Hafner. New York: Greenwillow.

Wolff, Ashley. (1993). *Stella and Roy.* New York: Dutton.

Wolff, Ferida. (1993). *Seven Loaves of Bread.* Illus. by Katie Keller. New York: William Morrow.

Wolff, Ferida. (1994). *On Halloween Night.* Illus. by Dolores Avendano. New York: Tambourine Books.

Wolestein, Diane. (1992). *Little Mouse's Painting.* Illus. by Jaryjane Begin. New York: William Morrow.

Wood, Jakki. (1998). *Across the Big Blue Sea: An Ocean Wildlife Book.* Washington, DC: National Geographic.

Woods, Andrew. (1996). *Young Squanto: The First Thanksgiving.* Illus. by Chris Powers. Mahwah, NJ: Troll.

Woolfitt, Gabrielle. (1992a). *Blue (Colors).* Minneapolis: Carolrhoda Books.

Woolfitt, Gabrielle. (1992b). *Red.* Minneapolis: Carolrhoda Books.

Wormell, Christopher. (1995). *A Number of Animals.* Orange Beach, AL: Creative Education.

Yektai, Niki. (1996). *Bears at the Beach: Counting 10–20.* Brookfield, CT: Millbrook Press.

Yenawine, Philip. (1991). *Colors.* New York: The Museum of Modern Art, New York/Delacorte Press.

Yeoman, John. (1995). *The Do-It-Yourself House That Jack Built.* Illus. by Quentin Blake. Colchester, CT: Atheneum.

Yolen, Jane. (1993a). *Jane Yolen's Songs of Summer.* Illus. by Cyd Moore. Honesdale, PA: Boyds Mills Press.

Yolen, Jane. (1993b). *Welcome to the Green House.* Illus. by Laura Regan. New York: G. P. Putnam.

Yolen, Jane. (1995). *Before the Storm.* Illus. by Georgia Pugh. Honesdale, PA: Boyds Mills Press.

Young, Ed. (1992). *Seven Blind Mice.* New York: Philomel.

Zagwyn, Deborah Turney. (1997). *The Pumpkin Blanket.* Berkeley, CA: Tricycle Press.

Zalben, Jane Breskin. (1995). *Pearl Plants a Tree.* New York: Simon & Schuster.

Zamorano, Ana. (1997). *Let's Eat!* Illus. by Julie Vivas. New York: Scholastic.

Zelinsky, Paul O. (1990). *The Wheels on the Bus: With Pictures That Move.* New York: Dutton.

Ziefert, Harriet M. (1992). *Clown Games.* Illus. by Larry Stevens. New York: Viking.

Ziefert, Harriet. (1996a). *Let's Get a Pet.* Illus. by Mavis Smith. New York: Puffin. (Paperback)

Ziefert, Harriet. (1996b). *Who Said Moo?* Illus. by Simms Taback. New York: HarperCollins.

Zolotow, Charlotte. (1995). *The Old Dog.* Rev. ed. Newly illus. by James Ransome. New York: HarperCollins.

Zolotow, Charlotte. (1998). *The Bunny Who Found Easter.* Boston: Houghton Mifflin.

Cassettes

All-Time Favorite Dances [CD or cassette]. (1991). Long Branch, NJ: Kimbo Educational.

Big Yellow School Bus [cassette]. (1991). Alfred Publishing.

Bingham, Bing. "The First Day of School." On *A Rainbow of Songs* [cassette]. Long Branch, NJ: Kimbo Educational.

Bingham, Bing. "Goober Peas." On *A Rainbow of Songs* [cassette]. Long Branch, NJ: Kimbo Educational.

Bingham, Bing. "Primary Colors." On *A Rainbow of Songs* [cassette]. Kimbo Records.

"Bingo." On *Six Little Ducks: Classic Children's Songs* [cassette or CD]. (1997). Long Branch, NJ: Kimbo Educational.

Brand, Oscar. (1994). *I Love Cats* [cassette]. Waterbury, VT: Alacazam!

Chanukah at Home [cassette]. (1988). Cambridge, MA: Rounder Records.

Child's Celebration of Showtunes [cassette]. (1992). Music for Little People.

De Paola, Tomie. (1991). *Merry Christmas, Strega Nona* [cassette]. Read by Celeste Holm. Old Greenwich, CT: Listening Library.

Do It Yourself Kid's Circus [cassette]. Long Branch, NJ: Kimbo Educational.

"Easter Egg Hunt." On *Holiday Songs for All Occasions* [cassette]. Long Branch, NJ: Kimbo Educational.

Epstein-Kravis, Anna. (1990). *Tot's Tunes* [cassette]. Anna Epstein-Kravis.

Fisher, Diana. (1996). *Wee Sing Wheels Sounds and Songs* [cassette]. New York: G. P. Putnam.

Gallina, Jill. *Holiday Songs for All Occasions* [cassette]. Kimbo Records.

Hartmann, Jack. (1990). *Make a Friend, Be a Friend: Songs for Growing Up and Growing Together with Friends* [cassette]. Freeport, NY: Educational Activities.

Holiday Action Songs [cassette]. Kimbo Records.

"I'm Going to Plant a Garden." On *Science in a Nutshell* [cassette]. Long Branch, NJ: Kimbo Educational.

Jack, David. (1990). *Gotta Hop* [cassette]. Leucadia, CA: Ta-Dum Productions.

James, Dixie, & Becht, Linda. *The Singing Calendar* [cassette]. Long Branch, NJ: Kimbo Educational.

Jenkins, Ella. (1990a). *Counting Games and Rhythms for the Little Ones* (Vol. 1) [cassette]. Rockville, MD: Smithsonian Folkways.

Jenkins, Ella. (1990b). *Growing Up with Ella Jenkins: Rhythms, Songs and Rhymes* [cassette]. Rockville, MD: Smithsonian Folkways.

Jenkins, Ella. (1990c). *Rhythm and Game Songs for the Little Ones* [cassette]. Rockville, MD: Smithsonian Folkways.

Johnson, Laura. (1987). "Puppet Pals" on *Homemade Games and Activities: Make Your Own Rhythm Band!* [cassette]. Long Branch, NJ: Kimbo Educational.

"Little Red Caboose." On *Toddler Favorites* [cassette]. (1998). Redway, CA: Music for Little People.

"Look Blue." On *There's Music in the Colors* [cassette]. Long Branch, NJ: Kimbo Educational.

Murphy, Jane. *Songs for You and Me: Kids Learn about Feelings and Emotions* [cassette]. Long Branch, NJ: Kimbo Educational.

Murphy, Jane Lawliss. (1993). *Songs about Insects, Bugs and Squiggly Things* [cassette]. Long Branch, NJ: Kimbo Educational.

"On a Rainy Day." On *A Rainbow of Songs* [cassette]. Long Branch, NJ: Kimbo Educational.

Palmer, Hap. (1991a). *Hap Palmer Sings Classic Nursery Rhymes* [cassette]. Freeport, NY: Educational Activities.

Palmer, Hap. (1991b). "Humpty Dumpty." On *Hap Palmer Sings Classic Nursery*

Rhymes [cassette]. Freeport, NY: Educational Activities.

Palmer, Hap. *Math Readiness—Vocabulary and Concepts* [cassette]. Freeport, NY: Educational Activities.

Palmer, Hap. *Walter the Waltzing Worm* [cassette or CD]. Long Branch, NJ: Kimbo Educational.

"Peter Cottontail." on *Holidays and Special Times* [cassette]. (1989). Sung by Greg Scelsa & Steve Millang. Los Angeles, CA: Youngheart Records.

"Puppy Dog." On *Walk Like the Animals* by Georgiana Liccione Stewart [cassette]. Long Branch, NJ: Kimbo Educational.

Raffi. (1983). *Raffi's Christmas Album* [cassette]. Long Branch, NJ: Kimbo Educational.

Rock 'N Roll Fitness Fun [CD or cassette]. (1989). Long Branch, NJ: Kimbo Educational.

Ronno. (1996). "Doctor Doctor." On *People in Our Neighborhood* [cassette]. Long Branch, NJ: Kimbo Educational.

Scelsa, Greg, & Millang, Steve. "I Like Potatoes." On *We All Live Together* (Vol. 5) [cassette or CD]. Long Branch, NJ: Kimbo Educational.

Scruggs, Joe. (1994). *Ants* [CD or cassette]. Shadow Play Records and Video/Educational Graphics Press.

Skiera-Zucek, Lois. (1989). *Halloween Fun* [cassette]. Long Branch, NJ: Kimbo Educational.

Stewart, Georgiana. (1987). *Good Morning Exercises for Kids* [cassette]. Long Branch, NJ: Kimbo Educational.

Stewart, Georgiana Liccione. (1991). *Children of the World: Multi-Cultural Rhythmic Activities* [cassette]. Long Branch, NJ: Kimbo Educational.

Traugh, Steven, et al. (1993). "Shapes." On *Music and Movement* [cassette]. Cypress, CA: Creative Teaching Press.

What's in the Sea: Songs about Marine Life and Ocean Ecology [cassette]. Long Branch, NJ: Kimbo Educational.

"A Yell for Yellow." (1976). On *There's Music in the Colors* [cassette]. Kimbo Records.

Cassettes Plus Books

The Ants Go Marching [cassette and book]. (1992). Bothell, WA: Wright Group.

Archambault, John. (1997). *Counting Kittens* [cassette and book]. Parsippany, NJ: Silver Press.

Auch, Mary Jane. (1995). *Easter Egg Farm* [cassette and book]. Pine Plains, NY: Live Oaks Media.

Bourgeois, Paulette. (1995). *Franklin Wants a Pet* [cassette and book]. New York: Scholastic.

Brown, Marc Tolon. (1998). *Arthur Makes the Team* [cassette and book]. Old Greenwich, CT: Listening Library.

Byars, Betsy. (1998). *My Brother Ant* [cassette and book]. Prince Frederick, MD: Recorded Books.

Griffith, Joelene. (1993). *We Like Bugs* [cassette and book]. East Wenatchee, WA: Learning Workshop.

Keats, Ezra Jack. *The Snowy Day* [cassette and book]. Kimbo Records.

London, Jonathan. (1997). *Froggy Gets Dressed* [cassette and book]. New York: Penguin Books.

Maestro, Betsy C. (1996). *Why Do Leaves Change Color?* Illus. by Loretta Krupinski [cassette and book]. Scranton, PA: Harper Audio.

McPhail, David M. (1986). *The Bear's Toothache* [cassette and book]. Pine Plains, NY: Live Oak Media.

Olde Mother Goose [cassette and book]. (1993). Performed by the Hubbards. Illus.

by Blanche Fisher Wright. Little Rock, AR: August House Audio.

Parker, Dan. (1988a). *Teach Me about Getting Dressed* [cassette and book]. Fallbrook, CA: Living Skills Music.

Parker, Dan. (1988b). *Teach Me about the Dentist* [cassette and book]. Fallbrook, CA: Living Skills Music.

Paterson, Katherine. (1996). *Smallest Cow in the World* [cassette and book]. Scranton, PA: Harper Audio.

Stanley, Leotha. (1994). *Be a Friend: The Story of African American Music in Song, Words and Pictures* [cassette and book]. Illus. by Henry Hawkins. Middleton, WI: Zino Press.

Compact Discs

All-Time Favorite Dances [compact disc or cassette]. (1991). Long Branch, NJ: Kimbo Educational.

"Ants on Parade." On *Songs about Insects, Bugs and Squiggly Things* [compact disc]. (1993). Long Branch, NJ: Kimbo Educational.

"Bingo." On *Six Little Ducks: Classic Children's Songs* [cassette or CD]. (1997). Long Branch, NJ: Kimbo Educational.

"Clean Rain." On *Evergreen Everblue* [compact disc]. (1990). Shoreline Records.

"Easter Time Is Here Again." On *Holiday Songs and Rhythms* [compact disc]. (1997). Freeport, NY: Activity Records, Inc.

Gold, Andrew. (1996). *Andrew Gold's Halloween Howls* [compact disc]. Redway, CA: Music for Little People.

Greg and Steve. "Muffin Man." On *We All Live Together* (Vol. 2) [compact disc]. Youngheart Records.

Jenkins, Ella. (1994). *This Is Rhythm* [compact disc]. Washington, DC: Smithsonian/Folkways.

Lavender, Cheryl. (1993). *Moans, Groans and Skeleton Bones* [compact disc]. Milwaukee, WI: Hal Leonard.

Louchard, Ric. (1993). *Hey, Ludwig! Classical Piano Solos for Playful Times* [compact disc]. Redway, CA; Music for Little People.

Murphy, Jane Lawliss. (1997). *Cars, Trucks and Trains* [compact disc]. Long Branch, NJ: Kimbo Educational.

"The Muffin Man." On *Toddler Tunes: Twenty-six Classic Songs for Toddlers* [compact disc]. (1995). Franklin, TN: Cedarmont.

Palmer, Hap. (1995). "The Mice Go Marching." On *Rhythms on Parade* [compact disc]. Baldwin, NY: Educational Activities.

Palmer, Hap. (1997a). "Hanukkah." On *Holiday Songs and Rhythms* [compact disc]. Baldwin, NY: Educational Activities.

Palmer, Hap. (1997b). "Have a Good Halloween Night." On *Holiday Songs and Rhythms* [compact disc]. Freeport, NY: Educational Activities.

Palmer, Hap. (1997c). *Holiday Songs and Rhythms* [compact disc]. Freeport, NY: Educational Activities.

Palmer, Hap. *Walter the Waltzing Worm* [cassette or CD]. Long Branch, NJ: Kimbo Educational.

Piggyback Songs: Singable Poems Set to Favorite Tunes [compact disc]. (1995). Includes 21 songs/poems for fall/winter. Kimbo Records.

Raffi. "Spring Flowers." On *Bananaphone* [compact disc]. (1994). Cambridge, MA: Shoreline, 1994. Available from Kimbo Educational.

Rock 'n' Roll Fitness Fun [compact disc or cassette]. (1989). Long Branch, NJ: Kimbo Educational.

Rosenthal, Margie. (1987). *Just in Time for Chanukah!* [compact disc]. Portland, OR: Sheera Recordings.

Rosenthal, Phil. (1996). "Little White Duck." On *Animal Songs* [compact disc]. Guilford, CT: American Melody.

Scelsa, Greg, & Millang, Steve. "I Like Potatoes." On *We All Live Together* (Vol. 5) [cassette or CD]. Long Branch, NJ: Kimbo Educational.

Scruggs, Joe. (1994). *Ants* [CD or cassette]. Shadow Play Records and Video/ Educational Graphics Press.

Sharon, Lois, & Sharon, Bram. (1984). "Three Blind Mice" and "Hickory, Dickory, Dock." On *Mainly Mother Goose* [compact disc]. Toronto: Elephant Records.

Stewart, Georgiana. (1992). *Multicultural Rhythm Stick Fun* [compact disc]. Kimbo Records.

"Take Me Out to the Ballgame." On *Six Little Ducks* [compact disc]. (1997). Long Branch, NJ: Kimbo Educational.

Tossing, Gaia. (1995). *Sing 'n' Sign for Fun!* [compact disc]. Glenview, IL: Heartsong.

Computer Programs

Bailey's Book House [CD-ROM]. (1995). Redmond, WA: Edmark.

Berenstain Bears Get in a Fight [CD-ROM]. (1995). New York: Random House/ Broderbund.

Berenstain Bears in the Dark [CD-ROM]. (1996). New York: Random House/ Broderbund.

Big Job [CD-ROM]. (1995). Bethesda, MD: Discovery Communications, Inc.

"Birds and How They Grow." (1993). On *Animals and How They Grow* [CD-ROM]. Washington, DC: National Geographic Society.

Brown, Marc. (1994). *Arthur's Birthday* [CD-ROM]. New York: Random House/ Broderbund.

Carter, David A. (1996). *How Many Bugs in a Box?* [CD-ROM]. New York: Simon & Schuster Interactive.

Children's Treasury II Rhymes, Poems, Stories [CD-ROM]. (1994). Fairfield, CT: Queue Inc.

Colors, Shapes and Size [CD-ROM]. (1995). Harbor, WA: StarPress Multimedia.

Community Construction Kit [CD-ROM]. (1998). Watertown, MA: Tom Snyder Productions.

Counting and Sorting [CD-ROM]. (1997). New York: DK Multimedia.

Firefighter [CD-ROM]. (1994). New York: Simon & Schuster Interactive.

Five A Day Adventures [CD-ROM]. (1994). San Mateo, CA: Dole Food Company.

From Moo to You [CD-ROM]. (1996). Westmont, IL: Dairy Council of Wisconsin.

Gryphon Bricks [CD-ROM]. (1996). San Diego, CA: Gryphon Software Corp.

If You Give a Mouse a Cookie [CD-ROM]. (1995). New York: HarperCollins Interactive.

JumpStart Preschool [CD-ROM]. (1996). Glendale, CA: Knowledge Adventure.

Kid Pix Studio [CD-ROM]. (1994). Broderbund.

K–6 Classroom Gallery [CD-ROM]. (1997). Lancaster, PA: Classroom Connect.

Let's Explore the Jungle with Buzzy the Knowledge Bug [CD-ROM]. (1995). Woodinville, WA: Humongous Entertainment.

Let's Start Learning [CD-ROM]. (1996). Freemont, CA: The Learning Co.

Macaulay, David. (1994). *The Way Things Work* [CD-ROM]. New York: Dorling Kindersley Multimedia.

Mercer Mayer's Just Me and My Dad [CD-ROM]. (1996). New York: GT Interactive Software.

Millie's Math House [CD-ROM]. (1992). Redmond, WA: Edmark.

Mixed-Up Mother Goose [CD-ROM]. (1995). Bellevue, WA: Sierra On-Line.

The Multimedia Bug Book [CD-ROM]. (1995). New York: Workman Publishing Co.

My Silly CD of Colors [CD-ROM]. (1995). Toronto: Discis Knowledge Research.

New Kid Pix [CD-ROM]. (1996). Broderbund.

The Night before Christmas [CD-ROM]. (1991). Toronto: Discis Knowledge Research.

Paint, Write and Play [CD-ROM]. (1996). Fremont, CA: Learning Company.

Peter's Colors Adventure [CD-ROM]. (1994). Arborescence.

Reader Rabbit's Preschool [CD-ROM]. (1997). Learning Company.

Reader Rabbit's Ready for Letters [computer program]. (1994). Learning Company.

Shape Up! [CD-ROM]. (1995). Cupertino, CA: Sunburst Communications.

A Silly, Noisy House [CD-ROM]. (1991). Santa Monica, CA: Voyager Company.

"Why Does It Rain." On *Our Earth* [CD-ROM]. (1992). Washington, DC: National Geographic.

Videos

The Adventures of Milo and Otis [video]. (1989). Culver City, CA: Columbia TriStar Home Video.

Adventures of Pinocchio [video]. (1994). Charlotte, NC: United American Video.

Ants: Hunters and Gardeners [video]. (1986). Washington, DC: National Geographic Society.

Apples [video]. (1996). DeBeck Educational Video.

At Home with Zoo Animals [video]. (1992). Washington, DC: National Geographic Society.

At the Post Office [video]. (1995). Tallahassee, FL: Dogwood Video.

Barney's Campfire Sing-Along [video]. (1990). Allen, TX: Lyons Group.

Be a Better Listener [video]. (1995). Pleasantville, NY: Sunburst Communications.

Bean, Norman and Sandy. (1992). *A First Look at Trees* [video]. Van Nuys, CA: AIMS Media.

"The Big Piece of Blue Corn." On *Tall Tales, Yarns and Whoppers* [video]. (1991). Atlas Video, Inc.

Big Red [video]. (1993). Mill Valley, CA: Fire Dog Pictures.

Building Skyscrapers [video]. (1994). New York: David Alpert Associates, Inc.

Colors, Shapes, and Counting [video]. Long Branch, NJ: Kimbo Educational.

Cat [video]. (1995). Eyewitness Video.

Cats [video]. (1985). Washington, DC: National Geographic.

Cats in the Cradle [video]. (1997). Bethesda, MD: Discovery Communications.

Child Safety Outdoors [video]. (1994). Chino Hills, CA: KidSafety of America.

Circle of Water [video]. (1995). Washington, DC: National Geographic.

Circus [video]. (1984). Edited by Steven Rosofsky. Chicago: Encyclopedia Britannica Educational Corporation.

"Circus Baby" by Maud and Miska Petersham. On *Max's Chocolate Chicken and Other Stories for Young Children* [video]. (1993). Weston, CT: Children's Circle Home Video.

Cleaver, Mary. (1993). "Rain Is Falling Down" and "The Incey Wincey Spider." On

Songs and Fingerplays for Little Ones [video]. Cleaver Productions.

Cole, Joanna. (1995). *Goes the Seed* [video]. New York: KidVision.

Coleman, Warren. (1993). *Valentine's Day* [video]. Niles, IL: United Learning.

Come See What the Doctor Sees [video]. (1994). Half Moon Bay, CA: Visual Mentor.

Cows [video]. (1995). Churchill Media.

Cranberry Bounce [video]. (1991). DeBeck Educational Video.

Cutting, Michael. (1990). *The Little Crooked Christmas Tree* [video]. Stamford, CT:ABC Video.

Daddy Doesn't Live with Us [video]. (1994). Pleasantville, NY: Sunburst.

Dance with Us: A Creative Movement Video [video]. (1994). Pleasantville, NY: Sunburst.

Deep Sea Dive [video]. Washington, DC: National Geographic.

Dig Hole, Build House [video]. (1994). Gig Harbor, WA: Real World Video.

Dogs [video]. (1985). Washington, DC: National Geographic.

Eastman, David. (1993). *What Is a Fish?* [video]. Northbrook, IL: Film Ideas.

Eastman, P. D. (1991). *Are You My Mother? Plus Two More P. D. Eastman Classics* video]. New York: Random House Video.

Emergency 911 [video]. (1994). Washington, DC: National Geographic.

Exciting People, Places and Things [video]. (1989). Washington, DC: Gallaudet University Press.

Exploring the World of Fish [video]. (1992). Troy, MI: Anchor Bay Entertainment.

Fire and Rescue [video]. (1993). Montpelier, VT: Focus Video Productions.

Fire Safety for Kids [video]. (1995). South Burlington, VT: Children's Video Development.

The Fire Station [video]. (1990). Washington, DC: National Geographic.

Fish [video]. Eyewitness Videos. Long Branch, NJ: Kimbo Educational.

Fish [video]. (1985). Washington, DC: National Geographic.

Flowers and Seeds [video]. (1994). Princeton, NJ: Films for the Humanities.

Flowers, Plants and Trees [video]. (1987). *Tell Me Why* series. Marina Del Rey, CA: Penguin Productions.

Flying, Trying, and Honking Around [video]. (1994). Washington, DC: National Geographic Kids Video.

Fruit: Close Up and Very Personal [video]. (1995). Geneva, IL: Stage Fright Productions.

Get Ready, Get Set, Grow [video]. (1987). Brooklyn Botanic Garden Children's Garden. Oley, PA: Bullfrog Films.

Goofy over Dental Health [video]. (1991). Newton, PA: Disney Educational Productions.

Groark Learns about Prejudice [video]. (1996). Featuring Randel McGee. Elkind & Sweet Communications/Distributed by Live Wire Media.

Halloween [video]. (1993). Niles, IL: United Learning.

Hanna, Jack. (1994). *A Day with the Greatest Show on Earth* [video]. Glastonbury, CT: VideoTours.

Harriet's Magic Hats IV series [video]. (1986). Edmonton, Alberta: Access Network, Alberta Educational Communication Corp. 25 videos. 15 min. Primary level. *Dog Trainer; Hat Maker; Hotel Manager; Librarian; Museum Curator; Naturalist; Newspaper Reporter; Palaeontologist; Pasta Maker; Photographer; Potter; Puppeteer; Rodeo Cowboy; Sheep Farmer; Ski Instructor; Telephone Installer; Toy Tester; Vegetable Processor; Veterinarian; Water Treatment Engineer; Weather Forecaster; Welder; Zookeeper.*

Holidays for Children: Hanukkah/Passover [video]. Schlessinger Media.

Hospital [video]. (1990). Washington, DC: National Geographic.

How a Car Is Built [video]. (1995). Think Media.

How Much Is a Million? [video]. (1997). Hosted by LeVar Burton. GPN/WNED-TV 120.

I Get So Mad! [video]. (1993). Pleasantville, NY: Sunburst Communications.

Insects and Spiders [video]. (1993). New York: Sony Kids' Video.

Introduction to Letters and Numerals [video]. (1985). Hightstown, NJ: SRA/McGraw-Hill.

Introduction to Puppet Making [video]. (1996). Jim Gamble Puppet Productions. Available from Library Video.

I Want to Be an Artist [video]. (1993). Glenview, IL: Crystal Productions.

Jack, David. (1991). *David Jack . . . Live! Makin' Music, Makin' Friends* [video]. Leucadia, CA: Ta-Dum Productions.

Jenkins, Ella. (1991). "One Two Buckle My Shoe." On *Ella Jenkins Live at the Smithsonian* [video]. Washington, DC: Smithsonian/Folkways.

K.C.'s First Bus Ride [video]. (1994). Chino Hills, CA: KidSafety of America.

Keats, Ezra Jack. (1987). *Pet Show* [video]. Norwalk, CT: Weston Woods.

Kids Get Cooking: The Egg [video]. (1987). Newton, MA: Kidviz.

A Kid's Guide to Personal Grooming [video]. (1989). Englewood, CO: Learning Tree Publishing.

Kunstler, James Howard. (1992). *Johnny Appleseed* [video]. Told by Garrison Keillor. Rabbit Ears.

Leokum, Arkady. (1988). *Tell Me Why: A Healthy Body* [video]. Marina del Rey, CA: Tell Me Why.

Let's Build a House [video]. (1996). San Diego, CA: Video Connections.

Let's Explore Water (*Science Is Elementary* Series) [video]. (1993). Agency for Instructional Technology.

Let's Find Out about Spring [video]. (1991). Hightstown, NJ: American School Publishers.

Let's Find Out about Summer [video]. Hightstown, NJ: American School Publishers.

Let's Find Out about Winter [video]. (1991). Hightstown, NJ: American School Publishers.

Let's Go Camping [video]. (1995). Burlington, VT: Vermont Story Works.

Let's Go to the Farm [video]. (1994). With Mac Parker. Burlington, VT: Vermont Story Works.

Let's Go to the Ice Cream and Yogurt Factory [video]. (1996). Burlington, VT: Vermont Story Works.

Lewis, Shari. (1995). *Lamb Chop's Special Chanukah!* [video]. Cypress, CA: Youngheart Music.

Lionni, Leo. (1987). "Frederick." On *Five Lionni Classics* [video]. New York: Random House Home Video.

Lonnquist, Ken, et al. (1994). *Sign Songs: Fun Songs to Sign and Sing* [video]. Madison, WI: Aylmer Press.

Magic School Bus Gets Ants in Its Pants [video]. (1997). New York: Kidvision.

Max's Chocolate Chicken and Other Stories for Young Children [video]. (1993). Weston, CT: Children's Circle Home Video.

Meter [video]. (1994). Princeton, NJ: Films for the Humanities & Sciences.

Milk Cow, Eat Cheese [video]. (1995). Gig Harbor, WA: Real World Video.

A Multicultural Christmas [video]. (1993). Niles, IL: United Learning.

My Family, Your Family [video]. (1994). Pleasantville, NY: Sunburst.

National Zoo [videodisc]. (1989). Washington, DC: Smithsonian Institution.

New Baby in My House [video]. (1993). Children's Television Workshop/distributed by Sony Wonder.

Nursery Songs and Rhymes [video]. (1993). Sandy, UT: Waterford Institute.

Oceans (*Science for You* series) [video]. (1992). Agency for Instructional Technology.

Palmer, Hap. *Learning Basic Skills* [video]. (1986). Freeport, NY: Educational Activities.

Pets: See How They Grow [video]. Sony. Long Branch, NJ: Kimbo Educational.

Pitch [video]. (1994). Princeton, NJ: Films for the Humanities & Sciences.

Polacco, Patricia. *Rechenka's Eggs* [video]. (1992). Lincoln, NE:GNP.

Polisar, Barry Louis. (1994). *Barry's Scrapbook: A Window into Art* [video]. ALA Video/Library Video Network.

Postal Station [video]. (1991). Princeton, NJ: Films for the Humanities.

Post Office [video]. (1991). Washington, DC: National Geographic.

Preschool Power! Jacket Flips and Other Tips [video]. (1991). Concept Associates.

Raffi. (1988). "Bathtime." On *Raffi in Concert with the Rise and Shine Band* [video]. Hollywood, CA: Troubadour Records.

Robertus, Polly M. (1992) *The Dog Who Had Kittens* [video]. Pine Plains, NY: Live Oak Media.

Rock 'N' Learn Colors, Shapes and Counting [video]. (1997). Conroe, TX: Rock 'N Learn.

Rogers, Fred. (1995). *Circus Fun* [video]. Beverly Hills, CA:CBS/Fox Video.

Rogers, Fred. (1996). *Mister Rogers' Neighborhood: Doctor* [video]. Beverly Hills, CA: CBS/Fox Home Video.

Rusty and Rosy Nursery Songs and Rhymes [video]. (1993). Sandy, UT: Waterford Institute.

Rylant, Cynthia. (1990). *All I See* [video]. Hightstown, NJ: McGraw-Hill Media.

Safety on Wheels [video]. (1994). Princeton, NJ: Films for the Humanities & Sciences.

Scullard, Sue. (1992). *The Flyaway Pantaloons* [video]. Pine Plains, NY: Live Oak Media.

Seat Belts Are for Kids Too [video]. (1987). AIMS Media.

See How They Grow: Farm Animals [video]. (1993). New York: Sony Music Entertainment.

Seuss, Dr. (1992). *Horton Hatches the Egg / If I Ran the Circus* [video]. Narrated by Billy Crystal. New York: Random House.

Snowplows at Work [video]. (1994). Truckee, CA: Bill Aaron Productions.

Sound the Alarm: Firefighters at Work [video]. (1994). Bohemia, NY: Rainbow Educational Media.

Squanto and the First Thanksgiving [video]. (1993). Rabbit Ears Productions.

Tell Me Why: Fish, Shellfish, Underwater Life [video]. (1987). Marina del Rey, CA: Tell Me Why.

Tell Me Why: Insects [video]. (1987). Marina del Rey, CA: Tell Me Why.

Tell Me Why Vol. 3: Flowers, Plants and Trees [video]. (1987). Marina Del Rey, CA: Tell Me Why.

Thanksgiving [video]. (1994). Schlessinger Video Productions.

There Goes a Bulldozer [video]. (1993). Van Nuys, CA: Live Action Video for Kids.

There Goes the Mail [video]. (1997). New York: KidVision.

Through the Seasons with Birds: Spring [video]. (1994). Evanston, IL: Altschul Group Corp.

Valentine's Day [video]. (1994). Schlessinger Video Productions.

Wagging Tails: The Dog and Puppy Music Video [video]. (1994). Forney Miller Film & Video / Distributed by New Market Sales.

We're a Family [video]. (1992). Pleasantville, NY: Sunburst.

We're Goin' to the Farm [video]. (1994). Minneapolis, MN: Shortstuff Entertainment.

Wet and Wild: Under the Sea with OWL/TV [video]. (1994). Toronto: Children's Group, Inc.

What Is a Leaf? [video]. (1991). Washington, DC: National Geographic Society.

When I Grow Up I Wanta Be [video]. (1994). Birmingham, AL: Five Points South.

Where Do Animals Go in Winter? [video]. (1995). Washington, DC: National Geographic Society.

White, Linda. *Too Many Pumpkins* [video]. (1997). Pine Plains, NY: Live Oak Productions.

Wonders of Growing Plants (erd ed.) [video]. (1992). Churchill Media/SVE.

World of Pets: Dogs [video]. (1985). Washington, DC: National Geographic Society.

World of Pets: Fish [video]. (1985). Washington, DC: National Geographic Society.

Appendix

Magazines for School-Age Children

Cricket
Carus Publishing Company
PO 7433
Red Oak, IA 51591-2433
1-800-827-0227
www.cricketmag.com

Ladybug
Carus Publishing Company
PO Box 7436
Red Oak, IA 51591-2436
www.cricketmag.com

Ranger Rick
National Wildlife Federation
8925 Leesburg Pike
Vienna, VA 22184
(703) 790-4000
www.nwf.org

Sesame Street
Children's Television Workshop
New York, NY 10023-7129
(212) 595-3456
www.ctw.org

Spider
Carus Publishing Company
PO Box 7435
Red Oak, IA 51591-2435
www.cricketmag.com

Stone Soup
Children's Art Foundation
PO Box 83
Santa Cruz, CA 95063
1-800-447-4569
www.stonesoup.com

Turtle
Children's Better Health Institute
1100 Waterway Boulevard
Indianapolis, IN 546206
(317) 636-8881
www.cbhi.org

Your Big Back Yard
National Wildlife Federation
8925 Leesburg Pike
Vienna, VA 22184
(703) 790-4000
www.nwf.org

Early Childhood Commercial Suppliers

Children's Press
5440 North Cumberland Avenue
Chicago, IL 60656
1-800-621-1115
www.publishing.grolier.com

Delmar Thompson Learning
3 Columbia Circle
Box 15-015
Albany, NY 12212-5015
1-800-477-3692
www.cengage.com/delmar

Discount School Supply
PO Box 7636
Spreckels, CA 93962-7636
1-800-627-2829
FAX: 1-800-879-2829

Earlychildhood.com
2 Lower Ragsdale Suite 200
Monterey, CA 93940
(831) 332-2000
www.earlychildhood.com

Gryphon House
3706 Otis Street
Mt. Rainier, MD 20712
1-800-638-0928
www.infoghbooks.com

Kimbo Educational
PO Box 477
Long Branch, NJ 07740
1-800-631-2187
www.kimboed.com

Photo Credits

Drawing: Page 31: Courtesy of EarlyChildhood.com

Collages, Arts & Crafts, and Gifts: Page 41: Courtesy of EarlyChildhood.com

Dough and Clay: Page 63: Delmar Thomson Learning

Painting: Page 77: Courtesy of EarlyChildhood.com

Sensory Experiences–Water and Sand Play: Page 93: Delmar Thomson Learning

Cooking: Page 101: Delmar Thomson Learning

Music and Movement: Page 139: Courtesy of Scott Calman Studio, Inc.

Play: Page 155: Delmar Thomson Learning

Games: Page 175: Delmar Thomson Learning

Math: Page 183: Delmar Thomson Learning

Science: Page 197: Delmar Thomson Learning

Storytelling and Fingerplays: Page 219: Delmar Thomson Learning

Social Studies and Excursions: Page 373: Courtesy of Steven Connor

Developmental Benchmarks

	Fine Motor Skills	Gross Motor Skills
Two-Year-Old	Turns pages in a book singly Imitates drawing a circle, vertical line, and horizontal line Fingers work together to scoop up small objects Constructs simple two- and three-piece puzzles Enjoys short, simple fingerplay games Strings large beads on shoelace Builds tower of up to eight blocks	Kicks large ball Jumps in place Runs without falling Throws ball without falling Walks up and down stairs alone Marches to music Tends to use legs and arms as pairs Usually uses whole arm to paint or color
Three-Year-Old	Cuts paper Builds tower of nine small blocks Pastes using a finger Pours from a pitcher Copies a circle from a drawing Draws a straight line Uses fingers to pick up small objects Draws a person with three parts Strings beads and can arrange by color and shape Uses a knife to spread food at meal or snack time	Catches ball with arms extended forward Throws ball underhand Completes forward somersault Walks up stairs with alternating feet Rides a tricycle skillfully Runs, walks, jumps, and gallops to music Throws ball without losing balance Hops on one foot
Four-Year-Old	Buttons or unbuttons buttons Cuts on a line with scissors Completes a six- to eight-piece puzzle Copies a "t" Buckles a belt Zips separated fasteners Adds five parts to an incomplete drawing of a man	Walks up and down stairs, one foot per step Skips on one foot Rides a bicycle with training wheels
Five-Year-Old	Uses a knife Copies most letters Traces objects Draws crude objects Colors within lines Copies square, triangle, and diamond shapes Models objects from clay Laces shoes	Tries roller and ice skating Catches ball with hands Jumps from heights Jumps rope Walks on stilts Skips Climbs fences
Six-Year-Old	Ties bows Establishes hand preference Reverses letters while printing Paints houses, trees, flowers, and clouds	Plays hopscotch Enjoys ball play Plays simple, organized games such as hide-and-seek

Developmental Benchmarks

	Emotional and Social Skills	Intellectual Skills
Two-Year-Old	Takes toys away from others Plays near other children, but not cooperatively Unable to share toys Acts negatively at times Seeks caregiver's attention Expresses fear of the dark Observes others to see how they do things Begins to show independence Joins in singing or telling simple stories	Identifies most body parts Talks mostly to self Uses "me" instead of proper name Enjoys showing and naming objects Uses a 200- to 300-word vocabulary Speaks in phrases or three-word sentences Answers yes/no questions Follows two-step commands Constructs negative sentence ("no truck, no truck") Uses modifiers such as "some," "all," and "one" Understands concepts of "big" and "little" Uses such adjectives as "red," "old," and "pretty"

Three-Year-Old	Cooperative, loving, and friendly
	Plays in groups of two or three children
	Begins to take turns
	Shares with friends
	Enjoys independence by doing things for self;
	   e.g., "let me do it," or "I can do it"
	Yells "stop it" at times as opposed to striking
	   another child
	Seeks approval of adults
		Asks how, what, when, and why questions
		Uses verb such as "could," "needs," "might," and "help"
		Uses adverbs such as "how about" and "maybe"
		Understands the pronouns "you" and "they"
		Understands "smaller" and "larger"
		Answers how questions appropriately
		Loves words such as "secret," "surprise," and "different"
		Uses words to define space, such as "back," "up," "out-
		   side," "in front of," "in back of," "over," and "next to"

Four-Year-Old	Independently makes friends with other children Loves other children and having a "friend" Bases friendships on shared activities Sometimes enjoys one particular friend Seeks approval of friends Plays with small groups of children Delights in humorous stories Shows more interest in other children than adults Excludes children who are disliked Loves to whisper and tell secrets	Experiences trouble telling the difference between reality and fantasy Exaggerates in practicing new words Loves hearing silly language and to repeat new silly words Uses a vocabulary of 1,200 to 1,500 words Begins to identify letters in name Begins to appreciate bugs, trees, flowers, and birds Learns simple card games and dominoes Develops an awareness of "bad" and "good"
Five-Year-Old	Prefers playing in small groups Prefers friends of same sex and age Protects younger children Plays well with older siblings Enjoys building and imagination play Washes hands before meals Respects other people's property Becomes competitive Develops sense of fairness Verbally expresses anger Boasts, shows off Shows generosity	Names the days of the week Writes numbers from 1 to 10 Retells main details of stories Recognizes the cause and effect of actions Uses a vocabulary of 2,000 or more words Uses sentence lengths of five to six words Tells original stories Follows three-step commands Recognizes square and rectangle shapes Recognizes the numerals for 1 through 5
Six-Year-Old	Prefers friends of the same sex Engages in cooperative play involving role assignments Enjoys being praised and complimented Enjoys "show and tell" time May be argumentative Is competitive and wants to win	Identifies penny, nickel, and dime Counts ten objects Completes a fifteen-piece puzzle Acts out stories Plays Chinese checkers and dominoes Recognizes letters and words in books Identifies right from left hand Prints numbers from 1 to 20 Repeats an eight- to ten-word sentence Counts numbers to 30

28965690R00251

Made in the USA
Lexington, KY
09 January 2014